CONTRACTUAL CERTAINTY IN INTERNATIONAL TRADE

Global business interacts efficiently despite the heterogeneity of social, economic and legal cultures which, according to widespread assumptions, cause insecurities and uncertainties. Breaches of contracts may occur more frequently and business relationships may be terminated more often in international than in domestic trade. But most business people engaged in exporting or importing products or services seem to operate in a sufficiently predictable environment allowing successful ventures into the global market. The apparent paradox presented by cultural/institutional diversity and contractual efficiency in cross-border business transactions is the focus of this volume of essays. The wide range of approaches adopted by contributors to the volume include: the Weberian concept of law as a tool for avoiding the risk of opportunism; economic sociology, which treats networks and relationships between contractual parties as paramount; representatives of new institutional economics who discuss law as well as private governance institutions as most efficient responses to risk; comparative economic sociologists who point to the varieties of legal cultures in the social organisation of trust; and national and international institutions such as the World Bank which try to promote legal certainty in the economy. The purpose of the volume is to build on this interdisciplinary exercise by adding empirical evidence to ongoing debates regarding enabling structures for international business, and by critically reviewing and discussing some of the propositions in the literature which contain interesting hypotheses on the effects of the internationalisation of markets on market co-ordination institutions and on the role of the state in the globalising economy.

Oñati International Series in Law and Society

A SERIES PUBLISHED FOR THE OÑATI INSTITUTE FOR THE SOCIOLOGY OF LAW

Titles in this Series

Social Dynamics of Crime and Control: New Theories for a World in Transition
Edited by Susanne Karstedt and Kai Bussmann

Criminal Policy in Transition
Edited by Andrew Rutherford and Penny Green

Making Law for Families
Edited by Mavis Maclean

Poverty and the Law
Edited by Peter Robson and Asbjørn Kjønstad

Adapting Legal Cultures
Edited by Johannes Feest and David Nelken

Rethinking Law, Society and Governance: Foucault's Bequest
Edited by Gary Wickham and George Pavlich

Rules and Networks
Edited by Richard Appelbaum, Bill Felstiner and Volkmar Gessner

Women in the World's Legal Professions
Edited by Ulrike Schultz and Gisela Shaw

Healing the Wounds
Edited by Marie-Claire Foblets and Trutz von Trotha

Imaginary Boundaries of Justice
Edited by Ronnie Lippens

Family Law and Family Values
Edited by Mavis Maclean

Contemporary Issues in the Semiotics of Law
Edited by Anne Wagner, Tracey Summerfield and Farid Benavides Vanegas

The Geography of Law: Landscapes, Identity and Regulation
Edited by Bill Taylor

Theory and Method in Socio-Legal Research
Edited by Reza Banakar and Max Travers

Luhmann on Law and Politics
Edited by Michael King and Chris Thornhill

Precarious Work, Women and the New Economy: The Challenge to Legal Norms
Edited by Judy Fudge and Rosemary Owens

Juvenile Law Violators, Human Rights, and the Development of New Juvenile Justice Systems
Edited by Eric L Jensen and Jørgen Jepsen

The Language Question in Europe and Diverse Societies: Political, Legal and Social Perspectives
Edited by Dario Castiglione and Chris Longman

European Ways of Law: Towards A European Sociology of Law
Edited by Volkmar Gessner and David Nelken

Crafting Transnational Policing: Police Capacity-Building and Global Policing Reform
Edited by Andrew Goldsmith and James Sheptycki

Constitutional Politics in the Middle East: With special reference to Turkey, Iraq, Iran and Afghanistan
Edited by Saïd Amir Arjomand

Parenting after Partnering: Containing Conflict after Separation
Edited by Mavis Maclean

Responsible Business: Self-Governance and Law in Transnational Economic Transactions
Edited by Olaf Dilling, Martin Herberg and Gerd Winter

Rethinking Equality Projects in Law
Edited by Rosemary Hunter

Contractual Certainty in International Trade

Empirical Studies and Theoretical Debates on Institutional Support for Global Economic Exchanges

Edited by Volkmar Gessner

Oñati International Series in Law and Society

A SERIES PUBLISHED FOR THE OÑATI INSTITUTE FOR THE SOCIOLOGY OF LAW

•HART•
PUBLISHING

OXFORD AND PORTLAND, OREGON
2009

Published in North America (US and Canada) by
Hart Publishing
c/o International Specialized Book Services
920 NE 58th Avenue, Suite 300
Portland, OR 97213-3786
USA
Tel: +1 503 287 3093 or toll-free: (1) 800 944 6190
Fax: +1 503 280 8832
E-mail: orders@isbs.com
Website: www.isbs.com

Hart Publishing Ltd, 16c Worcester Place, Oxford, OX1 2JW
Telephone: +44 (0)1865 517530 Fax: +44 (0) 1865 510710
E-mail: mail@hartpub.co.uk
Website: http://www.hartpub.co.uk

British Library Cataloguing in Publication Data
Data Available

ISBN: 978-1-84113-844-2 (hardback)
ISBN: 978-1-84113-843-5 (paperback)

Typeset by Columns Design Ltd, Reading
Printed by the MPG Books Group in the UK

Preface

The International Institute for the Sociology of Law, Oñati, Spain, was again the venue of a very productive workshop and the host for our small group of lawyers, sociologists and economists interested in interdisciplinary research on aspects of the emerging global legal culture. The meeting took place in September 2006 and was—as always in Oñati—perfectly organised by Malen Gordoa Mendizabal. We thank her and the highly supportive staff of the Institute for the lovely atmosphere and the tireless preparation both of the academic and of the pleasure parts of the conference. The event grew out of research at the Collaborative Research Centre, *Transformations of the State*, at the University of Bremen, Germany—a major academic enterprise generously supported by the German Science Foundation. We appreciate how Stephan Leibfried and Dieter Wolf have been able to bridge interdisciplinary gaps and offer the members of no less than 17 projects a creative working climate. One of the projects which deals with *New Forms of Legal Certainty in Globalised Exchange Processes* is proud of producing this collection of home-grown papers as well as scholarly contributions from invited guests.

We are grateful to two unknown reviewers whose recommendations led to major changes in the structure of the book and in individual chapters. John Flood has kindly read some of the manuscripts in order to eliminate linguistic errors of non-native English speakers. We also wish to acknowledge the fine editorial support of Hart Publishing. Our collection seems to be the last book under the general editorship of Bill Felstiner. For a period of more than a decade, he has done a tremendous job in creating and maintaining the high quality of the Oñati International Series in Law and Society.

Volkmar Gessner
Bremen, 10 March 2008

Contents

List of Contributors

Calliess, Gralf-Peter, Professor of International and Comparative Commercial Law and Legal Theory, University of Bremen, Germany. E-mail: <calliess@web.de>

Dietz, Thomas, Research Associate at the Collaborative Research Centre 'Transformations of the State' at the University of Bremen, Germany. E-mail: <thomdietz@hotmail.com>

Dorbeck-Jung, Bärbel, Associate Professor of Legal Governance, School of Business, Public Administration and Technology, University of Twente. E-mail: <b.r.dorbeck-jung@utwente.nl>

Flood, John, Professor of Law and Sociology, University of Westminster, TransState Adjunct Professor, Bremen University, and Visiting Professor of Law, University of Miami. Website: <http://www.johnflood.com>

Freiling, Jörg, Professor of Business and Economics, University of Bremen, Germany. E-mail: <freiling@uni-bremen.de>

Gessner, Volkmar, Professor Emeritus, Faculty of Law, University of Bremen, Germany. E-mail: <gessner@uni-bremen.de>

Hadfield, Gillian, Richard L. and Antoinette S. Kirtland Professor of Law and Professor of Economics, USC Gould School of Law, Los Angeles, California. E-mail: <ghadfield@law.usc.edu>

Heydebrand, Wolf, Professor Emeritus, Department of Sociology, Faculty of Arts and Science, New York University, New York, the United States. E-mail: <wolf.heydebrand@nyu.edu>

Konradi, Wioletta, PhD Candidate in the Department of Law at the University of Bremen, Germany. E-mail: <wioletta-konradi@web.de>

Nieswandt, Holger, economist, Research Associate at the Collaborative Research Centre 'Transformations of the State' at the University of Bremen, Germany. E-mail: <holger.nieswandt@gmx.de>

Richman, Barak, Professor of Law, Duke University, Durham, NC, United States. E-mail: <barak.richman@duke.edu>

Skordaki, Eleni, Partner, Olswang, London. E-mail: <eleni.skordaki@ olswang.com>

Sosa, Fabian, Dr jur, Attorney at law (Peltzer, Suhren and Meinecke) in Hannover, Germany. E-mail: <fabianpsosa@hotmail.com>

Part I

Introduction

1

Towards a Theoretical Framework for Contractual Certainty in Global Trade

VOLKMAR GESSNER

REGULATION AND SUPPORT OF ECONOMIC BEHAVIOUR

THE GLOBAL ECONOMY obviously suffers from enormous problems. It divides the world between the 'haves', who command the industrial, technological and financial heights, and the 'have nots'. It exploits natural resources to a maximum and resists environmental regulation. It violates human rights in disregarding health problems both at the levels of production and consumption. Similar concerns are raised in the current crisis of the financial markets since August 2007, when millions of institutional and private investors became aware of the risks of trusting the managers of their banks. The deficient formal system of monitoring the US financial market has disastrous consequences for most financial institutions worldwide. Conditions for US mortgages that are too generous and financial innovations for hiding these risks quickly lead to a global decline of growth rates. Whereas this list of sins could be easily extended, the equally obvious virtue of the global economy is its dramatic growth in recent decades.[1] Global business interacts efficiently despite the heterogeneity of social, economic and legal cultures which, according to widespread assumptions, causes insecurities and uncertainties. Breaches of contracts may occur more frequently and business relationships may be terminated more often in international than in domestic trade. However, most business people engaged in exporting or importing

[1] In global terms, the annual average compound growth rate between 1913 and 1950 was less than 1%. The following 23-year period was one of strong international trade expansion with annual compound growth averaging 7.9%, which then eased off to 5.1% over the 25-year period 1973—98 (<http://www.globalmarketbriefings.com> accessed 17 June 2008).

products or services seem to operate in a sufficiently predictable environment allowing successful ventures into the global market.

The ongoing debates about the declining role of the nation-state, the importance of multinational enterprises, the phenomenon of codes of conduct and the participation of non-governmental organisations (NGOs) in all kinds of regulatory regimes all refer to the (in the opinions of business people: ugly) face of regulatory governance. It is blamed as irrelevant to full employment, harmful to resource allocation and growth, counter-productive in a globalised market and harmful to income distribution (Shipman, 1999: 390–438). Deregulation, privatisation and 'minimising the state' are strategies recommended as recipes in order to reduce the over-extended role of government in the economy. At the same time, a different debate emerges in economic literature and reports of international financial institutions referring to public (state) responsibilities in supporting and securing market exchanges (Webb, 1999; Shihata, 1997). This style of government, the coordination (support) function of institutions, aims at establishing certainty and trust and the reduction of transaction costs.

The seemingly paradoxical picture of cultural/institutional diversity and contractual efficiency of cross-border business transactions has become an interesting research subject and this book will try to make a contribution to the debate. Cultural and institutional diversity has led to countless initiatives of state and/or private actors establishing legal and informal regimes towards corporate social responsibility in the global economic system. These are activities which try to deal with the above-mentioned social problems caused or aggravated by the globalisation of the economy. If successful, on the one hand, they limit the freedom of doing business, but on the other hand, they reduce some of the uncertainties in a world of multiple regulators. All other uncertainties of economic exchanges, despite regulatory interventions, continue to affect business people and are considered largely part of their way of life: business opportunities, innovations, markets, etc. Some ('developed') nation states also intervene in this 'private' realm of doing business, intending to facilitate contract enforcement. Through private law, the state offers a set of background norms and processes that can be used by private parties to make claims against each other. Private international law (consisting of domestic rules principally concerned with applicable law, jurisdiction of courts, and recognition and enforcement of judgments in civil disputes with aspects that cross jurisdictional borders) and unified private law (like the United Nations Convention on Contracts for the International Sale of Goods (CISG)) aim to extend this support for enforcement of cross-border contracts. The actual use of these 'facilitative' or 'enabling' instruments varies between legal cultures, between industries and social strata, leading to legal debates about best solutions (which is since Roman times the justification of legal scholarship) and legal initiatives to spread these best solutions worldwide (which also has a long tradition and is currently practised by the World Bank and many other international, state or private institutions).

More recently, the debates go beyond the details of best solutions by questioning the underlying assumption that an economy requires this legal support in order to be successful (mostly measured in growth rates) and efficient. Mainly (legal and economic) sociologists and economists take part in these debates, whereas legal science and neo-classical economy remain unaffected in their strong positions in favour of or against this assumption. For academic as well as for practising jurists, law is constitutional for society in general and for the economy in particular (ubi societas, ibi ius). Consequently, world trade 'needs' an international commercial law (Gopalan, 2004; World Bank, 2005). By contrast, neo-classical economy assumes that economic actors have no need for normative guidance in making rational decisions in markets. They have clear and consistent preferences and are able to render judgement on the probability of future outcomes. Neo-classical economics, with its reliance on the invisible hand paradigm, does not need institutions for efficient markets (Shipman, 1999: 429; critical North, 2005: 13). Neither of these two extreme positions explains the variance of economic behaviour within societies, let alone in a comparison of economic cultures and the world economy. The sociologists and economists currently involved in studying the role of law in the economy with more analytical and mostly empirical methodologies make use of Max Weber's insights on this subject, of New Institutional Economics, Evolutionary Economics and anthropological studies on the role of interpersonal relations and networks. These disciplines meet in 'varieties of capitalism' and 'law and economic development' research and have produced in the last decade knowledge highly relevant both for theory and practice. In studying the role of law in the global economy (which may be characterised as a 'developing' economy), it seems a good choice to take this knowledge as a frame of reference. The project leading to this book was just another occasion where disciplines located between the aforementioned extreme positions of doctrinal law and classical economics met, attempting both to follow their own agenda and learn from like-minded research in the academic neighbourhood.

CURRENT DEBATES ON LAW AND ECONOMIC DEVELOPMENT

In most social systems of production and exchange, the *coordination (support)* function of institutions occupies an important position, whereas regulatory aspects in fact play a minor role. In some sectors of economics and sociology it is common knowledge that market exchanges are not only contractually organised: they are embedded in social relationships and are also largely dependent on external coordination (governance). From this perspective, state law is one (although not the only) coordination structure and current debates on public-private modes of regulation also apply (Grande, 2005). Some states have established such structures or are in the process of creating them. Other states—either purposefully or due to lack of resources—refrain from building structures for market exchanges. Comparative economic sociology (Hollingsworth and Boyer, 1997) has provided many examples of cultural differences in organising markets. Support structures are in some cultures predominantly established by horizontal modes, whereas in others they are established by vertical modes of economic coordination. Horizontal modes of coordination are markets and communities; vertical modes are firms and the state. In addition—placed between the horizontal and vertical modes—networks and associations contribute to the governance system. Regulatory states, dominant developmental states, business corporatist states and inclusive corporatist states (Hall and Soskice, 2001) each develop distinctive ways of organising the institutional environment of the economy. Frequently made assumptions that the models can be ranged on efficiency and rationality scales are not supported by comparative economic research. A single best way to economic growth does not seem to exist (Boyer and Hollingsworth, 1997). Additional 'varieties of capitalism' (Hollingsworth and Boyer, 1997) emerge in globalised systems of exchange which develop their own culture and structure. This may then have repercussions on the economies of all nation states which take part in global trade regimes. Furthermore, globalisation may lead to new institutional arrangements.

Law and economic development research uses similar complex and comparative approaches in order to understand how economic behaviour is coordinated in situations of uncertainty. More attention than in comparative economic sociology is laid on the specific role of law as a potential support structure for the economy. Its central interest revolves around the questions of whether Max Weber's thesis needs qualification that 'modern' law characterised by formal legal rationality is uniquely suited to the demands of capitalism, and whether the relative informality that is so often said to characterise business relationships suggests that social institutions can provide at least a substantial portion of whatever stability and predictability capitalist development requires. Weber's idealised picture of how law operated in Germany, his 'England problem' and currently the narrow assumptions of promoters of the rule of law—biased again by an idealised picture of how law operates in the United States—are under scrutiny. In addition, economic theory contributes to this debate through the increasing influence of new institutional economics, which brings institutional structures and processes, explicitly including law, back into the picture.

We distinguish between and elaborate on five approaches which contribute to the debate on the role of law in economic development: (i) classical sociology of law; (ii) law and development; (iii) economic sociology; (iv) institutional economics; and (v) social capital discourses.

Max Weber is the classical reference for the argument that formal rational law, a politically independent bureaucracy and a predictable judiciary are prerequisites for a modern economy organised in anonymous markets (Trubek, 1972). A rational legal system should be autonomous from other social structures. It should be composed of systematically observable norms and rules that are purposively constructed. Such norms and rules must be applied with principled consistency to produce a system of predictable, systematic, formal and rational law, autonomous from prevailing political or religious considerations. The current discussion points in somewhat different directions: not only is Weber himself seen as much more open to informal and discretionary institutional support for the economy (Treiber, 1989; Gessner, 2007; Dorbeck-Jung, this volume), but his calculability and predictability premise is considered less relevant for economic performance (Heydebrand, 2007; Scheuerman, 1999; Teubner, 1997; Dorbeck-Jung, this volume). Like Peerenboom (2002), most participants in the actual reformulation of Weberian approaches—instead of insisting exclusively on state support and legalisation—search for 'the right combination of private and public ordering'. These new perspectives do not try to prove Weber wrong, but simply take dramatic changes in all developed or developing societies and their economies into account.

Law and development (Galanter and Trubek, 1974; Gardner, 1981; Carty, 1992; Cao, 1997; Larson-Rabin, 2007)—originally a scholarly movement which transformed later into a massive assistance programme of international financial institutions—initially gave priority to the role of the state in the economy and the development of internal markets. The perspective on law as an instrument for effective state intervention and regulation shifted in the 1990s to an approach more interested in legal certainty and legal structures facilitating market exchanges. Trubek (2006)—who himself was and still is one of the prominent activists of the movement— critically describes these two consecutive phases as inefficient and even counterproductive due to their application of an idealised Western rule of law concept, a strong belief in universal institutional models for market exchanges and the possibility of legal transplants imposed from the top. He currently perceives and advocates a third phase which considers the local context and local institution, avoids the 'one size fits all' approach and incorporates a social agenda in policy recommendations. Economic development requires the protection of human rights in addition to an effective system of property, contract, labour, bankruptcy, commercial codes, personal rights laws and other elements of a comprehensive legal system that is effectively, impartially and cleanly administered by a well-functioning, impartial and honest judicial and legal system. The role of private ordering in the third phase is not made explicit, but does not seem to be considered particularly relevant. Law and development is—at least predominantly—a legal agenda with recommendations for state policy-makers and international development assistance institutions.

Economic sociology always had as major intellectual sources Karl Marx, Max Weber and Karl Polanyi, with their discussion of legal elements in economic structures. However, for some decades the interest in law as a constitutive element of economic phenomena in modern society has been lost (Swedberg, 2003). The main research areas were organisations, enterprises, associations, networks, personalised economic relations, and informal norms and rules. In opposition to classical economics and its fictitious model of the rational and well-informed *homo economicus*, economic sociologists emphasised economic behaviour being embedded in social structures, cultural patterns and close-knit relationships. This private-order focus has only recently been amalgamated with economic (Zafirovski, 2000; Nee, 2005) and sociology of law (Swedberg, 2003) approaches, together with research on varieties of capitalism (Hollingsworth and Boyer, 1997)—the latter adequately covering all three disciplines. Most explicit in his interest in law and public rather than private governance structures is the economic sociologist Neils Fligstein (2001), who states bluntly that without law, states and the ability to find non-predatory legal methods of competition, firms cannot exist.

Institutional economics is among those approaches which have a quite balanced view on informal and formal governance structures. Douglass North (1990) explains economic performance as a dependent variable of efficient institutions. If the measurement of quality of whatever it is that is being produced or exchanged, the analysis and comparison of price, the enforcement of contracts and so forth cause transaction costs, economic actors can be, and in reality generally are, supported by institutions which reduce the investment in situations of choice. He posits that rationality, in the sense that economists talk about, works best when the choices of the players are most limited. As North (1999) notes: 'Markets have to be structured'. Whereas private, informal rules structure large sectors of the economy, these institutions tend to be legal institutions in impersonal markets. This balanced view gets somewhat lost in the literature where North's followers tend to focus their attention on formal institutions (for a critical discussion, see Knowles, 2005; Evans, 1995). It also gets lost in the course of research commissioned by policy-makers and international development institutions. By definition, private ordering and informal rules are not 'engineerable'. They cannot be created, imposed and legislated. This is why institutional economics appears to be biased in favour of legal institutions. Institutional economics also has a neo-liberal reputation because it is in the policy context more often used for creating opportunities for business (enabling law) than setting up constraints on business (regulatory law).

Although social capital approaches are similar to and overlap with discourses on informal institutions in institutional economics, they have their own research tradition across academic disciplines (Bourdieu, 1986; Coleman, 1988; Putnam *et al*, 1993; Lin, 2001; for an overview, see Woolcock, 1998). Higher levels of social capital—defined as the degree of trust, cooperative norms and associational memberships or networks in a society—are observed to influence economic performance: either improving performance by increasing the number of mutually beneficial trades, solving collective action problems, reducing monitoring and transaction costs and improving information flows (Knowles, 2005) or, on the contrary, prevent the market from functioning well. They can be ruinous not only for society at large (eg mafia communities), but even for the members of cooperative associations and interpersonal networks. As Dasgupta (2005, 12) notes, although networks and markets often complement each other:

> [T]here is nothing good or bad about interpersonal networks: other things being equal, it is the *use* to which a network is put by members that determines its quality.

A large number of studies have been carried out in order to assess these uses, in particular under the umbrella of the World Bank (which offers its own social capital website). The social capital is located somewhere between the individual and the state, the latter creating a positive or negative framework for its organisation and its influence on economic exchange. Effective states deliver rule-governed environments strengthening local organisations and institutions; ineffective states may cause the atomisation of society, leaving no space for self-organisation at the bottom. Most relevant are discourses on synergetic cooperation between public and private institutions (Evans, 1997), where state agencies rather than limiting local initiatives form dense networks of ties that connect state and social capital—making sure that embeddedness does not degenerate into clientelism, corruption and rent-seeking. Particularly in third-world communities, social capital is considered a resource that is at least latently available for economic development. State/network linkages seem to have played a central role in the transformation of East Asian economies from low-productivity agrarian to the most rapidly growing industrial regions of the world.

There is rich empirical literature produced or referred to in all of the above discourses. To mention only some examples: studies on the coordination through trust (Macaulay, 1963; 1985; Burt, 2001; McMillan and Woodruff, 1999) led to important theoretical discourses on relational contracting (eg Williamson, 1985). Equally important is empirical research on networks as a substitute for impersonal third-party institutional support that guarantees contracts and private property. Studies on the role of law in economic development have been carried out in Asia and Africa, as well as in Western and Eastern Europe. Feenstra *et al* (2001) deal with Taiwanese and South Korean business groups; Fafchamps (2004) with ethnic networks and indigenous market institutions in Sub-Saharian Africa; Kali (2001) with business networks in Eastern Europe; Aoki and Patrick (1994) with the Japanese Main Bank System (see a critical discussion in Miwa and Ramseyer, 2002; and Milhaupt, 2002); Milhaupt (2001) deals more generally with corporate governance in Japan; Kirman (2001) with the fish-market in Marseille; Padgett (2001) with the Renaissance Florentine Banking System; Greif (1993) with Mediterranean traders from the eleventh century known as the Maghribi; and again Greif (2006) with medieval trade. Finally, the compensation of weak court systems by endogenous dispute resolution institutions have been studied by Gessner (1976; 1984) in Mexico, and by Hendrix (1997) and Hendley (2001) in Russia. Dixit (2004) makes use of these and similar empirical data for law and economics and for his theory on behavioural consequences of lawlessness.

Recently, Trebilcock and Leng (2006) have made an extremely useful effort to summarise this empirical knowledge with regard to whether the existence of a formal contract law and enforcement regime significantly contributes to economic growth. They found that the existing empirical evidence on the correlation between a country's economic growth and legal enforcement of contracts suggests a strong correlation only in the financial sector. It turns out that both the proponents of contract formalism and of contract informalism offer supporting bodies of theory and empirical evidence, but that both risk overstating, or at least over-simplifying, their cases. In evaluating the literature from a developmental point of view, they conclude:

> ... that at low levels of economic development, informal contract enforcement mechanisms may be reasonably good substitutes for formal contract enforcement mechanisms. At higher levels of development, however, informal contract enforcement may become an increasingly imperfect substitute due to the presence of large, long-lived, highly asset-specific investments, as well as the prevalence of increasingly complex trade in goods and services that often occurs outside of repeated exchange relationships (at 1519).

Even these cautious attempts at generalising empirical research are challenged by the success stories of East Asian economies. Japan, South Korea, Taiwan and in particular China, with their rates of economic growth unknown in Western industrialised countries in the latter half of the twentieth century:

> ... failed to put judiciaries and problem-solving lawyers at the center of the governance process, failed to serve as convenient fora for private litigation to enforce property and contract rights, failed to protect minority shareholder

> rights, failed to take intellectual property rights, competition law, or insolvency law very seriously, and failed to legalise state-private sector relations through constitutional and administrative law (Ohnesorge, 2007: 290).

Most experts on Asian law agree that the 'Asian miracle' was accomplished largely without legal support on the private, administrative or constitutional law levels. Explanations were sought in particularities of the political system (Trebilcock and Leng, 2006, on China), in the absence of social conflict due to a homogeneous population (Trebilcock and Leng, 2006, on Japan), in substantive rationality approaches conducing to reasonable choices and trade-offs (Ohnesorge, 2007) and in cultural preferences for extra-legal relationships (Upham, 1987).

According to Ohnesorge (2007) and Mayeda (2006), East-Asian economies should not be treated as exceptional cases. Instead, they should be understood as alternatives to Western modernism and open our eyes to different normative systems that promote and coordinate social systems of production and exchange using alternative trajectories. To the extent that legal, sociological or economic theories on the role of law in the economy cannot accommodate the North-east Asian experience, they are considered inadequate. Ohnesorge's careful analysis of current knowledge on law and economic development leads to the conclusion that no general theory is available which either requires or rejects law as a constitutive institution for the operation of the economy. Max Weber's 'England problem' is today's 'China enigma'.

One issue that is not widely addressed in the literature on contract enforcement and development is the role of law, business coordination and contract enforcement in contemporary international trade. Since international trade has a comparably weak legal infrastructure and similar growth rates to East-Asian economies, this phenomenon of the 'world trade miracle' deserves equal attention and should be considered to be a similar theoretical challenge as the China enigma.

INTERNATIONALISATION OF MARKETS AND CONTRACTUAL CERTAINTY

The purpose of this collection is to build on this interdisciplinary exercise by: (i) adding some more empirical evidence to ongoing debates regarding enabling structures for *international* business; and (ii) critically reviewing and discussing some of the propositions in the literature which contain interesting hypotheses on the effects of the *internationalisation* of markets on market coordination institutions. Although the literature discussed above is a rich source for theory and empirical practices, its approaches and observations cannot easily be generalised with regard to the international field because actors and the social context differ in many important ways. In the global economy, there is no 'developmental state' (as in Asian national economies) and little interference by international financial institutions. Economic actors tend to be strong and experienced. Lawlessness is not always compensated by existing social norms, and culture is less relevant for either impeding or supporting market-efficient institutions. These and more differences between the domestic and global contexts will have to be elaborated in each of the papers collected in this volume.

There is little theoretical guidance for studies on the internationalisation of markets. From the position of economic sociology, Whitley (2003a) points to emergent global institutions for contract enforcement; Teubner (1997), as a prominent representative of systems theory, takes merchant law and the processes of international commercial arbitration as examples of how global functional systems are generating 'global law without a state'; and Hadfield (2001; 2002) suggests from an economic perspective that in order to achieve market efficiency, commercial and corporate law should be privatised. The competition of different private legal regimes is advocated as a first-best solution. In contrast are proponents of the law merchant (Berger, 2001), who advise the recognition of autonomous commercial norms by state courts. Our research question of whether law explains the 'world trade miracle' is only marginally addressed by these theoretical debates. If one looks for empirical research on the coordination of business exchanges in international markets, there is not much more to report. Dezalay and Garth (1996) provide useful information about the working of international arbitrators and their reluctance to create an autonomous *lex mercatoria*. Trebilcock and Leng (2006:1541) in their evaluation of empirical studies—after complaining that 'new institutional economics' scholars have paid inadequate attention to investigating the impact on contract enforcement mechanisms brought by the expansion of international trade and growing trend of economic globalisation—mention some studies on transnational business networks and on the increasing use of barter in both international trade and transition economies which their authors consider an optimal institutional response to contract enforcement problems in both settings. Berkowitz, Moenius and Pistor (2004) present evidence that a country's domestic legal institutions have strong explanatory power for its integration in international markets. Countries with higher ratings on rule of law scales experience greater international trade flows.

About one-half of the contributions to the present volume emerge from the Collaborative Research Unit, 'Transformation of the State', at the University of Bremen, Germany.[2] Previous research frequently referred to

[2] <http://www.sfb597.uni-bremen.de/?SPRACHE=en> accessed 17 June 2008. This large research project is funded by the *Deutsche Forschungsgemeinschaft* and generously supported by the University of Bremen.

in this volume documents the emergence of our topic and our emphasis on empirical studies.[3] The support function of domestic courts (Germany, Italy, the United States) for cross-border exchanges was the object of our initial curiosity (Gessner, 1996), followed by empirical research on cross-border debt-collection, cross-border maintenance claims, social security claims of European migrant workers, international disputes in the London reinsurance market, cross-border money transfer in the European banking sector and on support offered by (German) consulates and chambers of commerce abroad (Gessner and Budak, 1998).[4] The third publication in this series (Appelbaum, Felstiner and Gessner, 2001) offers—in addition to more theoretical debates[5]—empirical insights on international law firms, Chinese business networks (*guanxi*) and international arbitration. Sosa (2007)—the most recent dissertation emanating from the Bremen 'Transformation of the State' project—provides a balanced picture of the role of contract law in international business exchanges.

Our new volume now adds research on the coordination of international business in the diamond industry, the timber trade and the software industry by mid-sized and mega law firms, and by accounting firms.

A careful evaluation of this emergent empirical knowledge is useful in order to arrive at a better theoretical understanding of global law and global non-legal institutions in the worldwide varieties of capitalism (Gessner, 2007). It helps to avoid the selective use of data as it best fits the author's purposes—a fallacy particularly evident in globalisation of law discourses. It is fascinating to speculate about the 'world society' or 'global law', but this should be complemented by more down-to-earth—although mostly less spectacular—empirical research in areas affected by globalisation, in particular the economy. A complex understanding of coordination institutions of modern economies allows theory building about current or future changes in market coordination caused by globalisation processes.[6]

[3] Research started in the social science department of the Max Planck Institute for Comparative and Private International Law in Hamburg and was taken up when the entire department moved to a more interdisciplinary environment at the University of Bremen.

[4] During this project phase, dissertations with rich empirical data were written by Budak (1999), Grotheer (1998), Stammel (1998) and Vial (1999).

[5] These debates are structured on a continuum between universalist and particularist support institutions: law, *lex mercatoria*, law firms and networks (Gessner, Appelbaum and Felstiner, 2001). This is a differentiation also used in contributions to this volume.

[6] Comparative law, legal theory and legal history also deal from their perspectives with our topic (Michael and Jansen, 2006; Jansen and Michaels, 2007) and participate in conferences with similar titles ('Beyond the State? Rethinking Private Law' (Hamburg, 12/13 July 2007)). Despite being largely complementary, these legal discourses should develop separately from social scientific approaches in this early stage of reflection.

CONTRIBUTIONS TO THIS VOLUME

Empirical Studies

Diamond Trade

Barak Richman updates our knowledge about the diamond trade, the most frequently used example of a community of traders who coordinate their exchanges autonomously and have completely 'opted out of the legal system'. Recent developments challenge this trade, which has been stable for nearly a millennium. Indian diamond manufacture and trade traditions re-emerged with the opening of global market opportunities and the advantages of lower wages compared to wages paid in high-income nations, where Jewish diamond networks have operated in recent centuries. Consumer demands for a control of 'conflict diamonds' sold by African military warlords brought scrutiny to the previously secretive DeBeers monopoly and led to an international programme to certify the origin of each diamond. In addition, as a response to both developments, Richman describes revolutionary changes in the DeBeers marketing strategies from wholesale distribution to a vertically integrated marketing strategy supported by global branding campaigns. Whereas the Indian ethnic network using community institutions and ethnic-based extra-legal sanctions may be orchestrated similar to the Jewish diamond trade with no need for state law and public courts, the other two developments require legal regulation and contract law. Richman's surprising finding—similar to some of Konradi's observations in the timber trade—is that globalisation has brought more law, not less, to an industry that has been historically lawless.

Timber Trade

Wioletta Konradi has chosen the timber industry for a study on the governance of global business exchanges. She finds a mix of relational mechanisms and support structures ranging from trust in long-term relations, reputational sanctions in business networks, branch norms, autonomous commercial norms created by the International Chamber of Commerce and state law. Contract enforcement by third parties plays—as is common in business everywhere—a marginal role. Arbitration is popular (although the number of cases seems to be declining), whereas state courts are used less frequently for conflict resolution (mostly debt collection) in exchanges beyond the traditional (Western or Organisation for Economic Cooperation and Development (OECD)) timber markets. As her comparison with the diamond trade shows, the timber trade is far from reaching a kind of regulatory autonomy which, as Richman observes, is slowly disappearing even in previously close-knit communities such as the (Jewish) diamond traders community. This picture of economic institutions and economic behaviour supports most assumptions of economic sociology and institutional economics and is also shared by those approaches which Konradi calls traditionalist. No one holds or has ever held a position that contract enforcement is only possible by way of state support and through the application of state law. In search of traditionalists, one would rather find approaches at the opposite end—those which defend a complete autonomy of market behaviour from state and legal support—such as classical economy. Konradi offers valuable details of industry self-regulation, suggesting in her conclusions that this phenomenon is neither recent nor positively related to globalisation. Most interesting is her outlook on future developments. The data seem to indicate that globalisation has weakened private governance structures of the timber industry and that the cooperation between the state and private actors in developing support structures will increase considerably in the future.

Software Industry

Thomas Dietz and Holger Nieswandt summarise in their chapter an empirical study of contract enforcement in worldwide cooperations within the software industry. The software development carried out for German companies by Bulgarian, Indian and Rumanian firms appears to have a legal structure, since complex contracts are negotiated with choice of law and also mostly arbitration clauses. However, legal contract enforcement is almost impossible for the same uncertainties described in most other chapters in this volume. Some large firms have legal departments, but they do not take their controversies to domestic courts. Equally absent in this branch of business are autonomous rules of a *lex mercatoria* type. If disputes are arbitrated, it is (German) law which applies. Reputation and business network information— in most situations—puts enough pressure on contracting parties to honour previous agreements. The authors' most interesting finding is the bilateral contract management facilitated by almost daily electronic control, adaptation of expectations and reorganisation of next steps within the contractual cooperation. It seems as if high-speed information creates a kind of cognitive attitude to those unforeseen events which in previous non-electronic centuries have been defined as normative clashes, breach of contract and fraud. If the exchange cooperation develops in a way which was not anticipated, a speedy change of strategies on both sides mostly helps to avoid disappointments and turning to a 'naming, blaming, claiming' automatism.[7] This phenomenon of cognitive management of disappointments can certainly be generalised beyond the exchange within the trans-national software industry and may become a style element of a forthcoming global legal culture.[8]

International Law Firms

Fabian Sosa's detailed description and analysis of the handling of international cases in a German mid-sized law firm is the result of a unique opportunity of a participant observation. This method is generally (and more so in studying a legal context) far superior to data collection through interviews. The chapter provides an insider perspective of lawyers struggling with the uncertainties of cross-border arbitration. The transactions do not leave the sphere of influence of the law firms at any time. Lawyers draft complex contracts which are often the basis of coordination. They advise their clients on all matters concerning settlement, litigation or arbitration and they participate in the arbitration procedure as representatives of the parties or, if not involved as party representative, as arbitrators.

In all of those activities, state law is relevant, but somewhat shifted to the background. It is not the law—not even its shadow—nor the law merchant which offers the necessary institutional support for doing business, but the lawyer in his or her role as a manager of uncertainty. The typical client of a mid-sized law firm is a mid-sized company which has little experience in matters of international dispute resolution and no knowledge of foreign law or private international law. However, the company trusts the law firm to find an acceptable solution. Sosa not only describes the ways in which an experienced law firm earns this trust, but also how inexperienced law firms only pretend to be knowledgeable in international matters and advise a quick settlement in order to avoid embarrassing failures in dealing with foreign lawyers, foreign courts or experienced arbitrators. This study is complementary to other studies of the international legal profession, which deal mainly with the mega law firm advising big businesses with its huge experience and manpower. Sosa's participant observation is also complementary to research which conceives international arbitrators as an elite group with internal struggles rather than a profession with its specific methods as mediators and decision-makers.

[7] As the authors point out, they rely heavily on legal-sociological knowledge, in this context on Felstiner, Abel and Sarat, 1980.

[8] This again is a reference to legal sociology (Luhmann 1971; 1982).

International Investment and Financing

John Flood and Eleni Skordaki introduce us to the strange and (to most of us) unfamiliar world of real-estate finance. If the reader hardly understands this complex process of structuring 'pan-European' real-estate transactions and cross-collateralisations and if he or she is lost in the transaction structure of Canary Wharf 2001 financing given in Figure II, he or she only supports the authors' arguments: this world of capital flows and investment is impenetrable, opaque and uncontrollable, not only for the normal citizen, but also for most lawyers and even state bureaucrats. This gives a few specialised law firms (according to the authors, predominantly English firms) in collaboration with the Big Four accounting firms, banks and credit rating agencies a dominant position over all other actors like the Brussels administration, state regulatory agencies or tax offices. Security (for the money lent by the banks) is the main purpose of these efforts, but to call it legal certainty would seem overstated and a little euphemistic. State law and—in the case of the Sharía-compliant transactions— religious law are tools used unscrupulously in order to set up autonomous structures serving the interests of profit-seeking investors. Specialised law firms do not only support these cross-border capital flows, they create enabling structures without which investors would be confined to their domestic markets. The paper is written by two insiders, and so like Sosa's study, is a unique socio-legal opportunity for understanding the practice and the growing structural relevance of the legal profession.

Theoretical Debates

State-society Synergies in Economic and Legal Sociology

Volkmar Gessner starts by reviewing approaches in informal as well as formal and in endogenous as well as exogenous elements of market coordination. Market coordination may in part be achieved by contract enforcement institutions, but requires in addition a complex set of property rights protection institutions. They form the infrastructure of a market, a framework which is constitutive for any exchange before, during or after the specific transaction takes place. In a modern market economy, this protection is predominantly achieved through a *legal* infrastructure, although cultural institutions have an influence and informal (legal cultural) implementation patterns support or hinder the legal institutions to create the required trust in market relations. The importance of law as a constitutive element means that the state is a core player in establishing the institutional framework for markets. This constitutes then a description of the situation before the markets became more and more globalised and new actors and global institutions ready to replace or complement the traditional legal infrastructure emerged. A number of theories of change deal with this possible new situation and the role that the state plays in it, using as indicators most frequently contracts, international lawyering, dispute settlement, *lex mercatoria* and arbitration. Gessner concludes that there is no general theoretical consent or sufficient empirical evidence that nation-state support for the globalising economy is significantly changing by developments in the contract enforcement field. Such speculations under-estimate the complexities of social systems in general and of social systems of production in particular. Sufficiently complex theories for understanding domestic as well as global support for market exchanges seem to be those offered by economic sociology, in particular by Neil Fligstein.

Gralf-Peter Calliess recognises the existence of non-state normative orders in the transnational sphere as a social reality and attempts to reconstruct a legal approach beyond what he defines as traditional and transnational legal thinking. For the former, only state law has legal quality and the assumed weakness of state law in global dealings is deplored as lawlessness. For the latter, the private order created mostly by economic actors in order to facilitate global exchanges also qualifies as law. A critical discussion of both approaches is based on the normative argument that private and public law, coordination and regulation cannot be separated and that state law and non-state normative orders have comparable legal qualities. Neither lawlessness, with its lack of institutional support, nor private legislation, with its insufficient justice elements and protection of public goods, is a desirable model for global ordering. Callies prefers a model of transnational civil regimes which intermingles public and private governance mechanisms. This is, of course, a familiar and appreciated perspective for legal sociology and equally for economic sociology: both use this model of an institutional mix even for domestic legal cultures. Such a common perspective between normative and descriptive approaches seems to be a rare coincidence and will facilitate interdisciplinary cooperation between law and the social sciences in understanding and shaping global legal cultures—although all of those problems connected with the 'living law' concept will also be shared.

Efficient Private Legal Regimes in Law and Economics

Gillian Hadfield further develops her previously published—and in this volume frequently discussed—premise that the law governing commercial transactions need not be provided by the state, taking issue in particular with Callies' evolutionary perspective of emerging mixed public-private governance regimes generating transnational civil order. Distinguishing between the economic and democratic functions of law, she perceives a potential for identifying legal rules or mechanisms the functions of which are, or can be treated as, exclusively to achieve efficiency: the maximisation of gains from trade and the best use and allocation of resources. The rules governing contracts between corporate entities, for example, have only an efficiency dimension—even when fairness or due process emerge as a component of what the private market produces. Hadfield then emphasises that this efficiency dimension does not imply that the entire relationship is allocated to a private legal sphere. Three distinct ways are discussed in which privatising some aspects of commercial law will inevitably involve and may require elements of public law: legal services in adjudication and rule enforcement, a legal infrastructure of institutions and procedures without which contractual 'self-enforcement' cannot work, and public monitoring of market imperfections through, for example, competition law. In Hadfield's view, the public law elements directed to improving the efficiency of private legal regimes can and should be distinguished from those nation state or transnational regulatory institutions which aim to achieve democratic legitimacy.

Institution Building in Evolutionary Economics

Jörg Freiling's starting point is an institutional gap for international economic transactions. This approach follows the argument of new institutional economics in so far as institutional support is considered necessary for saving transaction costs. However, Freiling then takes his own direction by assuming that nation states are unable, unwilling or at least too slow to create the institutional structures, depriving business people of exogenous governance structures and forcing them to organise their own private order if they want to 'go international'. Important variables are business types, since needs for a specific governance structure vary according to what is exchanged: a product in a spot market, a product in a long-term relationship, a project or a system of prospective solutions. This process of institution building is analysed with the tools of evolutionary economics and their concepts of variation, selection and retention. The evolution is complex and characterised by trial and error and by historical accidents and contingencies. Second-best solutions and inefficiencies are maintained due to path dependencies, inertia, lack of information and—quite uncommon in economic discourses—due to the exercise of power. However, in the paper, somewhat pushed to the background, the variables used for analysing the evolution of economic institutions may also help to understand legal developments and the efforts of nation states and international agencies to build secure structures for global trade and for individual businesses. The approach does not seem superior to institutional economics in explaining the emergence of efficient institutions, but it offers interesting variables and better hypotheses for explaining the long life of inefficient institutions. Cooperation with legal sociology with its long tradition in researching this subject looks promising for both disciplines.

Updating Max Weber's Theory of Legal Certainty

Bärbel Dorbeck-Jung questions familiar concepts of legal certainty and goes back to the sources. Max Weber's most influential assumption that legal infrastructures facilitate modern capitalist developments by creating legal certainty (in the sense of a general, abstract, clear, hierarchic, coherent, uniform, predictable and stable legal order based on the state's monopoly of organised violence) is explained in the context of his economic sociology and confronted with its challenges. According to sophisticated and ongoing debates, Weber's model of the affinity between formal rational law and modern capitalism has lost its explanatory value due to globalisation processes, the emergence of multinational enterprises, technological innovations, decreasing relevance of nation states, legal pluralism and the decreasing role of legal instruments in public governance. Dorbeck-Jung, although supporting most of these challenges and suggesting a re-conceptualisation of economic needs for calculability and legal certainty, believes that Weber's 'iron cage' metaphor is not representative for his much more complex approach allowing for the recognition of non-state support structures for the economy and the materialisation of law (as opposed to formal law, which Weber is mostly identified with). A careful reading of Weber's great 90-year-old *oeuvre* still seems to be helpful in understanding legal developments in times of globalisation.

Wolf Heydebrand examines the concepts of contractual certainty and efficiency in global-local interaction in the historical context of pre-national, national, supra-national and post-national phases of economic globalisation and legal development. This analysis suggests that the goal of achieving contractual certainty was integral to the liberal legalism and formalism of the nienteenth century continental European nation states and their bureaucracies, but was gradually superseded by the goal of contractual efficiency in the post-national context of the late twentieth and early twenty-first centuries. The analysis also suggests that the assumption of the trans-historical stability and continuity of socially embedded legal and economic institutions is problematic in view of the disembedding consequences of globalisation. Temporarily established institutions and relatively autonomous practices may be exposed to a reversal of their embedded status under the impact of the pervasive neo-liberal quest for transnational economic and legal efficiency.

Some Important Limitations of our Collection

The contributions to this volume offer a variety of answers to our research question: why international trade prospers without a clear and predictive support structure comparable to institutions in economically successful nation states. The institutional gap is filled partly by law firms, trade associations and arbitrators, but also by a reliance on networks and close inter-firm relationships. This last aspect is reinforced by revolutionary developments in the field of information and communication technologies which enable companies to control certain actions of their exchange partners in real time. Legal support is present almost everywhere, but to a lesser degree than in domestic exchange relations, since economic actors tend to build their own structures that they can rely on and make future actions somewhat more predictable. Since this social organisation of distrust comes at considerable costs, only relatively wealthy firms are able to shield themselves from the risks and disappointments of global trade. One only has to compare the *de luxe* arbitration described by Sosa (2009, in this volume) with the picture of bread and butter litigation of international cases in domestic courts (Gessner, 1996). If our case studies offer mostly success stories of global uncertainty management, a caveat is necessary: the losers of globalisation are not represented in our sample. In order to obtain a balanced picture, one should also read previous research published within the Bremen project on 'small peoples' problems' in enforcing cross-border claims (Gessner and Budak (eds), 1998: 191–324). Schnorr (1994) observes the desperate situation of small law firms and sole practitioners in dealing with international cases, and Petzold (1996) describes the miserable legal support for 'small people' provided by consulates and foreign chambers of commerce. In Sosa's sample (2007), many cases are reported where inexperienced firms suffer losses in their import and export trades, and Gessner *et al* (2001:19) discuss a number of publications where international legal practice is presented as a failure rather than as an example of autonomous management of trust. A position of economic power prevents the breach of a contract by the weaker party. The best way towards contractual certainty is the establishment of dependency relations. More research in this direction will reveal that the success stories in this book, as well as the aggregate numbers of international trade expansion given in footnote 1 above, have to be taken with caution. The same applies to cultural elements in the social organisation of distrust like Russian, Italian and East-Asian ethnic networks, in particular *guanxi* networks of Chinese communities which have been extensively discussed in our previous collection on the legal culture of global business transactions (Appelbaum *et al*, 2001). The present volume only addresses this cultural aspect with regard to Jewish networks in the diamond industry.

Like domestic exchanges studied by authors of law and economic development research, global exchanges are also characterised by a mix of positive and negative experiences with institutional support structures. Theory building reflects this controversial picture and can at the current state of knowledge hardly be more ambitious than what has been attempted in the final part of this volume. The varieties of capitalism prevent us from formulating a universal theory.

REFERENCES

Aoki, M and Patrick, H (1994) *The Japanese Main Bank System* (Oxford, Oxford University Press).

Appelbaum, RP, Felstiner, WLF and Gessner, V (eds) (2001) *Rules and Networks—The Legal Culture of Global Business Transactions* (Oxford, Hart).

Berger, KP (2001) 'The New Law Merchant and the Global Market Place' in KP Berger (ed), (2001) *The Practice of Transnational Law* (The Hague, Kluwer).

Berkowitz, D, Moenius, J and Pistor, K (2004) 'Legal Institutions and International Trade Flows' 26 Mich. J. Int'l L. 163–98.

Bourdieu, P (1986) 'The Forms of Capital' in JG Richardson (ed), *Handbook of Theory and Research in the Sociology of Education* (New York, Greenwald Press).

Budak, AC (1999) *Making Foreign People Pay* (Aldershot, Ashgate).

Burt, RS (2001) 'Bandwith and Echo: Trust, Information, and Gossip in Social Networks' in JE Rauch and A Casella (eds), *Networks and Markets* (New York, Russel Sage).

Cao, L (1997) 'Law and Economic Development—A New Beginning?' 32 *Texas International Law Journal* 545.

Carty, A (ed) (1992) *Law and Development* (New York, New York University Press).

Coleman, J (1988) 'Social Capital in the Creation of Human Capital' *American Journal of Sociology* 94 Supplement at 95–120.

Dasgupta, P (2005) 'Economics of Social Capital' *Economic Record* 81 at 2–21.

Dezalay, Y and Garth, B (1996) *Dealing in Virtue, International Commercial Arbitration and the Construction of a Transnational Order* (Chicago, University of Chicago Press).

Dixit, AK (2004) *Lawlessness and Economics: Alternative Modes of Governance* (Princeton, Princeton University Press).

Evans, P (1995) *Embedded Autonomy—States and Industrial Transformation* (Princeton, Princeton University Press).

—— (1997) *State-Society Synergy: Government and Social Capital in Development* (University of California, University of California Press).

Fafchamps, M (2004) *Market Institutions and Sub-Saharan Africa: Theory and Evidence* (Cambridge, MA, MIT Press).

Feenstra, RC, Hamilton, GG and Huang, DS (2001) 'The Organisation of the Taiwanese and South Korean Economies: A Comparative Equilibrium Analysis' in JE Rauch and A Casella (eds), *Networks and Markets* (New York, Russel Sage).

Felstiner, WLF, Abel, R and Sarat, A (1980) 'The Emergence and Transformation of Disputes: Naming, Blaming, Claiming' *Law & Society Review* 15 at 631.

Fleischer, H (2001) *Informationsasymmetrie im Vertragsrecht: eine rechtsvergleichende und interdisziplinäre Abhandlung zu Reichweite und Grenzen vertragsschlußbezogener Aufklärungspflichten* (München, Beck).

Fligstein, N (2002) *The Architecture of Markets—An Economic Sociology of Twenty-First-Century Capitalist Societies* (Princeton and Oxford, Princeton University Press).

Galanter, M and Trubek, DM (1974) 'Scholars in Self-Estrangement: Some Reflections on the Crisis in Law and Development Studies in the United States' 1974 Wis. L. Rev. 1062.

Gardner, JA (1981) *Legal Imperialism: American Lawyers and Foreign Aid in Latin America* (Madison, The University of Wisconsin Press).

Gessner, V (1976) *Recht und Konflikt—Eine soziologische Untersuchung privatrechtlicher Konflikte in Mexiko* (Tübingen, Mohr).

—— (1984) *Los conflictos sociales y la administración de justicia en México* (México, UNAM).

—— (ed) (1996) *Foreign Courts—Civil Litigation in Foreign Legal Cultures* (Aldershot, Dartmouth).

—— (2007) 'Legalisation and the Varieties of Capitalism' in C Antons and V Gessner (eds), *Globalization and Resistance—Law Reform in Asia since the Crisis* (Oxford, Hart).

Gessner, V and Budak, AC (eds) (1998) *Emerging Legal Certainty: Empirical Studies on the Globalization of Law* (Ashgate, Dartmouth).

Gessner, V, Appelbaum, RP and Felstiner, WLF (2001) 'Introduction: The Legal Culture of Global Business Transactions' in RP Appelbaum, WLF Felstiner, and V Gessner (eds,) *Rules and Networks—The Legal Culture of Global Business Transactions* (Oxford, Hart).

Gopalan, S (2004) 'The Creation of International Commercial Law: Sovereignty Felled?' 5 *San Diego International Law Journal* 267–322.

Grande, E (ed) (2005) *Complex Sovereignty: Reconstituting Political Authority in the Twenty-first Century* (Toronto, University of Toronto Press).

Greif, A (1993) 'Contract Enforceablity and Economic Institutions in Early Trade: The Maghribi Traders Coalition' *American Economic Review* 83 at 525–48.

—— (2006) *Institutions and the Path to the Modern Economy: Lessons from Medieval Trade* (Cambridge, Cambridge University Press).

Grotheer, K (1998) *Kindesunterhalt im grenzüberschreitenden Rechtsverkehr—anwendbares Recht und Durchsetzungsmechanismen in der Praxis* (Baden-Baden, Nomos).

Hadfield, GK (2001) 'Privatizing Commercial Law' 24 *Regulation* 40–45.

—— (2002) 'Privatizing Commercial Law: Lessons from Icann' 6 *Journal of Small and Emerging Business Law* 257–83.

Hendley, K (2001) 'Beyond the Tip of the Iceberg: Business Disputes in Russia' in P Murrell (ed), *Assessing the Value of Law in Transition Economies* (Ann Arbor, The University of Michigan Press).

Hendrix, GP (1997) 'Business Litigation and Arbitration in Russia' *International Lawyer* 31 at 1075–103.

Heydebrand, W (2007) 'Globalization and the Rise of Procedural Informalism in Europe and America' in V Gessner and D Nelken (eds), *European Ways of Law* (Oxford, Hart).

Hollingsworth, JR and Boyer, R (1997) 'Coordination of Economic Actors and Social Systems of Production' in JR Hollingsworth and R Boyer (eds), *Contemporary Capitalism—The Embeddedness of Institutions* (Cambridge University Press, Cambridge).

Howells, G (2005) 'The Potential and Limits of Consumer Empowerment by Information' *Journal of Law and Society*, 32 at 349–70.

Jansen, N and Michaels, R (2007) 'Private Law and the State' *RabelsZ* 71 at 345–97.

Kali, R (2001) 'Business Networks in Transition Economies: Norms, Contracts, and Legal Institutions' in P Murrell (ed), *Assessing the Value of Law in Transition Economies* (Ann Arbor, The University of Michigan Press).

Kirman, A (2001) 'Market Organization and Individual Behavior: Evidence from Fishmarkets' in JE Rauch and A Casella (eds), *Networks and Markets* (New York, Russel Sage).

Knowles, S (2005) 'Is Social Capital Part of the Institutions Continuum?' Working paper No 05/11 (Center for Research in Economic Development and International Trade, University of Nottingham).

Larson-Rabin, L (2007) 'Introduction to the 25th Anniversary Issue: Happenstance and Memory: A Legacy of Law and Development Scholarship and Policy in Legal Education' 25 Wis. Int'l L.J. 209–33.

Lin, N (2001) *Social Capital—A Theory of Social Structure and Action* (Cambridge, Cambridge University Press).

Luhmann, N (1971) 'Die Weltgesellschaft' *Archiv für Rechts- und Sozialphilosophie* 57 at 1–35.

—— (1982) 'The World Society as a Social System' *International Journal of General Systems* 8 at 131–8.
Macaulay, S (1963) 'Non-Contractual Relations in Business: A Preliminary Study' *American Sociological Review* 55:1 at 86–104.
—— (1985) 'Symposium: Law, Private Governance and Continuing Relationships, an Empirical View of Contract' *Wisconsin Law Review* 5 at 465–81.
Mattli, W (2001) 'Private Justice in a Global Economy: From Litigation to Arbitration' *International Organization* 55 at 919–47.
Mayeda, G (2006) 'Appreciate the Difference: The Role of Different Domestic Norms in Law and Development Reform; Lessons from China and Japan' 51 *McGill Law Journal* 547–98.
McMillan, J and Woodruff, C (1999) 'Trust and Search in Vietnam's Emerging Private Sector' *Journal of Law, Economics and Organization* 15 at 637–58.
Michaels, R and Jansen, N (2006) 'Private Law Beyond the State? Europeanization, Globalization, Privatization' *American Journal of Comparative Law* LIV at 843–90.
Milhaupt, CJ (2001) 'Creative Norm Destruction: The Evolution of Non-legal Rules in Japanese Corporate Governance' 149 *University of Pennsylvania Law Review* 2083–119.
—— (2002) 'On the (Fleeting) Existence of the Main Bank System and Other Japanese Economic Institutions' *Law & Social Inquiry* 425–37.
Miwa, Y and Ramseyer, JM (2002) 'The Myth of the Main Bank: Japan and Comparative Corporate Governance' *Law & Social Inquiry* 401–24.
Nee, V (2005) 'The New Institutionalisms in Economics and Sociology' in NJ Smelser and R Swedberg (eds), *The Handbook of Economic Sociology* (Princeton and Oxford, Princeton University Press, New York, Russel Sage Foundation).
Newton, S (2006) 'The Dialectics of Law and Development' in D Trubek and A Santos (eds), *The New Law and Economic Development—A Critical Appraisal* (Cambridge, Cambridge University Press).
North, DC (1990) *Institutions, Institutional Change and Economic Performance* (Cambridge, Cambridge University Press).
—— (1999) 'Dealing With a Non-Ergodic World: Institutional Economics, Property Rights, and the Global Environment' 10 *Duke Environmental Law and Policy Forum* 1.
—— (2005) *Understanding the Process of Economic Change* (Princeton and Oxford, Princeton University Press).
Ohnesorge, JKM (2007) 'Developing Development Theory: Law and Development Orthodoxies and the Northeast Asian Experience' 28 *University of Pennsylvania Journal of International Economic Law* 219–308.

Padgett, JF (2001) 'Organizational Genesis, Identity, and Control: The Transformation of Banking in Renaissance Florence' in JE Rauch and A Casella (eds), *Networks and Markets* (New York, Russel Sage).

Peerenboom, R (2002) 'Social Networks, Rule of Law and Economic Growth in China: The Elusive Pursuit of the Right Combination of Private and Public Ordering' 31 *Global Economic Review* 2.

Petzold, A (1998) 'Obtaining Information on Foreign Legal Systems' in V Gessner and AC Budak (eds), *Emerging Legal Certainty: Empirical Studies on the Globalization of Law* (Aldershot, Ashgate).

Putnam, RD, Leonardi, R and Nanetti, R (1994) *Making Democracy Work. Civic Traditions in Modern Italy* (Princeton, Princeton University Press).

Scheuerman, WE (1999) 'Globalization and the Fate of Law' in D Dyzenhaus (ed), *Recrafting the Rule of Law* (Oxford, Hart Publishing).

Schnorr, T (1994) 'Einzelanwälte und kleine Anwaltsfirmen im internationalen Rechtsverkehr—eine empirische Untersuchung' *Anwaltsblatt* 98.

Shihata, IFI (1997) 'The Role of Law in Business Development' 20 *Fordham International Law Journal* 1577–88.

Shipman, A (1999) *The Market Revolution and its Limits—A Price for Everything* (London, New York, Routledge).

Sosa, F (2007) *Vertrag und Geschäftsbeziehung im grenzüberschreitenden Wirtschaftsverkehr* (Baden-Baden, Nomos).

—— (2009) 'Cross-Border Dispute Resolution from the Perspective of Midsized Law Firms: The Example of International Commercial Arbitration' in V Gessner (ed), *Contractual Certainty in International Trade* (Oxford, Hart).

Stammel, C (1998) *Waving the Gentlemen's Business Goodbye: from Global Deals to Global Disputes in the London Reinsurance Market* (Frankfurt am Main, Peter Lang).

Teubner, G (ed) (1997) *Global Law without a State* (Aldershot, Dartmouth).

Trebilcock, M and Leng, J (2006) 'The Role of Formal Contract Law and Enforcement in Economic Development' 92 *Virginia Law Review* 1517–80.

Treiber, H (1989) *Vollzugskosten des Rechtsstaates und andere Studien zum Recht* (Baden-Baden, Nomos).

—— (2006) 'Max Weber and Eugen Ehrlich: on the Janus-headed construction of Weber's ideal type in the Sociology of Law', paper presented at an Oñati Workshop.

Trubek, D (1972) 'Max Weber on Law and the Rise of Capitalism' *Wisconsin Law Review* 3 at 720–53.

—— (2006) 'The "Rule of Law" in Development Assistance: Past, Present, and Future' in D Trubek and A Santos (eds), *The New Law and Economic Development—A Critical Appraisal* (Cambridge, Cambridge University Press).

Trubek, D and Santos, A (eds) (2006) *The New Law and Economic Development—A Critical Appraisal* (Cambridge, Cambridge University Press).

Upham, FK (1987) Law and Social Change in Postwar Japan (Cambridge, Mass., Harvard University Press).

Vial, E (1999) *Die Gerichtsstandswahl und der Zugang zum internationalen Ziwilprozess im deutsch-italienischen Rechtsverkehr: Eine rechtssoziologische Untersuchung* (Baden-Baden, Nomos Verlagsgesellschaft).

Webb, D (1999) 'Legal and Institutional Reform Strategy and Implementation: A World Bank Perspective' 30 *Law and Policy in International Business* 161–70.

Williamson, O (1985) *The Economic Institutions of Capitalism: Firms, Markets, Relational Contracting* (New York, The Free Press).

Woolcock, M (1998) 'Social Capital and Economic Development: toward a Theoretical Framework' *Theory and Society* 27 at 151–208.

World Bank (2005) Doing Business in 2005: Removing Obstacles to Growth (Washington, DC, World Bank).

Zafirovski, M (2000) 'Economic and Sociological Approaches to Institutions: Economy, Society and Law' *European Journal of Law and Economics* 10 at 7–30.

Part II

Empirical Studies

2

Ethnic Networks, Extra-legal Certainty and Globalisation: Peering into the Diamond Industry

BARAK D RICHMAN*

INTRODUCTION

AS THE CONTRIBUTORS in this volume colourfully illustrate, it is no small task to ensure legal certainty in transnational commerce, and the challenge becomes increasingly acute as commercial exchange becomes ever more globalised. One might expect, however, that the diamond industry would remain largely unaffected by this trend of globalisation. Because diamonds are easily portable, universally valuable and virtually untraceable, state courts are incapable of enforcing executory contracts for diamond sales (Richman, 2004; 2006). In other words, the diamond industry has *never* enjoyed legal certainty. Instead, it has relied on *extra-legal* certainty—a non-state system of contract enforcement that rests on personal exchange and reputation mechanisms. What then does globalisation mean for diamond merchants?

In fact, globalisation has had, and is having, a striking impact on the diamond industry, and the millennia-old distribution system that relied on multiple layers of personal exchange is showing cracks, or growth marks, depending on the perspective. This chapter explores how globalisation has affected the diamond industry's distribution networks, and some extrapolation might inform how globalisation affects not just legal certainty, but even a well-developed system of extra-legal certainty. As increasing transnational commerce pushes many industries away from state-sponsored law and towards new forms of private ordering (Appelbaum *et al*, 2001),

* The author thanks Joy Hanson and Qasim Jami for their excellent research assistance, the participants of the Oñati workshop for their valuable insights and lively discussion and, especially, Volkmar Gessner for his spirited and steady leadership in organising both the conference at Oñati and this very useful volume.

the changing diamond industry can offer insights not only into how globalisation is affecting networks that rely on extra-legal enforcement, but also into globalisation itself.

ALTERNATIVE UNDERSTANDINGS OF PRIVATE CONTRACTUAL ENFORCEMENT

Two fairly distinct accounts have emerged from prior examinations of contractual enforcement in the diamond industry, and these separate, although not mutually exclusive, reports mirror alternative theoretical expositions of private contractual enforcement. The first account was made famous by Bernstein's (1992) seminal article explaining how diamond merchants have 'opted out' of employing the state-sponsored legal system to adjudicate contractual disputes. Bernstein's approach, which she later applied to the feed and grain (Bernstein, 1996) and the cotton industries (Bernstein, 2001), illustrates how merchant groups create tailored substantive contract law and private arbitration procedures to govern their transactions. In this account, social norms reinforce industry customs and trade rules to provide a private system of expert and efficient dispute resolution that is faster, more accurate and thus more reliable than enforcement in state-sponsored courts. Konradi (2009, in this volume) usefully applies this template to understand how industry associations, relational contracts and standardised arbitration support transnational transactions in the timber industry, and this approach has brought scholarly attention both to the pervasiveness and economic significance of industry contract rules and private arbitration.

A second account of the diamond industry focuses not on the attractiveness of private arbitration, but, rather, on the ineffectiveness of state-sponsored courts. This approach, which I chart in previous works (Richman, 2004; 2006), begins with the recognition that state courts simply cannot credibly enforce a diamond credit sale: a party that refuses to make payment can easily escape the reach of a particular court and enjoy the value of unpaid (stolen) diamonds in a foreign jurisdiction. According to this approach, the ineffectiveness of public courts compels the industry to devise its own system of extra-legal enforcement. Tailored systems of law and efficient arbitration procedures are thus built atop an enforcement system that employs social norms, community coercion and sharp reputation mechanisms. Reliance on extra-legal enforcement comes at considerable costs—entry is limited to parties, usually individuals with ethnic or family connections to current merchants, who are familiar to industry members; thus the industry is deprived of entrepreneurial newcomers and the dynamism that accompanies the threat of entry (Richman, 2004)—but extra-legal enforcement is the only credible governance mechanism available.

While the first account of the diamond industry offers a template that is readily applied to other industries with repeat players and standardised transactions (including the timber industry), the second account suggests that the diamond industry is rather unique, or is at least an extreme illustration of the limitations of public courts. The first account suggests that tailored law and specialised arbitration procedures can offer efficiencies to many industries, and thus explains the proliferation of industry-wide arbitration and a pervasive trend of 'opting out' of state court enforcement. Although the second account recognises the many inefficiencies created by state court procedures and the costliness of resolving disputes in public courts, it suggests that wholesale abandonment of public courts is an act of necessity that is required of very few, perhaps no, other industries.

This second approach explains why the diamond industry is insular, ethnically homogeneous and has remained largely unchanged for nearly one millennium. The industry resorts today to the same community enforcement mechanisms that it did before the rise of modern courts, when most other industries were transformed by the rise of credible impersonal exchange and the introduction of dynamic entrants (Greif, 2006a). This second approach also reveals the forces that determine the industry's structure. The central challenge in diamond transactions is enforcing the credit sale, and institutions that can assure credible exchange for such portable, untraceable and extremely valuable goods will play a role in the industry's future.

BACKGROUND—THE DIAMOND SUPPLY CHAIN, THE ECONOMICS OF CUTTING AND SORTING, AND THE PRIVATE ORDERING OF GLOBAL NETWORKS

Appreciating transactional governance in the diamond industry first requires an exploration of the industry's global architecture, which is illustrated by a diamond's path from the mine to the jewellery manufacturer. The journey for most diamonds begins in African, Russian, Australian and Canadian mines, with approximately 65 per cent of rough diamond production being controlled by DeBeers, either through direct ownership or long-term exclusive buying contracts. DeBeers distributes rough stones through its Diamond Trading Company (or DTC, formally known as the Central Selling Organisation, or CSO) in London, and the DTC sells the stones in pre-sorted boxes, with take-it-or-leave-it price offers, to approximately 100 specific merchants known as 'sight-holders'. The DTC's centralised distribution system enables DeBeers to control global supply and quality, and consequently diamond prices have remained remarkably stable compared to other commodities (Spar, 2006).

From this small collection of sight-holders, diamonds descend into a thick web of intermediaries and slowly make their way down the supply chain to jewellery manufacturers (rough diamonds not controlled by DeBeers, and sold directly from mines, descend into the same distribution network). Sight-holders and other players atop the distribution pyramid sell parcels of their rough diamonds to individual dealers, who in turn resell smaller parcels to other dealers. For many stones, and for approximately 80 per cent of the DTC diamonds, the second round of transactions takes place in Antwerp at its four large diamond bourses, and from there diamond dealers disperse to sell their stones throughout the world.

The primary activity in diamond distribution is sorting. Diamond dealers atop the distribution pyramid (a profitable location to occupy) have comparatively large inventories, and they sell parcels of gradually declining size to downstream dealers. The sorting process goes hand-in-hand with the process of cutting or polishing, which converts opaque rough diamonds into gem-quality diamonds for retail. Some Antwerp merchants arrange to polish the stones themselves, and many others sell rough diamonds to other dealers, who then orchestrate cutting in India, China, Israel, New York and other locations. Many merchants also use brokers, who work on small commissions, to assist these sales and find the best price for a given stone. Parcels are sold and resold, stones are cut and recut, and gradually they make their way to jewellery manufacturers for commercial sale.

The process of sorting and cutting adds significant value to the stones—the total value of diamonds in retail jewellery is approximately 75 per cent more than the value of mined stones. Since there is little retail demand for uncut diamonds, it is clear that cutting and polishing stones for jewellery manufacturing adds value. However, cutting raw diamonds is not a commoditised process, like refining oil into usable gasoline. It is both an art and a science. With the exception of cutting very small stones, which can be cut in large quantities through an industrial process, diamond cutting is done by hand. A cutter sits before a spinning grinding wheel and carefully applies the stone to the wheel. Although diamond cutting is a skilled occupation (there are cutting schools, run by 'master cutters', in several diamond centres throughout the world), the requisite skills vary significantly. Cutting small stones of relatively little value, for example, requires far less training and specialised skills than cutting large diamonds with few flaws. Accordingly, cutting factories vary significantly in the prices they charge, the labour they employ and the wages they pay.

A good amount of value is also created through the nuanced process of matching individual stones with the manufacturers and retailers who value them highly. Diamonds, especially high-end stones, feature subtle differences—beyond the standard qualities reflected in grading for the 'four Cs'—colour, cut, carat and clarity—that translate into significant variation in manufacturers' willingness to pay. Accordingly, the objective of the distribution chain is to find the optimal buyer for the individual stone, and the middlemen who can find the optimal match can secure a substantial profit. The process requires synthesising significant market information with inventory availability—hustling to know what sellers have and what buyers want. Like most open exchanges (including stock exchanges) that facilitate transactions between sellers and buyers, the matching process is significantly aided by organising trading in centralised locations, so most matching occurs at the 25 diamond bourses located in the world's major diamond markets.

Extra-legal enforcement is especially relied upon at these downstream locations on the supply chain, and thus the downstream supply chain is populated by ethnically homogeneous merchants who are subject to, and are acutely motivated by, extra-legal social sanctions that punish merchants who fail to comply with their contractual obligations. Accordingly, one of the most distinguishing features of the downstream distribution network is the predominance of Jewish merchants, and this predominance has deep historical roots. Jewish merchants enjoyed a virtual monopoly of Europe's diamond market for several centuries, reaching back as early as the late fifteenth century, when Jews escaping the Spanish Inquisition set up the world's largest diamond market in Amsterdam. Jewish merchants also dominated the German market in the seventeenth century, England's early diamond trading with India in the eighteenth century, and the DeBeers syndicate in the twentieth century. Jewish merchants remained deeply active in the twentieth century's downstream markets of cutting, polishing and brokering diamonds, and developed major diamond centres in New York, Antwerp and Tel Aviv (Grayzel, 1968; Baron, 1975; Richman, 2006). I have argued previously that the community ties that bond Jewish diamond merchants to each other give the community's merchants a comparative advantage over non-members. Core community institutions provide Jewish merchants with a reliable private contractual enforcement and enable Jewish merchants to commit credibly to credit sales (Richman, 2004; 2006). Thus, intimate and pervasive community institutions provide the extra-legal certainty that enables Jewish merchants to overcome the hazards of the diamond transaction.

In summary, the distribution chain collects uncut stones in London and Antwerp and matches them with high-valuing jewellery manufacturers located throughout the world. In the process, stones pass through the hands of several middlemen—cutters, brokers, and dealers—to find the ultimate buyer. Each middleman profits from each transaction—cutters are paid for their services, brokers earn commissions on sales, and dealers profit by mark ups—so the ultimate objective is to maximise the value created by an optimal match, while minimising the required cutting and sorting costs of doing so. This pyramidal distribution system, with monopolist DeBeers sitting at the top, has been in place and has remained largely unchanged since Cecil Rhodes founded the company in 1880. Furthermore, for centuries, including long before DeBeers controlled global supply, diamonds relied on an army of middlemen to reach the world's buyers. Until the entry of relative newcomers in the 1980s, this distribution system was dominated by Jewish merchants.

ENTER INDIA

Perhaps the most significant feature of economic globalisation has been the entry of low-wage labourers in developing countries into the labour market for producing goods that are marketed in developed economies. This has occurred in the diamond industry with tremendous force as India has become a major centre for diamond cutting, and in doing so it has transformed the diamond global distribution network.

India's recent entry into modern diamond production has by no means been the country's first encounter with the diamond industry. To the contrary, the Indian subcontinent was from 800 BC (the time of the first diamond discoveries on record) until 1844 (when diamonds were discovered in Brazil) the world's only source of diamonds. During the height of India's diamond production period in the late 1600s, approximately 50,000 to 100,000 carats were extracted annually from India's deposits.[1] India's rich past in diamonds is also reflected in many elements of Indian culture. Early Sanskrit manuscripts contain numerous references to diamonds, including elaborate descriptions of precious gemstones and associations with mythical figures at the foundation of Hinduism, and as Hindu symbols were incorporated into Buddhism, the diamond became a Buddhist symbol of religious virtue.[2] Diamonds have also played a role in India's caste system, as the different castes were only permitted to own

[1] Indian mines have also produced some of the world's most famous diamonds, including the Koh-i-Nur, which was the object of tribal battles from 1304 through 1850, when the East India Company presented it to Queen Victoria (it later adorned the crown worn by Queens Alexandria, Mary and Elizabeth), and the Hope Diamond, which was purchased by King Louis XIV, stolen during the French Revolution and eventually repurchased by Harry Winston, who donated it to the Smithsonian.

[2] The Ratnapariksa, a sixth century text on gems by Buddha Bhatta, noted: 'He who, having pure body, always carries a diamond with sharp points, without blemish, free from all faults; that one, as long as he lives, knows each day will bear some things: happiness, prosperity, children, riches, grain, cows and meat. He who wears [such] a diamond will see dangers recede from him whether he be threatened by serpents, fire, poison, sickness, thieves, flood or evil spirits.'

diamonds of a specific colour—Brahmins wore white, merchants wore yellow, lower classes wore gray, and only kings could possess diamonds of all colours.

Since the discoveries in African mines in the late nineteenth century, India's contribution to the world's diamond production has been extremely small, leaving control of the diamond market to DeBeers and the diamond merchants, mostly Jewish and Belgian, who controlled the downstream distribution chain. However, India's history and familiarity with gemstones permitted a re-emergence in the 1980s. For centuries, the Jains of Palanpur, a religious minority from a parched, dusty village in Northern Gujarat, served as India's diamontaires and harvested a centuries-old tradition for diamond cutting and polishing. The community maintained the tacit skills required for cutting and polishing diamonds even while India's role in the industry receded: before India's diamond boom, Palanpuri cutters owned and operated small cutting workshops even as they remained unconnected to the global market that was dominated by cutters in Israel and Antwerp. Subseqently, certain entrepreneurial Palanpuris sought to exploit their community's rich history and deeply rooted expertise with diamonds. They turned to the master craftsmen in their home villages and asked them to guide large-scale cutting operations. Led by this home-grown and hard-to-replicate expertise, comparatively low labour costs and a global family network, the Palanpuris' cutting operations quickly made India a leader in the diamond industry. Today, nine out of ten diamonds purchased annually are polished in India, Mumbai is home to an active bourse, Palanpuri diamond entrepreneurs are among the nation's wealthiest[3] and thousands of cutting factories, employing over 700,000 Indians, populate nearby Gujarat province.

This is a classic instance of globalisation, where the size of the global market for a good (in contrast to the national or regional market) dramatically heightens the value of certain skills or assets. In many respects, India's Palanpuri diamond cutters present the paradigmatic case of globalisation's success story—a small community in a remote location is able to exploit its unique skills to reap fortunes in the global marketplace. The inevitable flip side is paradigmatic as well, and the Palanpuris' success has come at the expense of higher-wage cutters in the West. In fact, the Palanpuri cost advantages are so significant, and their entry into the market has been so large, that they have sufficiently disrupted the global

[3] One of India's foremost business journalists remarked: 'Ordinary people cannot understand how a handful of families, all belonging to one small community—Palanpuri Jains—have become so rich, so quickly' (Piramal, 1996). India's successful Palanpuri families include Vijay and Bharat Shah, college drop-outs who now operate one of India's largest corporate empires. Their interests include operating construction companies and directing one of Bollywood's largest movie production companies.

distribution network to have transformed the face of the industry. Antwerp is now much less of a haven for wealthy Jewish merchants, while becoming home to a very substantial Indian community, and Israel's cutting industry has been in steady decline. Indian diamontaires have also become deeply embedded in New York's diamond market, with an Indian merchant recently getting elected to the board of New York's diamond bourse. India's success in diamond cutting has fuelled further globalisation, as many diamond dealers have opened cutting factories in low-wage countries in Eastern Europe and Southeast Asia.

India's diamond success also offers some generalisable insights into commercial globalisation. Relational exchange—exchange, such as ethnic exchange, that relies on the familiarity that commercial parties have with each other—is in many respects deemed to be inferior to systems of arms-length transactions and impersonal exchange. Personal exchange limits entry only to those who are familiar to trading partners, keeping out the market dynamism introduced by low-cost or innovative entrepreneurs, and such familiarity requirements also impose limits on the size and breadth that trading networks can achieve. For these reasons, scholars have explained that public courts and impersonal exchange have gradually replaced and supplanted systems that rely on private ordering (Greif, 2006a). The Palanpuris' success, however, reveals that ethnic trading networks can flourish in a globalising economy. Furthermore, the Palanpuris are not alone—it is well documented that the wildly successful Chinese ethnic trading networks, for example, continue to capitalise on extra-legal certainty to organise transnational commerce in South-East Asia (Landa, 1999). Palanpuri success and the success of other ethnic trading networks illustrate that ethnic networks continue to occupy an important place in the modern global economy.

However, a stronger point can be made. Commercial networks that can succeed in an industry like the diamond market, where routine transactions are beyond the reach of public courts and require extra-legal enforcement, are strongly suited to excel in global exchange since cross-national transactions are also routinely difficult to enforce. The Palanpuris' centuries-old experience with diamonds transactions, which were always imbued with legal uncertainty, prepared them for the legal uncertainty in transnational exchange. Since Palanpuris were adept at domestic extra-legal commerce, they were well equipped for international extra-legal commerce. It is nonetheless ironic that trading practices resting upon ancient family or ethnic traditions—thought to have been replaced by sophisticated government institutions—can suddenly offer an advantage in the ever-modernising global economy.

Nonetheless, even with its advantages, relational exchange has limits, and continued globalisation will pose a severe test to the durability of the diamond industry's ethnic networks. Since reputation-based exchange works only with familiarity, relational networks will fail when their expansions dilute the intimacy the members share. Economic history contains many illustrations of reputation-based systems of contractual enforcement that became victims of their own success—transactional credibility broke down when parties were sufficiently unfamiliar that they could (and did) misrepresent themselves as reliable, long-term commercial partners (Greif, 2006b). If the diamond market continues to expand, the relational constraints of diamond networks might fail to match the growth, and diamond merchants might have to find alternative systems to organise distribution.[4]

Globalisation's invitation to ethnic-based exchange also invites other challenges. Just as Palanpuri diamontaires found themselves capable of succeeding in the international marketplace, other ethnic networks that have excelled in transnational trade found themselves well positioned to thrive in the diamond industry. For example, the Palanpuris have been joined by other ethnic networks, including some recent entrants who sensed that ethnic connections offer a competitive advantage in the industry (Richman, 2006). This presents one of globalisation's more interesting challenges: how members of different ethnic networks can engage in commerce—and enforce contracts—with each other. If each member is beyond the reach of public courts, and thus can only be disciplined by other members of his or her network, then extra-legal methods are required to secure transactions between parties from different relational circles. Theoretically, communities will be incentivised to police their own members in trade with other groups. If a community's members are deemed to be credible business partners for merchants from all groups, then the business opportunities for each member expands and the community as a whole will benefit (Greif, 2004). Putting this into practice, however, will require substantial political resolve within each community, and coordinating transactional assurance becomes harder as each trading community grows and familiarity inevitably decreases.

Still, diamond centres such as Antwerp and New York have successfully organised cross-community exchange despite the substantial transaction costs, and many different ethnic networks succeed internationally. Ethnic networks might be ideally suited to enter and prosper in global exchange, but since they cannot rest on institutional supports, and instead must police exchange and compel contractual compliance on their own, they might be vulnerable to strain as globalisation moves forward.

[4] Diamond merchants who are most likely to feel the limits of personal exchange are those with limited family networks. One Indian dealer lamented: 'This business demands personal attention and trust. Only your family can give you both. I have remained a small diamond exporter because I do not have a brother whom I can send to live in Antwerp' (Piramal, 1990).

ENTER ANGOLA, AND DEMAND FOR INTERNATIONAL REGULATION

Globalisation has also meant the entry of diamond merchants of a very different kind. Rebel movements and warlords in war-torn African nations, such as Angola, Sierra Leone and the Ivory Coast, have exploited diamond mines in their countries to fuel their bloody campaigns. The diamond's immutable qualities make it the smuggler's and guerrilla's currency of choice.

Turning a blind eye to the unpleasant origins of a product that is marketed to affluent consumers in developed nations might also be a central feature of globalised commerce. Salient examples include sweatshops manufacturing designer clothing, children forgoing school to assemble athletic equipment, and natural resource exploration that pollutes farmland and natural habitats (Spar and La Mure, 2003). Stark inequalities in both wages and purchasing habits between the developing and developed worlds create tremendous incentives to produce in the former and sell in the latter. This understandably fuels the growing separation of a product's origins from its ultimate consumer (Kysar, 2004; Friedman, 2005).

However, this separation creates a particularly acute danger for the diamond industry. Diamonds are marketed, with remarkable success, as timeless ornaments to signify important emotional events—the sort of product that would be quickly spoiled if associated with a brutal warlord. The possibility that the purchase of the engagement ring heirloom might sponsor bloody civil strife threatened the core of the industry's highly successful advertising efforts and attacked the root of a diamond's romantic appeal. It became a grave concern for the entire industry.

However, an easy solution is not obvious. Because the structure of the diamond industry's distribution network relies on many layers of middlemen, and because of the diamond's essential features, tracing a diamond's origins is profoundly more difficult than following other goods, such as designer apparel manufactured by sweatshop labour. Consequently, for many decades the industry turned a blind eye to the ugly origins of much of its product. Diamond dealer networks have long operated in Africa and purchased diamonds from military warlords. Those 'conflict diamonds' were then funnelled to Antwerp and other diamond centres and mixed in with diamonds from less controversial sources. The independence and multitude of the diamond dealers, the industry's lack of vertical integration and the inability to trace a diamond's origins made prohibiting and policing such diamond sales extremely difficult.

The threat to global demand eventually was too severe to ignore, particularly as NGOs and social activists—Global Witness in the lead—organised a highly effective media campaign. The industry, led by DeBeers, was compelled to develop a sweeping response. The end solution arrived in 2002 with the creation of the Kimberley Process, a vast international program to certify the origin of each diamond and to prohibit trade with countries that could not confirm that their diamond exports did not finance entities seeking to overthrow a UN-recognised government. The Kimberley Process requires that each international shipment of rough diamonds must be transported in a tamper-resistant container and accompanied by a government-verified certificate that indicates the origin of each stone. The importing state's customs must then confirm that the contents of the shipment are in accord with the certificate, and each individual who thereafter handles the stone is obligated to maintain the identity tag. Although enforcement, the integrity of the certifications and the overall effectiveness of the Kimberley Process remain unknown and are a matter for ongoing debate, in theory it provides jewellery manufacturers, reflecting the interests of engagement ring purchasers and other romantics, proof that the diamonds they purchase come from wholesome origins. Peddlers of conflict diamonds should have much greater difficulty in finding buyers and slipping into the mainstream pipeline.

For a number of reasons, DeBeers's cooperation with global activists demanding restraints on industry leaders is self-explanatory. The Kimberley Process reduced diamond output and aided DeBeers's ongoing efforts to control global supply; it cleansed DeBeers's brand name of very sordid associations (although DeBeers has quite a chequered history of its own); and it created a global infrastructure that adds highly valued assurance to diamond purchasers. However, it also represents DeBeers's adjustment to the politics of globalisation and its willingness to become a partner in an increasingly typical political manoeuvre.

The lack of public governance in global exchange has prompted a rise in what some have called 'private governance' (Gereffi and Mayer, 2006). Private governance includes self-regulation by multinational corporations, codes of conduct promulgated by international organisations and trade associations, and consumer standards—including the famous 'fair trade' movement—that impose minimum labour or production standards. It is not unprecedented, nor is it unreasonable, for for-profit corporations to join those demanding private governance and collaborate with social activists to bring reform: such cooperation was been dubbed 'the NGO-industrial complex' (Gereffi *et al*, 2001).

However, this sort of international scrutiny and regulation is quite new to the diamond industry even though, unlike other industries that have only recently globalised, international distribution networks had always been required to bring diamonds from mines to jewellery stores. The globalisation of industries such as textiles and chemicals prompted consumer alarm and the mobilisation of international private governance because the internationalisation of those industries meant less legal and political oversight. The diamond industry, in contrast, was always globalised and had received relatively little scrutiny (despite brutal treatment of workers in diamond mines, poor labour relations in many cutting factories and, of course, the prevalence of conflict diamonds). Thus, the politics of globalisation has meant something very different to the diamond industry. Ironically, globalisation has meant the involvement of more, not less, consumer regulation and political scrutiny. Moreover, the regulatory structures arose to create a legal certainty of a different kind: global oversight mechanisms now provide consumers with regulatory compliance certainty. They aim to reduce information assymmetry between the diamond seller and the uninformed but socially aware consumer.

What lessons can be drawn from the diamond industry's experience with the politics of globalisation? Prior to the swell of globalisation, the diamond industry seemed to avoid the scrutiny it probably deserved. Just as its transactions remained beyond the reach of public courts, the industry's practices remained largely beyond the attention of social activists and constituencies that demand regulatory oversight. These parallel trends of nesting outside the public arena are interconnected. Since the industry was forced to rely on self-governance to police transactions and enforce contracts, it assumed a self-regulatory governance structure that distrusted outsiders and demanded regulatory autonomy. However, when globalisation enabled multinational corporations (MNCs) to escape the regulation of the industrialised democracies, the political backlash fuelled scrutiny towards all MNCs active in the developing world, and that included DeBeers. Diamond sellers now need global private governance to assure consumers, and instruments of regulatory certainty replace the unsupported anonymous transaction. In short, the general lawlessness of globalisation has meant the end to lawlessness in the diamond industry.

ENTER LOUIS VUITTON AND THE POWER OF BRANDS

In 2000, DeBeers launched its own 'millennium' diamond, limited edition stones of the highest quality, of substantial size, and with a microscopic laser-inscribed DeBeers 'centenary logo' etched along the side (each millennium diamond came with its own viewing lens, certificate of assurance from De Beers and a time capsule). Later that year, DeBeers announced a plan to market 'designer diamonds' with unusual shapes and sizes, with promises that each stone would exhibit top grades in colour and clarity. And in January 2001, DeBeers created a joint venture with LVMH Moet Hennessy Louis Vuitton, a leader and trend setter in the luxury goods market, to create a network of own-brand stores that would sell, under the DeBeers brand, exclusive lines of diamonds (Handleman, 2000; Weber, 2001). These initiatives—the first to bring the company towards the retail market—were a response to several years of declining DeBeers market share,[5] a sense that DeBeers was not fully capturing value from its brand name and a decision to execute a change in corporate strategy (Spar, 2006).

Although DeBeers's strategic initiatives have garnered complimentary press coverage, the business world has yet to appreciate how dramatic this departure is from past practices. For years, DeBeers's focus on wholesale distribution was explained by the transaction costs of 'block booking'. A famous paper by Roy Kenny and Benjamin Klein observed that for goods that varied significantly in quality but required substantial measurement costs to evaluate quality, transaction costs are economised when the good is sold in bundles in which the price for each individual item is the average price. Thus, block booking would economise on over-searching and make productive use of items of below-average quality (Kenny and Klein, 1983). The Kenny and Klein explanation has been the most generally accepted understanding of DeBeers's operations (Hanssen, 2000). It explains both DeBeers's unusual distribution methods—selling pre-sorted bundles to individual sight-holders, sight unseen—and DeBeers's decision to remain atop the distribution system as a wholesaler without vertically integrating downstream.

However, with the DeBeers-LVMH joint venture, Kenny and Klein's explanation no longer applies. Instead, DeBeers now finds value in integrating downward into the retail market. It also means that DeBeers, in dealing directly with the ultimate consumer, is bypassing the many layers of middlemen who had organised the industry's distribution system for nearly one millennium.

It is possible that DeBeers's moves are products of new technologies. Perhaps the art of diamond cutting has been refined such that DeBeers can credibly claim that all of its hallmarked stones achieve a certain quality. If DeBeers can now produce homogeneous branded diamonds, but was previously unable to, then the branded effort obviates the requisite search and inspection costs in diamond sales. Thus, whereas before diamond buyers needed to inspect each stone carefully, now they might trust DeBeers. A second explanation points to technological developments of a different sort. Perhaps the internet and the rising facility to share information has offered low-cost replacements for the army of middlemen. If a major value-added activity of these middlemen—a swarm of aggressive brokers and resellers who gobble and relay market information on available inventories and the particularities of demand—was to match individual diamonds with optimal buyers, then a branding campaign

[5] DeBeers's declining market share was largely attributable to the opening of new diamond mines, including large finds in Canada and Australia that did not sell through DeBeers's DTC, and the periodic departures by Alrosa, Russia's large mining operation, from the DeBeers cartel.

would obviate this as well. The DeBeers brand would reflect known characteristics, and buyers demanding stones of that kind can purchase them directly from the manufacturer.[6] A third explanation is the simplest, that DeBeers is losing global market share and now has to compete more vigorously against other suppliers, and its competitive advantage over other mines is its name recognition. Whereas before, DeBeers invested in advertising for the entire industry—its 'Diamonds are Forever' campaign, in addition to being hailed by *Advertising Age* as the slogan of the century, marketed all diamonds, not just DeBeers diamonds—now it also advertises its own wares. Capitalising on its brand name in the retail market might simply be the competitive response of a former monopolist.

However, DeBeers's transformation might also shed insight into the economics of globalisation. Previously, DeBeers stood atop the distribution chain and relied on ethnic networks to disperse diamonds to local markets. With globalisation's convergence of regional markets, the effect of branding is magnified. A unifying global market decreases the likelihood of brand confusion, increased communication extends the reach of brand marketing, and improved brand recognition enables brand holders to build and capitalise on a reputation for quality. One might also argue that if globalisation has lead to a homogenisation of preferences for luxury goods, DeBeers's offering of specific designer stones might, despite the limited variation, meet the demands of the high-end market as it never could before. The true lesson is that these globalising forces have created a third type of legal certainty: the certainty of quality assurances that trademarks and trademark law are designed to promote. These assurances are useless if a brand is unfamiliar, but cultural and commercial globalisation might enable DeBeers to extract previously unattainable value from its brand.

Although it is too early to determine whether DeBeers's strategy will be successful, the significance of its reorientation for the rest of the industry cannot be understated. With its focus on its brand name, DeBeers is using a vertical integration strategy to supplant the trust-based exchange that for generations has been organised by ethnic networks.

[6] These developments in information technology also suggest that internet sites could similarly create a forum of information exchange and create virtual diamond exchanges, thus further obviating the role of middlemen. In fact, several such internet brokerages have emerged, featuring an inventory of diamond with GIA-certified features and high-resolution pictures. By some measures, internet sales are growing and have already achieved 15% of all US sales, but many remain sceptical that internet pictures will erode the perceived need to personally inspect a diamond before purchase (Berger, 2001; Rozhon, 2005).

CONCLUSION

The diamond industry's distribution system had remained intact and relatively stable for nearly one millennium. It emerged long before the DeBeers cartel arrived and it has survived technological booms, continental wars and economic shocks of every sort. However, it is now threatened by certain forces of globalisation. Globalisation has meant entry by low-wage ethnic groups that have displaced incumbent Jewish merchants who had long dominated the downstream market. It has brought political scrutiny to an industry that previously enjoyed secrecy, autonomy and lawlessness. And it has enabled DeBeers to pursue marketing strategies that skip the middleman. These developments might mean the end of 1,000 years of Jewish predominance.

However, watching the diamond industry change with globalisation also yields insights into globalisation itself. The lawlessness of transnational exchange means that ethnic networks that have historically shunned public courts and have instead employed extra-legal mechanisms to enforce transactions are particularly well suited to excel in the globalised economy. The absence of public regulation to govern global commerce has led to consumer-driven private governance, which ironically can reach and influence secretive international networks, such as the diamond networks, much more than state-sponsored regulation. And globalisation has changed the economics of brand names such that branding strategies can now reach larger markets and exploit profit opportunities as never before. De Beers's recent ventures suggest that vertical integration strategies that focus on maximising value from brand reputations might offer a superior organisational form than the historic use of multiple middlemen, personal reputations and trust-based exchange.

Moreover, changes in the diamond industry illustrate new paths through which globalisation will bring legal certainty. Ethnic networks able to create transactional certainty in domestic markets have brought additional security to international commerce. The politics of globalisation and the corresponding demand for private governance has brought attention to the origins of diamonds that are later sold in developed nations, and the Kimberley Process was constructed to provide the regulatory certainty to assure consumers of their purchase. And the expanded reach of trademarks, which spread on the commercial and cultural currents of globalisation, give additional meaning to brands and thus bring greater quality certainty to the global marketplace.

The diamond industry, to be sure, is an unusual industry—few others can boast features such as a predominance of ethnic networks, artificially created demand, the rejection of sophisticated public courts in developed economies and an organisational structure that has remained largely unchanged for one millennium. However, since 'the study of extreme instances often provides important leads to the essentials of the situation' (Behavioral Sciences Subpanel, 1962; Williamson, 1976), peering into the diamond industry, with all its refractions and distortions, produces revealing insights on the legal, political and economic challenges of the globalising world.

REFERENCES

Appelbaum, RP, Felstiner, W, and Gessner, V (2001) *Rules and Networks—The Legal Culture of Global Business Transactions* (Oxford, Hart Publishing).

Baron, S (1975) *Economic History of the Jews* (New York, Schocken Books).

Behavioral Sciences Subpanel, President's Science Advisory Committee (1962) 'Strengthening the Behavioral Sciences' 136 *Science* 233.

Berger, S (2001) 'Diamonds in the Rough' *The Jerusalem Post* (6 April 2001) 4B.

Bernstein, L (1992) 'Opting Out of the Legal System: Extra-legal Contractual Relations in the Diamond Trade' 21 *Journal of Legal Studies* 115.

—— (1996) 'Merchant Law in a Merchant Court: Rethinking the Code's Search for Immanent Business Norms' 144 *University of Pennsylvania Law Review* 1765.

—— (2001) 'Private Commercial Law in the Cotton Industry: Creating Cooperation Through Rules, Norms, and Institutions' 99 *Michigan Law Review* 1724

Friedman, T (2005) *The World is Flat* (New York, Ferrar, Strauss and Giroux).

Gereffi, G, Garcia-Johnson, R and Sasser, E (2001) 'The NGO-Industrial Complex' 125 *Foreign Policy* 56.

Gereffi, G and Mayer, F (2005) 'Globalization and the Demand for Governance' in G Gereffi, *The New Offshoring of Jobs and Global Development* (International Institute for Labour Studies: ILO Social Policy Lectures).

Grayzel, S (1968) *A History of the Jews* (New York, Jewish Publication Society).

Greif, A (2004) 'Impersonal Exchange without Impartial Law: The Community Responsibility System' 5 *Chicago Journal of International Law* 109.

—— (2006a) *Institutions and the Path to the Modern Economy Lessons from Medieval Trade* (Cambridge University Press).

—— (2006b) 'The Birth of Impersonal Exchange: The Community Responsibility System and Impartial Justice' 20 *The Journal of Economic Perspectives* 221.

Handleman, L (2000) 'The Once-in-a-Millenium Gift' *Princeton Packet* (2 January 2000) <http://www.pacpubserver.com/new/news/1–2-00/diamonds.html> accessed 17 June 2008.
Hanssen, A (2000) 'The Block Booking of Films Reexamined' 43 *Journal of Law and Economics* 395.
Kenny, R and Klein, B (1983) 'The Economics of Block Booking' 26 *Journal of Law and Economics* 497.
Konradi, W (2009) 'The Role of *Lex Mercatoria* in Supporting Globalised Transactions: An Empirical Insight into the Governance Structure of the Timber Industry' in V Gessner (ed), *Contractual Certainty in International Trade* (Oxford, Hart).
Kysar, D (2004) 'Preferences for Processes: The Process/Product Distinction and the Regulation of Consumer Choice' 118 *Harvard Law Review* 525.
Landa, JT (1999) *Trust, Ethnicity, and Identity* (Ann Arbor, University of Michgan Press).
Piramal, G (1996) *Business Maharajas* (New Dehli, Viking).
Richman, B (2004) 'Firms, Courts, and Reputation Mechanisms: Towards a Positive Theory of Private Ordering' 104 *Columbia Law Review* 2328.
—— (2006) 'How Communities Create Economic Advantage: Jewish Diamond Merchants in New York' 31 *Law and Social Inquiry* 383.
Rozhon, T (2005) 'Competition is Forever' *New York Times* (9 February 2005) C1.
Spar, D (2006) 'Markets: Continuity and Change in the International Diamond Market' 20 *Journal of Economic Perspectives* 195.
Spar, D and La Mure, LT (2003) 'The Power of Activism: Assessing the Impact of NGOs on Global Business' 45 *California Management Review* 78.
Weber, L (2001) 'The Diamond Game' *New York Times* (8 April 2001) ss 3 and 1.
Williamson, OE (1976) 'Franchise Bidding for Natural Monopolies—In General and with Respect to CATV' 7 *Bell Journal of Economics* 73.

3

The Role of Lex Mercatoria *in Supporting Globalised Transactions: An Empirical Insight into the Governance Structure of the Timber Industry*

WIOLETTA KONRADI[1]

INTRODUCTION

THE GLOBALISATION OF trade discussed in this book has considerably affected the character of economic exchanges. Whereas for many centuries commerce was domestic, nowadays a considerable proportion of transactions transcends the legal frames of nation states. Numerous companies, including those of medium size, have become global players and transact with business partners from different countries around the world. Risky cross-border exchanges, especially those with partners from states of low political and economic stability, can only be ventured if traders gain trust in long-term effective exchange. As explained in Gessner's introduction, the question of an effective support of cross-border exchanges is of great interest for current theoretical debates and empirical research.

The high level of certainty needed in global business transactions can hardly be achieved by classical legal means, as assumed by the traditional approach (Weber, 1976: 187). Even if the involvement of state institutions in the enforcement of contracts is seldom necessary, modern nation states,

[1] I would like to thank Volkmar Gessner for his helpful comments on an earlier version of this chapter. Many thanks also to other participants of the conference on 'Legal Certainty beyond the State? Autonomous Structures in Globalised Exchange Processes', held at the International Institute for the Sociology of Law, Oñati, Spain, 25–26 September 2006, for their valuable comments, as well as to Doerthe Hauschild and John Flood for language support.

which constitute their internal markets by providing national laws and courts, may be able to secure only domestic transactions. Transnational trade lacks a comparable degree of institutionally guaranteed legal certainty (Calliess, 2004: 162). The empirical literature dealing with this problem shows that the practical problems of the contractual parties trying to legally enforce their claims outside their home turf remain considerable (Gessner, 1996: 207) and that alternative governance mechanisms supporting cross-border transactions may be more relevant.[2]

A potential universal order of economic exchanges is known as *lex mercatoria*, the new law merchant or the autonomous commercial law.[3] Generally speaking, the concept *lex mercatoria* describes a pluralistic mix of commercial norms, contracts and customs, as well as arbitral awards, which tend to govern international business transactions. The diverse terms and definitions used for the descriptions of the same body of autonomous rules mirror the different perceptions of the phenomenon.[4] The legal discourse regarding the existence, nature, scope and autonomy of *lex mercatoria* has been in existence for more than 40 years. The extensive theoretical literature available in this field offers a valuable tool for the legal analysis of this phenomenon and often assumes its considerable practical relevance in supporting globalised exchanges.

However, due to the scarce empirical research[5] and contradictory evidence, there is no complete and coherent picture regarding the *lex mercatoria* approach towards globalisation. Most empirical studies of *lex*

[2] The term 'governance' is similarly applied to the notion of 'private ordering' in the field of institutional economics and sociology of law. It means the coordination of transactions using an alternative to state law coordination mechanisms, eg relational contracts (Macaulay, 1963; 1985; Macneil, 1985; 2000) or self-regulation within different industries (Bernstein, 1992; 2001). The theoretical background of the term 'governance' makes it best suitable to explain the focused research topic. It justifies its use in order to describe different coordination mechanisms of the investigated industry.

[3] *Lex mercatoria* is traditionally the notion of the autonomous merchant law which existed in the Middle Ages and lost its autonomous character due to the national codifications in the eighteenth and nineteenth centuries. The notion 'the new law merchant' is used to emphasise the revival of the *lex mercatoria* discussion after the Second World War. Both notions are well established in the scientific community and will be used interchangeably in this article in order to participate in the ongoing discourse.
For the historical development of *lex mercatoria,* see especially Schmitthoff, 1964: 48 *ff*; Dasser, 1989: 32 *ff*; Weise, 1989: 8 *ff*; Stein, 1995: 4 *ff*; Lopez, 2002: 85 *ff*; Calliess, 2004: 163; Milgrom, North and Weingast, 1990; and Greif, 2006.

[4] The discussion of the *lex mercatoria* doctrine would go beyond the scope of this chapter. For different concepts of the phenomenon, see particularly Schmitthoff, 1961; 1964; 1968; 1982; Berman and Kaufman, 1978; Goldman, 1983; 1986; Berger, 1996; Teubner, 1997; De Ly, 2001; and Calliess, 2002.
A functional concept of *lex mercatoria*, which allows recognising its approach to globalisation, is an underlying factor in this chapter. The aspects concerning the origin, scope and autonomy of *lex mercatoria* will be discussed below.

[5] For an overview of existing empirical research related to *lex mercatoria*, see Konradi and Fix-Fierro, 2005.

mercatoria focus, like many theoretical approaches, on international arbitration as a worldwide accepted method of alternative conflict resolution.[6] In particular, there is only scarce research on the production and implementation of autonomous rules within close-knit industries. The most convincing empirical evidence for the existence of autonomous regulated industries was provided by Lisa Bernstein, who studied the international diamond trade (Bernstein, 1992). She showed that risky diamond transactions are coordinated merely by means of network mechanisms, thus allowing the involved traders an 'opting out of the legal system'.[7] Bernstein's findings have been confirmed and completed through the valuable economic examination of Barak Richman, who described the last developments within the diamond industry and appreciated them in the context of globalisation (Richman, 2006; 2009, in this volume). However, other empirical studies reason that autonomous rules play only a marginal role in transnational exchanges (Bernstein, 1996; Stammel, 1998; Bond, 1990). Despite the contrary findings of these studies, they clearly show that complex cross-border transactions are supported by both state and merchant-created law, as well as by other extra-legal governance mechanisms.

A deficiency of the *lex mercatoria* discourse is that it tends to ignore the existing empirical findings and other theoretical approaches, for example on relational contract management (eg Macaulay, 1963; 1985; Macneil, 1974; 1978; Williamson, 1985; Freiling, 1995; 1996; Kiedaisch, 1997; Sosa, 2007), on the contribution of international law firms to the protection of cross-border business relationships (eg Silver, 2000; Flood, 1996; 2007; Flood and Sosa, 2008; Sosa, 2009, in this volume), as well as on institutions, which govern and facilitate economic action (eg Williamson, 1985; 2005; Nee, 2005; Greif, 2005; 2006). A more comprehensive and interdisciplinary perspective leads us to ask the following questions: Can *lex mercatoria* be seen as a functional equivalent to state law or does it rather play a marginal role while completing and supporting national laws? Which other governance mechanisms play an important role in the globalised economy and what relationship do they have to state law and the *lex mercatoria*? The last important question regards the supposed changes in the governance structure of close-knit industries, which could result from the globalisation of trade.

This chapter tries to contribute to this discussion by presenting the results of an empirical study on the timber industry conducted within the

[6] For theoretical approaches, see Carbonneau, 1998; and Zumbansen, 2003. Empirical evidence is available in Dasser, 1989; Dezalay andGarth, 1996; Drahozal, 2000; and Berger, 2001; 2002.

[7] Bernstein also found self-regulation within the cotton industry (Bernstein, 2001).

framework of the research of the 'Transformations of the State' Collaborative Research Center 597 at the University of Bremen.[8] The timber industry was chosen for a number of reasons. The first and most important aspect relates to this industry's extensive traditions, which allow us to observe changes in the governance structure over a long period of time.[9] Secondly, most timber trade crosses borders.[10] A third aspect is its network-like structure facilitating the industry's self-regulation.[11] Fourthly, the characteristics of timber as a commodity may influence the governance of transactions by state law and ordinary courts.

The empirical results presented below are based on 30 expert interviews with managers of German companies involved in international timber trade, as well as with representatives of timber trade federations and intra-industry arbitrators. This chapter is not confined to a presentation of the findings of the branch study: it also tries to compare the achieved results with those of the studies on the international diamond trade,[12] on the mid-sized law firms and on the software industry.[13] The comparison should show similarities and differences in the governance structure of those industries and allow the appreciation of the results in the context of the globalisation discourse.

THE STRUCTURE OF THE TIMBER INDUSTRY

The network-like organisation of the timber industry results from the affiliation of most companies to a number of national and international associations. Almost all German importers and exporters are represented by the German Timber Trade Federation, *Gesamtverband Deutscher Holzhandel* (GD Holz), which is located in Wiesbaden and Berlin. In 2004, GD Holz had 1,200 members. Most of these are medium-sized, family-owned companies with sales ranging between €100,000 and €175 million.

[8] <http://www.staatlichkeit.uni-bremen.de/www.state.uni-bremen.de> accessed 1 December 2006.

[9] The first cross-border transactions in the field of timber trade were conducted in the Middle Ages, especially the timber trade between the current territory of Germany and the Nordic countries, which occurred one thousand years ago; see Speth, 2004: 54.

[10] Germany, in addition to the UK, belongs to the leading timber import nations in Europe (see Speth, 2004: 56) and participates in worldwide timber transactions (see import and export statistics in the report of the German Timber Federation, 2004: 44–63). For this reason, Germany was chosen for the empirical investigation.

[11] According to existing empirical studies, the creation and implementation of autonomous rules occurs as a rule within close-knit branches of trade. This increases the possibility of finding *lex mercatoria* in the timber industry.

[12] See 'Timber Industry and Diamond Industry Compared' in this chapter.

[13] See 'Conclusions' below.

Additionally, the German Timber Trade Federation represents members in Switzerland, Austria, Luxembourg and Belgium.[14]

The *Gesamtverband Deutscher Holzhandel* offers a wide range of services which are of great importance to the international timber trade. These services especially include information about international markets, making contact with foreign companies and providing information on foreign business conventions and grading rules, the modification and transfer of contract forms to be used for external trade, advice for contract drafting for exchange with foreign companies, support for handling external trade transactions, organisation of expositions, dealing with issues concerning customer complaints, as well as the provision of an intra-industry arbitration (see Speth, 2004: 85–6). The membership of GD Holz in the *Fédération Européenne du Néoce de Bois* (FEBO), as well as the maintenance of good relations with national and international timber trade associations, is essential to the functioning of the network.

FEBO[15] currently represents 13 countries: Germany, France, Great Britain, Italy, Latvia, Finland, Sweden, Austria, Belgium, Denmark, the Netherlands, Switzerland and Luxembourg, 15 national associations and about 3,500 timber trading companies. FEBO's duties particularly include the promotion of the cooperation within the European timber trade and the support of the information exchange between national associations, as well as the representation of the interests of the European timber industry in facing the European Commission. Other international intra-industry organisations which help to interlink the timber industry in Europe are, for example: the *Union pour le Commerce des Bois Résineux dans l'UE* (UCBR) and the *Union pour le Commerce des Bois Durs dans l'UE* (UCBD). Both organisations represent a number of companies, operating in a certain field within the timber industry.

Another organisation that contributes to the integration of the timber industry at the international level is the *Association Technique Internationale des Bois Tropicaux* (ATIBT), a non-political non-governmental organisation located in Paris.[16] It represents the interests of more than 200 direct members from 39 countries. Among the members are worldwide operating national organisations of producers and importers, international organisations, for example, the International Tropical Timber Association (ITTO) and the African Timber Organisation (ATO), scientific institutes of the timber industry and tropical-timber-producing firms, as well as service suppliers and suppliers of accoutrements for the tropical timber divisions.

[14] See GD Holz Geschaeftsbericht, 2004 <http://www.holzhandel.de/img/upload/gf_bericht/gf-bericht2004.pdf> accessed 17 June 2008.

[15] <http://www.febo.org> accessed 17 June 2008.

[16] <http://www.atibt.com> accessed 17 June 2008.

ATIBT plays a significant role concerning the recommendation and implementation of feasible solutions for the sustainable management of tropical timber resources and furthers the worldwide use of products made of tropical timber. A significant part of the work carried out by ATIBT is characterised by the technical standardisation of the tropical timber products. The fact that ATIBT maintains an arbitration board of worldwide reputation is of eminent importance for the international tropical timber trade. The arbitration chamber is in charge of resolving all potential disagreements arising in the field of tropical timber trade. It offers a judicial service and expert arbitration (association representative, interview no 22).

The network structure of the timber industry has an enormous impact on the governance of the international timber transactions. It permits the autonomous norm generation and implementation and also enables network mechanisms to operate. This will be laid out in the following parts of the chapter. Most Organisation for Economic Cooperation and Development (OECD) countries have well developed association structures to represent the companies involved in domestic and external timber trade. This holds true especially for Western European and Northern American countries, which are particularly oriented towards the international timber trade. All Scandinavian countries,[17] France, England,[18] Scotland[19] and Ireland, as well as the United States[20] and Canada,[21] have established well-functioning trade organisations, which support cross-border timber transactions. On the other hand, there are no branch associations in non-OECD African and Asian countries. Trade associations are an indispensable prerequisite for the generation and implementation of autonomous intra-industry norms. In most cases, such norms are developed in the course of cooperation of different timber associations. Complex normative achievements like the framework agreement 'Germania 1998'[22] are, for instance, products of close cross-border interactions of a number of national trade associations.

[17] In Finland, there is, for example, the Suomen Sahat, the Association of the Independent Sawmill Industry (<http:www.suomensahat.fi/ger/index.htm> accessed 17 June 2008); in Sweden the Sagverkens Riskfoerbund, the umbrella organisation of the Swedish Kaufsaegewerke (<http://www.sagverk.se> accessed 17 June 2008); in Norway Treindustrien, the Association of the Saw Industry in Norway (<http://www.treindustrien.no> accessed 17 June 2008).

[18] Information on the English Timber Trade Federation is available at <http://www.ttf.co.uk> accessed 17 June 2008.

[19] See the homepage of the Scottish Timber Trade Association (STTA) at <http://www.stta.org.uk> accessed 17 June 2008.

[20] For example, the American Plywood Association in Washington.

[21] Canadian Lumber Standards Administrative Board, Ganges.

[22] The contract will be analysed in the following part of this chapter.

THE GOVERNANCE MECHANISMS OF THE TIMBER INDUSTRY

Relational Contract Management

The first governance mechanism of the timber industry being of great importance in all analysed business relationships is the *relational contract management*, which is well known and discussed in the fields of jurisprudence and economics.[23] The timber trade is (especially in Germany) composed of middle-sized, family-owned companies that have been operating in this business for many generations (Konradi and Fix-Fierro, 2005: 224). The reason why mainly middle-sized companies are engaged in timber trade can be explained by the fact that this commodity cannot be easily standardised. Despite the existence of some technical standards, the quality inspection of timber products often takes place in connection with a meeting of the business partners, which renders the business a personal matter. According to one interviewee, large companies are not able to handle such a commodity because they are bound to products which can be completely standardised and sold in an impersonal way (company representative, interview no 11).

Owing to the fact that the trade in a commodity makes it necessary to put some energy into learning how to handle it and finding appropriate suppliers, many business relationships develop into long-term connections. These connections are based on trust that the business partners will meet the needs concerning the quantity and grading of materials (company representative, interview no 17). Individual transactions occur sporadically in the timber industry, since those interviewed said company representatives try to establish long-term business relationships with a strong personal character (company representatives, interview nos 9, 10, 11, 17 and 18). The personal connections to foreign suppliers and clients are maintained for generations. Generally, companies have an average of 20 to 40 years in operation (company representatives, interview nos 7, 15 and 19). However, there are also relationships which have lasted over a period of 70 years.

[23] The starting point of the economical and legal approaches that deal with this coordination mechanism is the assumption that most transactions occur in connection with business relationships which are built on mutual trust and appreciation of the products and can develop into business friendships. This concept of transactions is contrary to '*spot transactions*', which occur once between individual market participants and lead much more often to an opportunistic behaviour of the contractual parties. The best-known approaches in the field of *relational contract management* have been taken by the sociologists of law Ian Macneil and Stewart Macaulay (Macaulay, 1963; 1985; and Macneil, 1974; 1978). Their theses have been recently confirmed by Fabian Sosa (2007). Other interesting approaches were developed by Freiling, 1995; 1996; and Kiedaisch, 1997.

The following quotation from the manager of one of the most successful German timber trade companies best represents the personal character of business relationships in the timber industry:

> You can only be successful in this industry if you are able to build business relationships that have a strong personal character. The term 'business friendship' really means friendship: the connections to most of our suppliers and clients are intense friendships which we strive to maintain. A friendship is a value you do not easily deceive whereas it is easy to break up a business relationship if there are no personal bonds … . Hence, we try to build personal relations to create an atmosphere which guarantees that problems in everyday situations can be solved in a way that both parties feel comfortable with. This is vital to make sure the business relationship does not break up. Buy once and never again: this is not our practice; this is not an option in our company … . No doctoral degree, no studies, no computer, nothing, only fostering the relations with our clients and suppliers is the key to our success (company representative, interview no 16).

It makes clear that the businessmen who conceive their business relations as friendship do not care much about detailed contracts or legal methods to enforce their rights. All participants in the study underline that they favour simple solutions. In their eyes, the bureaucracy connected with drafting detailed contracts is not worth the time and energy and is viewed as rather damaging (company representatives, interview nos 1 and 10). However, whereas contracts by handshake are common in the domestic timber trade, where the same circle of people meet like a club, written contracts are drafted for cross-border transactions characterised by a diversity of suppliers and clients (company representative, interview no 10).

In many long-term business relations, contracts are first entered into through a handshake and then supplemented by a document. Such a supplemented contract does not have the purpose to determine the rights and obligations of the parties in detail. Mostly, it is rather simple in its form and only includes the *essentialia negotti*, as there is mention of the parties, specification of the product and prices, etc. Such a contract serves to render the transaction transparent and proves that the concessions and certificates necessary in cross-border trade have been obtained (company representative, interview no 12). In addition, the contract ensures that the goods, which are worth a considerable amount of money, will be paid, as this can, if necessary, be claimed before a public or arbitral court. Businessmen, who work out more detailed contracts including *force majeure* clauses or regulations regarding warranties, mostly do not put much importance on these provisions. One interviewee explained:

> You may in principle avoid a lot of eventualities and hide behind regulations specified by the contract, but in real life the business turns out to be incompatible

> with strict regulations: a contract—this is not much more than a piece of paper, when it comes to practice. In practice a lot of things are handled completely differently (company representative, interview no 15).

The empirical study shows that businessmen always strive to find a solution with which both parties feel comfortable should complications arise, ie financial difficulties or a delay in delivery. Customer complaints can often be sorted out by a simple phone call or fax. More often, the business partners agree on financial compensation. It is also common to waive a certain sum in order not to jeopardise the business relationship (company representatives, interview nos 12, 14 and 16). In most cases, private solutions are sufficient to settle the differences between the parties. However, sometimes the involvement of a third party to resolve the conflicts will be necessary. Arbitration is usually conceived as a proper form of conflict solution in cases in which parties cannot settle a conflict on their own.[24]

To summarise, it can be said that relational contract management is of eminent importance in cross-border timber trade. Apart from the coordination of transactions by means of the *lex mercatoria*, it functions by stabilising expectations[25] and is an integral part of the philosophy of most companies in the timber trade. This exemplifies the statement of one of the most successful German importers, who puts it this way: 'We do not deal in timber, we deal with people' (company representative, interview no 9).

Lex Mercatoria

The second governance mechanism of the timber industry which supports cross-border exchanges is the autonomous norm creation occurring in the community of international merchants. The numerous trade organisations being active in the timber industry have developed standard contracts and grading rules for the trade in diverse timber sorts and products. Additionally, the organisations write down some of the commercial customs applied in the practice of the international timber trade. The development of international standard contracts, commercial norms and customs unique to the timber trade began in the 1950s. This process is characterised by the continuous improvement of normative solutions in order to adapt them to the new reality of global trade.

[24] The issue concerning the involvement of a third party will be discussed in more detail in 'Arbitration' and 'National Legislations and Jurisdictions' below.

[25] See Luhmann, 1983.

Complex contracts that are applied in international timber transactions are—especially: 'General Conditions of sale Germania 1998', 'Japan-Timber 1998 General Conditions', 'General Conditions-European Plywood Contract Form 1997', 'General Conditions for Plywood Contracts Bremensia 1957' and the 'Plywood Cif Contract Form 1957'. These standard contracts explicitly govern the trade in special timber sorts and products available in different regions and are used by the contractual parties in order to govern their cross-border transactions. In addition, drafted model contracts are applicable in cross-border timber exchanges. The above-mentioned standard contracts belong to the most important normative achievements of the timber industry and considerably facilitate global exchanges. All standard contracts have been developed by different branch organisations and are adjusted to the special requirements of timber trade. The analysis of these contracts shows that German timber traders can recourse to diverse contract forms supporting global timber exchanges.

The most complex and popular framework contract applied within the lumber industry is the 'Germania 1998' contract. This has been developed by German and Scandinavian timber trade associations: the German Timber Trade Federation (GD Holz), the Finnish Forest Industries Federation (FFIF), the Swedish Timber Export Federation (STEF) and the Norwegian Sawmill Industries Association (NSIA), and governs the import of sawn wood from Finland, Sweden and Norway to Germany. 'Germania 1998' covers detailed regulations regarding all aspects of the above-mentioned trade. This complex contract form does not stipulate any applicable law. All disputes arising from the contract should be settled by means of arbitration. The arbitrators shall decide merely on the basis of 'Germania'. The arbitral awards are declared as final and binding. Thus, this contract intends to replace state laws and circumvent the involvement of ordinary courts. All German businessmen interviewed consider the 'Germania 1998' as a perfect framework contract which is effectively used in business transactions with Scandinavia (company representatives, interview nos 8, 9, 13, 17, 18 and 22). The high quality and popularity of the contract also resulted in its application in other European countries. Meanwhile, the contract is applied to deliveries from Baltic countries and Poland (company representatives, interview nos 14 and 22), although these countries were not involved in its drafting. Thus, 'Germania 1998' provides legal certainty for many European countries involved in foreign trade in sawn timber. Other aforementioned standard contracts have also gained popularity in cross-border timber transactions. However, they cannot be compared with 'Germania 1998', which is considered by all interviewed timber traders to be the best drafted contract form.

A further issue to be discussed here concerns the content and autonomy of the available timber contracts. The contracts are without any doubt autonomous with regard to their creators, because they have been developed by intra-industry experts. All contracts drafted for the support of international timber trade contain technical details regarding the traded goods. These technical provisions could only be drafted by the industry's insiders and do not result from any national legal order, but from the practice of trade. The stipulations regarding the transport and insurance inherent in contracts applicable in cross-border timber transactions refer to the current version of Incoterms developed by the International Chamber of Commerce in Paris and considered as one of the most important sources of *lex mercatoria*. The terms for delivery and pick up of goods are different in some contracts, for example in 'Germania 1998', from the usual terms stipulated in national civil laws, for example, in the German Civil Code (BGB). In actual fact, the terms are adjusted to the specific features of the trade in a commodity. All contracts described contain a *force majeure* clause which is typical for international contracts and can be considered to be an important element of *lex mercatoria*. Regarding payment securities, the contracts provide either retention of title, which is usually drafted on the basis of national laws, or special securities developed for the needs of international trade, for example, documentary credit.

In addition, some of the contracts stipulate recourse to the Uniform Customs and Practices for Documentary Credits, thus again allowing the use of *lex mercatoria*. Furthermore, all contracts applied in the practice of international trade stipulate the arbitration proceedings. They foresee either intra-industry arbitration, for example 'Germania', 'Bremensia' and 'Europly', or international commercial arbitration, for example 'Japan-Timber'. The 'Germania' contract form does not contain any provisions concerning applicable law. The contract governs all aspects of the respective trade and provides a perfect basis for possible conflict solutions without the necessity of recourse to national legal systems. Thus, the framework contract can be considered as a self-regulatory contract ('*contrat sans loi*' or '*rechtsordnungsloser Vertrag*'), which is not related to any national legal system, yet generates much discussion in the literature.[26]

[26] Main objections against the self-regulatory contracts are connected to the incompatibility of the *lex mercatoria* with the clasical doctrine concerning sources of law. It is argued that the parties can not declare '*legibus soluti*'. This point of view is supported by the decisions of the highest European courts, which claim for international contracts the 'unlimited submission to a particular national legislative' (RG JW 1936, S. 2058, 2059; English House of Lords in *Amin Rasheed Shipping Corp v Kuwait Insurance Co* (1983) WLR 241, 249; 'Contracts are incapable of existing in a legal vacuum. They are mere pieces of paper devoid of all legal effects unless made by reference to some system of private law'; OLG Wien, 26 January 1982, *Norsolor v Pabalk Ticaret AG 1982*, P. 165, 166 (the description of the *lex mercatoria* as a global law with a questionable validity)). The national law-makers argue that they cannot abdicate in the field of international business law and leave the coordination of the legal relationships completely to the power of the contractual parties. For discussion on this topic, see Berger, 1996: 38 *ff*; Dasser, 1989: 18; and Reimann, 1970.

However, the 'Germania' contract form contains a provision regarding the competence of the appeal court in Bremen for the possible execution of arbitral awards. Although the executions of arbitral awards occur only in exceptional cases (arbitrator, interview no 24), the possibility of involving state institutions may sometimes be relevant. There is no such execution clause in the 'Bremensia General Conditions', which declare arbitration awards as final and binding and do not stipulate any courts responsible for their execution. Consequently, the 'Bremensia General Conditions' are also an example of a '*contrat sans loi*'. The 'Europly' contract also foresees the arbitration proceedings while acting as a conflict resolution method that can be applied to all disputes. However, the contract contains a clause which allows the contractual parties and arbitrators recourse to the laws of the state in which arbitration took place. The application of national laws is also permitted in the 'Japan Timber' contract.

The analysis of the contracts used within the timber industry shows that international merchants developed largely autonomous contracts, which are very well adjusted to the needs of international timber trade. Most contracts do not allow recourse to state laws and courts and foresee arbitration as a preferred method of conflict resolution. Notwithstanding, there are also some contracts with provisions that allow the application of national laws and the involvement of ordinary courts. These contracts mostly apply to transactions with risky countries which are non-members of the OECD and have not developed stable legal systems.

There are also many uniform grading rules and quality standards, for example, the 'National Lumber Grades Authority (NLGA) Standard Grading Rules for Canadian Lumber' and the 'Standard Grading Rules for Southern Pine Lumber', which have been produced by branch organisations and are applied in the practice of international trade. These technical standards have been created in order to facilitate the trade in particular timber sorts and cannot be compared with the complex contracts described above. An increasing number of standards are nowadays created by international standardisation committees like the International Organisation for Standardisation (ISO) and European Committee for Standardisation (CEN) in order to achieve international harmonisation of these product norms. Intra-industry experts are not the only ones involved in the development of these norms: there are also representatives of science and politics and others.

In addition to the above-mentioned norms and contracts, there are several unwritten and codified commercial customs in the international timber trade. There are, for example, specific practices of identification of the owner of bought logs. These practices are used in the field of hardwood trade in some African and American countries (company representative, interview no 20). The '*Tegernseer Handelsbraeuche*' belong to the best-known codified commercial customs, which were primarily developed by

GD Holz for German domestic trade. Nevertheless, because of their high quality, these customs are also applied in transnational trade in exceptional cases.

Because of the variety of traded timber, which requires separate normative regulation, the contracts, grading rules and commercial customs presented above usually apply only in particular countries. Exceptions are Incoterms and General Principles of Law, which are universally applicable in global trade. Nevertheless, the above-presented norms, customs and contracts are so widespread in the international community of merchants that international traders trust their application and compliance in the *business community*. The acceptance of these private rules also results from the fact that they are produced by highly accepted intra-industry experts. The special provenance of merchant-created rules and their reapplication in the practice of international trade cases is such that they can be considered as highly effective coordination mechanisms facilitating globalised timber exchanges.

Arbitration

The timber industry not only operates by its own rules, but has also established its own intra-industry arbitration. Settling disputes with the aid of arbitration is always preferred to litigation. Apart from very few exceptions (company representatives, interview nos 14 and 18), all participants of the survey claimed to have never involved a lawyer or an ordinary court in connection with international trade. This is due to the high costs and time which need to be invested herein. Moreover, the outcome of legal processes carried out abroad cannot be easily assessed. The problems regarding the enforcement of claims hold true not only for developing countries, but also for some OECD countries which have well-functioning legal systems. In Spain, for example, a legal process may require six or seven years for adjudication; in Italy it may even be more than 10 years. This is conceived of as unacceptable, so a reasonable solution within a short time frame is required (company representatives, interview nos 4 and 6).

Arbitration is only taken into consideration when an amicable agreement could not be found. Intra-industry arbitration is organised by different branch organisations, for example GD Holz or ATIBT. Apart from this, the business people are free to appeal for ordinary arbitration, which is open to all commercial fields by national or international chambers of commerce, ie the International Chamber of Commerce (ICC) in Paris. Which arbitral court is competent for dispute resolution is determined by the respective contract in the form of an arbitration clause. The reasons mentioned by the timber traders regarding the preference for arbitration over legal processes are: the party's interest in having the conflicts settled by acknowledged and experienced intra-industrial experts; the shorter time frame that arbitration takes; and the lower costs compared to the costs of lawyers and courts (company representatives, interview nos 9, 10, 21 and 22). A legal process may run for years and cannot be concluded without the involvement of an intra-industry expert. Arbitration usually takes two weeks to produce a decision. This is essential since the goods which need to be inspected *in toto* cannot be held in store for the lengthy period a legal process can take (arbitrator, interview no 24).[27]

The particular procedures concerning arbitration differ slightly from each other. The procedure applied by the Parisian Chamber of Commerce is more complicated than the German regulations, which are, for example, laid down in the *Bremer* or *Hamburger Freundschaftliche Arbitrage*. Both are, in practice, competent and are preferred to regular courts. The reason why arbitration is called for may be the same worldwide. Apart from disputes concerning quality, technical arguments, ie about measures or contract fulfilment, can arise and be the object of arbitration.

Arbitration ends with a legally binding award which is usually accepted by the parties (company and association representatives, arbiter, interview nos 3, 10, 22 and 24) without the necessity to involve state courts for execution. The general acceptance of the arbitral awards is not only due to the good reputation of the arbiters and of the alternative method of conflict resolution itself: it is also the matter of reputation which has a high value within the timber industry (company representative, interview no 3). The certainty that an arbitral award can be executed by an ordinary court adds to the wide acceptance of arbitral awards. The businessmen are sure to have received an award which can be executed in the case of non-compliance of the other party. Whereas it is seldom carried through in practice,[28] the participants of arbitral proceedings obviously bear in mind the possibility to call state institutions if necessary (company representatives, interview nos 10 and 21).

The description of the role of arbitration in the timber industry can be illustrated by the words of a highly renowned arbiter:

> The timber industry functions brilliantly with their self-made rules and private arbitration. It functions as a rule without the involvement of ordinary courts (arbiter, interview no 24).

[27] For this situation, in some countries like Germany there is a special judicial procedure available (§ 485 of the German Code of Civil Procedure). This does not change the fact that timber traders do not want to have disputes resolved by state judges and use courts only in exceptional cases.

[28] None of the company managers has ever tried to have a judgment executed by a court or has heard of any colleague having done so.

This is not only the opinion of an arbitrator: he is supported by association representatives (association representatives, interview nos 22 and 23) and company managers (company representatives, interview nos 9, 10 and 21), who assign arbitration the status of a worldwide accepted method for conflict resolution within the timber industry. More than one-half of the interviewed company representatives (14 persons) have already involved an arbitrator in order to settle a dispute (company representatives, interview nos 1, 2, 3, 5, 9, 10, 12, 14, 15, 16, 17, 21, 26 and 27). Although most contractual parties find a compromise without the involvement of a third party, there is evidence of a more frequent use of arbitration by particular timber traders (company representatives, interview nos 9 and 21). Merchants using arbitration more often than their colleagues can better afford the costs of the proceedings and are experienced in carrying out arbitrations in different countries and by different institutions.

Interestingly, it can be inferred from the interviews that the number of arbitrations generally has declined in recent years. The above-quoted arbitrator, who has carried out approximately 20 to 40 arbitrations per year, claims that he hardly gets any requests at present. He assumes that it is common nowadays to reach an amicable agreement. He is supported by the head of the foreign commerce division at GD Holz, who states that in the last five or six years he only initiated two or three arbitrations on the basis of 'Germania 1998' (association representative, interview no 22).

These statements confirm opinions of experienced company managers on developments in alternative conflict resolution:

> Well, in my opinion arbitration is a sensible method of conflict resolution, but it is not as common as it was 20, 30 years ago when many more arbitrations were carried out. We ourselves have initiated the last arbitration 15 years ago (company representative, interview no 14).

This quotation shows that timber traders prefer to settle differences privately and that they are usually able to settle without the involvement of third parties. The infrequent involvement of arbitrators in recent years can be explained not only by the preference for friendly exchanges, but also by the current transparent normative situation of the timber industry. Clear product standards help to avoid disputes.[29]

The above statements concerning the advantages of arbitration are made not only by arbitrators—who could have their own biased view of arbitration—but also by the companies and the associations' representatives who reported their positive experiences with arbitration. Surprisingly, there are even some judges voicing the opinion that state courts should not be involved in specific trade disputes. Due to high court case loads, they

[29] See 'The Changes in the Governance Structure of the Timber Industry Caused by Globalisation of Trade' below.

are reluctant to collect the special knowledge necessary to decide disputes concerning international commodity trade. An experienced German judge interviewed in order to explain the role of state courts in the conflict resolution within the timber industry could not report a situation in which she or her colleagues decided cases concerning international timber trade. The judge was convinced that this special field is and should remain the domain of arbitrators (judge, interview no 28).

These empirical findings confirm that arbitration is still the preferred method of conflict resolution within the timber industry and that the involvement of state courts in order to settle timber disputes is hardly ever practised. The number and categories of the cases which are brought to state courts will be explained below.

National Legislations and Jurisdictions

In rare cases, national laws are applied in order to govern transnational exchanges of the timber industry. Moreover, in some situations national courts may be involved, even though this may be prove impractical, as is shown above. Company managers mostly opt for this way in new business relations with partners from riskier countries in order to secure payments. Such transactions are either secured by means of letter of credit or a bank guarantee. In addition, business people often apply the clause: *cash against documents*. In some cases in cross-border timber trade, the extended forms of the retention of title are applied (company and association representatives, interview nos 4, 6, 11 and 23).

These mechanisms have been created by international commerce as private methods to ensure payments. In case of financial difficulties of a contractual party, a third party, ie a bank, has to pay the amount due. Even if these mechanisms are instruments of international trade, they often contain elements of the national legal systems or must be applied according to national laws. The letter of credit, for example, represents a contract which is specifically regulated by some legal systems (Zuericher Kantonalbank, 2004).[30] As adequate legal norms for the international credit business have not yet established, the ICC in Paris has created standardised directives and conventions for letters of credit.

Since there is no international standardised legislation for the bank guarantee, it works according to the national legislation in question. Due to the needs that arise in practice, similar conventions have developed. There are of course national particularities which have to be observed. In

[30] <http://www.osec.ch/Osec_Internet_root/marktinformationen/Topics/Financing/das_dokumentar/akkreditiv_einfaehrung/ge/das_dokumentar-akkreditiv_internet.pdf> accessed 1 August 2006.

Germany, the principle of contractual freedom and the general regulation regarding the law of obligation laid down in the BGB have to be considered (Hypovereinsbank, 2004).[31] According to the rules of international private law (compare paragraphs 43 et seq. of EGBGB),[32] the effectiveness of retention of title which is also widespread within external trade depends on domestic property law. In addition, extentions of the retention of title to cross-border transactions are not necessarily recognised.

As the examples above show, the use of private methods to secure payments in cross-border transactions can often lead to the application of national legislation. In case payment is not made, business people engaged in transnational exchanges might consider taking legal action (company representatives, interview nos 6, 14 and 18). Most of the interviewees view a legal process as a worst-case scenario. They would only take legal action when they do not want to maintain the particular business relationships. According to the statements of the international merchants, simply the threat to engage a lawyer or take legal action may cause the end of the business relation (company representative, interview no 13).

However, four of the interviewed company representatives stated that they have already been involved in judicial proceedings (company representatives, interview nos 2, 11, 14 and 18). A telephone interview with a lawyer from an international law firm in Hamburg confirmed that some cases concerning timber trade are brought to state courts. Nevertheless, in these cases, it was not clear whether they had a truly international character, since the connections to foreign countries could hardly be recognised and were without any relevance for the pending disputes (lawyer, interview no 28). The few legal processes regarding timber trade are taking place in OECD countries, where litigation may be time consuming, but not completely ineffective. These cases deal almost exclusively with cash loss. It is mostly clients and not suppliers who are sued.

Network Mechanisms

As a consequence of its network structure, the timber industry makes use of the established network-based sanction mechanisms, as there is the circulation of information concerning the credibility of the trading companies as well as the switching and exclusion mechanism.[33] The German Timber Trade Federation, for example, blacklists foreign companies that

[31] <http://www.hypovereinsbank.deportal?view=media/pdf/fk_auha_gage_Bankgarantie_Brosch.pdf> accessed 1 August 2006.

[32] The Introductory Act to the German Civil Code.

[33] For discussion on network mechanisms in more detail, see Granovetter, 1985; Powell and Smith-Doerr, 1994; Castells, 1996; and Aviram, 2003; 2004.

have cheated German traders. In addition to this, members of GD Holz can be excluded from the trade association if they have damaged their commercial reputation (§ 2.4.1 of the GD Holz Bylaws). This has never happened in practice, but it serves as a deterrent in preventing opportunistic behaviour. In the course of intra-industrial conferences, information on colleagues and business partners is exchanged. This makes reputation an effective governance mechanism playing a significant role within the timber industry (Konradi and Fix-Fierro, 2005: 223).

Actors in the lumber industry describe the effect of reputation as following:

> I am not aware of any other industry which is only nearly as gabby. Many hypotheses could be thought of to explain why this is so, but the fact is, that if I wanted everybody in the industry to take notice of certain circumstances, I would exactly know with whom to talk to in order to inform everybody within a short period of time what's on (company representative, interview no 20).

In other words:

> Our industry is so small that a black list is in effect redundant. Everybody knows everybody. It just needs one day to spread information and reaction will follow promptly. The information mechanism works very well (company representative, interview no 16).

Nevertheless, the timber market cannot be regulated only by means of reputation mechanisms, blacklisting and fear of exclusion from trade associations. Some of the actors in the industry even report that the influence of reputation on the market has declined within the last few years (arbitrator, interview no 24). The contract by handshake, as put into practice within the diamond industry, is as stated before only used in exceptional cases. Most cross-border transactions are secured by contracts, which can become authoritative when a conflict cannot be solved without the involvement of a third party. Possible explanations for the differences in the governance structure in the diamond and in the timber industry will be given below.

TIMBER INDUSTRY AND DIAMOND INDUSTRY COMPARED

One could expect that the timber industry, which at first glance resembles the diamond industry, would coordinate its transactions by exactly the same governance mechanisms. Both industries have a very long tradition,[34] are characterised by a considerable amount of external exchanges and are hallmarked by a network structure. Most of the companies within these

[34] The trade in timber and diamonds has endured through millennia, see Speth, 2004: 54; and Richman, 2006: 410 *ff*.

industries are of small or medium size and family-owned. In addition, both industries are concerned with the trade in commodities, which require on-site quality inspections and familiarity with the handled goods. Consequently, most of the business contacts develop into long-term relationships characterised by relational contracting. There is also a similarity concerning the time-inconsistent exchange occurring in the timber and diamond trades (Richman, 2006: 384). Thus, the probability of being cheated in the course of these exchanges is quite high. Since the disputes concerning diamonds and timber can, due to the uniqueness of the commodities, hardly ever be resolved with the aid of ordinary courts, there is also in both cases a strong need for arbitration.

Nevertheless, there are also some differences in the institutional structure of the industries causing the different governance of the relevant exchanges and circumventing the coordination of trans-border timber trade by complete exclusion of state law. The phenomenon of self-regulation occurring within the diamond industry has been explained in a very convincing way by Bernstein and Richman (Bernstein, 1992; Richman, 2006; 2009, in this volume). Both researchers argue that the *opting out of the legal system* observed within the diamond industry can be explained with the dominance of orthodox Jews who established a private legal system by recourse to the pre-existing Jewish law and the foundation of specific industry, family and community institutions, which allow enforcement of executory agreements beyond the reach of public courts.

The analysis of Bernstein's and Richman's descriptions regarding the diamond industry clarifies that this sector fulfils conditions which are not met in the timber industry. The last has never been dominated by a particular ethnic group of merchants. The pioneering role of German and Scandinavian traders in cross-border timber exchanges (see footnote 9) has only the consequence that these countries still belong to the main participants of the international timber trade. The German and Scandinavian merchants have never tried to incorporate the elements of their laws in the international timber trade, even when they are leading in drafting standard contracts that facilitate cross-border exchanges of many European countries. A further proof for the leading role of Germany and Scandinavia in the fostering of intra-industry self-regulation is the establishment of a private arbitration system of the timber branch. These achievements are considerable and replace in most cases the use of state laws and courts in international transactions. However, they cannot be considered as 'opting out of the legal system'. The private arbitration system of the timber industry is, despite its high acceptance and effectiveness, voluntary and confined to traders governing their transactions with the aid of 'Germania 1998'. The arbitrations are carried out on the basis of this framework contract, thus circumventing the far-reaching discretionary decisions that are typical for the diamond arbitrators (Bernstein, 1992: 127). As it has become clear from the proceeding discussion, there are very few executions of arbitral awards occurring in the timber industry. It may also happen that contractual parties which did not include an arbitration clause in their contract will search redress by a public court in a case of non-payment. This is not imaginable within the diamond trade, where such behaviour would be sanctioned with the exclusion from the DDC (Bernstein, 1992: 119; Richman, 2006: 395 *ff*).

The lower ability of the timber traders to enforce executory contracts is obviously connected to the less dense network structure of the industry and to the lack of religious elements and indispensable club goods that are available within the diamond industry. The existing networks developed on the basis of long-term business relationships and cooperation between particular timber trade associations. The main purpose of the networks is to connect merchants being a part of the same industry and represent their economic interests. Although the timber traders prefer to transact with their old friends and children of well-known, trustworthy families being active in this sector for generations, the access to the network is not limited in any way. Everybody who is involved in timber trade can become a member of the German Timber Trade Federation by paying the due amount. This is clearly different from the regulation of the DDC Bylaws, which impose easier membership requirements for spouses, widows, sons, daughters, and sons- and daughters-in-law of current members (Richman, 2006: 403). This example shows that the value of families' reputation in the timber sector has other economic implications than in the diamond industry, where entering the market without family connection is hardly possible.

In contrast to the diamond industry, in the field of the international timber trade there is no high concentration of the industry-specific institution in one place, for example, specific country or city. Many companies trading in timber are located in Northern Germany and there are also a number of international timber trade organisations settled in Brussels. Nevertheless, such a high concentration of the industry like the one known from New York, Mumbai or Antwerp (Richman, 2006: 410 *ff*) is not typical for timber trade. This explains why network mechanisms, which are effectively used in the field of diamond trade, prove to be less effective in governing cross-border timber transactions. The German Timber Trade Federation includes 1,200 members and governs 80 per cent of sales, thus being capable of providing information exchange within the industry. However, this information mechanism is aimed at providing the members with details concerning foreign markets or important branch meetings rather than focusing on merchants' reputations. The blacklist drafted by GD Holz may damage the reputation of cheating traders, but the maintenance and effectiveness of this list depends on the cooperation of members of the trade organisation. Since members are not always willing to inform GD Holz about cases of opportunistic behaviour, the list cannot easily be updated. This leads to the consequence that market participants who cheated once in the past and started then to transact honestly will never be removed from the blacklist. Furthermore, this system of blacklisting does not seem to be adequate and fair, since it is often based on the subjective opinions of particular traders and cannot be effectively controlled. These objections are known to the representatives of the trade organisations and their members and entail that the described mechanism does not belong to the most effective enforcement mechanisms of the timber industry.

GD Holz also forgoes the posting of pictures, backgrounds and references of its members in order to provide referral for potential business dealings. In this respect, it differs from the practice of the New Yorker Diamond Dealers Club (Bernstein, 1992: 119; Richman, 2006: 397). The information about reputation of potential business partners must by obtained by private actors in the course of informal meetings with their colleagues. A gossip concerning a particular market participant may diminish his or her chances to profit from the business, but it seldom leads to his or her exclusion from the market. Since the timber market is not as dense as the diamond industry, there are many possibilities for potential cheaters to establish new companies and business relations in order to continue the transacting.

The honesty behaviour of timber traders cannot be enforced by offering valuable club goods either, as those available in the diamond community. Since the timber traders do not build a religious network comparable to that established by the orthodox Jewish diamond merchants, there are no excludable community goods like common prayers, honours in life-cycle ceremonies, access to classes or teachers or enrolment in particularly selected educational institutions. Nor are there rabbinical courts to impose sanctions (Richman, 2006: 407). The timber traders have succeeded in building diverse industrial organisations, but they have never built social institutions comparable to those known from the Jewish diamond communities. Consequently, the membership in timber networks has many advantages described in the second part of this chapter, but it is not indispensable for being successful in the business, as is the case in the diamond trade.

The timber traders have not succeeded in the enforcement of credit sales, which is considered as the key success of the Jewish diamond traders. The supply and demand of lumber is more regular than of diamonds, where most sales occur in November and December, making the role of credit a central one (Richman, 2006: 391, 392). Numerous timber traders also prefer credit sales, but they are not the rule in the timber industry. Moreover, the credits are not offered by the business partners, but by third parties, for example, banks. The payment deadlines are contractually stipulated and are in most cases very short.[35] Moreover, the sales are often secured by different mechanisms assuring payments and requiring the involvement of third persons (see 'National Legislations and Jurisdictions' above).

The practice of the timber industry compared with that of the diamond industry (Bernstein, 1992; Richman, 2006; 2009, in this volume) aims to stress that *opting out of the legal system* is only practised in extremely specific cases. The governing of transactions by means of blacklisting and fear of exclusion from trade associations must be seen as bound to closed social, ethnic and religious networks which build on special prerequisites and strictly control the access to the network. This view is supported by the diamond researcher Richman, who considers the diamond industry to be an unusual industry and states that only few others can boast similar features (Richman, 2009, in this volume).

The differences in the governance structure of the international timber trade and diamond trade as well as the possible explanation for them can be summarised with the words of an experienced timber trader and arbitrator:

> The timber industry is not at all like the diamond industry. It is not as exclusive and also consists of a variety of suppliers and clients who do not work as exclusively as the diamond trade, which in turn does still have its own ethics. On the contrary, the timber trade has, in my opinion, adapted to the harder conditions of the business having developed over the last 30 years. The solidarity of earlier times has vanished—but this is no problem, unless contracts are breached.

As the timber trade is not as exclusive as the diamond industry, the combination of several coordination mechanisms becomes necessary in order to secure transactions effectively. On the other hand, the fact that the timber trade does not share the same prerequisites as the diamond trade makes the existence of self-regulation in this industry a noticeable matter.

THE CHANGES IN THE GOVERNANCE STRUCTURE OF THE TIMBER INDUSTRY CAUSED BY GLOBALISATION OF TRADE

The above-mentioned quote of the experienced timber trader and arbitrator and the aforementioned necessity to secure international transactions with mechanisms assuring payments indicate the changes in the governance structure of the timber industry, which are the consequence of the globalisation of trade. The changes which can be observed regard first of

[35] The payment occurs mostly immediately after the transferring of documents according to the clause *cash against documents*. Typical for timber contracts is also the deadline of 14 days.

all the increasing extension of the international timber trade and the discovery of new markets. Furthermore, there are visible changes in the structure and management of some timber companies and in the coordination of international transactions by the above-described means.

The timber market became much larger due to globalisation. There was only a small circle of companies that participated in timber exports and imports after the Second World War. These few companies possessed a special knowledge required to carry out trans-border timber exchanges. Nowadays, there are considerably more participants in the international timber trade. An easier participation in this business is not at all possible through the current transparent normative situation in the lumber industry. Clearly formulated product norms and standardised contracts available for international timber trade allow the newcomer to deal with the specific commodity without previous experience gained within the industry. According to the sophisticated timber traders, the timber exchanges became much easier after the globalisation of commerce (supplement to interview no 24). New relevant markets such as Eastern Europe, Asia and Africa emerged. Consequently, new timber providers, importers and customers are available, thus guaranteeing more choice in respect of different lumber sorts and products and to potential business partners.

The change regarding the new markets in the trans-border timber trade can be well illustrated with the example of Germany's exports and imports. Whereas in the 1970s most timber trade was domestic or limited to few countries such as the Scandinavian countries, Germany or Russia, we can observe truly globalised exchanges today. In recent years, a considerable increase in German timber exports to China occurred. However, since the Chinese traders have oriented towards North American timber classes, which they are currently importing, the market collapsed for Germany. Most German exports in sawn wood are nowadays going to Japan, the United States, Spain and Portugal (association representative, interview no 22). Most German imports of tropical timber nowadays come from different African countries, especially Gabon, Cameron, Congo and Ghana. Providers of tropical deciduous sawn timber are also Malaysia and Indonesia. At present, the import of veneers occurs not primarily from Europe and Asia, but from the United States and Canada (GD Holz Geschaeftsbericht, 2004: 17). The changes caused by globalisation of commerce and described above relate not only to the spatial extension of timber trade. There are also demands for new sorts of timber or timber products, which affect cross-border exchanges and cause the search towards new markets.

Furthermore, the fact that there is a turning away from export of untreated lumber towards subsequent processing of the commodity before exporting is of special importance. As a result, finished products rather than crude lumber are often exported today (association representative, interview no 22). The demand for specific products causes a strong need for new product norms in the lumber industry (supplement to the interview no 24). The coordination of international timber trade by means of trade usages did not result from globalisation: it is a very old phenomenon. Some trade usages have been used in Germany for 200 years due to the traditional import of softwood from Sweden, Finland, Norway, Denmark and Russia (association representative, interview no 23). Written standard contracts described above (see 'Lex Mercatoria' above), characteristic for the international timber trade, have developed since the 1950s and proved to be very practicable. For this reason, the contracts have been updated by the relevant trade organisations and are successfully used in current trans-border exchanges (interview nos 23 and 24). The most prominent example for the development of such contracts and adjustments that are usually made in order to consider the new basic conditions of globalised trade is the framework contract 'Germania 1998', which has been described above (see 'Lex Mercatoria' above).

One aspect which should also be mentioned in the context of changes and which occurred in the international timber trade due to globalisation is the increasing cooperation between the industrial and political organisations. Timber trade organisations are nowadays working together with the European Union in order to develop new product norms, which should facilitate trans-border exchanges and protect consumers. The commissions responsible for the development of these norms assign industry experts, who write down norms that already exist in the practice of international timber trade. These norms result from the ongoing business relationships between the timber traders and the nature of the trade, and are adjusted to the new practice of globalised trade. In other words, the current norm standardisation at EU-level is based on what already exists in the timber trade practice going back many years or decades. The European Union itself does not develop any new standards

The cooperation of industrial organisations and political bodies in order to set international standards, which can facilitate trans-border timber exchanges, is typical for the European countries (especially for the EU-members) and other OECD countries such as the United States or Canada. Some English and US timber standards which proved to be useful in the practice of international trade have been exported to South-East Asia. Malaysia also developed useful standards in recent years. The necessity to develop such kinds of norm still exists in China. In this country, problems with the fulfilment of contracts often occur, which emerge due to the lack of relevant norms.

The increasing standardisation of timber products prevents in many cases disagreements in international timber trade. The number of quality arbitrations decreased, for instance, in recent years due to exact standardisation (arbitrator, interview no 24). The settlement of differences in trans-border timber trade is a clear result of the use of modern information and communication technology, which is meanwhile common in the timber industry. Many doubts or disagreements can be clarified by telephone, fax or email, without the necessity to visit the business partner abroad. Disagreements and claims in long-lasting business relations are mostly clarified on the basis of pictures of the rejected goods, which are sent to the business partners.

Nevertheless, there are also some problems arising in trans-border exchanges and caused by globalisation. As already mentioned, the globalisation of trade caused a high fluctuation in the timber market. Some family-owned companies, involved for generations in the international timber trade, have been sold and filled with foreign managers who are not familiar with the unique character of timber exchanges or the rules established within the industry. Many of the young managers of the timber companies reject the on-site quality inspections that have for a long time been characteristic for most timber transactions. The new generation of traders tends to rely on quality descriptions based on established norms and grading rules or on buying some products via the internet. This facilitates and accelerates international timber exchanges, but at the same time limits the role of human beings in that business. In several countries, such as the United States and Finland, more complex firm structures are developing. Meanwhile, numerous corporate groups are active in the timber industry. People who have been well known and proved as trustworthy are often replaced by new players. The latter must first gain a good commercial reputation in order to profit from relational contracting.

The changes in the structure of timber companies, the extension of the market to new countries and participants, and the development of modern information and communication technology considerably affects the nature of cross-border exchanges. It has the consequence that network mechanisms are not sufficient to govern these kinds of transaction and that normative regulations are increasingly necessary. Another effect of the more complex market structure is that the market participants are more likely to take legal action, which is, for example, not an option in the trans-border diamond trade.

Interestingly, many of the described developments concerning the globalised timber trade resemble changes in the structure of the diamond industry, which have been recently observed by Richman (2006; 2009, in this volume). The researcher argues that recent trends in the globalisation of commerce have introduced pressures that may cause the 1,000-year-old system to unravel (Richman, 2006: 415; 2009, in this volume).

The described changes in the structures of the timber and diamond industries, as well as modifications concerning the governance of cross-border transactions, are without any doubt the result of the globalisation of the economy. The extension of markets to new countries and the modern communication and information technology greatly facilitate trans-border exchanges. Nevertheless, they also make some well-established governance mechanisms redundant, which have supported cross-border trade for many centuries. Network mechanisms, especially personal reputation, are less important since most commodities can be described and certified. An exact description of products and the possibility to sell them via the internet make interpersonal exchange less important. This could cause the end of relational contracting in the future. The described changes occur very slowly in such close-knit branches of trade like the diamond and timber industries. It is obviously difficult to challenge long and well-accepted trading traditions of such industries. Nevertheless, the first effects of globalisation are already visible within the industries and it is highly probable that the changes will continue.

Recent developments show that the dense network structures of the diamond trade are increasingly open to persons who are new in the industry and that these kinds of network will hardly survive globalisation. The less exclusive network of the timber industry seems to be more immune against the changes caused by globalisation. The traditional networks between German and Scandinavian traders have not been threatened by globalisation. There is still a strong demand for timber sorts available in Scandinavia and very good cooperation between the business partners. Furthermore, business relations in the Baltic States and Poland remain very stable and are even getting closer. German timber traders, especially the middlemen who realised the importance of stable business relations, are keen to integrate the new participants in the trade and motivate them to play by the established intra-industry rules. These traders, who have for a long time profited from well-functioning domestic networks, are networking now at the international level in order to establish business friendships which as a rule assure effective trans-border exchanges.

According to the interviewees, such business-networking works well in most of the OECD countries such as France, Spain, Italy, Belgium, Netherlands and Japan. Nevertheless, there are often problems with the integration of Russian or Chinese traders. Even if these two countries are well-known examples of relational contracting (Landa, 1981; Hendley, Murrell and Rytermann, 2001: 67, 68), the traders from these countries do not seem to be interested in relational contracting at the international level. This different behaviour of market participants can be explained by different business cultures and diverse basic conditions of the respective exchange. While the business culture of the OECD countries grew over a long time in the international exchange environment and is based on stable institutions today, there is, for example, no comparable development in Russia or China. Both countries were for a long time isolated politically and economically and experienced primarily domestic exchanges. The post-war German-Russian timber trade has been handled by a state institution, 'Exportless', and by fixed one-year contracts. There has been no incentive to establish business friendships in order to continue the exchanges. Even if the trade is no longer regulated by the state, the mentality of business friendships at international level is not very common in Russia.

The problem with Chinese traders is of different nature. They represent the new market players who are not ready to accept the rules of the timber industry and establish stable business connections. The main motivation to exchange with particular foreign traders is in most cases the price of the timber products. Since fashions for timber products are changing and there are possibilities of buying the products in different countries for divergent prices, the incentive to establish business networks is lacking. Under these circumstances it can be assumed that the networking of the timber industry will continue in the future and that the well-established business networks will survive the globalisation. However, they remain limited to these exchange partners and countries which have already proved to be reliable and prefer to transact in a friendly business atmosphere. The exchanges with traders and countries which are oriented towards rapid profits and short-term business relations will still require additional safeguards, which are available within network structures.

CONCLUSIONS

The previous discussion has shown that the international timber trade is characterised by a low influence of national legal systems on industry's regulations. The cross-border timber trade works very well on the basis of the established long-term business relationships, self-created rules and intra-industry arbitration. The network-like structure of the timber industry and the trade in a specific commodity positively further the generation and implementation of self-made rules. The relatively small, well-integrated timber industry is an example which illustrates that international trade is far too specific to be regulated through national legislations.

The fragmentation of world society and the differentiation of diverse subareas, for example, law, politics and economy, as set out by Teubner (1997), render global transactions difficult to handle through national laws. The above-mentioned aspects also impede that breach of contracts can be sanctioned by ordinary courts. Private norms, by contrast, have been shaped in accordance with the specific needs of the business community. They are applied and executed according to the needs of the international *societas mercatorum* (Goldman, 1983: 3), which contributes to their popularity.

These rules and the mechanisms for executing them autonomously are so widely accepted in the timber industry that they must be regarded as a highly feasible supporting mechanism for cross-border timber transactions. The available norms, contracts and customs as well as the intra-industry arbitration accomplish their purpose of securing expectations of effective transnational exchange at least in the OECD countries, mainly in Western and Northern Europe, as well as in Northern America. Several European countries handle their trade exclusively on the basis of the basic purchase agreement 'Germania 1998', which completely excludes national legislations and courts. Thus, within these limits the *lex mercatoria* functions well as an effective supporting mechanism for international commerce.

Nevertheless, in non-OECD African and Asian countries there is a lack of institutions which could further the generation and execution of autonomous rules. As a consequence, no standard contracts or industry-specific norms could be identified in these regions. In Africa, there are a few exceptional conventions which are applied in individual fields of commerce, but, generally, the trade with African countries takes place within the limits of well-established long-term business relationships with the suppliers. The above analysis shows that the existing timber trade rules do not have the quality of a global legal order which is assumed by numerous theoretical legal and socio-legal approaches as dealing with *lex mercatoria*.[36]

Many of the identified rules, for example, standardised contracts, are only applied on the basis of individual agreements, thus in the scope of the freedom of contracts. Others, for example, quality standards, do not have a quality of legal norms and can only be classified as '*lex*', ie a universally applicable law with strong reservations. Moreover, the norms, contracts and customs peculiar to international timber trade are due to the diverse sorts of timber only applied within the limits of certain countries and regions. The obvious lack of universality does not allow conferring these rules with the status of a global commercial law. Such status could be at least conferred to the Incoterms of the ICC in Paris which are very popular within international commerce, including the investigated timber trade. Other universal rules and principles, especially the UNIDROIT Principles, which belong to the most prominent elements of *lex mercatoria*, are not applied within the timber industry.

The co-existence and interaction of different self-regulating mechanisms in the timber industry almost renders national legislations and courts

[36] The legal quality of *lex mercatoria* is, for example, assumed by Gralf Peter Calliess, who usually uses the notion 'transnational law' for describing that phenomenon. A different, sceptical view of the existence, legal quality and practical relevance of the *lex mercatoria* is characteristic for Volkmar Gessner. For more detailed points of view of these authors, see their contributions to this volume.

dispensable, as these are only relevant in connection with imports from unstable countries and trade with new business partners. As a renowned arbitrator put it: 'The more anonymous the business relation, the more likely it is that national laws will be applied' (arbitrator, interview no 24).

The findings of the study on international timber trade show that state law works more ineffectively in an international context than within the national scope. In this respect, these findings correspond with the results of the empirical research of Fabian Sosa as well as Thomas Dietz and Holger Nieswandt presented in other chapters of this book. Both studies show that the coordination of globalised transactions occurs mainly with the aid of private coordination mechanisms and with exceptional recourse to state laws and courts. The extra-legal governance mechanisms, which are used by medium-sized law firms in order to support cross-border transactions as well as the private CEIs identified in cross-border outsourcing transactions, are identical or at least very similar to the private governance mechanisms described in this chapter. All empirical studies emphasise, for example, the relevance of relational contracting and arbitration in globalised exchanges. Even though in all described structures the private governance mechanisms obviously lead to only infrequent use of public governance mechanisms, I do not share the opinion of the authors of other empirical studies which argue that law recedes almost completely from the minds of international merchants.

It should be emphasised that none of my interviewees in the timber industry could imagine doing globalised business completely without law. The statutory framework created by the national legal systems obviously has a reassuring effect. In addition, although private solutions are always favoured, national laws are applied if no compromise is found. If payment is not made, for example, legal action may be taken in the international timber trade. What does this mean in relation to the existence and autonomy of the *lex mercatoria*? It means that self-regulating mechanisms do not substitute national legislations, but render them the *last resort*. The international timber merchants evidently act *in the shadow of the law* even though they often do not make use of the available legal means. There can be no other reasonable explanation why written contracts are drafted in this area and international transactions are not only handled on the basis of relational and network-like mechanisms, as is, for example, common in the international diamond trade. Moreover, many of the analysed international contracts contain permeability for state laws and courts. Even such high quality framework contracts like 'Germania 1998' do not dispense with execution clauses. Accordingly, *lex mercatoria* can be at least considered as semi-autonomous, but not as a fully autonomous legal order.

The '*shadow of the law*' and the identified links between private and public structures are not only visible in the timber industry. We have to consider the successful combination of legal and extra-legal tools used by the medium-sized law firms as described by Sosa. Furthermore, Dietz and Nieswandt, who investigated the software industry, reported in their contribution to this book that contracts used in cross-border outsourcing transactions are exclusively drafted under German law. These empirical findings confirm the obvious links to state laws existing in all studied industries and structures and cannot be overseen by the description of globalised trade. Consequently, the above-mentioned arguments that law recedes from the minds of international merchants are not convincing. An additional aspect is that the changes caused by globalisation can be observed much better within traditional branches of trade like the timber or diamond industries than within such young industries like the software industry. Generally, considering that globalisation already affected the so far privately organised traditional industries, one can expect that it will also increase the pressure for public regulation in many other industries, including the software industry.

The findings of the empirical study on the international timber trade also underline that global exchanges cannot be handled through one coordinating mechanism only. On the contrary, it is necessary for business people to combine different available governance mechanisms in order to achieve the best results. Actors in global commerce learn according to evolutionary economics from their past experience (Dopfer, 1990; 2005; Kappelhof, 2004; Sydow, 2005; Freiling and Reckenfelderbaeumer, 2004; Freiling, 2006). On that basis they choose a strategy for governing the trading operations, and this strategy may differ according to the region in which the trade takes place. '*Traditionalists*'[37] still claim that commercial exchange can only be coordinated by means of state mechanisms, but this view has been shown to be out-dated. However, it also seems exaggerated to claim that the *lex mercatoria* is always the basis for cross-border transactions, as held by the '*transnationalists*'.[38] As the empirical study shows, the order of commerce cannot only be established by national or non-national law. The embeddedness of particular business actors in social structures often goes unnoticed in the course of scientific arguments.[39] However, in fact, this aspect plays a significant role in global commerce. This is especially true for closely interrelated industries such as the timber industry.

[37] This notion is used by Zumbansen in order to describe the authors which emphasise the continuing important role of the state in coordination of international transactions and in enforcing arbitral awards; see Zumbansen, 2006: 741.

[38] 'Transnationalists' are sometimes called the proponents of the *lex mercatoria* which embrace the emergence of a self-producing legal order among commercial actors; see Zumbansen, 2006: 741.

[39] Granovetter is the key author who has dealt with the problem of social embeddedness; see Granovetter, 1985. He resumed the embedded approach as a central element of the new economic sociology; see Nee, 2005.

Current research shows that neoclassical economics is limited in its conception of *homo economicus*. As the new institutionalist economic sociology (Nee, 2005; Fligstein, 2002; Swedberg, 2003; Evans, 1999) rightly emphasises, rationality is context bound. Economic actors are motivated by interests usually shaped by shared beliefs, norms and network ties. The study in the field of the international timber trade confirms that individuals articulate their interests within different organisations and networks. The timber industry, especially in the OECD countries, consists of diverse branch organisations, which build domestic and worldwide networks. Timber traders profit from their membership in these organisations since they provide them with useful information concerning the governance of international trade. The merchants can also use intra-industry arbitration and participate in meetings with colleagues, learning in passing about the reputation of other market participants. Finally, members of industrial organisations can, with the aid of their representatives acting as their agents, influence political decisions concerning laws affecting the timber trade. For these reasons, membership in industry-specific networks can be seen as a welfare-maximising measure.

As has been shown, international merchants not only rely on formal industry's organisations, but also establish long-term business-relations, which can endure for many generations. In these kinds of relationship, factors like trust play an important role. All of these elements—both formal and informal—can be considered as institutions which are interrelated to each other, motivate and govern economic action. As a rule, economic actors articulate their interests within internal and external network structures, but sometimes they leave these socially embedded structures to undertake market transactions. This occurs especially when they search for new business partners and markets. In such situations, the network regulation common to the timber industry does not work. Consequently, actors are forced to use more detailed contracts and secure transactions by means of letters of credit, bank guarantees, etc. A breach of the contract committed by a stranger would be sanctioned by a law suit, while this mechanism is usually not used within the intra-industry networks. The macro-level mechanisms (for example, state and market regulation) described by the new economic sociologists are remote from individuals embedded in social groups, but they are not completely absent. Like network regulation, both mechanisms offer proper sanction means for breaches of contract and are therefore accepted by the international traders.

The state regulation which affects individuals acting within networks is not only visible in the enforcement of contracts and provision of environmental laws.[40] States and their institutions are also responsible for organising the whole infrastructure governing international trade.[41] In international and intra-industry arbitration, the use of privately produced *lex mercatoria* norms is sometimes combined with state execution. Neither companies trading in timber nor arbitrators would be able to operate without the structures provided by nation states. Although the functionality and effectiveness of classical state legal support structures (in particular contract law and the court system) are significantly reduced in the field of globalised exchanges, the state still provides an important infrastructure which is vital for running cross-border transactions.

It can be argued that modern nation states are responsible for providing the infrastructure described above, but they must not necessarily intervene in supporting cross-border transactions, since this challenge has been successively taken by private actors. However, in the international timber trade an increasing tolerance of private and state structures can be observed. This tolerance is based on the common intention of the actors involved. The private mechanisms governing international timber exchanges described in this chapter are not the result of the globalisation of trade. The timber trade was organised privately long before globalisation. However, the networks that previously existed within national frames have recently been extended to take up other market participants due to the internationalisation of trade. The growth of the timber market has caused the creation and implementation of private norms also to be extended to new countries. However, the empirical investigation of the timber industry also clarified that the globalisation of trade has caused an increasing inclusion of execution clauses in international contracts. The execution of arbitral awards has become more frequent since new market participants who are unfamiliar with the intra-industry rules entered the market. This

[40] There is a strong political pressure for public regulation in order to allow tropical forest protection and stop illegal logging. While the EU Commission negotiates with particular countries that deliver lumber to Europe in order to sign international conventions, national and international timber organisations, eg FEBO, support the legal timber trade by formulating voluntary codes of conduct and using different certification systems like FSC (Forest Stewardship Council). Official national and international forestry laws, which are drafted by political institutions, are opposed by traders who know that global exchanges will be constrained by these regulations. In Germany, there was considerable opposition to the implementation of the so-called '*Urwaldschutzgesetz*', a law protecting the destruction of virgin forests and outlawing the illegal timber trade. The German Trade Federation lobbied for a long time against the law and obstructs its implementation. Instead, it implemented a private code of conduct.
This aspect refers to the regulation of business transactions (see the distinction between the support and regulation of global exchanges explained in the introduction to this book).

[41] The globalisation of trade was facilitated by the opening of national markets. Many legal solutions, especially the law of the European Union providing a single European Market and the General Agreement on Tariffs and Trade, facilitated international trade. In addition, the state organises markets by providing an infrastructure in the form of property laws, different forms of companies, chambers of commerce, etc.

fact indicates that the process of globalisation has affected the previously private governance structure of the timber industry.

There is also a second indication that state intervention in the governance structure of close-knit branches of trade has increased due to globalisation, namely the new collective development of norms governing cross-border transactions. The pioneers in the development of the normative solutions of the timber industry in terms of drafting standard contracts are branch organisations resident in the OECD countries. However, recently, product norms are also created on the initiative of the European Commission in international standardisation committees. The Commission does not develop any new standards by merely writing down the norms that have existed in the trade practice for a long time. Nevertheless, it initiates the harmonisation of merchant-created rules and encourages the still inchoate codification of *lex mercatoria.*

This example illustrates that state-like institutions (for example, the EU and UN) are increasingly interested in supporting global exchanges, thus extending their primary function to regulate cross-border trade. If this trend will continue, one can expect that at least some elements of *lex mercatoria* will be integrated in particular national commercial laws or in the international commercial law. This would have the consequence that the *new law merchant* would lose its autonomous character completely, thus repeating its sad history from the eighteenth and nineteenth centuries.[42]

Furthermore, interlocking of public and private structures, especially the cooperation between state and private actors in developing normative solutions, will increase considerably in the future. This development is essential in order to stabilise permanently expectations for effective cross-border exchanges. Power struggles between different providers of norms governing and facilitating cross-border transactions may foster the competition for a short time, thus contributing to the improvement of the proposed solutions. However, in the long term, this behaviour would definitely impede transnational trade. There are no doubts that an intensive cooperation between state and private actors and institutions is indispensable in order to secure complex global transactions in the long term.

REFERENCES

Aviram, A (2003) 'Regulation by networks' *Brigham Young University Law Review* 1179 *ff* <http://ssrn.com/abstract=387960> accessed 17 July 2008.

[42] See footnote 3 and the explanation by Calliess, 2002: 185–216.

—— (2004) 'A Paradox of Spontanous Formation: The Evolution of Private Legal Systems' 22 *Yale Law & Policy Review* 1–65 <http://www.law.uchicago.edu/Lawecon/index.html> accessed 17 June 2008.

Berger, KP (1996) *Formalisierte und "schleichende" Kodifizierung des transnationalen Wirtschaftsrechts* (Berlin and New York, Walter de Gruyter).

Berger, KP, Dubberstein, H, Lehmann, S and Petzold, V (2001) 'The CENTRAL Enquiry on the Use of Transnational Law in International Contract Law and Arbitration' in KP Berger (ed), *The Practice of Transnational Law* (The Hague, Kluwer).

—— (2002) 'Anwendung des Transnationalen Rechts in der internationalen Vertrags- und Schiedspraxis. Hintergrund, Methode und ausgewählte Ergebnisse einer Umfrage des Center for Transnational Law (CENTRAL)' 101 *Zeitschrift für vergleichende Rechtswissenschaft* 12–37.

Berman, HJ and Kaufman C (1978) 'The Law of International Commercial Transactions (*Lex mercatoria*)' 19 *Harvard International Law Journal* 221–77.

Bernstein, L (1992) 'Opting Out of the Legal System: Extra-legal Contractual Relations in the Diamond Trade' 21 *Journal of Legal Studies* 115–57.

—— (1996) 'Merchant Law in a Merchant Court: Rethinking the Code's Search for Immanent Business Norms' 144 *University of Pennsylvania Law Review* 1765–821.

—— (2001) 'Private Commercial Law in the Cotton Industry: Creating Cooperation Through Rules, Norms, and Institutions' 99 *Michigan Law Review* 1724–90.

Bond, SR (1990) 'How to Draft an Arbitration Clause (Revisited)' 1 *ICC International Chamber of Commerce International Court of Arbitration Bulletin* 20–27.

Calliess, GP (2002) 'Reflexive Transnational Law. The Privatisation of Civil Law and the Civilisation of Private Law' 23 *Zeitschrift für Rechtssoziologie* 185–216.

—— (2004) 'Transnationales Handelsvertragsrecht. Private Ordnung und staatlicher Rahmen' in Zürn and Zangl (eds), *Verrechtlichung-Baustein für Global Governance* (Bonn, Dietz).

—— (2009) 'An evolutionary theory of transnational law' in V Gessner (ed), *Contractual Certainty in International Trade* (Oxford, Hart).

Carbonneau, TE (1998) *Lex mercatoria and Arbitration. A Discussion of the New Law Merchant* (Kluwer Law International, Juris Publishing).

Castells, M (1996) *The Rice of the Network Society* (Oxford, Blackwell).

Dasser, Felix (1989) *Internationale Schiedsgerichte und lex mercatoria* (Zürich, Schulthess Polygraphischer Verlag AG).

DeLy, F (2001) 'Lex mercatoria (New Law Merchant): Globalization and international Self-Regulation' in RP Appelbaum, WLF Felstiner and V Gessner (eds), *Rules and Networks: The Legal Culture of Global Business Transactions* (Oxford, Hart Publishing) 159–88.

Dezalay, Y and Garth, B (1996) *Dealing in Virtue: International Commercial Arbitration and the Construction of a Transnational Legal Order* (Chicago, University of Chicago Press).

Dietz, T and Nieswandt, H (2009) 'The emergence of transnational cooperation in the software-industry' in V Gessner (ed), *Contractual Certainty in International Trade* (Oxford, Hart).

Dopfer, K (1990) 'Elemente einer Evolutionsökonomik: Prozess, Struktur und Phasenübergänge' in U Witt (ed), *Studien zur Evolutorischen Ökonomik I* (Berlin, Duncker & Humbold) 19–47.

—— (2005) *Economics, Evolution and the State: The Governance of Complexity* (Cheltenham, Edward Elgar).

Drahozal, CR (2000) 'Commercial Norms, Commercial Codes, and International Commercial Arbitration' 33 *Vanderbilt Journal of Transnational Law* 79–146.

Evans, P and Rauch, JE (1999) 'Bureaucracy and Growth: A Cross-National Analysis of the Effects of "Weberian" State Structures in Economic Growth' 64 *American Sociological Review* 748–65.

Fligstein, N (2001) *The Architecture of Markets: An Economic Sociology of Twenty-First-Century Capitalist Societies* (Princeton and Oxford, Princeton University Press).

Flood, J (1996) 'Megalawyering in the Global Order: The Cultural, Social and Economic Transformation of Global Legal Practice' 3 *International Journal of the Legal Profession* 169–214.

—— (2007) 'Lawyers as Sanctifiers: The Role of Elite Law Firms in International Business Transactions' 14 *Indiana Journal of Global Legal Studies* 35–66.

Flood, J and Sosa, F (2008) 'Lawyers, Law Firms and the Stabilization of Transnational Business', *North-Western Journal of International Business and Law*, forthcoming.

Freiling, J (1995) *Die Abhängigkeit der Zulieferer. Ein strategisches Problem* (Wiesbaden, Deutscher Universitäts-Verlag).

—— (1999) 'Management Strategischer Allianzen' in 40 *Swiss Export* 10–15.

—— (2004) 'Competence-based View der Unternehmung' 58 *Die Unternehmung* 5–25.

Freiling, J and Engelhardt, W (1996) 'Prekäre Partnerschaften—Gefahren, die aus Geschäftsbeziehungen erwachsen' 39 *Absatzwirtschaft* 145–51.

Freiling, J, Gersch, M and Goeke, C (2006) 'Eine "Competence-based Theory of the Firm" als marktprozesstheoretischer Ansatz—Erste disziplinäre Basisentscheidungen eines evolutorischen Forschungsprogramms' 16 *Managementforschung 'Management von Kompetenz'* 37–82.

Gessner, V (ed) (1996) *Foreign Courts—Civil Litigation in Foreign Legal Cultures* (Aldershot, Dartmouth).

—— (2009) 'The governance of business transactions in globalising economies: Theories of Change' in V Gessner (ed), *Contractual Certainty in International Trade* (Oxford, Hart).

Goldman, B (1983) '*Lex mercatoria*', *Forum Internationale*, 3 (Deventer).

—— (1986) 'The Applicable Law: General Principles of Law—*Lex mercatoria*' *Contemporary Problems* 113–25.

Granovetter, M (1985) 'Economic Action and Social Structure: The Problem of Embeddedness' 91 *American Journal of Sociology* 481–510.

Greif, A (2006) *Institutions and the Path to the Modern Economy. Lessons from Medieval Trade* (Cambridge, Cambridge University Press).

Hendley, K, Murrell, P and Ryterman, R (2001) 'Law Works in Russia: The Role of Law in Interenterprise Transactions' in P Murrell (ed), *Assessing the Value of Law in Transition Economies* (Ann Arbor, Mich., University of Michigan Press) 56–93.

Hypovereinsbank (2004) 'Die Bankgarantie im Aussenhandel' <http://www.hypovereinsbank.deportal?view=media/pdf/fk_auha_gage_Bankgarantie_Brosch.pdf> accessed 1 August 2006.

Kappelhoff, P (2004) 'Kompetenzentwicklung in Netzwerken: Die Sicht der Komplexitäts- und allgemeinen Evolutionstheorie', Arbeitspapier am Lehrstuhl für empirische Wirtschafts- und Sozialforschung (Wuppertal, Universität Wuppertal).

Kiedaisch, I (1997) *Internationale Kunden-Lieferanten Beziehungen* (Wiesbaden, Gabler).

Konradi, W and Fix-Fierro, H (2005) '*Lex mercatoria* in the mirror of empirical research' 2/3 *Sociologia del Diritto* 205–27.

Landa, J (1981) 'A theory of the ethnically Homogenous Middleman Group: An Institutional Alternative to Contract Law' 10 *Journal of Legal Studies* 349–62.

Lopez, AM (2003) *Lex Mercatoria and Harmonization of Contract Law in the EU* (Copenhagen, DJOF Publishing).

Luhmann, N (1983) *Rechtssoziologie* (Opladen, Westdeutscher Verlag).

McConnaughay, PJ (2001) 'Rethinking the Role of Law and Contracts in East-West Commercial Relationships ' 41 *Virginia Journal of International Law* 427 et seq.

Macaulay, S (1963) 'Non-Contractual Relations in Business: A Preliminary Study' 28 *American Sociological Review* 55 et seq.

—— (1985) 'An Empirical View of Contract' 5 *Wisconsin Law Review* 465–82.

Macneil, I (1974) 'The Many Futures of Contract' 47 *Southern California Law Review* 691 et seq.

—— (1985) 'Relational Contract: What We Do and Do Not Know' *Wisconsin Law Review* 483–525.

—— (2000) 'Relational Contract Theory: Challenges and Queries' 94 *Nothwestern University Law Review* 877–907.

Milgrom, PR, North, DC and Weingast BW (1990) 'The Role of Institutions in the Revival of Trade: The Law Merchant, Private Judges, and the Champagne Fairs' 2 *Economics and Politics* 1–23.

Nee, V (2005) 'The New Institutionalisms in Economics and Sociology' in NJ Smelser and R Swedberg (eds), *The Handbook of Economic Sociology* (Princeton and Oxford, Princeton University Press, New York, Russel Sage Foundation) 49–74.

Reimann, T (1970) *Zur Lehre vom 'rechtsordnungslosen' Vertrag* (Bonn, Ludwig Röhrscheid Verlag).

Richman, BD (2006) 'How Community Institutions Create Economic Advantage: Jewish Diamond Merchants in New York' 31 *Law & Social Inquiry* 383–420.

—— (2008) 'Ethnic Networks, Extra-legal Certainty, and Globalisation: Peering into the Diamond Industry' in V Gessner (ed), *Contractual Certainty in International Trade* (Oxford, Hart).

Schmitthoff, C (1961) 'International Business Law: A New Law Merchant' *Current Law and Social Problems* 129–53.

—— (1964) 'Das neue Recht des Welthandels' 28 *RabelsZ* 47–77.

—— (1968) 'The Unification of the law of International Trade' *Journal of Business Law* 105–19.

—— (1988) 'Nature and evolution of the transnational law of commercial transactions' in N Horn and C Schmitthoff (eds), *The Transnational Law of International Business Transactions*' (Boston, Daventer).

Silver, C (2000) 'Globalization and the US Market in Legal Services—Shifting Identities' 31 *Journal of Law & Policy in International Business* 1093 et seq.

Smelser, NJ and Swedberg, R (eds) (1994) *The Handbook of Economic Sociology* (New York, Princeton University Press).

Sosa, F (2007) *Vertrag und Geschäftsbeziehung im grenzüberschreitenden Wirtschaftsverkehr* (Nomos, Baden-Baden).

—— (2009) 'Cross-Border Dispute Resolution from the Perspective of Midsized Law Firms: The Example of International Commercial Arbitration' in V Gessner (ed), *Contractual Certainty in International Trade* (Oxford, Hart).

Speth, H (2004) *Der Erklärungswert der Transaktionskostentheorie für den Handel mit nordischem Nadelschnittholz* (Hamburg, Universität Hamburg).

Stammel, C (1998) *Waving the Gentlemen's Business Goodbye: From Global Deals to Global Disputes in the London Reinsurance Market* (Frankfurt/Main, Peter Lang).

Stein, U (1995) *Lex mercatoria. Realität und Theorie* (Frankfurt/Main, Klostermann).

Swedberg, R (2003) *Principles of Economic Sociology* (Princeton and Oxford, Princeton University Press).

Teubner, G (ed) (1997) *Global Law without a State* (Aldershot, Dartmouth).

Weber, M (1976) '*Wirtschaft und Gesellschaft. Grundriss der verstehenden Soziologie*' 5. rev. Aufl. Tübingen.

Weise, PF (1990) *Lex mercatoria. Materielles Recht vor der internationalen Handelsgerichtsbarkeit* (Frankfurt/Main, Peter Lang)

Williamson, OE (1985) *The Economic Institutions of Capitalism-Firms, Markets, Relational Contracting* (New York and London, The Free Press).

—— (2005) 'The Economics of Governance' 95 *American Economic Review*, Papers and Proceedings 1–18 <http://groups.haas.berkeley.edu/bpp/oew/TheEconomicsOfGovernance.pdf> accessed 17 June 2008.

Zumbansen, P (2003) '*Lex mercatoria*, Schiedsgerichtsbarkeit und Transnationales Recht' 67 *RabelsZ* 637–82.

—— (2006) 'Transnational Law' in J Smits (ed), *Encyclopedia of Comparative Law* (Edward Elgar Publishing) 738–54.

Zuericher Kantonalbank (2004) 'Das Dokumentar-Akkreditiv mit den einheitlichen Richtlinien und Gebraeuchen. Mit Incoterms. Ausgabe 2' <http://www.osec.ch/Osec_Internet_root/marktinformationen/Topics/Financing/das_dokumentar/akkreditiv_einfaehrung/ge/das_dokumentar-akkreditiv_internet.pdf> accessed 17 June 2008.

4

The Emergence of Transnational Cooperation in the Software Industry

THOMAS DIETZ AND HOLGER NIESWANDT

INTRODUCTION

IN MANY CASES, firms buy and sell products without reflecting much on the possible risks of opportunistic behaviour inherent in economic transactions. Rather, exchange occurs as a routine practice which is based on mutual trust and relational norms (Collins, 1999; Macneil, 1980; Morgan und Hunt, 1994; Gessner, 1996: 203). However, trust and relational norms are not unlimited. Both mechanisms require certain social structures—for example, long-term business relations or close-knit communities—which are not always present in fast developing market economies[1] (Macaulay, 1985; Williamson, 1985). In these situations, when trust and relational norms are absent, the exchange partners feel the risks of being vulnerable to the action of the other and as a result draft detailed contracts and plan for enforcement institutions to safeguard their transactions against opportunistic behaviour (Hadfield, 2005: 178).

Both in economics and sociology we find a large body of literature focusing on the role of contract enforcement institutions (CEI) in economic transactions.[2] Interestingly, across both disciplines the pertinent literature can be divided into two groups. On the one hand, much economic and social theory underlines the role of state-based sanctions to enforce contractual claims. Thomas Hobbes already developed this idea in the

[1] Macaulay asserts 20 years after his classical study at the beginning of the 1960s: 'Relational sanctions still played a significant role but economic change has exposed their limits' (1991: 189).

[2] A good introduction to this topic is given by Deakin *et al.* (See Deakin, Land and Wilkinson, 1994).

middle of the seventeenth century.[3] Later, the concept of a legally enforceable contract played a prominent role in the writings of the most influential classical social theorists, including Durkheim and Weber[4] (Durkheim, 1992; Weber, 1976). Today, the impact of public courts and state sanctions to enforce contracts is particularly highlighted by authors who are interested in the relationship between law and economic development,[5] for example, Douglass North[6] and the so-called 'legal centralists', for example, Eric Posner (North, 1990; Posner, 2002).

On the other hand, we find literature which argues that legal sanctions only play a minor role in enforcing contractual agreements.[7] Sociologists of law—for example, Stewart Macaulay and Marc Galanter—criticise the state-centred view and articulate the broad significance of private enforcement mechanisms (Macaulay, 1963; 1985; 2006; Galanter, 1981). Likewise, Robert Ellickson and Lisa Bernstein highlight the importance of community sanctions to enforce contractual agreements, and Hugh Collins argues that legal sanctions only play a peripheral role in the construction of market exchange in modern economies (Ellickson, 1994; Bernstein, 1992; Collins, 1997). In the field of economics, many researchers apply game theoretic models to illustrate the functioning of non-state-based contract enforcement institutions.[8] An example developed by Avner Greif shows that Jewish traders in the eleventh century organised exchange relations long before the existence of modern legal systems (Greif, 1994). Similarly, authors like McMillan and Woodruff show how today private ordering works in countries where no effective state sanctions are available (McMillan and Woodruff, 2000). Yet, also with regard to modern western nation states, Oliver Williamson argues—in line with the findings of Macaulay—that non-legal sanctions by far

[3] An often cited passage in Thomas Hobbes' Leviathan is: 'he that performeth first, has no assurance, the other will perform after; because the bonds of words are too weak to bridle men's ambition, avarice, anger and other Passions, without the fear of some coercive power; which is the condition of her Nature, where all men are equal, and judges of the justness of their own fears cannot possibly be supposed' (Hobbes, 1955: 89–90) (first published 1651).

[4] The best-known discussion of the relationship between legal institutions and the economy is Max Weber's. A classic Weberian formulation of the role of legal institutions in the economy states: 'The universal predominance of the market consociation requires on the one hand, a legal system the functioning of which is *calculable* in accordance with rational rules. On the other hand, the constant expansion of the market, which we shall get to know as an inherent tendency of the market consociation, has favoured the monopolization and regulation of all "legitimate" coercive power by one universalist coercive institution through the disintegration of all particularist status-determined and other structures which have been resting mainly on economic monopolies' (Weber, 1978: 337).

[5] For a list of representative studies in this field, see Rubin (2005).

[6] Douglas North asserts that 'impersonal exchange with third party enforcement [via an effective judicial system] has been the crucial underpinning of successful modern economies involved in the complex contracting necessary for modern economic growth' (1990: 35).

[7] See also the contribution of Gillian K Hadfield (2009, in this volume).

[8] For an overview, see Dixit (2004).

outweigh the importance of legal sanctions to guarantee the fulfilment of contractual agreements (Williamson, 1983).[9]

As this indicates, both in sociology and economics there is a controversial discussion about state-based and non-state-based enforcement mechanisms. However, despite the large body of literature, surprisingly little is known about the functioning of CEIs in exchange processes that transcend the borders of nation states.[10] Empirical research in this field predominantly looks at transactions that are conducted within the context of western nation states or within the context of the so-called transformation countries. In other words, research interested in the enforceability of contractual agreements is either conducted in a lawful or lawless political environment. Less research exists regarding the enforceability of contractual agreements in cross-border transactions, which often take place neither in an exclusively lawful nor exclusively lawless political environment.[11]

Among the few studies that deal with the specific circumstances of cross-border transactions, we particularly want to mention the work of Fabian Sosa. In 2007, he published his results about economic transactions between German and Spanish companies in the engineering, chemical and food industries. His findings show that state-based CEIs are of very low importance to back up cross-border transactions. Rather, Sosa's results demonstrate both a high relevance of safeguards like letters of credit, bank guarantees and prepayments and a high usage of non-legal sanctions like the threat to terminate a business relation or exclude a party from a business network. In contrast to domestic transactions in cross-border transactions, state-enforced contracts even seem to loose their function as a *last resort* (Sosa, 2007).

In this chapter, we build on Sosa's results and focus our attention on the functioning of CEIs in globalised exchange processes. We examine cross-border contractual agreements in the field of outsourcing software development between legally independent companies and try to assess the relative importance of both state-based and autonomous CEIs. We have chosen the software industry as a case study because of two reasons. First, the worldwide outsourcing of business processes certainly belongs to the

[9] A very good short summary of the literature on non-legal sanctions can be found in Panther, 2002.

[10] Volkmar Gessner asserts with regard to this research gap: 'Theoretically, sociology of law tends to concentrate on municipal law and eventually to generalize national legal phenomena (legalization, informalization, materialization, decentralization, and so on) without taking global interaction, between states, between firms, or between individuals, or the legal activity of international organizations as an object of analyses' (Gessner, 1996: 1). See also the same point from an economic viewpoint (Schmidt-Trenz, 1990).

[11] Volkmar Gessner, Fabian Sosa and Gralf-Peter Calliess belong to the small group of researchers in Germany who conducted empirical studies in this field. (See Gessner, 1996; Sosa, 2007; and Calliess, 2006).

most characteristic features of the actual period of economic globalisation. The software industry has been a pioneer in this development. India alone in 2005/06 exported software products worth US $13.3 billion.[12] Secondly, the outsourcing of software development is a knowledge-based transaction which is heavily supported by the revolutionary developments in information and communication technology. From the beginning of our research project, we were interested in the impact of the new technological possibilities on the governance structures of business transactions.

We present results of 31 expert interviews that we conducted with executives of German, Bulgarian, Indian and Romanian software companies in the period from May 2005 through to February 2006. The interviews were conducted in a qualitative way. Therefore, it is not our intention to draw universally valid conclusions by evaluating a great number of samples with the help of statistic means; rather, we aim to deepen the understanding of a few particularly interesting cases. In other words: our research interest does not concern the testing of verifiable hypotheses, but adding some innovative knowledge to an emerging scientific debate. Moreover, the qualitative interviews were conducted in a non-standardised way. We did not choose standardised, guided interviews because we wanted to remain open to potentially novel CEIs that are employed by economic actors in order so safeguard cross-border economic transactions against opportunistic behaviour. Nonetheless, we divided the interviews into three parts as follows:

a) transaction risks: questions about the major risks and uncertainties that occur in cross-border transactions;
b) state legal system: questions about the meaning of the state legal systems to safeguard cross-border transactions; and
c) private CEIs: questions about the meaning of private enforcement mechanisms to guarantee the fulfilment of contractual agreements.

In contrast to very intense qualitative pieces of research, the following study does not aim to reconstruct entirely the way people experience the world in which they live. Rather, it focuses on the practice of globalised exchange processes. Therefore, it was not necessary to transcribe all interviews completely. In many cases it was sufficient to protocol the interviews according to the three main topics mentioned above. To interpretate the interviews we applied an approach that was developed by Philip Mayring (qualitative content analysis) (Mayring, 2007). According to his method, we first reduced the database until only the relevant parts of the interviews remained. We subsequently developed a theoretical framework (taxonomy of CEIs) to

[12] <http://www.nasscom.in/Nasscom/templates/NormalPage.aspx?id=28833> accessed 17 June 2008.

structure the interviews in a systematic way. What stands below are only the highly condensed results of an extensive research process.

In this chapter we hypothesise that in cross-border economic transactions the relevance of autonomous CEIs surpasses the relevance of state-based CEIs for two reasons: first, state-based sanctions are unable to keep pace with the territorial expansion of economic globalisation; and secondly, revolutionary innovations in the field of information and communication technologies largely enhance the effectiveness of autonomous CEIs.

The chapter is organised as follows. As mentioned above, in the second part we establish a set of terms and develop a taxonomy of six possible contract-enforcement institutions which can be used by the transaction partners to enforce contracts in cross-border transactions. The analytical framework will then be applied in the third part of the chapter to describe our empirical findings. In this part, we analyse the relevance of the six types of CEIs depicted above and try to assess the relative importance of the state legal system compared to autonomous CEIs. In the fourth part, we draw a conclusion and link our findings to the ongoing economic and sociological debates about the relative importance of state-based and autonomous sanctions to enforce contractual agreements.

We realise that our sample is small (31 interviews) and that we cannot assess the role of different CEIs in cross-border transactions in general. We have not yet tested to what extent the picture we draw for the software industry can be generalised. Thus, at this point in our research, we are unable to develop a consistent theory about the relative importance of state-based and autonomous CEIs in globalised exchange processes. Furthermore, we are aware of the fact that exchanging goods and services requires a complex social interaction. Looking exclusively at the aspect of enforcement certainly does not give a full picture of contractual relations. However, despite these limitations we think that our research contributes to showing some general trends concerning the relative importance of state-based and autonomous CEIs in cross-border exchanges. Our results can then be studied in more depth if this is considered worthwhile.

THEORETICAL FRAMEWORK

The development of a taxonomy of different CEIs requires the establishment of a common set of terms which enables us to classify the pertinent literature. As we show in the following paragraphs, to be effective, any type of CEI consists of at least three different elements:[13]

[13] Our set of terms derives from Stephan Panther. He writes: 'Any system of sanctions faces the same issues. At a first level these are: who decides about the sanction, how, and who administers the sanction?' (Panther, 2000: 0780).

a) an instance, which is capable of:
   i) assessing whether a breach of contract has been committed by one of the contractual parties; and
   ii) deciding to impose a sanction on a defaulting party (*decision-maker*);
b) a structure, which determines:
   i) which information the decision-maker takes into consideration; and
   ii) how the information is interpreted in preparing a decision (*information processing structure*);
c) a power mechanism which is capable of enforcing the sanction that has been imposed on the defaulting party (*enforcement mechanism*).

The specification of the three elements (*decision maker*, *information processing structure* and *enforcement mechanism*) makes it now possible to distinguish taxonomically between six different types of CEIs. With regard to the focus of our research, it is important to mention that three of the six types of CEIs we depict below are state-based, whereas the remaining three are autonomous in the sense that they work without any backing of the state legal system.

State-based Contract-enforcement Institutions

The first type of a CEI in our taxonomy is the *state legal system*. This type is exclusively based on state action with regard to all three elements specified above. The decision to impose a sanction on a defaulting party is made by a state court (*decision-maker*). Concerning the process of decision-making, the state court applies state law. Thus, also the *information processing structure* is characterised by state action. Finally, the sanction that is imposed on the defaulting party is enforced with the support of the state's coercive power (*mechanism of enforcement*) (Behrens, 2001).[14]

The second type we admit to our taxonomy is the *public-private legal system*. This type differs from the state legal system only with regard to one element, ie the *decision-maker*. The decision to impose a sanction on a defaulting party in the case of the public-private legal system is not made by a state court, but by a private arbitration court. Since the private arbitration court applies state law to come to a decision, the *information*

[14] The so-called 'legal centralists' have accomplished a detailed analysis of the role of state legal system with regard to contract enforcement. See, eg Posner, 2002; and Coase, 1998. Regarding cross-border transactions, the role of state courts has been assessed by, among others, Volkmar Gessner. He concluded that 'in terms of internationalization of legal thinking, globalization simply has not reached German civil procedure' (Gessner, 1996: 206).

processing structure is still dominated by the state. According to the 'UN Convention on the Recognition and Enforcement of Foreign Arbitral Awards', the judgments of private arbitration courts can be enforced with the support of the state's power.[15] Thus, also with regard to the *enforcement mechanism*, the state still plays the dominant role.

The *private-public legal system* differs from the exclusively state-based type not only with regard to the *decision-maker*—as is the case with the public-private system—but also with regard to the *information processing structure*. It is a special feature of the private-public legal systems that private arbitration courts apply private commercial rules instead of state law (*information processing structure*) to come to a decision whether or not to impose a sanction on a defaulting party. Only the enforcement of sanctions is still conducted according to the above-mentioned UN Convention with the support of the state's coercive power (*enforcement mechanism*) (Calliess, 2004; Berger, 1996).

As we have shown above, the first three types of our taxonomy, at least with regard to the element of enforcement, imply the existence of a state as a prerequisite. In the following subsection, we show that, in addition to the state-based types, there exist types of CEI which function autonomously without the backing of state power.

Autonomous Contract-enforcement Institutions

The first type of a CEI that works without any state support is the *private legal system*. This type is autonomous with regard to all three dimensions mentioned above. The decision to impose a sanction is made by a private arbitration court (*decision-maker*). The process of decision-making takes place in line with private rules (*information processing structure*) and even the enforcement of a judgment is carried out autonomously without the backing of the state's power. In contrast to the state-based types, the enforcement of a sanction in the case of the private legal system is carried out by the actors of a specific business network. The network excludes from future business opportunities any party that does not adhere to a judgment of a private arbitration court (*enforcement mechanism*) (Bernstein, 1992; Panther, 2000; Ellickson, 1994; 2001).

The second type of an autonomous CEI we admit to our taxonomy is the *reputation network*. With regard to the enforcement of sanctions, this type of CEI functions in a similar way to the type of private legal system. The business network reacts to a breach of contract by excluding the defaulting

[15] The convention was drafted in 1958. At present, more than 120 nations have signed and ratified the convention.

party from it (*enforcement mechanism*). In contrast to the above-mentioned legal types of CEIs, the decision to impose a sanction on a defaulting party in the case of the reputation network comes about without any involvement of a court. Rather, the decision to impose a sanction on a defaulting party arises from a vital flow of information within a particular business network (*information processing structure, decision-maker*) (Dixit, 2004; McMillan, 2000; McMillan and Woodruff, 1999; Murrell, 1996; Greif, 1993).[16]

The last type of a CEI we admit to our taxonomy is the *bilateral contract management*. In contrast to the five types we have depicted so far, this type of a CEI is capable of enforcing contractual agreements without the support of a third party. Only the contractual partners are capable of deciding whether or not to impose a sanction on their counterparts (*decision-maker*). The decision to impose a sanction usually consists of the termination of an ongoing contractual relation. Since in many cases the exchange partners evaluate the future value of an ongoing contractual relation higher than a present breach of contract, they tend to adhere to their contractual obligations (*enforcement mechanism*). The decision to terminate an ongoing relation in the case of the bilateral contract management is based on information, which is gathered by the contractual parties in the course of their common business relation. Thus, in contrast to the reputation network, third-party information only plays a minor role with regard to the *information processing structure* (Williamson, 1985; 2005; Macaulay, 1963).

Taxonomy of Contract-enforcement Institutions

Summarising the CEI described above, we obtain the following taxonomy (see Table 1).

[16] Avner Greif illustrates this mechanism very clearly: 'The Maghribis employed each other as agents, and all retaliated against any agent who had cheated a coalition member. Their social and commercial network provided the information required to detect and announce cheating, and the multilateral punishment was self-enforcing, since the value of future relations with all Maghribis kept an agent honest' (Greif, 1992: 128, 130).

Table 1—A Taxonomy of CEIs

Elements of contract enforcement institutions

Contract enforcement institutions	Enforcement mechanism	Information procession structure	Decision maker
State legal system	State power	Litigation according to state law	State courts
Public-private legal system	State power	Litigation according to state law	Private arbitration courts
Private-public legal system	State power	Litigation according to private law	Private arbitration courts
Private legal system	Exclusion	Litigation according to private law	Private arbitration courts
Reputation network	Exclusion	Gathering and interpretation of information within the business community	Business community
Bilateral contract management	Contract termination	Gathering and interpretation of information within the contractual relation	Contractual partners

EMPIRICAL FINDINGS

In the following section, we apply the taxonomy of contract enforcement institutions developed above to our empirical findings. In presenting the empirical findings, we will highlight the relevance of each contract enforcement institution in our sample, ie global outsourcing cooperation in the field of software development.

Available Contract-enforcement Institutions

In the cross-border transactions of the software industry we examined, we found four of the six types of CEI as being available in principle, even though the functionality of some of them was limited. Two CEIs could not be detected: the private-public legal system and the private legal system. We did not find private courts applying and enforcing private (autonomous) law. Contracts are exclusively drafted under German law. In addition, parties agree upon an arbitration clause in most cases.

Distinction Between Types of Actor

Different types of actor can have entirely different views on the question of whether a specific CEI is available in a transaction and whether it can successfully stabilise expectations. A specific CEI can imply transactional certainty to one actor, whereas it might be without any relevance to his or her cooperation partner. This issue has been so far neglected by the literature on governance. For a better understanding of the relevance of different CEIs in the transactions examined, we considered it to be crucial to differentiate between different types of actors according to their usage of CEIs. Thus, three groups of actors can be distinguished. The first group of actors relevant for our study consists of the German clients in software development transactions. They are mostly medium-sized or large companies, which either belong to the software industry or base their processes heavily on software services (banks, insurance companies, travel organisations, automotive manufacturers, etc). The second group of actors comprises medium-sized and large foreign (non-German) software companies. These companies have between 500 and 50,000 employees and usually have their own—often quite small—legal department. The process of software development in these companies is commonly characterised by a high degree of rationalisation following standard procedures that are generally accepted in the industry. Small foreign software companies constitute the third group of actors worth distinguishing in our study. Their number of employees ranges from 10 to 500 and they do not have a legal department. In most cases, they have very limited access to legal expertise.

Prominent Role of ICT for the Governance of Contractual Relations

A far-reaching impact on the functionality of different CEIs can be attributed to the revolutionary developments in the field of information and communication technologies (ICT). Generally speaking, the capacity and speed of data transfer has increased to such an extent that it has become possible for companies to control certain actions of their exchange partners in real time (real-time controlling). Thus, in exchange processes which require an intensive interaction between client and supplier, as is the case in the software industry, the purchaser can check on a daily basis whether his or her supplier has progressed in the development of a software product according to the schedule agreed upon. The transparency of the exchange process enables the cooperation partner to detect immediately any deviances from the contractual agreements. As both parties are capable of responding promptly to deviances, conflicts can be kept low and be dealt with within the exchange relation. Hence, in most cases conflict resolution can be accomplished without the aid of third parties, especially courts.

Real-time controlling spans both quality management and time lines. For German clients, variations in either of the two issues can cause severe problems regarding their own products and delivery commitments to third parties. Even though real-time controlling is an efficient means to avoid conflicts, it still needs the backing of a CEI in order to stabilise expectations. Otherwise, there could be no certainty that parties conduct countermeasures in case of deviance from an initial agreement, pay compensatory fees or refrain from deliberately violating contracts.

Standard Processes

To be functional, trilateral CEIs rely heavily on the transparency and traceability of the processes carried out in an exchange relation. Third parties need to understand the contents of a contractual relation in order to solve conflicts and to administer the law. As already discussed, transparency can be achieved in the software industry by interlinking the exchange partners during the entire transaction with the help of modern ICT. How about traceability? At least for technical experts, traceability is given to a high degree if the software development process follows certain accepted standard processes. For the last 10 years, intensive efforts have been undertaken in the industry to standardise the processes of software development. Different models exist that specify guidelines for the structuring of software development. The ISO 9001 standard and the Capability Maturity Model (CMM) rank among the best known and most widely applied models. All models originally aim at the same goal: controlling the process of software development. In order to achieve this goal, different kinds of measure are to be taken: the process of software development is to be standardised, properly documented and to made subject to quantitative control. From a governance perspective, standardisation to such a degree is of crucial importance: malpractice can be disclosed easily by comparing specific procedures to the industry standards. Detailed documentation of processes facilitates the participation of external experts in the solution of legal conflicts.

The Relevance of the State Legal System

In looking at CEIs in global exchange processes, one assumption stands to reason: private CEIs are better suited to support global transactions than state-based CEIs by the mere fact that, from the outset, private CEIs are not territorially confined. Our empirical results confirm the hypothesis that global actors often do not rely on the enforceability of contractual claims before state courts: from the perspective of the German clients, uncertainty prevails with regard to the enforceability of a judgment rendered by a German court in the home country of the client. Conversely, foreign software companies also barely rely on the support function of German courts. For small foreign software companies, pursuing contractual claims in Germany often implies unbearable costs. Furthermore, in most cases these companies have too little legal expertise to be able to assess the chances and risks of going to court in Germany. Thus, the state legal system is in principle more readily accessible to the medium-sized and especially the large foreign companies. First, they have sufficient legal know-how in order to ponder whether or not it is worth taking legal action against an exchange partner. Secondly, they have the financial means to engage in a legal procedure. Although software companies most generally consider the capacity of state courts to correctly grasp the complex substance of contractual relations in software development as limited, state courts still provide certainty for foreign software suppliers regarding the enforceability of certain essential framework agreements which can be vital for these companies. One typical example of such an agreement are non-solicitation agreements between German clients and Eastern-European software companies. Still, recourse to the purely state-based CEIs—the state legal system—is mostly limited to the smaller foreign companies, since the medium-sized and larger companies—if they decide to take legal means at all—generally resort to arbitration courts for the solution of contractual conflicts. German clients are expected by their counterparts to follow judgments rendered by German state courts without recourse to actual enforcement unless, of course, the client is in financial distress. Suppliers believe that German companies intending to stay in business could not afford to refuse compliance. The loss of reputation would in most cases weigh much higher than the amount in dispute. As a matter of course, if the German company is in financial distress, even state courts could not provide sufficient legal certainty for foreign software companies.

Thus, paradoxically as it may appear, we found that if contracts are drafted under German law, the German state legal system is better suited to give support to foreign software companies than to German companies in their global exchange processes, since German courts can enforce claims much easier vis-a-vis German companies than vis-a-vis foreign companies.

Still, one significant advantage for German companies remains, which induces them to insist on the use of German law when drafting contracts: because of their familiarity with the law of their home country, German companies can assess ambiguities and risks associated with a contract far better than their foreign counterparts.

The Relevance of the Public-private Legal System

In the business transactions we examined in our study, contracts were, as already mentioned above, exclusively drafted under German law. Additionally, in most cases parties agreed on an arbitration clause. As a matter of course, companies always try everything to solve their conflicts outside the courts. Still, obtaining a neutral judgment by a third party can become crucial if a conflict escalates. Here, arbitration courts offer an essential support, much more than in the physical enforcement of their judgment. A neutral and generally accepted judgment is especially important for the foreign (non-German) software suppliers. Since they usually dispose of less reputation capital than their German counterparts, it is only by referring to a generally recognised third-party judgment that they can credibly prove to the software industry that they have acted in line with contractual agreements. A reputation as a reliable cooperation partner constitutes an important means of existence for foreign suppliers of out sourcing. Thus, restoring their clean record by resorting to an arbitration court can be crucial for foreign software companies if they want to attract new customers. Still, not all foreign software companies can afford to go to an arbitration court. Thus, as an effective CEI, the public-private legal system is better suited for the group of medium-sized and large foreign companies than for the small ones.

With regard to the enforcement of arbitration awards, a similar reasoning applies as for the state legal system. Although it is theoretically possible to have an arbitration award recognised and enforced in Germany and elsewhere, the loss of reputation in the industry associated with a refusal to accept an award constitutes a much larger threat for the parties than the prospect of state enforcement. In the case of an official award by a generally accepted arbitration court, this rationale applies to German clients as much as to foreign software companies.

The Relevance of Reputation Networks

When analysing why companies adhere to contracts in the software industry, reputation is definitely a key issue. As discussed earlier, and especially for foreign suppliers of outsourcing services, a reputation as a reliable exchange partner represents a part of their means of existence. Certainly, the German clients have a reputation to loose as well, vis-a-vis clients and other exchange partners. They cannot afford to blatantly break contracts either. Still, when looking at the relevance of reputation networks as a CEI there is a difference between foreign software suppliers and German clients, which lies in two main aspects. One of them is that the initial reputation of being trustworthy is often higher for the German clients than for the foreign software companies. The second is that, more generally, the loss of reputation stemming from a breach of contract in an outsourcing cooperation is usually more harmful to the supplier than to the client.

Regarding the first aspect, two main reasons are pertinent: German clients have often been longer in business than their foreign counterparts and they are often better organised in formal or informal networks. This gives them additional leverage in terms of reputation capital. Thus, if there is a conflict between two parties that becomes known in the software industry, chances are high that without a neutral proceeding to settle the claims, actors will tend to believe the statements of the German side. With respect to the second aspect—a loss of reputation being more harmful to the supplier than to the client—the rationale is that in software outsourcing the client is king. At the outset of an exchange relation, the client is much more likely to demand references on, or from, the supplier than the other way around. Good references are the key to success for any outsourcing company. Thus, a bad reference because of a prior breach of contract will harm the supplier more than the client. The client will probably find other suppliers, who either do not know about the incident or are willing to take the risk. The supplier, on the other hand, will have serious problems in finding new clients. If, for example, a German client gives a bad account of a foreign company at a German trade association, the supplier will face serious problems finding new clients in Germany.

For the foreign software companies, utility gains from opportunistic behaviour usually cannot outweigh the disutility associated with bad references. This is why reputation networks without formal proceedings are of significant relevance as a CEI for German clients. As mentioned before, in the software industry a key mechanism constituting the reputation network is the exchange of references. Before entering a contract, the parties do a thorough evaluation of each other. The clients in particular demand references on past exchange relations, which they usually contact personally. Again, developments in the field of ICT play a decisive role in this context. The effectiveness of a reputation network as a CEI depends largely on the flow of information. If actors feel that they are part of a network in which opportunistic behaviour is disclosed quickly and securely, it strongly influences their incentive structure. Given the intensive usage of ICT in the software industry, the exchange of cooperation-specific information is extremely high.

The Relevance of Bilateral Contract Management

Our empirical results confirm that bilateral contract management is an important CEI for all groups of actor involved. Since bilateral contract management is operational as a CEI without being embedded in an institutional framework, it is particularly well suited for global transactions. The settlement and enforcement of claims takes place within the exchange relation. The nationalities of the exchange partners are of no importance. Non-payment is the bilateral enforcement mechanism available to the German clients and non-delivery to the foreign software suppliers. The ultimate sanction for both parties would be an early termination of the contract.

Especially for the small foreign software companies, bilateral contract management is often the only CEI available, as they neither have the financial means for resorting to a formal conflict-settlement procedure, nor sufficient reputation capital to use informal reputation networks for securing their rights. However, bilateral contract management is also the most important CEI for the larger foreign software companies. It draws its effectiveness out of the fact that, at a certain point in the exchange relation, the German clients become highly dependent on their software suppliers. Either they have adapted their own production processes to a new software application and need continuous support from their supplier to run the software (maintenance and support), or they have integrated a specific software solution into one of their products (embedded software) and must rely on punctual delivery and high quality. Once the exchange relation has progressed in time, it becomes increasingly difficult and expensive for the client to replace the supplier, since the latter has gathered much cooperation-specific knowledge about the client.

Bilateral contract management is also useful as a CEI for the German clients. Still, their sanctioning power is limited to non-payment of services already rendered. Non-payment is of course a sanction, but usually not as powerful as the sanctioning possibilities given to the clients in the reputation network.

Considering the relevance of bilateral contract management, it is important to note that contractual agreements in software development are usually structured into milestones. The overall contract is split into a succession of smaller assignments (deliverables). At the end of each assignment, the delivered product or service is checked and if it is in accordance with the agreement a milestone payment is effected. Once the final milestone is reached, the overall contract is completed. If the deliverable is not supplied on time or the client does not pay after successful delivery, the parties can cease to cooperate using an exit option integrated into the contract (exit clause). Such a detailed structuring of the contract is only possible if the parties are closely linked, enabling them to discuss specific deliverables regularly. This is of course time-consuming, but very effective from a governance point of view. The risk for suppliers of not being paid is reduced to the next milestone payment. In projects where small foreign software companies are involved, milestone payments usually range between €10,000 and €20,000, which is a bearable risk even for small companies. On the other hand, suppliers have a strong disincentive for opportunistic behavior in the early phase of an exchange relation, as they are interested in carrying out the following assignments laid out in the overall contract. Thus, at each milestone, there is a shadow of the future, ie the milestones yet to be accomplished.

Overall Results

Our overall results are summarised in Table 2. For the German clients, the reputation network serves as a decisive CEI, as their exchange partners are highly dependent on their reputation as reliable suppliers. Foreign software companies gain certainty of transaction mostly on the basis of bilateral contract management. In the course of an exchange relationship, clients become increasingly dependent on their suppliers and the products to be delivered. Switching costs rise and become a disincentive for the client to act opportunistically. In the view of small software companies, the state legal system retains a function for securing existential agreements. For medium-sized and large software companies, this function is fulfilled by the public-private legal system.

Table 2—Relevance of CEI According to Groups of Actor

	State legal System	Public-private legal system	Private-public legal system	Private legal system	Reputation network	Bilateral contract management
German clients						
Medium-sized and large foreign suppliers						
Small foreign suppliers						

High Relevance
Medium Relevance
Low Relevance

CONCLUSION

In the field of outsourcing, we found a high significance of private contract enforcement institutions. Two CEIs play an outstanding role: bilateral contract management and reputation networks. Only these two mechanisms can unrestrictedly keep pace with the territorial expansion of economic globalisation. They owe their global functionality to the revolutionary innovations in the field of ICT.

Whether the low relevance of the state legal system constitutes a temporary or long-ranging phenomenon must be the subject of future research. What may be possible state reactions to the increased acceptance of private CEIs? Are nation states willing to transfer competencies to private actors or will they try to regulate contracts in cross-border transactions, as, for example, demanded by international organisations like the World Bank or the International Monetary Fund? The first option would apply if states accompany the privatisation of contract enforcement in economic exchange processes with establishing rules that govern the conditions of acceptance of private governance mechanisms. The second option would apply if states increase their efforts for the establishment of an international private legal system. Which option the international community of states will choose vis-a-vis the intensive use of private CEIs in the global outsourcing of software development is an important subject for further research.

REFERENCES

Behrens, P (2001) 'Die Bedeutung des Kollisionsrechts für die "Globalisierung" der Wirtschaft' in J Basedow (ed), *Aufbruch nach Europa: 75 Jahre Max-Planck-Institut für Privatrecht* (Tübingen, Mohr Siebeck).

Berger, KP (1996) *Formalisierende oder 'schleichende' Kodifizierung des transnationalen Wirtschaftsrechts: zu den methodischen und praktischen Grundlagen der lex mercatoria* (Berlin, de Gruyter).

Bernstein, L (1992) 'Opting Out of the Legal System: Extralegal Contractual Relations in the Diamond Trade' 21 *Journal of Legal Studies* 115.

Calliess, GP (2002) 'Reflexive Transnational Law. The Privatisation of Civil Law and the Civilisation of Private Law' 23 *Zeitschrift für Rechtssoziologie* 185.

—— (2006) *Grenzüberschreitende Verbraucherverträge. Rechtssicherheit und Gerechtigkeit auf dem elektronischen Weltmarktplatz* (Tübingen, Mohr Siebeck).

Coase, RH (1988) *The Firm, the Market and the Law* (Chicago, The University of Chicago Press).

Dixit, AK (2004) *Lawlessness and Economics. Alternative Modes of Governance* (Princeton, Princeton University Press).

Durkheim, E (1992) *Über soziale Arbeitsteilung* (Frankfurt am Main, Suhrkamp).

Ellickson, RC (1994) *Order without Law: How Neighbors settle Disputes* (Cambridge MA, Harvard University Press).

—— (2001) 'The Evolution of Social Norms: A Perspective from the Legal Academy' in M Hechter and KD Opp (eds), *Social Norms* (New York, Russell Sage).

Gessner, V (1996) 'International Cases in German First Instance Courts' in V Gessner (ed), *Foreign Courts—Civil Litigation in Foreign Legal Cultures* (Aldershot, Dartmouth).

Gessner, V, Appelbaum, RP and Felstiner, WLF (2001) 'Introduction: The Legal Culture of Global Business Transactions' in RP Appelbaum, WLF Felstiner and V Gessner (eds), *Rules and Networks* (Oxford, Hart).

Greif, A (1993) 'Contract enforceability and economic institutions in early trade: the Maghribi traders' coalition' 83 *American Economic Review* 525.

—— (2005) 'Commitment, Coercion and Markets: The Nature and dynamics of Institutions Supporting Exchange' in C Ménard and MM Shirley (eds), *Handbook of New Institutional Economics* (Dordrecht, Springer).

—— (2006) *Institutions and the Path to the Modern Economy. Lessons from Medieval Trade* (Cambridge, Cambridge University Press).

Hadfield, GK (2005) 'The Many Legal Institutions that support Contractual Commitments' in C Ménard and MM Shirley (eds), *Handbook of New Institutional Economics* (Dordrecht, Springer).

Mayring, P (2007) *Qualitative Inhaltsanalyse. Grundlagen und Techniken* (Weinheim, UTB).

McMillan, J (2000) 'Private Order under dysfunctional public order' 98 *Michigan Law Review* 2421.

McMillan, J and Woodruff, C (1999) 'Dispute prevention without courts in Vietnam' 15 *Journal of Law, Economics and Organization* 637.

Murrell, P (1996) 'How far has transition progressed' 10 *Journal of Economic Perspectives* 25.

North, DC (1990) *Institutions, Institutional Change and Economic Performance* (Cambridge, Cambridge University Press).

Panther, S (2000) 'Non-legal Sanctions' in B Bouckaert and G de Geest (eds), *Encyclopedia of Law and Economics* (Cheltenham, Edward Elgar).

Posner, EA (2002) *Law and Social Norms* (Cambridge Mass, Harvard University Press).

Schmidt-Trenz, H-J (1990) *Außenhandel und Territorialität des Rechts. Grundlegung einer neuen Institutionenökonomik des Außenhandels* (Baden-Baden, Nomos).

Sosa, F (2007) *Vertrag und Geschäftsbeziehung im grenzüberschreitenden Wirtschaftsverkehr* (Baden-Baden, Nomos).

Weber, M (1976) *Wirtschaft und Gesellschaft. Grundriss der verstehenden Soziologie* (Tübingen, Mohr Siebeck).

Weingast, BR (1997) 'The Political Foundations of Democracy and the Rule of Law' 91 *American Political Science Review* 245.

Williamson, OE (1985) *The Economic Institutions of Capitatlism: Firms, Markets, Relational Contracting* (New York, The Free Press).
—— (2005) 'The Economics of Governance' 95 *American Economic Review* 1.

5

Cross-Border Dispute Resolution from the Perspective of Mid-sized Law Firms: The Example of International Commercial Arbitration

FABIAN P SOSA

INTRODUCTION

IN MODERN SOCIETIES, it is widely believed that the state has a central support function to perform in enabling economic cooperation, ie by determining and enforcing the rules of economic exchange. However, today, in the age of globalisation, many transactions go beyond the legal framework of the nation states. This leads to an incongruity between economic activity and territorial law. As a consequence, the question arises of whether the protection of exchange processes in cross-border commerce can still be guaranteed by state law, or whether this task has been taken over by private actors. According to the legal approach, the deficit of legal certainty can be compensated by the transnationalisation of law, eg the modernisation of law in all nation states on the basis of Western law. However, the frequent notion that law can be unified is highly questionable. Even if it is possible to observe a tendency in this direction, it is important to emphasise that the development of international civil and procedural law is not even visible in highly regulated regions like the European Union. International private and procedural law is a useful instrument for the determination of the applicable law and jurisdiction, but it does not solve the practical problems faced by parties in the enforcement of cross-border contractual claims. Consequently, many factors indicate that the classical legal instruments are less effective in the international or global context. Many practitioners and researchers are very sceptical with regard to the efforts at legal unification and the resort to state courts in cross-border commerce. In this context, it is worth mentioning the discourse regarding the new law merchant (Berman and Kaufman, 1978; Berger, 1997; DeLy, 2001; Konradi, 2008), as well as the *relationship management*, which emphasises the significance of business relationships for the coordination of transactions (eg Williamson, 1975; 1979; 1981; 1985; Macaulay, 1963; 1985; 1991; Macneil, 1971; 1974; 1975; 1981; Dwyer *et al*, 1987; Kiedaisch, 1997; Gundlach and Murphy, 1993; Morgan and Hunt 1994; Sosa 2007). A third approach, which is at the centre of the following research concept, discusses the contribution of international law firms to the protection of cross-border business relationships.

A THEORETICAL APPROACH

Flood and Sosa have developed a theoretical approach to describe the role of law firms in a globalised economy. This is based on Niklas Luhmann's idea of the stabilisation of normative expectations (Flood and Sosa, 2008). They criticise current literature that still supports Max Weber's thesis that the state legal system provides the central support structure in modern economies. A stabilisation of behavioural expectations on the basis of general legal provisions (programmes) is only possible if sufficient legal structures exist. This is highly questionable with regard to the international context (Gessner, 1996; Gessner *et al*, 2001; Sosa, 2007). As a consequence, the stabilisation of normative expectations will occur at a lower level of abstraction. Where lawyers cooperate with international economic actors to realise cross-border transactions, the stabilisation of expectations occurs at the level of law firms, which have developed their own legal and non-legal structures to support global exchanges (Flood and Sosa, 2008). Business actors are aware of the legal system's weakness when it comes to cross-border transactions. Consequently, they do not rely on the state legal system as a last resort. They rely on the assumption that the lawyer who can make use of the international structures of his or her law firm will be able to provide adequate legal or non-legal solutions for any type of conflict that can arise out of the transaction (Flood and Sosa, 2008).

According to Flood and Sosa, the abstract Luhmann approach has to be complemented by current approaches in law firm literature, because Luhmann does not adress the phenomenon of (international) law firms. Several approaches in current law firm literature point out the diminishing role of the state and the growing influence of lawyers in the international context (McBarnet, 1994; Powell, 1994; McBarnet, 1987; Flood, 1991). However, these approaches focus on very specific aspects of the lawyers' work. A more general approach can be derived from the works of Lawrence Friedman, who has argued that the significance of lawyers and their indispensability increase the weaker and lumpier existing legal structures (Friedman, 1989). This argumentation has also been used to explain the dominance of Anglo-American mega law firms (MLF) in the global context and the growing Americanisation in the global legal field (Silver 2000; Trubek *et al*, 1994; Shapiro, 1993). The fragmentariness of the global legal system leads to a comparative advantage for US law firms because they are familiar with the openness of the legal system in the common law and the coexistence of different legal systems. In this context, they were able to develop a particular style of lawyering, much more creative and business-oriented than in civil law countries. Consequently, these firms were the first to be able to provide a pragmatic and creative approach to lawyering necessary for facing the current changes of the global economy (Silver, 2000; Flood, 2004).

This assumption is certainly correct with regard to the shifting of responsibility in the international context from the level of the state to that of lawyers. However, its focus on US mega law firms needs to be modified. Current studies show very clearly that the global legal field comprises different types of law firms. Flood and Sosa have described this for the German market (Flood and Sosa, 2008). Their analysis shows that US and UK firms exercise an important position at the level of large firms that advise multi-national and large national companies. However, even at this level there is a strong competition between Anglo-American MLF and large German firms (Flood and Sosa, 2008). However, the vast majority of the top 60 law firms are traditional German firms with 40 to 100 lawyers. We refer to these firms as mid-sized law firms.[1] Most of these firms have developed competence and experience in international transactions (Flood and Sosa, 2008).

It can be assumed that some areas of international commerce are dominated by the Anglo-American MLF, but there is no universal, optimal type of law firm for every international transactional context. A very interesting approach that makes it possible to integrate these different types of law firms into the discourse can be derived from Morgan and Quack (2005), who have tried to combine the socio-economic approach of the varieties of capitalism (Hollingsworth and Boyer, 1997) with current research on law firms.

METHODS

In order to present a more accurate picture of the work of international law firms, we have decided to carry out a study on international law firms that involves MLF from the US and UK, as well as mid-sized law firms (MidLF) from continental Europe. Consequently, our project—carried out

[1] See Appendix, p00

at Bremen University and the University of Westminster—involves a sub-project on MLF and a sub-project on MidLF. In the context of the study on mega law firms, approximately 100 in-depth interviews with representatives of different professional service firms involved in complex projects, eg mega law firms, investment banks, consultants, accountants, etc, were carried out. The empirical data in the context of the study on MidLF was gathered during a one-year participant observation in a mid-sized German law firm with approximately 90 lawyers (hereinafter: 'the law firm'). Their clients are largely small and mid-sized companies, who carry out national as well as international activities. During the participant observation, 40 case studies were produced, supplemented by the analysis of contracts, participation in the daily work of the law firm, participation in negotiations, interviews with lawyers, etc. The study describes four central areas of work for the law firm (litigation, arbitration, negotiation and complex projects). It has a very strong focus on German-Spanish commerce, but is also related to other countries (such as the US, France, United Arab Emirates, Mauretania, etc).

This chapter is part of the above-described larger project and will only focus on the results of those case studies which are related to international commercial arbitration.[2]

CONFLICT RESOLUTION IN THE INTERNATIONAL CONTEXT

The weakness of the legal system in the international context leads to a situation where litigation will only provide adequate solutions in exceptional cases. High costs and time expenses, unpredictability of decisions, lack of competence of judges and many other factors significantly limit the scope for litigation. Consequently, litigation is often not an appropriate solution for cross-border conflicts when small amounts are at stake, because the costs will often exceed the benefits (Gessner, 1996; Sosa, 2007; Flood and Sosa, 2008). The same occurs in the context of complex transactions, where the stakes are usually very high, because state courts have great difficulties in handling conflicts arising out of those transactions (Sosa, 2007; Flood and Sosa, 2008). Whereas litigation has lost its superiority when compared with other forms of conflict resolution, lawyers must select between different alternative forms of conflict resolution to provide adequate results for their clients. This leads to a higher complexity, but also creates a much greater scope for innovative solutions, which is often exploited by law firms in favour of their clients.

The empirical studies that we have carried out revealed that it is often the *specific combination* of different legal and non-legal sources that

[2] See also Calliess *et al*, 2007.

provides optimal results. International lawyers have become conflict managers, who decide on the use and combination of different mixes to solve a cross-border conflict. Legal and non-legal instruments are not used alternatively: they are combined (Flood and Sosa, 2008). Upon a closer look, the different instruments themselves appear to be composed of a variety of legal and non-legal elements.

Even if lawyers resort to state courts in the international context, they rarely exclusively operate within the support structures provided by the nation state. Lawyers have to take into account legal aspects of different jurisdictions, select between different solutions or combine them. In many situations, state law can only provide the raw material for a solution (Flood and Sosa, 2008; Calliess *et al*, 2007). Lawyers use their creative lawyering skills to develop new legal arguments or completely new legal structures for the handling of new types of problem. However, most cases taken to a state court end with a settlement. In these cases, the role of the state is often limited to the creation of a fear of possible sanctions for both parties. The success of the settlement depends crucially on the lawyer's ability to summarise all legal and non-legal aspects of the conflict and integrate them into the process (Flood and Sosa, 2008).

International commercial arbitration is a very good example for the specific need to *combine* legal and non-legal elements to provide adequate solutions for cross-border commerce.

ARBITRATION: AUTONOMOUS OR HYBRID?

Previous studies have shown that arbitration is often considered by many practitioners to be the only appropriate form of conflict resolution in the international context. The most obvious characteristic of the increasing importance of lawyers and the decreasing role of the state in the context of international commercial arbitration is certainly the fact that lawyers can take over the role of judges. However, it is the enormous influence exercised by lawyers on the entire structure of the arbitration system which demonstrates their growing importance in this field and their contribution to the stabilisation of expectations. At present, very few socio-legal investigations have been carried out in the area of international arbitration. The most prominent study, conducted by Dezalay and Garth (1996), has produced tremendous insight into international arbitration. It provides information about the arbitrators, the network structure of the International Chamber of Commerce (ICC), the relation between law and business, etc. However, it is based on interviews of arbitrators and not on the analysis of the transactions itself; the focus is on the infrastructure rather than the actual practice of arbitration. Consequently, aspects with regard to the actual handling of arbitral disputes remain unknown.

CHARACTERISTICS OF ARBITRATION CASES AND OF PROFESSIONALS INVOLVED IN ARBITRATION PROCEDURES

Types of Transaction Subject to Routine Arbitration

The type of arbitration where MidLF are involved, which I will refer to as 'routine' arbitration, does not involve the large arbitration cases described in the literature, with enormous amounts of money at stake. The following table gives an overview over the amounts at stake in the analysed cases.

Table 1—Amounts at Stake in the Analysed Arbitration Procedures

Case Study	Amount at Stake in US$
7	7,500,000
9	4,500,000
12	7,200,000
13	957,000
17	57,000,000
23	32,000
24	556,000
25	7,400,000
38	1,230,000

A comparison with the average amount at stake in ICC procedures shows that the cases analysed in this study can be located at a medium level.

Table 2—Percentage of Cases Presented to the ICC in Relation to the Amount at Stake

Amount at Stake US$	Percentage of Cases			
	1997	1999	2001	2003
≤ 50,000	2.9	2.6	1.1	4.0
> 50,000	15.9	11.3	9.8	7.6
> 200,000	11.2	9.6	11.1	10.0
> 500,000	7.7	10.4	10.9	10.3
> 1,000,000	32.1	33.7	31.4	34.8
> 10,000,000	11.4	9.7	15.0	13.1
> 50,000,000	2.2	3.4	4.4	4.0
> 100,000,000	2.2	1.7	3.0	3.4
> 1,000,000,000	0	0.2	0.2	0.2
Not indicated	14.4	17.4	13.1	12.6

Source: ICC International Court of Arbitration Bulletin 1998, 2000, 2002, 2004.

'Routine arbitration' is not an appropriate way of conflict resolution for all kinds of transaction, despite statements to the contrary in the literature on international commercial arbitration (Risse, 1999; Günther and Höffer, 2000). Previous studies show that most arbitration procedures are carried out in the context of transactions with very high amounts at stake (eg Sosa, 2007; see also Table 2), typically long-term and complex long-term contractual relations. The advantages of arbitration have full effect and the costs are irrelevant with regard to the high amounts at stake. In cases with smaller amounts at stake, the arbitration procedure is usually too expensive. The fact that arbitration is not used in the case of low amounts at stake can be attributed to the costs of the procedure. Table 3 demonstrates that the costs of arbitration are comparatively high if the amount at stake is low, but they are comparatively low in the case of high amounts.

Table 3—Costs of Arbitration Procedure in Relation to Amount at Stake

Number of Arbitrators	Amount at Stake in US$/Percentage of Amount at Stake					
	100,000		1,000,000		10,000,000	
1	13,975	14	56,485	5.6	157,635	1.6
2	32,625	32.6	130,455	13	370,105	3.7

Cost estimated using the Online-Calculator of the ICC Court <http://www.iccwbo.org/court/arbitration/id4097/index.html> accessed July 30, 2008.

Additional expenses for lawyers, travelling, expert reports, etc will usually lead to a situation where the costs exceed the benefits in the case of low amounts at stake. The tendency not to use arbitration in this case is explained by one of the interviewed lawyers:

> ... if the amount at dispute is over EUR 600,000 I take arbitration into consideration, if the amount is lower than that I force the parties to find an agreement.

Arbitration is also rare in business relationships characterised by the dominance of one of the parties, because the stronger party will usually be able to dictate the contractual provisions favourable to it, which usually leads to the selection of the law and jurisdiction of the stronger party. In addition, in such constellations conflicts are rarely taken to court (Kenworthy, Macaulay and Rogers, 1996). There is no need for the stronger party to resort to court because it has the power to give instructions to the weaker party. By contrast, the weaker party will try to avoid judicial procedures, because this will cause the ending of the business relationship, and will very often endanger the existence of the firm itself. However, in the area of long-term and complex long-term contracts, arbitration seems to be the central form of conflict resolution. This makes it indispensable for MidLF to provide arbitration services if they work in this field. This very general analysis shows that, contrary to the general opinion in the literature (eg Berger, 1997; Dezalay and Garth, 1996; Risse, 1999; Günther and Höffer, 2000), international commercial arbitration is not an adequate instrument for international commercial dispute resolution in general, but rather is limited to relatively few complex conflicts with high stakes. On the other hand, approaches that tend to attribute a very limited role to international arbitration also have to be corrected.

Professionals Involved in Routine Arbitration

A strong indicator for the enormous importance of private actors (especially lawyers) in arbitration is the fact that they can take over the role of party counsel as well as the role of judges. The following table shows the dominance of law firms, indicated by the fact that with few exceptions all key positions in the analysed cases are held by lawyers.

Table 4—List of Participants in Arbitration Procedures

Case Study	Chairman	Arbitrator	Arbitrator	Party counsel 1	Party counsel 2
7	Lawyer from a mid-sized German-Spanish firm	–	–	Mid-sized Spanish firm	Large Spanish firm International boutique firm
9	Lawyer from a mid-sized German firm	Lawyer from a mid-sized German-Spanish firm	Lawyer from a mid-sized German firm	Mid-sized German law firm	Mid-sized German law firm
12	French Judge/ Professor	Lawyer from a mid-sized Spanish law firm	Lawyer from a mid-sized German law firm	Mid-sized Spanish law firm	Mid-sized German law firm
13	No information about arbitrator	–	–	Large Spanish firm Mid-sized German law firm	Mid-sized Spanish firm

17	Lawyer from a Mid-sized German law firm	Lawyer from a Mid-sized Swiss law firm	Spanish Professor	Large Spanish firm Mid-sized Spanish firm	Large Spanish firm Mega law firm
23	–	Businessman	Businessman	Small law firm	Mid-sized law firm
24	Lawyer from a mid-sized Italian law firm	–	–	Mid-sized German law firm	Mid-sized Spanish law firm
25	Mauretanian Professor	Lawyer from a mid-sized German-Spanish law firm	Lawyer from a mid-sized French law firm	Mid-sized German law firm	Mid-sized French law firm
38	Lawyer from a mid-sized Italian law firm	Lawyer from a mid-sized Spanish law firm	Lawyer from a mid-sized German-Spanish law firm	Mid-sized Spanish law firm	Mid-sized German law firm

Lawyers draft the complex contracts which are often the basis of a transaction; they advise their clients on all matters of arbitration and they participate in some arbitration cases as party counsel and in others as arbitrator (Calliess *et al*, 2007). The law firms involved are often linked to each other by networks and sub-networks within and outside of the arbitration system. The mere fact that the largest group of key players comprises lawyers indicates the high level of privatisation of the arbitration system (in contrast, a higher involvement of judges and university professors would indicate stronger links to the state). Another important factor is the dominance of mid-sized law firms as a specific type of law firm and the relatively low level of participation of large law firms and MLF. This contradicts an important thesis of Dezalay and Garth who observe an increasing Americanisation in the field of international arbitration. A comparison with examples of non-routine arbitration supports the notion that the international arbitration field comprises different types of arbitration with different types of law firms involved. A typical example for non-routine arbitration is case study 17. The parties are two large telecommunication companies, the amount at stake is much higher than in all other cases, and the main party counsels on both sides are large law firms. This observation is supported by the following two tables which provide a list of the 10 largest contract and treaty disputes in international arbitration and show the central players in non-routine arbitration.

Table 5—Top 10 Contract Disputes

Stakes*	Parties	Arbitrators	Party Counsel 1	Party Counsel 2
13	*OAO NK Yukos (Russia) v Shareholders in OAO Sibneft*	Marc Lalonde of Stikeman Elliott in Montreal (Chair); Jeffrey Hertzfeld of Salans in Paris; Kenneth Rokison, QC, of 20 Essex Street in London	Fulbright & Jaworski in Houston	Skadden, Arps, Slate, Meagher & Flom in London
8	*The National Property Fund of the Czech Republic and The Czech Republic v Nomura Principal Investment Plc (Japan)*	Pierre Tercier of Fribourg in Switzerland (Chair); Yves Derains of Derains & Associés in Paris; Bernard Hanotiau of Hanotiau & van den Berg in Brussels	Squire, Sanders & Dempsey	Freshfields Bruckhaus Deringer
7.65	*IDT Corp (US) v Telefónica SA (Spain)*	John Wilkinson of Fulton, Rowe, Hart & Coon in New York (Chair); Mark Kantor (Retired) of Milbank, Tweed, Hadley & McCloy in Washington DC; David Kay of Gardner, Carton & Douglas in Chicago	Debevoise & Plimpton	Winston & Strawn

6	*German Federal Ministry of Transport, Building and Housing v Toll Collect Consortium*	Günther Hirsch of the Federal Court of Justice in Karlsruhe (Chair); Horst Eidenmüller of Munich University; Claus-Wilhelm Canaris of Munich University	Linklaters Oppenhoff & Rädler Beiten Burkhardt	Shearman & Sterling Hengeler Mueller and Henning Bälz in Berlin
2	Rumeli Telefon Sistemleri AS (Turkey) v. Motorola Credit Corporation (U.S.)	Daniel Wehrli of Gloor & Sieger in Zurich (Chair); Niklaus Mueller of Hartmann Mueller Partner in Zurich; Marc Blessing of Bär & Karrer in Zurich	Bratschi Emch & Partner	Pestalozzi Lachenal Patry Steptoe & Johnson
2	*Telsim Mobil Telekomünikasyon Hizmetleri AS (Turkey) v Motorola Credit Corp (US)*	Daniel Wehrli of Gloor & Sieger in Zurich (Chair); Hans Rudolf Steiner of Walder Wyss & Partner in Zurich; Marc Blessing of Bär & Karrer in Zurich	Bratschi Emch & Partner in Zurich	Pestalozzi Lachenal Patry Steptoe & Johnson
2	*Vivendi Universal SA (France) and Vivendi Telecom International SA (France) v Elektrim SA (Poland)*	Wolfgang Peter of Python Schifferli Peter & Associés in Geneva (Chair); Alan Redfern of One Essex Court in London; Jerzy Rajski of Warsaw	Salans	Soltysinski Kawecki & Szlezak
1.9	*Gruppo Banca Intesa (Luxembourg) v Slovakia*	Gunther Frosch of Petsch, Frosch & Klein in Vienna; Peter Draxler of Draxler & Partner in Vienna; Jozef Maly of Detvai Ludik Maly in Bratislava	Allen & Overy	Bohm and Partners

1.6	*Electricité de France (France) v Capitalia SpA (Italy), Banca Intesa SpA (Italy), IMI Investimenti SpA (Italy)*	Laurent Levy in Geneva (Chair); Klaus Sachs of CMS Hasche Sigle Eschenlohr Peltzer Schäfer in Munich; Pietro Trimarchi in Milan	Shearman & Sterling	Studio Legale Carbonetti
1.5	*Elf Aquitaine SA v Banco Santander Central Hispano SA*	Guillermo Aguilar Alvarez of SAI Abogados in Mexico City (Chair); Henri Alvarez of Fasken Martineau DuMoulin in Vancouver; Horacio Grigera Naon of Washington DC	Freshfields Bruckhaus Deringer	Uría & Menéndez in Spain Derains & Associés in Paris

*Amount at stake in billion US$
Source: Goldhaber 2005 <http://www.americanlawyer.com/focuseurope/scorecard0605.html> accessed July 30, 2008.

Table 6—Top 10 Treaty Disputes

Stakes*	Parties	Arbitrators	Party Counsel 1	Party Counsel 2
27	*Hulley Enterprises Ltd (Cyprus) v The Russian Federation*	Chair not selected; Daniel Price of Sidley, Austin, Brown & Wood in Washington DC; Stephen Schwebel of Washington DC	Shearman & Sterling in Paris	Cleary Gottlieb Steen & Hamilton
9.4	*Generation Ukraine Inc. (US) v Government of Ukraine*	Jan Paulsson of Freshfields Bruckhaus Deringer in Paris (President); Eugen Salpius of Austria; Jürgen Voss of Germany	Barrister-at-Law in Dublin McKeever Rowan in Dublin	Proxen in Kyiv Grischenko and Partners in Kyiv
4.8	*Veteran Petroleum Trust (Cyprus) v The Russian Federation*	Chair not selected; Daniel Price of Sidley, Austin, Brown & Wood in Washington DC; Stephen Schwebel of Washington DC	Shearman & Sterling	Cleary Gottlieb Steen & Hamilton

4.0	*Offshore Power Production CV, Travamark Two BV, EFS India-Energy BV, Enron BV and Indian Power Investments BV (Netherlands) v Government of India*	Chair not selected; Marc Lalonde of Stikeman Elliott in Montreal; Lord Cooke of Thorndon of New Zealand	Simpson Thacher & Bartlett in New York Sidley Austin Brown & Wood in Washington	Fox Mandal & Co in New Delhi
2.9	*France Telecom Group (France) v Republic of Lebanon*	Bernard Audit of the University of Paris (Chair); Marc Lalonde of Stikeman Elliott in Montreal; Antoine Akl of Akl & Akl in Beirut	Freshfields Bruckhaus Deringer	Robin et Korkmaz in Paris
2.5	*Hussein Nuaman Soufraki (Italy) v The United Arab Emirates*	L Yves Fortier of Ogilvy Renault in Montreal (President); Aktham El Kholy of Egypt; Stephen Schwebel of Washington DC	Freshfields Bruckhaus Deringer	Allen & Overy
2.5	*Hussein Nuaman Soufraki (Italy) v The United Arab Emirates*	Florentino Feliciano of the Philippines (President); Omar Nabulsi of Jordan; Brigitte Stern of the University of Paris	Arnold & Porter in Washington	Allen & Overy
2.0	*Motorola Credit Corporation, Inc (US) v Republic of Turkey*		Steptoe & Johnson in Washington	Ministry of Finance in Turkey

1.5	*Saluka Investments BV (The Netherlands) v The Czech Republic*	Sir Arthur Watts, QC, of 20 Essex Street in London (Chair); Peter Behrens of Hamburg; L Yves Fortier of Ogilvy Renault in Montreal	Freshfields Bruckhaus Deringer	Sanders & Dempsey in Cleveland Squire, Sanders in Prague
1.4	*Aguas Argentinas, SA (Argentina), SUEZ (France), Sociedad General de Aguas de Barcelona, SA (Spain), Vivendi Universal, SA (France) v Argentine Republic*	Jeswald Salacuse of Tufts University (President); Gabrielle Kaufmann-Kohler of Schellenberg Wittmer in Geneva; Pedro Nikken, former president of the Inter-American Court of Human Rights	Freshfields Bruckhaus Deringer	Osvaldo César Guglielmino, Attorney General of Argentina

*Amount at stake in billion US$
Source: Goldhaber, 2005.

Even if it is possible to observe a mix of boutique, mid-sized, large, mega law firms and solo-practitioners, the dominant position in the group of party counsel is held by well-known MLFs such as Freshfields, Shearman & Stearling, Clifford Chance, Allen & Overy, etc. The following table of the top 10 party counsel supports this.

Table 7—Top 12 Law Firms Appearing as Arbitration Counsel

Top 12 Law Firms Appearing as Arbitration Counsel	**No of Arbitrations in 2005**
Freshfields Bruckhaus Deringer	18
Shearman & Sterling	18
White & Case	13
Debevoise & Plimpton	11
Cleary Gottlieb Steen & Hamilton	10
Clifford Chance	8
Sidley, Austin, Brown & Wood	8
Skadden, Arps, Slate, Meagher & Flom	8
Allen & Overy	7

Herbert Smith	7
King & Spalding	7
Winston & Strawn	7

Source: Goldhaber, 2005.

Most of these law firms are mega law firms based in the US or UK. All four leaders have arbitration practice groups in New York and Paris; Freshfields and Debevoise field arbitration stars in London, Shearman in Singapore, and White & Case in Washington (Goldhaber, 2005). However, the group of professionals that participate as arbitrators has very different origins. The top 10 belong to the full range of settings, from MLF to mid-sized national firms, boutiques, one-man offices and universities (Goldhaber, 2005).

Table 8—Top 10 Arbitrators Worldwide

Top 10 Arbitrators	No of Arbitrations in 2005
L Yves Fortier Ogilvy Renault (Canada)	12
Stephen Schwebel Independent practice (US)	8
Gabrielle Kaufmann-Kohler Schellenberg Wittmer (Switzerland)	7
Marc Lalonde Stikeman Elliott (Canada)	7
Albert Jan van den Berg Hanotiau & van den Berg (Belgium)	7
Francisco Orrego Vicuña University of Chile (Chile)	7
Jan Paulsson Freshfields Bruckhaus Deringer (France)	7
Charles Brower White & Case and 20 Essex Street (US and UK)	6
Karl-Heinz Böckstiegel University of Cologne (Germany)	6
Yves Derains Derains & Associés (France)	5

Source: Goldhaber, 2005.

This leads to three important conclusions: First of all, the findings confirm the penetration of MLFs into the field of arbitration and their dominant position in the area of disputes with high stakes (already identified by Dezalay and Garth, 1996). MLFs have obviously accepted international arbitration as an important form of international conflict resolution. Secondly, even if MLFs dominate the sector of high stakes, they do not operate independently of other key players. There are strong links between the MLFs and the 'grand old men' (already identified by Dezalay and Garth, 1996) and other types of law firms. The 'grand old men' (mainly from mid-sized or small firms) still play a crucial role as arbitrators in this type of arbitration. In addition, MLFs and MidLFs cooperate as party counsel. Thirdly, a comparison of Table 4 with Tables 5 and 6 shows very clearly that different firms with different types of organisational structure seem to be successful in international arbitration. In the first group, it is possible to observe a dominance of mid-sized law firms (most of them specialised in German-Spanish commerce). In the second group, it is possible to observe a dominance of MLFs. It is not very likely that MLFs will move into the routine arbitration business, simply because their operation is too expensive in terms of cost. In addition, most of the analysed cases are derived from German-Spanish business transactions, where specialised law firms which dominate the market may be able to provide a better service at a lower price than the MLFs. This makes it unlikely that they will be displaced by MLFs.

Another exception from the list of analysed cases is case study 23, which relates to an arbitration procedure in the cotton industry. The cotton industry is a typical branch with a long tradition, its own standard contracts, arbitration system and extra-legal sanction mechanisms such as blacklisting and damage of reputation. The amount at stake and the costs of the procedure are much lower than in ICC procedures. The arbitrators are cotton traders themselves and have no legal education. The texts of the awards are not very legalistic and are considered to be of inferior quality. Awards in this area are usually enforced with the help of the specific enforcement mechanisms of the particular branch. If parties try to execute these awards in a state court, there are often problems with regard to their enforceability. The court's decision in case no 23 was based on the contractual agreement and the General Conditions of the Bremen Cotton Exchange (no resort to state law). The court assumed that according to the customs of the parties, the General Conditions of the Bremen Cotton Exchange formed the basis of the contractual relation. Claimant G tried to execute the award in Spain according to the New York Convention of 1958, but the Spanish Court adopted a very formalistic position and refused to execute the award because G was unable to prove the existence of an explicit arbitration agreement between the parties. Since it was not possible to have the award executed by a state court, the claimant threatened to put the defendant on a black list of the Committee for International Cooperation between Cotton Associations (CICCA) and to announce the non-fulfilment in the Cotton Report (which is published by the Bremen Cotton Exchange), which ultimately led to the fulfilment of the obligation by the defendant.

The case shows that the arbitration system of the cotton industry is a typical branch institution which works with branch members but not necessarily outside of it.[3] It is not linked to the ICC or other important institutions of international arbitration with international or global reputation. It is rather located at the periphery of the international arbitration system. Similarities can be observed between branch arbitration and domestic arbitration, which also has a relatively low prestige because it is perceived to be too close to business and lacking in legal expertise (Dezalay and Garth, 1996: 124). In contrast, 'international arbitration claims to be learned, in part because it involves relationships with many legal systems' (Dezalay and Garth, 1996: 124).

In summary, it is highly questionable whether the tendency towards Americanisation claimed by Dezalay and Garth and supported by the literature on international mega law firms (eg Flood 2005; Trubek *et al*, 1994; Silver, 2000; Shapiro, 1993) can be maintained. Instead, what we observe at the international and global level is rather a mixture of different law firms with different approaches to lawyering that can be described as the *varieties of capitalism of law firms* (Morgan and Quack, 2005). International arbitration is a very good example of this: there are different areas of international commercial arbitration in which different types of law firm dominate. A first differentiation has to be made between non-routine arbitration and more standardised arbitration cases that involve less complex and cost-intensive transactions. However, our findings also indicate the existence of sub-groups specialising in commerce between particular countries. The emergence of sub-groups is also very likely in specific areas of law with a high level of technical complexity (eg intellectual property law). In addition, it is possible to observe that different types of law firm do not work independently, but have developed strong links and are dependent on each other. This supports our thesis that it is not possible to view the support structures of the MLFs independently from the support structures of other types of law firms.

THE SHIFT OF RESPONSIBILITY TO PRIVATE ACTORS AND THE CONTINUING IMPORTANCE OF THE STATE LEGAL SYSTEM IN THE ARBITRATION PROCESS

Together with complex contracts drafted by MLFs, international commercial arbitration is probably the most important example of a shift of responsibility from the state legal system to private actors within the context of contractual support structures. In fact, both subjects are closely

[3] A further analysis of branch arbitration is provided by Konradi, 2008; and Konradi and Fix-Fierro, 2005.

linked to each other, because most complex contracts contain an arbitration clause. The following sections will examine this notion by looking at some selected findings of the study with regard to substantive law, the process of decision-making, the characteristics of arbitrators and their networks and the quality assurance system of the ICC. The cases do not support Dezalay and Garth, who have argued that commercial arbitration can be characterised by a trend from charisma to routine. It is rather a mixture between the new, more formalised form of arbitration introduced by the Anglo-American MLFs and old-style arbitration, ie a specific mix of routinisation and preservation of relational aspects, which explains the tremendous success of commercial arbitration and its advantages with regard to state legal procedures.

Participation of the Parties in the Arbitration Process

One of the central reasons for the increasing dominance of private actors is the high level of participation of the parties that characterises the entire arbitration procedure. The fact that the parties have much more autonomy than in a state legal procedure (Lew, Mistelis and Kröll, 2003) is evident: they possess the right to select the place of arbitraton, the applicable procedural and substantive norms, etc. The most important aspect with regard to this issue is the fact that the parties can nominate the arbitrators. They can:

> ... choose from a palette of potential arbitrators according to the nature of their problems, their affinities, and above all their strategies. The parties—and their advisers—thus choose their terrain, their arms, and the rules of the game that will govern their confrontation (Dezalay and Garth, 1996).

In the case of three arbitrators, every party is allowed to select one arbitrator, while the chairman is usually nominated by the ICC; in the case of a sole arbitrator they have the possibility to agree on a specific arbitrator (art 8, nos 3 and 4 of the ICC Rules). Even if they leave the selection of the arbitrator to the ICC Court, they are usually asked to indicate the criteria for the nomination of an arbitrator. This also happened in case study 7, where a lawyer from the law firm was nominated as sole arbitrator. In his request for arbitration, the claimant expressed that:

> ... the arbitrator should be independent of the Parties and their respective groups of companies, of a neutral nationality, fluent in English and Spanish, and have knowledge and experience of Spanish law.

The respondent agrees to this and adds an additional criterion:

> ... furthermore, Respondent 2 agrees with the criteria expressed by the Claimant in its Request for Arbitration. In addition to those criteria, and given that the

law applicable to this proceeding is Spanish law, the Respondent would like to see the knowledge and experience in Spanish law cited by the Claimant confirmed by the arbitrator's admission to a Spanish bar.

The central instrument that allows the parties to influence the arbitration process is the terms of reference in which the major elements of the arbitration procedure are determined (Lew, Mistelis and Kröll, 2003: 528). According to the ICC Rules[4] (art 18 of the Rules), the terms of reference should contain the following parts:

a) the full names and descriptions of the parties;
b) the addresses of the parties to which notifications and communications arising in the course of the arbitration may be made;
c) a summary of the parties' respective claims and of the relief sought by each party, with an indication to the extent possible of the amounts claimed or counterclaimed;
d) unless the Arbitral Tribunal considers it inappropriate, a list of issues to be determined;
e) the full names, descriptions and addresses of the arbitrators;
f) the place of the arbitration; and
g) particulars of the applicable procedural rules and, if such is the case, reference to the power conferred upon the Arbitral Tribunal to act as amiable compositeur or to decide *ex aequo et bono*.

The terms of reference provide a possibility of summarising counterclaims and defences, creating a framework for the proceedings and bringing the parties together at the outset of the proceedings (Lew, Mistelis and Kröll, 2003: 531). This helps to reduce the enormous complexity immanent to conflicts that arise out of complex business transactions. The process becomes more transparent and the risk of misunderstandings is reduced. Case study 7 refers to a large arbitration in the telecommunication industry. It involved the construction of the infrastructure for a fibre-optic network which was supposed to connect 45 European cities. The particular transaction is limited to the part of the network that runs through Spain. The basis of the transaction was a contract of 80 pages with numerous anexes. The parties involved were two large telecommunication companies and several construction companies. The professional service firms involved in the dispute were a Spanish mid-sized law firm specialising in intellectual property, unfair competition and internet law, a large Spanish law firm, an MLF and another large Spanish firm. It is evident that the design, construction, installation and inspection of the work was subject to

[4] Terms of reference are not only referred to in the ICC Rules, but also in other arbitration institutions: CEPANI art 24; AIA art 24; JCAA art 15; and Euro-Arab Chamber of Commerce art 23(7). Source: Lew, Mistelis and Kröll, 2003.

numerous technical difficulties and unforseeable contingencies. Nevertheless, the arbitrators were able to summarise the positions and claims of the parties and the issues to be determined in very few pages.

The process of establishing the terms of reference is usually carried out in intense cooperation between the representatives of the parties and the arbitrators. Usually, the tribunal drafts a first version of the terms of reference. Afterwards, the parties suggest changes or reformulate them. The tribunal and the parties often plan a separate meeting for final discussion and the signing of the terms of reference.

If the parties are unable to reach an agreement on the terms of reference, they must be submitted to the ICC Court for approval (art 18, no 3 of the ICC Rules), but this only occurs very rarely (a submission of the terms of reference to the court was unnecessary in any of the analysed cases), which indicates the tendency to decide as many issues as possible on the basis of consensus.[5] The time frame of two months for the establishment of the terms of reference provides an advantage in comparison to court proceedings, where the preliminary proceedings often take more than a year because parties are often granted extensions to present their pleadings.

Due to the fact that the contested issues are determined at a very early stage in the arbitration proceedings, it is possible for all participants to focus on the same issues. The necessity to cooperate at the outset of the proceedings (Lew, Mistelis and Kröll, 2003: 531) leads to a much higher level of acceptance. The summary of claims and reliefs sought makes the conflict more transparent, thus promoting a better understanding of the opposite party's position. As a matter of fact, the establishment of the terms of reference is often a first step for a settlement of the dispute (Lew, Mistelis and Kröll, 2003: 531).

The Legal Sources of Arbitration: Emergence of a Truly International Law, Continuing Importance of State Law, or a Combination of Both Sources?

The first part of the analysis has shown that the arbitration process is largely in the hand of private actors (especially lawyers). However, the state may still play a crucial role as provider of a legal infrastructure (ie procedural rules, substantive rules and private international law). Consequently, the legal sources of arbitration have to be analysed in more detail. The purpose here is not to give a full overview of the sources of the entire arbitration process, but to show the combination of different sources used in specific examples. This perspective gives a more accurate picture of the

[5] A principle which is also used in the area of international organisations where a 'rough-consensus-strategy' is observed (Calliess, 2006).

different sources used in international commercial arbitration than many abstract and theoretical approaches, which claim that certain types of norms (eg national or anational law) dominate in the field of arbitration. Due to the limited space in this chapter, we will focus exclusively on the substantive norms.

Substantive Rules

The Need to Find Particularistic Solutions in International Business Conflicts

A central problem of the state legal system is its lack of flexibility, which stands in opposition to the need of business to reach particular solutions for particular problems. Business conflicts are usually very complex and cannot be removed from their economic, technical and social background. Internationality and rapid technological changes make it even more difficult for the law to comprehend the contextual factors of a business conflict. In some cases, the contextual factors are of minor importance (eg an isolated sales contract or an isolated contract for specific services). However, many business relationships in the international context tend to be of longer duration (eg Sosa, 2007) and more complex than in the national context. Consequently, they are more like a marriage than a one-night stand (Macneil, 1981). The need to take different contextual factors into account persists after the termination of the contractual relation (typical issues in case of the termination of a business relation are the transfer of the right to use customer networks, compensation for specific investments, etc). As a consequence, business actors have a need for particular solutions created by individual decision-makers and they try to avoid general solutions provided by the law. However, what sources do arbitrators use and how are the different sources mixed? Dezalay and Garth argue that the sources consist of an 'amalgamation of the state legal system and the ad hoc, custom-tailored justice' (Dezalay and Garth, 1996: 309), but this thesis has never been clarified sufficiently. Consequently, the focus of the following text is not to give an overview of the existing theoretical discussion on the use of different sources of law such as complex contracts, national law, general principles or the *lex mercatoria*, but rather to analyse the specific mix of different sources which arbitrators use to find adequate solutions for business conflicts as well as the process of decision-making using the evidence from the empirical examples in this study.

The Use of Different Sources of Law in the Empirical Examples

The nine different case studies on arbitration produced during this study include the analysis of entire files, (complex) contracts, pleadings, correspondence, awards and interviews with lawyers, as well as the participation in some of the arbitration procedures. The low number of cases does not allow a generalisation of the findings. However, they are able to produce some insight into the mix of sources used in arbitration procedures. The following table gives a short overview of the different sources used as a basis of the decision.

Table 9—Factual Resort to State Law

Type of Transction	Type of Contract	Choice of Law	Resort to State Law	General Principles	Use of Discretionary Power	Extra-legal Expertise
Construction of a fibre-optic network	Complex	Spanish	–	Principle of good faith/*pacta sunt servanda*	Express discretion in several contract clauses	Construction expert
Sales contract, non-performance	Standardised	German	§ 326 BGB/arts 81 and 82 EC Treaty	Contract interpretation	Discretionary decision with regard to loss profit	–
Licensing agreement	Standardised/ complex clauses	German	§ 89b HGB/arts 81 and 82 EC Treaty	–	Discretionary decision on compensation	–
Shareholder agreement	Complex	German	–	Contract interpretation	Discretion with regard to use of general principles	Expert report from a tax consultant
Stock purchase agrement	Complex	New York	Principle of *res iudicata*	–	–	Tax consultant, two Spanish professors (both tax)

Supply of cotton	Standardised	–	–	Trade usage, custom between the parties	–	Technical expert for cotton quality
Purchase of machines	Standardised/ complex clauses	CISG	–	–	–	Technical expert
Purchase of railway tracks	Standardised/ complex clauses	Maure-tanian	Art 284 *Code des Contrats et Obliga-tions*	Trade usage, custom between the parties	Discretion-ary decision on compen-sation	Three technical experts
Purchase of company shares	Complex	Spanish	–	Good faith/*culpa in contra-hendo*	Discretion with regard to use of general principles	Financial expert

Notes: BGB = Bürgerliches Gesetzbuch (German Civil Code); EC = European Community; HGB = Handelsgesetzbuch (German Commercial Code); CISG = UN Convention on the International Sales of Goods
Source: Callies *et al*, 2007.

Complex Contracts

In an *ex ante* situation, economic actors often resort to the (large) law firms to draft complex contracts which regulate any detail of a transaction and make a resort to substantive national law obsolete (Dezalay, 1990; Daly, 1997; Flood, 1996; 2005; 2007). Arbitration often becomes an integral part of the contractual conflict resolution system. Conflict resolution clauses in complex contracts often provide a conflict resolution system with different levels. A typical example is the contract in case study 7. The conflict resolution clause provides that the parties have to give notice to the other party in the case that a dispute is considered to have arisen. The operating directors have to meet to find a solution within 14 days. If a solution cannot be found, the managing directors have to meet. If the managing partners are unable to find a solution, any party is entitled to refer the dispute to arbitration.

It may be possible that this contract works largely independently of any state legal system as indicated by Dezalay, Daly, Flood and many others. However, the dispute resolution clause contains a referral to national Spanish law not only with regard to the content, but also with regard to the interpretation of the contract.[6] On the other hand, the referral to national law may be largely symbolic (Flood, 2007). Cases 7, 13, 17 and 38 are typical complex contracts which do not leave much room for resorting to national law (Flood 2001; 2005; 2007).

The contract in case study 7 (construction of a fibre glass network for the telecommunication industry) contains a glossary in which all central terms used in the contract are specified. For example, it contains a complete list of documents which can be categorised under the term 'drawings', it lists all events that lead to '*force majeure*' and it even defines the term 'day' ('day means calendar day').

Owing to the high complexity of the transaction, it is impossible to cover all possible contingenies in the contract, but several clauses in the contract regulate the handling of unforseen contingencies. One of the central problems in this project was adverse physical conditions and artificial obstructions which may be encountered during the execution of the works. According to the contract, the constructor of the network is responsible for all adverse physical conditions. This responsibility includes the proposal and implementation of a 'work around plan', which has to be agreed with the principal. The contract contained a clause of several pages' length in which the procedure of the elaboration of the 'work around plan' was specified in detail. There is no visible gap in these clauses which would allow a resort to national civil law.

On the other hand, the complexity of the transaction (the contract contains 72 different clauses and several annexes) makes it impossible to determine *ex ante* every aspect of the transaction, which makes it inevitable to concede a certain level of discretion to the parties. A good example is clause x, which stipulates that the parties shall agree a *fair and reasonable* valuation (of the costs). In fact, many of the stipulations in this contract contain similar unspecified terms: the contractor shall carry out the work 'diligently ... in a good, proper, careful and workmanlike manner'; 'in accordance with good industry standards', the employer shall take steps 'in a timely manner'; 'the security shall be provided by a bank or institution reasonably satisfactory'; the contractor shall obtain 'for himself all necessary information'; the 'Employer's Representative's reasonable request'; 'the approval shall not be unreasonably withheld'; the contractor shall keep the site 'in an orderly state appropriate to the avoidance of danger'; the parties shall 'resolve the dispute or difference in good faith', etc. Finally, the contract contains a clause in which the general responsibilities are fixed.

[6] ie the parties do not want the arbitrators to interpret the contract according to general principles of international law.

The fact that the parties use such a general clause indicates that they are aware of the fact that the specific clauses will not be able to cover all possible contingencies. Thus, even though the contract may not leave much room for the application of national civil law, it does contain a variety of 'gaps' that make it necessary to resort to other sources (of law) to resolve conflicts that can arise with regard to these aspects. In fact, the probability of the existence of gaps is much higher in complex transactions than in standard transactions even if the contractual documents in the former will be much more complex. A typical instrument to fill these 'gaps' is the implementation of general principles of law, which will be described below.

National and International Law

Generally, one can say that international actors using arbitration are advised by experienced, internationally operating law firms, which urge their clients to use sophisticated, often tailor-made international contracts that contain a detailed regulation of all contingencies which can arise during the realisation of a transaction. Thus, typical problems such as delay, non-delivery, breach of warranty, etc are regulated in every detail in most general conditions attached to the contract or in the contract itself. Consequently, national civil law, which is largely non-mandatory in this area,[7] plays a very small role in conflicts which arise out of these types of problem. However, this does not mean that national civil law is completely irrelevant. First of all, the contractual solutions are created within the freedom of contract granted by most national legal systems. Secondly, there are many situations when arbitrators resort to non-mandatory law. This happened, for example in case 9, where the parties had not agreed on the consequences of the non-delivery of the product. In this case, the arbitration court applied § 326 BGB. In another case (25), the arbitrators resorted to article 284 of the Mauretanian *Code des Contrats et Obligations* to decide on the prerequisites of *force majeure* which were not stipulated in the contract. Thus, even if most of the contracts subject to arbitration do not leave much room for national law, there are still many examples where national law is used as subsidiary in the area of non-mandatory law. It may be argued that the relevance of contract law is decreasing because international actors continually produce new types of contractual agreements which will completely replace national contract law in the long term (see, for example, Shapiro, 1993), but this is not an accurate picture of actual business practice.

In addition, it was possible to observe that *mandatory national law* is often subject to arbitration. The ignorance of mandatory law may lead to

[7] Except for the norms on general conditions of contracts, eg §§ 305 *ff* BGB, in Spanish law: *Ley 7/1998, de 13 de abril, sobre condiciones generales de la contratación.*

the unenforceability of an award. The prevention of this situation has always been a key issue, especially in ICC arbitration (Derains, 2001: 44; 2005: 313) and is the central reason for the introduction of the final scrutiny procedure (art 27 of the ICC Rules). A typical example regarding the application of mandatory law is EC competition law. A considerable body of commentary and case law considers that mandatory public laws (especially anti-trust law) are applicable to a dispute irrespective of the choice of law made by the parties (for example, Lew, Mistelis and Kröll, 2003: 483; Derains, 2005: 239; Derains, 1987: 227; Lazareff, 1996: 538). Thus, allegations of competition law infringements are a common feature in international arbitration, which was also the case in two case studies subject to this analyis (nos 9 and 12). The legal sanction in the case of an infringement is the voidness of the contract. Consequently, parties often refer to articles 81 and 82 of the EC Treaty to avoid legal consequences of non-performance (Lew, Mistelis and Kröll, 2003: 482). In the *ECO Swiss v Benetton* decision,[8] the European Court of Justice held that article 81 of the EC Treaty is a mandatory provision of public policy character. Thus, the failure of an arbitral tribunal to recognise the applicability of article 81 of the EC Treaty justifies the annulment of the award under national laws and a refusal of enforcement under the New York Convention of 1958 (Lew, Mistelis and Kröll, 2003: 483). This decision made it clear that articles 81 and 82 are arbitrable (Lew, Mistelis and Kröll, 2003: 483). Whereas the claim on the basis of a breached contract requires the existence of the contract, the arbitral tribunal should apply these norms *ex officio* even if none of the parties has invoked them (Lew, Mistelis and Kröll: 2003: 488). Articles 81 and 82 (formerly 85 and 86) of the EU treaty have been applied by ICC arbitrators for many years (Derains, 2005: 239; Derains, 1982: 39).

Another factor which supports the still existing relevance of national law is the fact that arbitrators usually spend much time doing research on legal questions (in contrast to national judges who often do not have the time to analyse all existing sources). Legal argumentation is usually very detailed and contains many references to the case law of the nation states. In contrast to state courts, arbitrators will also compare the case law in different states. Arbitrators are usually from different nationalities. As a consequence, there is usually only one expert for the applicable law, who is usually the one responsible for the research. An investment of 100 working hours per arbitrator is not rare. In case 7, the chairman of the arbitral tribunal invested 92 working hours; in case 17, as much as 527 working

[8] ECJ, 1 June 1999, Case C-126/97 *Eco Swiss China Time Ltd v Benetton International NV* [1999] ECR I-3055.

hours. This amount of time could obviously never be invested by a state judge (however, the arbitrator received a compensation of US $171,000).

General Principles as an Independent Body of Law?

A third source of law used in international arbitration is general priniciples. While it cannot be denied that arbitrators make use of national law, it could be argued that in many situations complex contracts and the use of general principles generally accepted in international commerce, such as the principle of good faith or of fair dealing, are sufficient for deciding a case. In these cases, the remaining function of national law may be largely symbolic. A study from Nassar (2001) indicates the great relevance of general principles in commercial arbitration, such as the principles of good faith and fair dealing, *rebus sic stantibus*, etc (see also Dezalay and Garth, 1996). Nassar confirms that arbitrators take extra-contractual circumstances into account in order to interpret or adjust contractual agreements. Usages of trade and customs of the parties are used to interpret the contract, and they can also be the source of obligations for the parties. Finally, arbitrators acknowledge the existence of extensive obligations of information, cooperation and renegotiation independently of the contractual stipulations. They resort to the principle of *rebus sic stantibus* in order to dissolve a contract or to adjust it in exceptional cases (Nassar, 2001). Some authors argue that these general principles are part of a completely independent body of rules, the *lex mercatoria*, which has become the dominant source of substantive law in international commercial arbitration (eg Berman and Kaufman, 1978; Berger *et al*, 2001; Teubner, 1997); others assume that the relevance of the *lex mercatoria* has decreased in the last decades (Dezalay and Garth, 1996). However, these studies rely on anecdotal evidence or on interviews with different types of international actor (eg Berger *et al*, 2001; Dezalay and Garth, 1996) rather than on a detailed analysis of files, awards or the observation of the arbitration procedure itself.

In order to compare the importance of these general principles with national law, it is necessary to develop a categorisation of cases where general principles are used. Derains makes a difference between five different categories:

a) situations in which the parties have not selected the applicable law and the arbitrators come to the conclusion that they only want to apply general principles;
b) cases in which the parties have selected the application of *lex mercatoria* or general principles;
c) situations in which the parties have selected national law, but arbitrators resort to general principles to fill gaps;

d) cases where arbitrators use general principles to supplement national law; and
e) cases where general principles prevail over national law pursuant to international public policy (Derains, 2001).

According to Derains, the first, second and fifth categories are exceptional. The first and the second cases are very rare, because most contracts contain a choice-of-law clause in which national law is selected (eg ICC Statistical Reports 2005 and 2006). Even if this is not the case, an exclusive recourse to transnational law rarely occurs. This has been observed in situations when arbitrators where unable to decide on the applicable national norms because the dispute concerned a contract that had contact with numerous countries.[9] Another typical example relates to complex projects that often involve several parties, such as oil and gas projects in third-world countries that cannot provide the necessary legislation. The fifth category refers to cases where international principles exclude national law. According to Derains, the only example known in this context is the case in which a state law prohibits a resort to international arbitration (eg article 139 of the Iranian Constitution, which submits the validity of a reference to arbitration by the state to the consent of the Iranian Parliament (Derains, 2001)). In contrast, there are numerous examples for the third and the fourth cases. Arbitrators have referred to a number of general principles on many occasions. In these situations, national law is not replaced, but *supplemented* by general principles:

> However, what happens is that the arbitrators apply French law and then add some reference to some general principles. And obviously, the award could be set aside if it applied a principle contrary to International Public Policy or a principle directly contrary to French law—which in the majority of cases will be very difficult to establish (Derains 2001: 45).

These principles include the principles of *pacta sunt servanda*, *rebus sic stantibus* and *culpa in contrahendo*, obligation to perform the contract in good faith, unenforceability of contracts designed to achieve an illegal object or obtained by bribes or other dishonest means, obligation to negotiate in good faith to overcome unforeseen difficulties in the performance of the contract, entitlement of a party to treat itself as discharged from its obligations if the other has committed a substantial breach, obligation of party which has suffered a breach of contract to mitigate the loss, etc.[10] Arbitrators will often refer implicitly or explicitly to the general

[9] Derains names two examples: (i) a cruise in the Mediterrainan Sea, including seven different countries; and (ii) a contract between a Japanese producer and a distributor in the Middle East covering four different countries (Derains, 2001: 46).

[10] For a detailed list of various principles that have been applied in international arbitration, see Lew, Mistellis and Kröll, 2003: 458.

principles of international business law when they apply these principles. Thereby they usually try to strengthen the decision (Derains, 2001: 50). However, the same solution can usually be found under national law by reference to the general principle developed within a national context (Derains, 2001: 50). The application of these principles does not run contrary to national law, because most national laws explicitly allow the application of these principles (eg § 242 of the German Civil Code). This is also supported by Derains:

> Second, if somebody criticized the arbitrators by saying 'the arbitrators had the mission to apply French law—they did not do it!' a more subtle analysis would reach the conclusion that in fact they did not come to a result that is *contrary* to French law. Therefore they could do it, although they approached the problem referring to a general principle and not to the national legal system which should be applied (Derains, 2001: 49).

The analysed cases support the thesis that general principles play a crucial role in international arbitration to supplement other sources of law (eg national law and complex contracts). As shown in Table 9, the arbitrators have referred to typical general principles, such as the principle of good faith, *pacta sunt servanda*, general principles for contract interpretation and *culpa in contrahendo*. Whereas *they do not run contrary to national law*, the categorisation of these principles (national versus anational) is reduced to a conceptual discussion which is completely irrelevant for the functional approach in this chapter. Therefore, it is much more interesting to analyse the situations in which arbitrators apply general principles that run contrary to national law.

The most interesting examples are related to the application of transnational general principles that run contrary to national law in the interpretation of contracts. In this case, the arbitrators can decide whether they should apply national general principles of interpretation or international (transnational) principles of interpretation (eg article 4 of the Unidroit Principles[11]). However, there are differences with regard to the general principles of interpretation of contracts between different countries. Of course, a variety of differences can be observed between the more formalistic common law and the more flexible civil law approaches to contract interpretation.[12] One of the central problems is the extent to which trade usage, prior negotiations and subsequent conduct have to be considered when interpreting a contractual stipulation.[13] According to German case law, customs should be taken into consideration in the interpretation of

[11] <http://www.unidroit.org/english/principles/contracts/principles2004/blackletter2004.pdf> accessed 18 June 2008.

[12] For a detailed analysis, see Nassar, 2001: 35.

[13] For a detailed analysis, see Nassar, 2001: 35.

contractual obligations,[14] they can define additional obligations[15] or even *suspend* contractual provisions (Schmidt, 1999: 607).

Case 13 indicates that arbitrators and party counsel hesitate to resort to general principles of international law if the parties have selected a specific national law in their contract. This is an arbitration procedure between a Spanish (S) and a German telecommunication company (G) regarding a conflict in the context of selling of shares from a third company from S to G. The central question to be addressed by the tribunal is whether S had to exercise its put option granted in the shareholder agreement on 1 January or from 1 January. The corresponding clause reads as follows: 'On January 1, 2003, D grants S the right to sell and transfer a 20% share stake in SD to D'.

Whereas the parties had agreed that German law was applicable to the contract, the clause was interpreted in accordance with the principles of interpretation developed in German case law. The expert report drafted by the law firm (which was confirmed by the tribunal in its final decision) interprets the contract clause on the basis of the different methods for contract interpretation. While some methods provide specific instructions for interpretation (among others the concept of prohibition of literal interpretation and the theory of reference[16]), the most common concepts such as the requirement to take into consideration all the circumstances, the historical, systematic and teleological interpretation, interpretation according to the reasonable interests of the parties, and interpretation according to the principle of good faith and to commercial customs, leave a wide scope for discretion for the interpreter. It is necessary to take into account the economic and technical circumstances of the transaction, the commercial customs, other agreements, the correspondence between the parties, etc. The arbitrator dedicated by far the largest part of the award to this specific question. Even if this stipulation is part of a large complex contract that leaves no room for the applicable national law, it is necessary to consider the entire relationship between the parties for the interpretation of one short word in this contract.

Technical Expert Reports

Most of the analysed conflicts are not only complex, but involve economic and technical issues. A good example for the tight interrelation with economic issues is case study 7. A US company (A) has established a stock purchase agreement (SPA) with a Spanish company (S), on the basis of

[14] BGHZ (Sammlung der Entscheidungen des Bundesgerichtshofes in Zivilsachen—Collection of decisions of the German Federal Court of Justice) 57, 1105.

[15] BGHZ 107, 331.

[16] Every interpretation needs to be indicated in the contract clause.

which all shares of a third company (E) where supposed to be transferred from S to A. S had provided different documentation about E, among others the financial statements for the years 1992, 1993 and 1994 and a report from the tax consultant. Company A makes the following assertions:

a) company S has given wrong information about the financial and economical situation of E;
b) the calculation of the net value of company E by the tax consultant was incorrect;
c) the financial statements for the years 1992, 1993 and 1994 were not established in accordance with the applicable accounting rules;
d) company S has retained documentation;
e) company A has purchased the shares on the basis of the wrong information; and
f) company S has made a high profit on the basis of this transaction.

On the basis of these assertions, company A claims that the SPA should be dissolved and that it should receive indemnification. The very tight relationship between the legal and economic aspects of the case is obvious: the issues are based on economic aspects such as the financial and economic situation of company E, incorrect accounting and incorrect information about these issues. It is almost impossible to differentiate between the legal and economic issues of the case, which makes it necessary for the different actors involved to have an understanding of both. Similar observations could be made in case study 13, which also handled the purchase of stock. The close connection between economy and law is also shown in the cooperation of lawyers with accountants, tax consultants, etc. In case study 17, the parties involved were one MLF, two large law firms and one MidLF that acted as party counsel, two lawyers from MidLFs as arbitrators, another MidLF as consultant of the arbitrators, two international tax consultants and two professors. In addition, most of the analysed cases require the involvement of a technical expert (see Table 9) because they involve either very complex technical projects (case no 7, the construction of a fibre glass network for the telecommunication industry) or because the product itself is highly complex (eg case studies 5, 24 and 25). In case 25, the question of the defect was solved with the help of three different experts: two party experts and a third expert from the International Centre of Expertise of the ICC. The following picture attempts to sketch the participation of the different professional service firms involved in case study 17.

Obviously, the involvement of technical experts is not exclusively limited to international arbitration. In many situations, state judges will have insufficient technical expertise and cannot resort to pre-existing structures. In addition, high costs often prevent the parties from using experts. In

Figure I—Participation of Different Professional Service Firms in the Creation of Particular Solutions (Case Study 17)

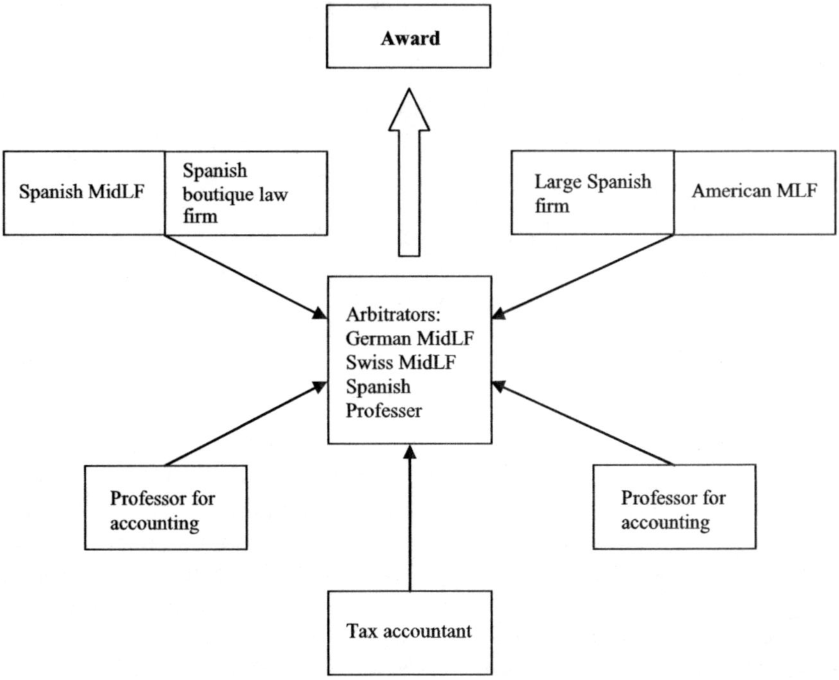

contrast, in international commercial arbitration, lawyers and arbitrators are used to cooperating with technical experts frequently and they can resort to pre-existing structures such as the ICC centre for expertise, which also guarantees a relatively high quality of technical reports, because experts who have not provided a satisfactory service in former arbitration procedures will disappear from the expert list. Due to the fact that the amounts at stake are usually very high, the parties will only rarely abstain from using technical experts. Expert reports are obviously one of the central sources for the integration of context factors into a decision. Similar to the situation with regard to the use of general principles, expert reports are not an instrument unknown in state court procedures, but the use of technical reports is much better integrated in the system of international arbitration, and actors show a higher level of experience with regard to its use.

Conclusion

Typical conflicts taken to arbitration are end-game situations in complex cooperation processes (ending of distributor agreement, failure of a stock purchase, etc), which require very particular solutions that cannot be provided by the state legal system. Due to the complexity of the transactions and the diversity between different types of transaction, it is very unlikely that case law will be able to fill these gaps (in addition, commercial conflicts are only rarely taken to courts, and this prevents the establishment of precedents). The cooperation process itself is so complex that parties rarely take a conflict to court as long as the cooperation process has not ended. The complexity of the transaction is also reflected in the end-game situation. The resulting questions cannot be isolated from its economical and technical background, but have to be solved in accordance with it. Consequently, pragmatic, technical and economic considerations have to figure in the decision-making balance (Dezalay and Garth, 1995). Arbitration awards are created in an intensive process of cooperation between highly qualified experts, typically found in international commercial arbitration. Only these experts are capable of finding pragmatic solutions through consideration of technical, economic and social context factors (Calliess *et al*, 2007). Awards are based on rules of civil and commercial law (often used as raw material), complex contracts, general principles of law and expert reports, which play a crucial role in most decisions. Through the combination of these sources, it is possible to take into account context factors better. This makes it possible to create more particularistic solutions that are better suited to the parties' interests and provide a higher level of fairness (Calliess *et al*, 2007). In addition, arbitrators spend an enormous amount of time in the legal analysis, the establishment of the facts, the understanding of the non-legal context, etc.

In contrast to many opinions in literature, there was no indication of the use of completely new legal structures for the global economy such as the *lex mercatoria* (eg Berger *et al*, 2001; Teubner, 1997). All analysed contracts contain a choice of national law. Arbitrators resort to national or international law which is applicable in a concrete case and they carry out a detailed and extensive legal analysis. Their assistants are usually asked to draft complex legal reports on particular matters, which would be impossible for state judges. Contracts have to be agreed between individuals, have no validity for other actors and can consequently not be attributed to an autonomous law merchant. The application of general norms is certainly of tremendous importance for the arbitration system. In addition, Nassar's study illustrates that arbitrators apply these mechanisms frequently and have a certain experience with the usage of these principles. However, general principles only complement other sources of law such as contracts and national law. When arbitrators resort to general principles of international commerce, these principles usually do not run contrary to national law. In situations where this would be the case, arbitrators tend to use general principles developed in the correspondent national context. Thus, the prevalence of general principles over national law cannot be observed in the empirical data.

The cases also prove that a relational law which has been claimed by many prominent scholars such as Macneil, Campbell and Harris or Nicklisch is not necessary to decide these conflicts, because the existing law leaves enough scope for the consideration of relational factors (Sosa, 2007). This does not mean that an analysis of the *lex mercatoria* in international commercial arbitration is obsolete, because there are some rare cases where arbitrators have decided not to apply national law and to resort to transnational law,[17] but the empirical analysis of *lex mercatoria* should be limited to these very specific cases. With regard to more standardised cases, the advantage of arbitration does not lie in the ability to use completely new legal structures, but in the possibility to resort to experts who are experienced in the use of existing legal structures with the necessary flexibility. The entire picture shows that these solutions can only be created by individuals (*ex ante* by the lawyers and *ex post* by the arbitrators who are often lawyers themselves, both in close cooperation with other professionals) and not by abstract programmes. This leads to a shift of responsibility from the state (legal system which provides the basis for the decision) to the private actor who influences the decision (party counsel) or decides the case (arbitrator). The openness of arbitration for particular solutions, which can be considered to be its central advantage, automatically leads to a shift of responsibility from the level of programmes (law) to the level of lawyers who are the key players in this system.

The Key Players in the Field of International Commercial Arbitration

One of the central elements of the success of international commercial arbitration is the involvement of certain key players. The effectiveness of state legal systems is usually analysed without paying any attention to this aspect. However, especially when it comes to the resolution of cross-border conflicts, the key players become one of the central elements of analysis. As mentioned before, the key players in the files that I have analysed are not Anglo-American MLF-lawyers. The respective arbitration procedures are carried out by well-known Spanish or German MidLFs and most arbitrators also belong to this group. Only 1 of 21 participants (counsel and arbitrators) was a judge; the rest were lawyers. My findings also indicate that parties prefer a general practitioner with long-standing experience and

[17] Interesting cases are arbitration awards where arbitrators have exclusively applied the UNIDROIT Principles; see Lew, Mistelis and Kröll, 2003: 464.

high reputation to a highly specialised expert, who may lack the ability to capture the nuances of international trade that cannot be handled adequately by legal means. The following tables display some examples of profiles of different arbitrators:

Table 10—Profile no 1

Profession:	Spanish lawyer
Experience:	Civil law, common law and European law.
Expertise:	International trade, joint ventures (JV), industrial cooperation, agency and distribution, IP, finance and banking
Languages in which arbitrator has carried out arbitration procedures:	French, German, English and Spanish
Link to university:	PhD from a German university, honorary doctor in a Spanish university, honorary professor in a Spanish university
Member of international associations:	Chamber of Commerce and different international associations
Number of arbitration procedures:	150

Table 11—Profile no 2

Profession:	Lawyer admitted to the German and Spanish bars
Experience:	Civil law (German and Spanish), international law and European law
Expertise:	International trade, JV and industrial cooperation
Languages in which arbitrator has carried out arbitration procedures:	German, English, Spanish and French
Link to university:	PhD from a German university
Member of international associations:	Member of different international organisations and chambers of commerce
Number of arbitration procedures:	13

Table 12—Profile no 3

Profession:	Italian lawyer
Experience:	Civil law (Italy, Germany, France, Spain), international and European law
Expertise:	International trade, JV, industrial cooperation, agency and distribution, and industrial property
Languages in which arbitrator has carried out arbitration procedures:	French, English, Spanish, German and Italian
Link to university:	PhD from an Italian university, honorary professor in an Italian university
Member of international associations:	–
Number of arbitration procedures:	13 as arbitrator, large number (not specified) as party counsel

Typical characteristics of arbitrators are experience in civil law, common law as well as European law, experience in different areas of international law such as international trade, joint ventures, industrial cooperation or agency and distribution. However, none of the arbitrators is a true specialist in a particular area of law (a typical attribute of highly specialised MLF lawyers). All arbitrators described in the above tables are general practitioners with a wide scope of experience in different areas of commercial law. Another outstanding aspect is the cosmopolitan character of most arbitrators: a typical example is the arbitrator from the firm, who has spent a year in Paris after high school graduation and received a one-year scholarship to study at a US law school. All lawyers command several languages (not only English) and most of them have already conducted arbitration procedures in different languages. The ability to move from one language to another is taken for granted among these people. Most lawyers assume that French is no longer a relevant language for global business, but at least in the leading circles of the ICC it seems to be important to command fluency in this language. The ability to command different languages may be considered to be part of a cosmopolitan culture of international arbitrators which may be compared to the common culture of international managers that creates a certain sense of unity independently of the existing networks which will be discussed in the next part. Flexibility, adaptability and open-mindedness have been part of their education and it now becomes an essential part of their work. Their experience in the international context gives them a specific aura of respect. Even if the arbitrator from the firm cannot compete with the legal expertise of Spanish lawyers with respect to Spanish law, he or she is always considered to be the head of the team in the German as well as Spanish offices, and he or she usually leads the deliberation process among the different lawyers involved in a project. Finally, it is possible to observe strong links to universities. Most arbitrators are lawyers, but most of them have a PhD (which indicates that many of them are outstanding scholars), they are often linked to universities as honorary professors and have published books in the area of international law or arbitration. In fact, most of the literature which is used in law firms in arbitration procedures has been written by practitioners, not by full-time university professors. The fact that many arbitrators work as honorary professors is also an indication of a certain link to the state, because a large part of their reputation is derived from this work. In addition, they are linked to different international associations such as bars and chambers of commerce.

Networks

Personal Networks as the Basis for a More Cooperative Process of Conflict Resolution

Another central reason for the success of arbitration is attributed to the fact that key players seem to share very friendly contacts, leading to a reduction of conflict in the atmosphere between key players in comparison with state court procedures (Eger, 1995; Risse, 1999) and to a more cooperative form of conflict resolution. In the ideal case, this type of friendly conflict resolution makes it possible to re-establish the harmony between the parties, which could make a continuation of the cooperation process possible (Frick, 2001). A central reason for this is the still-existing networks not only between arbitrators, but also between arbitrators and counsel, which are still of crucial importance for the arbitration system in spite of its increasing institutionalisation. Due to the mixing of roles, individuals belonging to the network are also found in the role of lawyers, co-arbitrators or chairs (Dezalay and Garth, 1995). Despite conflicts with regard to the conduct of arbitration, all participants are still members of a community (Dezalay and Garth, 1995). This means that the key players have very tight relationships and, as Dezalay and Garth suspect, they develop a certain connivance in the role held by the adversary. Due to the fact that members often nominate each other, it is quite difficult for external professionals to enter this network structure. Dezalay and Garth describe this phenomenon as *mafia-like structures* (Dezalay and Garth, 1996).

Different Types of Network in International Commercial Arbitration

Dezalay and Garth have described the existence of tight networks among different participants in international commercial arbitration. A closer look reveals the existence of sub-networks inside and outside of the ICC networks and the existing links between different types of networks. First of all, it is possible to observe the creation of sub-networks in specific areas of trade, such as German-Spanish business. The German-Spanish legal market is dominated by a few mid-sized firms that have a high reputation and often share the same history. Most bilateral law firms are well known because of the high reputations of their pioneers. These 'grand old men' have known each other for a long time, often have personal relationships and are members of different organisations with a specific focus on German-Spanish commerce (eg the German-Spanish Chamber of Commerce and German-Spanish Lawyer Association). These firms cooperate frequently at different levels (litigation, negotiation, arbitration) and meet in trial or arbitration procedures as party counsel. It is obvious that only very few arbitrators fulfil the specific prerequisites for participating in a German-Spanish arbitration procedure—for example, high reputation, legal competence in both jurisdictions, experience with commercial disputes, linguistic competences—which means that the sub-networks are much smaller, but have a high social density. This shows that there are tight links between the ICC Network and other networks that play a crucial role.

The possibility for the parties to select an arbitrator grants them an indirect access to the arbitrator networks: the parties will usually select an arbitrator in whom they have confidence. This arbitrator, in turn, is connected to the other professionals through the arbitration network. This is exemplified by case study 12. In this case, arbitrator A (Spanish) is selected by the claimant; arbitrator B (German) was selected as arbitrator by the respondent. Both arbitrators have known each other for a long time as lawyers in German-Spanish commerce and as members of the ICC network. The relationship between both arbitrators creates an indirect relationship between the parties. Arbitrator C, the chairman, is a French arbitrator who does not share close links between A and B, but who is still linked to both of them through the ICC. At least B and C have cooperated before as arbitrators on the same tribunal.

A similar situation occurs in case study 38: Arbitrators are arbitrator A (Spanish), arbitrator B (German), and arbitrator C (Spanish). Arbitrator A and B have known each other for a long time. Party counsel for the

German company is a lawyer from one of the well-known German-Spanish firms, who has a long standing personal relation with arbitrator B.

Thus, arbitration is strongly characterised by its network structure, which consists of the general network and different sub-networks, for example, for German-Spanish business, where the same people seem to be nominated with a high frequency. It is obvious that the pioneers of German-Spanish business exercise a strong influence on ICC arbitration in this area. In addition, the networks of large and smaller firms are obviously not completely independent, but highly linked, which leads to the conclusion that all law firms and other professional service firms provide a common support structure for international business that should be analysed as a whole.

The Quality Assurance System of the ICC

The trend towards routinisation is also visible in the growing importance of the ICC's control system. The court attaches particular importance to the rapid resolution of arbitrations conducted under its rules and the maintainance of the high-quality level of ICC awards. In addition, it creates different incentives for the arbitrators to perform in the most diligent manner. The analysis of awards supports the thesis that arbitrators usually invest more time in a case than state judges and that they try to perform in the most diligent manner. The enormous investment in legal research has already been described above. Another outstanding characteristic of the arbitration procedure seems to be the fact that arbitrators attach much greater importance to the establishment of the facts of the case than state courts do. In contrast to state courts, arbitrators are obliged to establish the facts of the case in close cooperation with the parties. Article 20 of the ICC Rules states:

> The arbitral Tribunal shall proceed within as short a time as possible to establish the facts of the case by all appropriate means.

Arbitrators spend enormous amounts of time in the investigation of the facts, analyse all existing documents, examine witnesses from different countries and carry out judicial inspections if necessary. The ICC's 'quality assurance system' is a mix of formal and informal elements which can be compared to similar systems in consultant firms and other professional service firms that constantly control and evaluate the performance of their collaborators. The different elements are incentives, sanctions and control.

The incentive structure consists of reputational and financial aspects. First of all, the fact that a lawyer is an arbitrator at the ICC contributes to his or her reputation. Nowadays, most large and mid-sized firms emphasise their experience in international arbitration on their websites. Obviously, in many cases this contradicts the reality of the practice of most smaller firms. However, lawyers who practice international arbitration are frequently usually well known and do not need to advertise this. Owing to the fact that ICC arbitrators in general have the reputation of being among the best in their practice, participation in these circles almost automatically leads to an increase of reputation. The reputation of an arbitrator is also the decisive factor in his or her nomination in future arbitration proceedings. Of course, his or her reputation depends strongly on his or her performance in prior arbitration procedures.

Another central aspect relates to, of course, the high fees paid to the arbitrators. In one of the analysed files, the amount at stake was US $7,000,000 (which is an average amount in ICC procedures). The ICC Court settled the total costs at US $188,000, which was distributed as follows: administration fees—$28,000; Chairman—$64,000; and both co-arbitrators received an amount of $48,000 each. In case 17, the court settled the costs at US $535,000, which was distributed as follows: administrative expenses— $75,800; fees for the Chairman—$171,000; and fees for the co-arbitrators—$128,460 each. This shows that an arbitrator can earn more money in a single arbitration procedure than a state judge in Germany for the entire year (in the case of study 17, it is even three times as much). The quality of arbitration awards is usually very superior to that of state courts' decisions. Reasons for this include the ICC Rules, which impose the duty to establish the facts of the case on the arbitrator, the control system of the ICC, the fact that arbitrators spend much more time on the analysis of the case, the support of assistants and the high fees, which provide an important incentive to perform with the highest possible diligence within very strict time limits.

The court attaches particular importance to the rapid resolution of arbitrations conducted under its rules and the maintainance of the high quality level of ICC awards. Although the court may grant extensions of time, avoidable delay in the completion of the terms of reference may be taken into account by the court in fixing the arbitrator's fees. In addition, all arbitrators are advised at the beginning of an arbitration procedure that they may be replaced when the court decides they are prevented *de jure* or de facto from fulfilling their functions, or that they are not fulfilling their functions in accordance with the rules or within the prescribed time limits. This shows that arbitrators, in contrast to judges in national courts, are paid according to their performance, which gives them a peculiar incentive to perform in the best possible and effective way.

In addition, the tribunal has to submit the award to the ICC for final scrutiny (article 27 of the ICC Rules). The purpose of scrutiny is to identify possible defects of form and substance in order to produce an award with the highest possible quality that the parties will accept, and which is capable of enforcement (Derains, 2005: 313). Indications of the court with regard to the substance are often related to the argumentation of the tribunal, which may be confusing, insufficiently reasoned or contrary to provisions of the applicable law (Derains, 2005: 313). With regard to the wide discretion arbitrators usually have in complex business disputes, argumentation is often the central part of the award. The tribunal has to integrate modifications of form, but it is free to disregard any suggestions of the court with regard to defects of substance. However, the indications will usually lead to a new deliberation of the arbitrators (Derains, 2005: 313). The court makes full use of its right, as shown in case 12, where the tribunal's first draft was not accepted and had to be revised by the arbitrators. The court criticised different legal and factual aspects.

The tribunal managed to handle the indicated problems under very high time pressures and handed a second version of the award to the court that was finally approved. This case shows that the court does not limit its control to formal aspects (which could be expected), but that it also evaluates the substantive argumentation of the tribunal. The importance of the final scrutiny procedure is shown by the fact that today nearly two-thirds of the awards are returned to the arbitrators with comments on formal or substantive aspects (Derains, 2005: 314).[18] It would probably be an exaggeration to claim that the ICC control system is comparable to an incidental second instance procedure in the national court system, but there is no question that the control system provides another instrument to secure the high quality of awards.

The quality assurance system of the ICC is a combination of reputational and financial incentives, formal and informal (economic and reputational) sanctions and control. Similarities can be observed with regard to other private institutions such as consultant firms that constantly evaluate the performance of their colaborators, or even the German Science Foundation, which frequently evaluates the performance of the university institutes that have received funds from this institution. The quality assurance system may not be the only reason for the consistently high quality of awards and high level of acceptance. However, it can be considered as an important element in modern international arbitration. It shows that more emphasis must be attributed to the analysis of the specific formal and informal structures of international arbitration.

[18] In 2004, 345 awards where approved by the court; in 252 the court has asked for modifications (Derains, 2005: 314).

Acceptance of Awards

Most actors seem to accept ICC awards without further need of execution proceedings. In fact, the senior partner at the firm who works as an arbitrator cannot remember a single case where an award was not accepted.

The mere possibility of enforcement of awards before national courts is not sufficient to explain the high level of acceptance of ICC awards. However, it would be a mistake to neglect this factor. As shown above, the ICC and the arbitrators themselves attach a particular importance to the enforceability of awards, as demonstrated by the strict application of national mandatory law and the final scrutiny of awards by the court. In fact, the ICC forces compliance because many actors resort to ICC arbitration with the central intention to obtain an arbitral award which is enforceable in any country related to the dispute. This may be one of the exceptional elements of ICC arbitration which distinguishes it from branch arbitration (see case study 23 above).

The quality assurance system of the ICC, which consists of a combination of reputational and financial incentives and formal and informal (economic and reputational) sanctions and control, may be another important factor which contributes to the high level of acceptance. The significance of an award can be significantly improved because the parties are aware of this very efficient quality assurance system.

Reputational factors still seem to be of crucial importance for international commercial arbitration. The ICC is still considered to be trustworthy and respectable because of its long history and senior status (Dezalay and Garth, 1995: 47). The ICC offers an image of neutrality and legitimacy; it has benefited from its close relations with international business and the state (Dezalay and Garth, 1995: 47). The acceptance of the ICC as an outstanding institution in global commerce by most actors was already confirmed by the interviews in other studies (Dezalay and Garth, 1996; Sosa, 2007). Another factor is obviously the high reputation of most arbitrators. In addition, most lawyers who participate in arbitration procedures as arbitrators or counsel are repeat players who wish to be nominated in the future as arbitrators or counsel. This creates a strong incentive to urge the client to comply with arbitration awards.

Another central factor seems to be the high level of participation of the parties in the arbitration procedure, which may be one of the central reasons for the high acceptance rate of awards. A good example for this is the cooperation in the drafting of the terms of reference, which makes the process more transparent and reduces the risks of misunderstandings. The possibility for the parties to select an arbitrator grants them indirect access to this network even if they are unaware of it. The parties will usually select an arbitrator in whom they have confidence. This arbitrator, in turn, is connected to the other professionals through the arbitration network. It can be argued that the contract itself creates a link between different support structures necessary to realise a complex transaction (for example, the business relation between the parties, the contract, the arbitration court and the existing networks between different professionals involved). This makes it easier for the parties to consider the arbitration system to be an integral and not external part of their support structures.

SUMMARY

My findings confirm the assumption that arbitration is the most suitable form of conflict resolution in global commerce in the area of complex transactions involving high amounts of money. On the one hand, it is certainly based on the technical aspects of the arbitration system (flexibility, neutrality, etc) and the high profile arbitrators. On the other hand, the relational factors described are of crucial importance for the functioning of the arbitration system. However, the central result of my study is the confirmation of the predominant position of lawyers, especially MidLFs, in this type of arbitration. The transactions subject to arbitration do not leave the law firms' sphere of influence. Lawyers draft complex contracts which are often the basis of coordination. They advise their clients on all matters concerning the arbitration procedure and participate in the arbitration procedure as representatives of the parties or as arbitrators (Calliess *et al*, 2007). States are still visible in this context, but are no longer the central figure; their position is reduced to a 'position equivalent to more mundane actors' (Flood, 2005). Most arbitrators resort to civil law from different nation states, thus indicating the prevailing importance of national legal systems in private arbitration. However, the parties can select the applicable law or establish complex contracts that do not leave any room for resorting to the applicable state law, which reduces this influence significantly. Although national law is selected in most of the cases, complex contracts do not leave much room for resorting to national law. On the other hand, the examples also show that non-mandatory national law is used when necessary. In addition, arbitrators strictly adhere to mandatory national and international law. Many awards are exclusively based on the terms of the contract and general terms (which are not autonomous from national legal systems). The common argument against the autonomy of the arbitration system has always been that the possibility of court enforcement is a necessary prerequisite for the acceptance of awards, even if they rarely have to be enforced. It is quite doubtful that this assumption holds true. It is very likely that the reputation of the ICC and the authority of arbitrators, together with the high level of participation of the parties, provide a very high incentive for acceptance. This is also supported by a statement of one of the lawyers, who argued that awards from other arbitral institutions have to be enforced much more frequently than ICC awards. However, the mere fact that the nation states have accepted arbitration as an alternative form of conflict resolution may have contributed to its high reputation. Finally, state actors such as professors or high court judges endow international arbitration with the necessary credibility. Nevertheless, it is obvious that the resolution of conflicts depends crucially on the key players who are mainly lawyers. The ICC as an outstanding institution of international commerce provides the necessary credibility, but the international lawyers with their personal characteristics, experience, reputation and personal relations to other key players, constitute the lifeblood of this system.

REFERENCES

Abel, R (1994) 'Transnational Law Practice' 44 *Case Western Reserve Law Review* 737.

Berger, K (1997) 'The Lex Mercatoria Doctrine and the Unidroit Principles of International Commercial Contracts' 28 *Law and Policy in International Business* 923.

Berger, K, Dubberstein, H, Lehmann, S and Petzold, V (2001) 'The CENTRAL Enquiry on the Use of Transnational Law in International Contract Law and Arbitration—Background, Procedure and Selected Results' in P Klaus, *The Practice of Transnational Law* (The Hague, Kluwer).

Berman, H and Kaufman, C (1978) 'The Law of International Commercial Transactions (Lex Mercatoria)' 19 *Harvard International Law Journal* 221.

Calliess, GP (2006) *Grenzüberschreitende Verbraucherverträge* (Tübingen, Mohr Siebeck).

Calliess, GP, Dietz, T, Konradi, W, Nieswandt, H and Sosa, F (2007) 'Transformations of Commercial Law: New Forms of Legal Certainty for Globalized Exchange Processes?' in A Hurrelmann, S Leibfried, S Martens and P Mayer (eds), *Transforming the Golden-Age Nation State* (Houndmills, Palgrave Macmillan).

Daly, M (1997) 'The Cultural, Ethical, and Legal Challenges in Lawyering for a Global Organization: The Role of the General Counsel' 46 *Emory Law Journal* 1057.

DeLy, F (2001) 'Lex Mercatoria (New Law Merchant): Globalization and International Self-Regulation' in RP Appelbaum, LF Felstiner and V Gessner (eds), *Rules and Networks* (Oxford, Hart).

Derains, Y (1972) 'L'application cumulative par l'árbitre des systèmes de conflit des lois interessés au litigé' *Review de l' Arbitrage* 99.

—— (1982) 'Arbitrage et droit de la concurrence' 14 *Revue Suisse du Droit International de la Concurrence* 39.
—— (1987) 'Public Policy and the Law Applicable to the Dispute in International Arbitration' 3 *ICCA Congress Series* 227.
—— (2001) 'Transnational Law in ICC Arbitration' in KP Berger, *The Practice of Transnational Law* (The Hague, London, New York, Kluwer).
—— (2005) *A Guide to the New ICC Rules of Arbitration* (The Hague, London, New York, Kluwer).
Dezalay, Y (1990) 'The Big Bang and the Law: The Internationalization and Restructuration of the Legal Field' 7 *Theory, Culture & Society* 279.
Dezalay, Y and Garth, B (1995) 'Merchants of Law as Moral Entrepreneurs: Constructing International Justice from the Competition for Transnational Business Disputes' 29 *Law & Society Review* 27.
—— (1996) *Dealing in Virtue, International Commercial Arbitration and the Construction of a Transnational Order* (Chicago, University of Chicago Press).
Dwyer, R, Schurr, P and Oh, S (1987) 'Developing Buyer-Seller Relationships' 51 *Journal of Law, and Marketing* 11.
Eger, T (1995) *Eine ökonomische Analyse von Langzeitverträgen* (Marburg, Metropolis).
Flood, J (1991) 'Doing Business: The Management of Uncertainty in Lawyer's Work' 25 *Law & Society Review* 41.
—— (1996) 'Megalawyering in the Global Order: The Cultural, Social and Economic Transformation of Global Legal Practice' 3 *International Journal of the Legal Profession* 169.
—— (2001) 'Capital Markets: Those Who Can and Cannot Do the Purest Global Law Markets' in R Appelbaum, W Felstiner and V Gessner (eds), *Rules and Networks* (Oxford, Hart).
—— (2004) 'International Law Firms: Guardians of Globalization' (unpublished manuscript).
—— (2005) 'Rating, Dating, and the Informal Regulation and the Formal Ordering of Financial Transactions: Securitizations and Credit Rating Agencies' in M Likosky, *Privatising Development: Transnational Law, Infrastructure and Human Rights* (Leiden, Boston).
—— (2007) 'Lawyers as Sanctifiers, The Role of Elite Law Firms in International Business Transactions' 14 *Indiana Journal of Global Legal Studies* 35.
Flood, J and Sosa, F (2008) 'Lawyers, Law Firms, and the Stabilization of Transnational Business' 28 *Northwestern Journal of International Law & Business* 489.
Frick, J (2001) *Arbitration and Complex International Contracts* (The Hague, New York, Kluwer).

Friedman, L (1989) 'Lawyers in Cross-Cultural Perspective' in R Abel and P Lewis, *Lawyers in Society*, Vol 3, *Comparative Theories* (Stanford, Stanford University Press).

Gaillard, E (1985) 'L'Interdiction de se contredire au detriment d'autrui comme principe général du droit du commerce international' *Review de l' Arbitrage* 241.

Galanter, M (1983) 'Mega-Law and Mega-Lawyering in the Contemporary United States' in R Dingwall and P Lewis, *The Sociology of the Professions: Lawyers, Doctors and Others* (London, Macmillan).

Gessner, V (1996) 'International cases in German First Instance Courts' in V Gessner (ed), *Foreign Courts—Civil Litigation in Foreign Legal Cultures* (Aldershot, Dartmouth).

Gessner, V, Appelbaum, RP and Felstiner, LF (2001) 'Introduction: The Legal Culture of Global Business Transactions' in RP Appelbaum, LF Felstiner and V Gessner (eds), *Rules and Networks* (Oxford, Hart).

Goldhaber, M (2005) 'Arbitration Scorecard' <http://www.americanlawyer.com/focuseurope/scorecard0605.html> accessed 18 June 2008.

Gundlach, GT and Murphy, PE (1993) 'Ethical and Legal Foundations of Relational Marketing Exchanges' 57 *Journal of Marketing* 35.

Günther, K and Hoffer, H (2000) 'Mediation im Zivilrecht, insbesondere im Wirtschaftsrecht' in Henseller and Koch, *Mediation in der Anwaltspraxis* (Bonn, Deutscher Anwaltsverlag).

Hollingsworth, JR and Boyer, R (1997) *Contemporary Capitalism: The Embeddedness of Institutions* (Cambridge, Cambridge University Press).

ICC, 'ICC Statistical Report 1997' (1998) *International Court of Arbitration—Bulletin.*

—— 'ICC Statistical Report 1999' (2000) *International Court of Arbitration—Bulletin.*

—— 'ICC Statistical Report 2001' (2002) 13 *International Court of Arbitration—Bulletin.*

—— 'ICC Statistical Report 2003' (2004) 15 *International Court of Arbitration—Bulletin.*

Kenworthy, L, Macaulay, S and Rogers, J (1996) 'The More Things Change. Business Litigation and Governance in the American Automobile Industry' 21 *Law and Social Inquiry* 631.

Kiedaisch, I (1997) *Internationale Kunden-Lieferanten-Beziehungen* (Wiesbaden, Gabler).

Konradi, W (2009) 'The role of *lex mercatoria* in supporting globalised transactions: An empirical insight into the governance structure of the timber industry' in V Gessner (ed), *Contractual Certainty in International Trade* (Oxford, Hart).

Konradi, Wand Fix-Fierro, H (2005) 'Lex Mercatoria in the Mirror of Empirical Research' *Sociologia del Diritto* 205–27.

Lalive, P (1976) 'Les Regles de Conflit de Lois Appliquees au Fond du Litige par l'Arbitre International Siegeant en Suisse' *Revue de l'Arbitrage* 155.

Lazareff, S (1996) 'Mandatory Extraterritorial Application of National Law Rules' 7 *ICCA Congress Series* 538.

Lew, J, Mistelis, L and Kröll, S (2003) *Comparative International Commercial Arbitration* (The Hague, London, New York, Kluwer).

Luhmann, N (1983) *Rechtssoziologie* (2nd edn, Reinbeck, Opladen).

Macaulay, S (1963) 'Non-Contractual Relations in Business: A Preliminary Study' 55 *American Sociological Review* 86.

—— (1985) 'Symposium: Law, Private Governance and Continuing Relationships, an Empirical View of Contract' 5 *Wisconsin Law Review* 465.

—— (1991) 'Long-Term Continuing Relations: The American Experience Regulating Dealerships and Franchises' in C Joerges, *Franchising and the Law, Theoretical and Comparative Approaches in Europe and the U.S.* (Baden-Baden, Nomos).

Macneil, IR (1971) *Contracts: Exchange Transactions and Relationships* (Mineola, Foundation Press).

—— (1974) 'The Many Futures of Contract' 47 *Southern California Law Review* 691.

—— (1975) 'A Primer of Contract Planning' 48 *Southern California Law Review* 627.

—— (1981) 'Economic Analysis of Contractual Relations: Its Shortfalls and the Need for a "Rich Classificatory Apparatus"' 75 *Northwestern University Law Review* 1017.

McBarnet, D (1987) 'The construction of legal devices: Legal entrepreneurs and private law making', abstract presented at the Law and Society Association Conference, Washington (June 1987).

—— (1994) 'Legal creativity: law, capital and legal avoidance' in M Cain and C Harrington, *Lawyers in a Postmodern World* (New York, New York University Press).

Morgan, G and Quack, S (2005) 'Institutional Legacies and Firm Dynamics: The Growth and Internationalization of UK and German Law Firms' 26 *Organization Studies* 1765.

Morgan, R and Hunt, S (1994) 'The Commitment-Trust Theory of Relationship Marketing' 58 *Journal of Marketing* 20.

Nassar, N (1995) *Sanctity of Contracts Revisited: A Study in the Theory and Practice of Long-Term International Commercial Transactions* (Dordrecht, Martinus Nijhof Publishers).

Powell, M (1993) 'Professional Innovation: Corporate Lawyers and Private Lawmaking' 18 *Journal of Law and Social Inquiry* 423.

Risse, J (1999) 'Die Rolle des Rechts in der Wirtschaftsmediation' *Betriebsberater* 1999' Annex 9.1.

Schmidt, K (1999) *Handelsrecht* (Köln, Carl Heymanns Verlag KG).
Shapiro, M (1993) 'The Globalization of Law' 37 *Global Legal Studies Journal* 37.
Silver, C (2000) 'Globalization and the U.S. Market in Legal Services—Shifting Identities' 31 *Law & Policy in International Business* 1093.
Sosa, F (2007) *Vertrag und Geschäftsbeziehung im grenzüberschreitenden Wirtschaftsverkehr* (Baden-Baden, Nomos).
Teubner, G (ed) (1997) *Global Law without a State* (Aldershot, Dartmouth).
Trubek D, Dezalay, Y, Buchanan, R and Davis, J (1994) 'Global Restructuring and the Law: Studies of the Internationalization of Legal Fields and the Creation of Transnational Arenas' 44 *Case Western Reserve Law Review* 407.
Weber, M (1980) *Wirtschaft und Gesellschaft* (5th. edn, Tübingen, Mohr Siebeck).
Williamson, O (1975) *Markets and Hierarchies: Analysis and Antitrust Implications* (New York, The Free Press).
—— (1979) 'Transaction-Cost Economies: The Governance of Contractual Relations' 22 *Journal of Law and Economics* 233.
—— (1981) 'The Economics of Organization: The Transaction-Cost Approach' 87 *American Journal of Sociology* 548.
—— (1985) *The Economic Institutions of Capitalism: Firms, Markets, Relational Contracting* (New York, The Free Press).

APPENDIX

The following table, which is based on Galanter, 1983, displays differences between mega, mid-sized and small law firms:

	Small LF	**MidLF**	**MLF**
Lawyers in one office	1–5	15–20	50–100
Lawyers nationwide	–	100	1,000
Lawyers worldwide	–	–	2,000
Site of operation	Local	Local, national, sometimes international	Local, national, international
Clients	Private citizens	Small and medium-sized business	Large business

Range of services	Narrow	Wider	Full service
Specialisation of lawyers	Low	Higher	High
Creative lawyering	Ordinary lawyering	Ordinary and creative lawyering	Creative lawyering

6

Structuring Transactions: The Case of Real Estate Finance

JOHN FLOOD AND ELENI SKORDAKI

COMPLEX ECONOMIC TRANSACTIONS, especially those engaging multiple jurisdictions, are creating considerable problems in regulation and management that are taxing states' resources. The result is that alternative support structures are generated to resolve these difficulties and lacunae (Gessner, 2009a, this volume). While states provide some legislative frameworks, the vast majority of the support structures are brought into existence by other sources. Among them are candidates such as *lex mercatoria* (Konradi, 2009, this volume), real-time contract evaluation (Dietz and Nieswandt, 2009, this volume) and large and medium-sized law firms (Flood and Sosa, 2008).

The liquidity crisis originally prompted by the 2007 sub-prime mortgage debacle in the United States is an exemplar of the type of complexity referred to here that has caused chaos in international financial markets. Here, although the individual steps in the creation of the sub-prime market and its extension and amplification through the collateralised debt obligation market were carried out legitimately, the cumulative effect of the steps combined with the lack of necessary regulatory oversight by the authorities produced a series of effects that rippled out worldwide and that most states were unable to manage competently or foresee, or even begin to calculate how to prevent their future re-occurrence.[1] Indeed, the regulatory conundrum was such that whichever way governments acted, they would be accused of participating in the creation of moral hazards by rescuing institutions or failing to insure weak, unprotected investors from the seamy side of market exploitation.

[1] By the first quarter of 2008, the 'credit crunch' had caused one major British mortgage bank to threaten bankruptcy and ultimately be nationalised by the government, and at least two German banks to be rescued by state authorities to avoid insolvency. In both cases, their exposure to sub-prime mortgage hazards through their dealings in asset-backed paper was the genesis of their problems.

Although a number of institutions participated in the creation of the market (for example, investment banks, mortgage banks, credit rating agencies, hedge funds and mono line insurers), crucial to the piecing together of the market was the documentation produced by the law firms that enabled the participants to engage in this uncertain venture. Due to the inherent complexity of these transactions, they cannot be conceived without the assemblage of documents that accompany them (Flood, 2007). They would be impossible to do 'on a handshake'. The role of lawyers and law firms in structuring these types of transaction is vital and necessary to their accomplishment.

In this chapter, we examine how a particular kind of transaction is structured to enable actors from a variety of countries and jurisdictions to co-manage and create a communal perspective that incorporates complexity, yet produces certainty and calculability. It also enables us to answer one question to which the solution remains elusive: what do lawyers do (Abel and Lewis, 1989)? Although academics have pursued this question (for example, Gilson, 1984; Felstiner, 2001; Flood, 1991; Sosa, 2009, this volume; Flood and Sosa, 2008), practitioners rarely write on the topic (but see, for example, Freund, 1975; and Neate, 1987). It has been suggested that lawyers manage uncertainty in their roles as practitioners, providing solutions that enable business to capitalise on its ventures. The problem is exacerbated in the context of cross-border business where the parties are attempting to reach agreement but must overcome the insecurity inherent in the fallibility of their knowledge of the other's system (Gessner, 2009b, this volume). In this chapter, we draw on Luhmann's ideas of the stabilisation of expectations (1985).

Luhmann defines the function of law as the stabilisation of normative expectations through regulation of its temporal, social and material generalisation. The primary means here for the stabilisation of expectations or risk reduction is through the construction of typified solutions which correspond to legal instruments, in that they contain the full panoply of guarantees, warranties, default clauses, arbitration clauses, and so on (cf Gilson, 1984). In doing this, lawyers create a series of private legal systems that effectively have the force of the state legal system. In part, they have this effect because they are constructed within the shadow of the law (since they have to refer to national legal systems), and also because they are produced by highly qualified experts whose imprimatur is widely accepted. The authority and legitimacy of their licence is conferred in two ways: one is by virtue of their individual expertise; and the other is through the status of their law firm. These are interrelated in that each derives to an extent from the other. Expertise comes from training and experience, which have to be acquired in the right place and under the right people. Thus, obtaining the benefits of another's human capital can only be maximised in the appropriate law firms that contain the leading experts. Moreover, the law firm then confers legitimacy on its members and simultaneously has its authority augmented by the presence of experts. This double legitimation process enables the movement of experts from firm to firm so that alternative sites of expertise can be established and nurtured. While it has an enabling effect, it can also be destructive in that if an expert or group of experts leave one firm for another, although the new firm acquires heightened status, the previous firm can be left bereft of appropriate expertise and so suffer a loss of authority in that field. The balance between lawyer and firm is a delicate one.

In this chapter, we illustrate some of these processes in the case of real estate finance lawyers and their structuring of transactions. The crucial term is 'structure', because the way in which a transaction is put together determines its outcome. It works within the confines of law, it takes account of law; but, ultimately, structure is guided by the requirements of the transaction, which for business lawyers means what the participants desire from the deal.

Real estate finance is an area which captures many aspects of traditional legal thinking. It is concerned with real immoveable property (for example, title, covenants and easements), security, mortgages, financing and tax. The area is one in which little global harmonisation has occurred. Indeed, even inside the European Union, local rules on property rights vary enormously from Member State to Member State. In countries external to the EU, rules involving property ownership can be even more obscure (EBRD, 1995: 101–17).[2] Yet varieties of real estate finance are creating enormous value. Furthermore, real estate finance has ballooned as the complex derivatives markets have soared. Therefore, much of what occurs in real estate finance is in the nature of off-balance sheet transactions and deals with risk planning versus realisable expectations. It is the intersection of real estate and capital markets that is driving innovation in this field.

Real estate finance is concerned with ways of enabling investment in commercial property. It brings together a number of specialisms, banking, real estate, securitisation, tax and derivatives. Although the core is property, the manner in which it is financed and structured is the concern of banking and corporate lawyers. They have created new ways of importing techniques from their areas into new fields. Because property has enduring value, it provides for the creation of novel means of arranging its holding and financing.

Secured lending started with 'vanilla-flavoured' lending, ie lending backed by security over specific assets. Over time, secured lending has become increasingly complex, with the introduction of concepts such as

[2] For example, in Hungary, land ownership is permitted, although foreigners may own land only through local companies; whereas in Georgia, foreigners or foreign-owned local companies may not own land (EBRD, 1995: 110–12).

the floating charge, where the creditor is not restricted to specific existing assets. With the advent of securitisation and derivatives, markets have developed to exploit more marginal risks and earn potentially greater rewards. For example, new types of investment include, as Davies (2006: 43) describes:

> Commercial real estate collateralised debt obligations, or CRE CDOs, mostly pool together the riskier slices of commercial mortgages with the more junior bits of commercial mortgage backed securities, which by themselves repackage pools of property debt.[3]

It is also possible to incorporate other kinds of debt into these complex packages so that their apparent complexity is hedged over a number of elements. Yet, as Davies argues:

> ... commercial property can be a volatile asset and many of the instruments set to be included in CDOs have not been tested in a downturn.[4]

Most transactions handled by real estate finance lawyers are carried out in conjunction with a series of repeat players, including banks and clients, who may be real estate investment trusts or funds, or companies. Their key attribute is their continuous interplay. Their embedded ties comprise both social contacts and network positions which aid the construction of trust that tends to override arm's length ties (Uzzi *et al*, 2007). The heavy repeat nature of this market creates high barriers to entry for many lawyers. While they may have substantial reputations in banking or corporate law, unless they have been part of a law firm that has traditionally done real estate finance or been mentored by a lawyer so engaged, it is very difficult to break into the market as banks and clients are risk averse. The market for real estate finance, therefore, is constrained to a relatively small number of law firms and lawyers. Identifying them is relatively straightforward, as the legal directories (for example, *Legal 500* and *Chambers UK*) now rank real estate finance lawyers separately from banking and property lawyers. Moreover, both directories rate lawyers by canvassing opinions in the profession and among clients. *Chambers*, for example, ranks lawyers on a scale of one to six (one being the highest) and states:

> The qualities on which rankings are assessed include technical legal ability, professional conduct, client service, commercial awareness/astuteness, diligence, commitment and other qualities most valued by the client.[5]

[3] See the implications of this statement in the discussion of the sub-prime crisis above and in Gessner (2009a, this volume).

[4] Despite the guarded optimism of these commentators, the viability of CDOs and other securitised structures have been tested and found wanting in a downturn.

[5] <http://www.chamberssecure.com/global/research-ranking.aspx> accessed 18 June 2008.

The initiation of a transaction is usually the beginning of a series of actions. Once a deal is completed, it commits itself to future restructurings when the same—but not always—parties collaborate on extending the deal and leveraging it further.[6] In addition, it will continue to be restructured even if the property is sold to others. Efficient minimising of tax liabilities, changes in interest rates by central banks and intensification of leveraging, among other things, drive restructuring.

For the purpose of this chapter, we focus on real estate financing in Europe. The market is driven both by the banks who lend and the investors who are seeking fresh opportunities for their money. The investors seem to pull along the debt providers. Since the majority of both are situated in London, there is an enormous advantage given to UK lawyers as the providers of expertise. Once lenders and investors step outside their home markets, their risk expectations soar. The need for the lawyer's guiding hand is correspondingly increased. What is clear to all of the actors is the lack of uniformity in the European real estate market. It can broadly be divided into 'mature' and 'secondary' markets with, for example, Paris, Madrid and Barcelona in the former category and cities in Croatia, Romania, Greece, Slovenia and Bulgaria in the latter. Different types of property investment are favoured in different markets. The mature market attracts investors in shopping centres, retail parks, hotels and offices, whereas in the secondary market, industrial properties and also some residential properties are selected in preference to others.

Despite the interest in the European market, there is little harmonisation to aid cross-border acquisitions, nor is there much initiative towards convergence. Certain aspects of property transactions cause major problems for investors when transplanted outside of the UK. Local property laws, as mentioned above, and tax laws have resolutely escaped all moves to harmonisation. For example, Swiss laws on leases cause considerable angst to investors, as they are exceedingly specific in their requirements when compared to English law. In addition, most debt providers insist on as full a security package as they would obtain under English law. However, both banks and investors have realised that attempting to reproduce an entire English property transaction when venturing beyond the borders of Britain is a fruitless task because local rules render it impossible. This puts the real estate finance lawyer in a key position: it is up to the lawyer to create a structure that will satisfy not merely the immediate needs of investors and funders, but accommodate local jurisdictional needs without compromising the essential aspects of the transaction.

[6] See Regan (2004) for a dramatic version of what happens to a company when its finances are continuously restructured, thus endangering its existence.

It is at this juncture that the role of structure comes to the foreground. Although there are significant differences between jurisdictions and systems, English common law enables an assembly of structures that are transportable across borders. The structure can be compared to a prefabricated building delivered to the relevant site which is then adjusted in order to stand securely. In some instances, only minor adjustments are needed, but in other cases, where the peculiarities of local property and tax laws show the structure to be less than stable and likely to collapse unless serious modifications are made, the tweaking stage is most critical. For example, the regulatory regime for Portuguese closed-end property funds delivers an extremely tax-efficient means of property ownership, but also makes it nigh impossible to grant security over such property. The lawyers here had to act as mediators between conflicting demands. Although they acted for the London branch of an international bank, they had to explain the requirements of an English-based debt structure to the fund managers of a Portuguese closed-end property fund who had to accept that 'London' did business in a particular way, while convincing the bank that the deal could not be structured as if it were an English property transaction.

How, then, does structuring function? Property is peculiar in that most people think in terms of 'location' as the prime attribute of the transaction. For lawyers, however, structure is paramount. Two main types of structure come into play:

a) tax-led structures:
   i) these entail tax withholding issues on interest payments to non-resident lenders;
   ii) there are issues involving withholding tax in respect of dividends to an international parent; and
   iii) they involve tax-efficient vehicles and local regulatory restrictions;
b) corporate structures:
   i) the movement of income and gains across groups;
   ii) thin capitalisation (interest re-characterised as dividends); and
   iii) the changing role of the real estate finance lawyer, moving to structuring as opposed to servicing property transactions.

None of these structures would be feasible without the ability of the English common law to create and innovate in ways difficult, if not at times impossible, for civil law.[7] They escape the formalism of the logically rational and reside with the norms of material rationality in accordance with:

[7] One important feature, often neglected in the academic study of law, of the use of common lawyers, and English and American in particular, is their use of the English language, which market participants welcome and encourage. Cf the use of German law in the software contracts discussed by Dietz and Nieswandt (2008, this volume).

> ... ethical imperatives, utilitarian and other expediential rules, and political maxims, all of which diverge from the formalism of the 'external characteristics' variety as well as from that which uses logical abstraction (Weber, 1978: 657).

Although the London lawyer is in charge of the overall drafting of the agreements that integrate the transaction, the local jurisdictional elements are sub-contracted to local lawyers. One problem for London lawyers is ensuring that local lawyers understand what 'London' needs. London lawyers are essentially commercially minded, but this is not always the case with, for example, Portuguese or Italian lawyers. Having a network of law firms that can adopt the London mentality when required is a necessary part of the London lawyer's armoury. Developing such networks is thorny when investors and funders are moving into new markets where sophisticated property financing techniques are completely unknown.[8]

We illustrate the role of these structures in the following examples. Assume, in a simple 'vanilla-flavoured' transaction, company A wants to buy company B by taking a loan from a bank. The key for the bank is to obtain security for its loan by, say, taking a charge of a pool of assets. Some jurisdictions, for example, France and Italy, have legal impediments that prevent banks from doing this. A way around these impediments is to have B create a limited liability partnership or a special purpose vehicle and transfer the assets for value to the orphan company, thereby protecting the assets in case of B's default and enabling the bank to take a charge. See Figure I.

This type of transaction becomes even more complex when more than one or two jurisdictions are involved. Assume company A wants to buy company B in France, company C in Luxembourg and company D in Italy, all with bank funding. Each country has its own rules regarding legal and beneficial ownership and the ability of the bank to obtain security.[9] Thus, the real estate finance lawyer has to structure the deal to give the bank the required security and yet honour each country's particular rules. Problems arise when investors and lenders tackle problems of cross-collateralisation and cross-guarantee. In English law, these create no difficulties in their application. However, in countries such as Belgium, France and Italy, companies can only cross-guarantee and cross-collateralise obligations owed by wholly-owned subsidiaries. If a company wants to cross-collateralise or guarantee the obligations of a sister or parent company in these civil code countries, problems arise unless corporate benefit is shown,

[8] The problem is not necessarily resolved by using the foreign branch of a law firm. Smets' (2006) research on banking lawyers in the London and Frankfurt branches of an English law firm showed frequent misunderstandings and misinterpretations when English and German lawyers worked on the same transaction.

[9] The UK security regime allows various self-help remedies that do not require the intermediation of a court, but in civil code countries this type of self-help is rarely available.

Figure I—The Structure of a Company Purchase

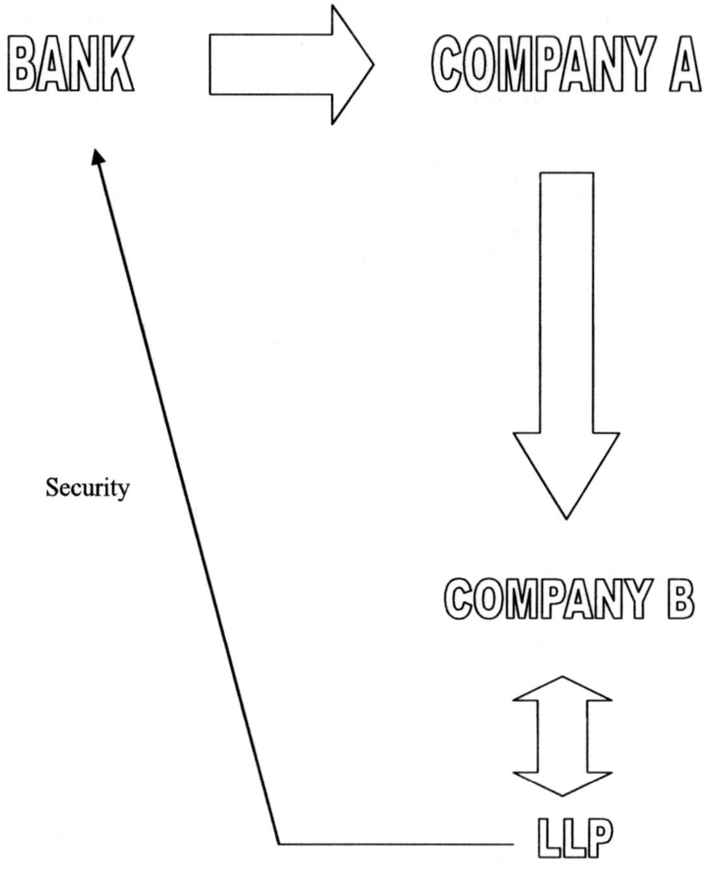

leading in the case of France to criminal penalties against the directors of the company. Typically, in the UK all properties would be in one company, where cross-collateralisation could be accomplished. Figure II illustrates how the transaction might operate under these constraints.

In this transaction, the ideas from the first example are translated into the different jurisdictions. Each individual jurisdiction carries out the procedures in its particular way by creating a series of special purpose vehicles (SPVs) that collectively enable the bank finally to obtain security. By importing the Anglo-American concept of SPVs, the peculiarities of the individual jurisdictions were sidestepped and the ultimate aim of granting security was achieved. Risk and uncertainty were minimised without appearing to compromise the integrity of the individual jurisdictions' competences.

Figure II–The Structure of a Multi-jurisdictional Company Purchase

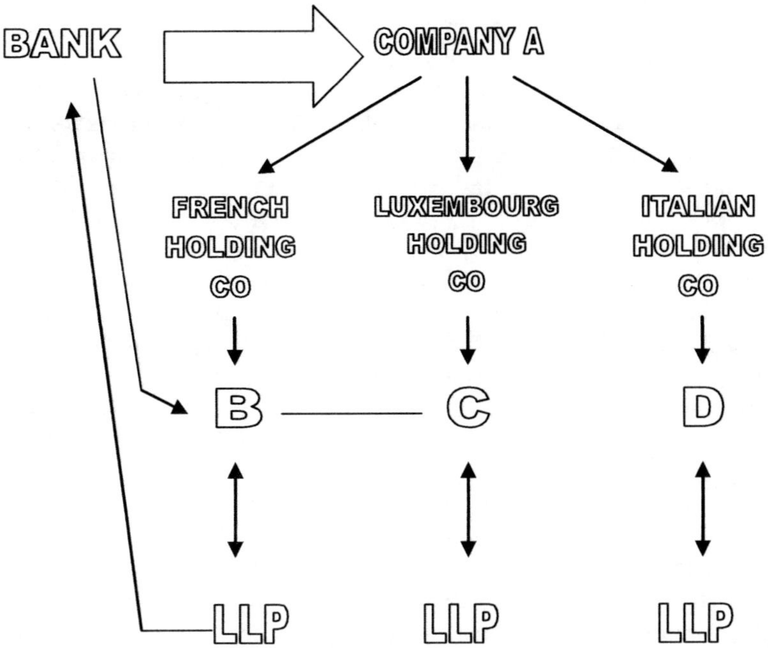

On occasion, real estate finance projects are combined with corporate acquisitions so that the financing bank moves from its 'normal' range of financing into areas where it has less expertise. In this situation, the lawyers have to create structures that satisfy both real estate and corporate issues. In one such transaction, a sports equipment company was bought by its management with the backing of a private equity fund. The majority of the debt was provided by the bank, which also had a recurring relationship with the private equity fund that was providing equity, and was therefore familiar with its own approach to transactions. On this transaction, in addition to the usual requirement of a commercial property valuation, the bank and the private equity investors required a commercial due diligence review of the sports equipment business. Estimates were arrived at for future potential retail and wholesale growth, based on detailed qualitative and quantitative surveys of participants in the company's key areas of sailing, shooting and riding. Both the bank and the investors required a thorough understanding of the value of the sports equipment brand and its potential for growth.

In addition to the usual security over the real estate assets of the company and security over the shares of the group companies, the transaction needed to consider taking security over other classes of assets, including intellectual property rights or rights under commercial agreements, such as agency and distribution agreements, trade mark licences and certified manufacturer agreements. As the business had a specialist technical clothing focus, the terms of agreements entered into by the company relating to the use of other brands (for example, the Gore-Tex brand) were of particular interest, not only to the private equity investors, but also to the bank. For this type of business, it was also important to consider the large number of trademarks held by the company worldwide and any practical issues arising in connection with registering security over these trademarks as a condition precedent to completion.

In more traditional real estate finance transactions, the term 'financial covenants' has come to mean two main types of financial test: 'loan to value' (the ratio of the fair market value of the real property assets to the amount of the loan financing the purchase of such assets) and 'interest cover' (the amount of interest and other finance costs paid by a company on its borrowings against the income generated by the properties that are the subject of such borrowings in the same period). In a transaction such as this—involving real estate, but also other types of assets owned in the course of an operating business—a more complex approach to financial covenants was required. In addition to the usual 'loan to value' test (in relation to the company group's warehouse assets), the financial test of 'EBITDA to loan' (earnings before interest, taxes, depreciation and amortisation) aimed to test the consolidated profits of the company against the aggregate amount of the bank's loan facilities. The requirements of this test reflected the projected growth of EBITDA in the company's business plan.

In addition to this 'acquisition facility' financing the acquisition of the sports equipment company, the bank provided ancillary facilities to assist the operating activities of the company. These included the employment of a 'capex facility' (capital expenditures) to fund approved capital expenditure projects carried out in the company's retail sites. To enable the company and its management to plan for growth, the capex facility was also made available for 'immature' retail sites where return on capital was expected to be below a certain threshold.

Transactions such as these are no longer exceptional in the specialist real estate finance field. The financing of real estate has expanded to include a set of practices that recognises the value of an operating business alongside a pool of real estate assets, but also responds to the need of a business to be allowed to continue its operations with minimal intervention by funders. No lender can take much comfort from the expertise of its borrower's management unless it is prepared to allow the management to manage its business. Examples of operating businesses that have become particularly suitable for this type of financing (due to their ownership of substantial real estate assets integral to the operation of the business) include care and nursing homes, restaurants, petrol stations and private educational institutions.

Some projects are so large that their financing structure becomes a *sui generis*. Canary Wharf in the Docklands of East London is one such project. The Thatcher Government in the 1980s considered ways of regenerating run-down neighbourhoods and increasing the influence of the City of London. In 1987, the Docklands area was created to construct a second City of London. It had few zoning restrictions and also had favourable tax treatments, thus allowing rapid development of the land. By 1991, the main buildings had been erected and let. Within one or two years, the developer Olympia & York was caught up in the worldwide recession and entered administration in the UK and Chapter 11 in the US (Flood and Skordaki, 1997). After considerable restructuring, the original investors were able to buy their way back into Canary Wharf. The purpose of this particular refinancing was to fund the construction of the remainder of the Canary Wharf property. The transaction raised over £1 billion in a series of notes to be redeemed in 2033, some with fixed interest rates and others with variable ones, and including various kinds of swap agreement. Because of the huge tax liabilities that can be incurred in such transactions, the planning of the structure was crucial to minimising these costs while preserving the rights of the interested parties, especially those of the funding banks. Figure III shows the complexity of the structure and how it was created.

The transaction document ran to 135 pages. In order to complete the package, two Magic Circle law firms—one for the issuer, borrower and charging subsidiaries; and one for the managers, trustee and liquidity facility provider—were involved, together with five banks, two real estate valuers and one Big Four firm of accountants. There would be other law firms, not listed in the document, who would have acted for various other involved parties.

The rapid development of real estate finance markets has created a push to innovation, partly in response to new entrants to the market and also to generate new returns from existing assets. One example of the former is the growth in Sharia-compliant transactions.[10] For example, a Middle Eastern investment fund based in London wanted to establish a German real estate fund to allow Arabs to invest in German property. (Again, the use of the English language is important here in the structuring of the transaction.) The key to enabling the setting up of the fund was to adopt the '*ijara wa iqtina*', 'in which a bank buys an item and leases it to the purchaser, who agrees to buy the item at the end of a pre-agreed period. Rental payments

[10] The *Qur'an* warns against the evils of usury and, in particular, *riba*, the charging of interest for loans. Since money has value and entails costs, Islamic finance has developed a number of techniques to avoid interest payments, yet reward banks and other lenders for financing projects. Some of these may involve building the payment of fees or some other means of acknowledging the cost of money. *Sharia* is the law revealed in the *Qur'an*.

Figure III—The Transaction Structure of the Canary Wharf 2001 Financing

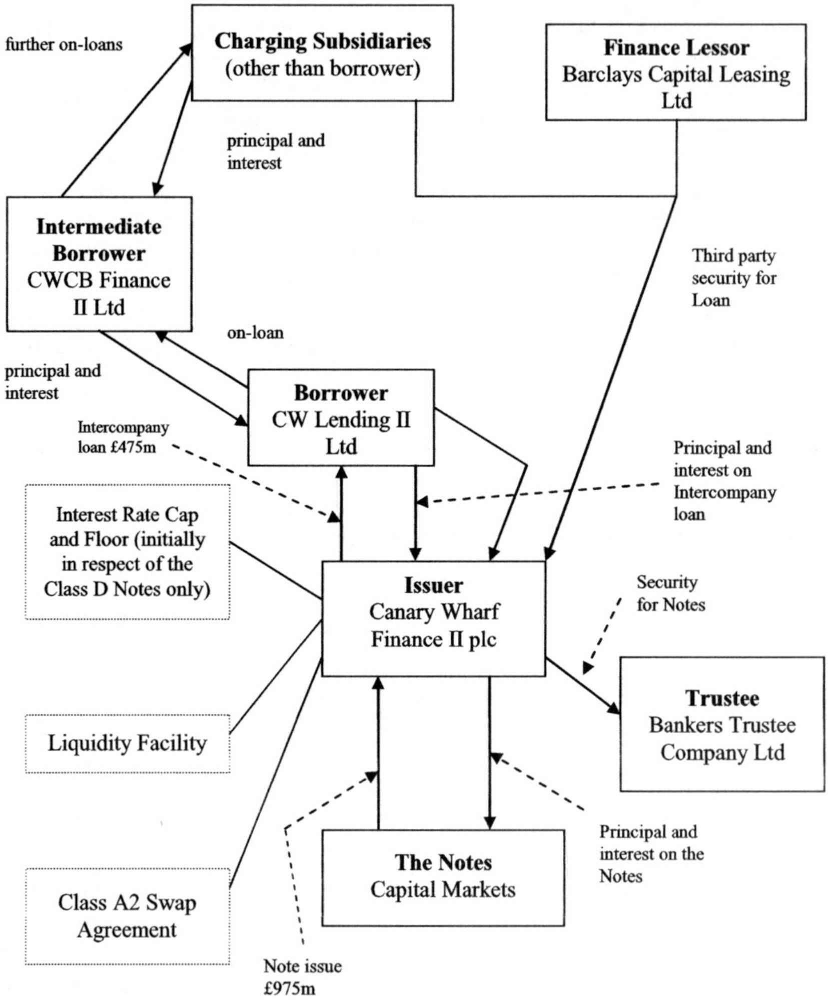

include an amount towards the value of the item, so that the final payment is generally a token amount. Thus, a profit is earned by the lender, but, technically, interest is not collected.[11] The structure of this fund allowed the investors to benefit from Western-style bank financing and leveraging without violating Sharia. The structure crossed legal jurisdictional, cultural and religious boundaries.

[11] <http://www.everything2.com/index.pl?node_id=1771357> accessed 18 June 2008.

When transactions reach these levels of complexity, they become private ordering systems with their own forms of governance. The role played by the credit rating agencies is crucial to their effectiveness (Flood, 2005). As issues involve various kinds of derivative and securitisation, external monitoring is carried out by the agencies, such as Standard & Poors and Moodys. Without their imprimatur of a triple-A rating, a transaction cannot successfully conclude. Moreover, where orphan companies (SPVs) are implicated, the rating agencies oversee their activities during their intended life-spans to ensure compliance with the transaction.

The cross-border aspects of transactions are often a matter of reconciling some jurisdiction-specific issues within a UK-based legal document, thus harmonising differences so that a bank has the confidence to rely on the structure captured in the document. Alternatively, the transaction may be a case of using several different jurisdictions as key attributes of the structure. In this type of transaction, the relationship of the jurisdictions is based on their relative merits to the entire structure. This occurs typically when bank accounts are located in offshore regimes and tax-efficient countries are used to channel funds.

Transactions take their character and shape from the initial driver, which in the case of real estate finance is most often a bank. Banks seek to minimise the risk of the strange and maximise their range of normality. In the examples provided in this chapter, the majority of the banks were UK-based, which meant that their strong preference was for structures to be documented ultimately in some form of English law. Ideally, other jurisdictions would be subordinated to the overall rule of the primary legal system. However, given the contingent nature of these structures, future restructurings could easily provide for different approaches. From that perspective, as solid as these structures appear, they are ultimately noumenal with the appearance of the phenomenal.

It is clear that the analysis and discussion presented strongly support the fact that international legal structures are weak and fragmentary, which follows Gessner's findings on international cases in courts (1996: 155). Moreover, the legal coordination structures available are few and many lawyers and other actors instead rely on relational coordination structures. However, these are unable to provide effective protection under all circumstances and so the risk increases as business crosses borders. The lack of such established structures emphasises the importance of the lawyer as the creator and provider of contingent structures that fill the gaps. Thus, what we observe is lawyers simulating the proximity of the state legal system when they use typified solutions to resolve conflicts. Gilson (1984) augments the argument when he refers to lawyers as transaction cost engineers who manage the process of contracting between the parties: in adjusting, modifying and tweaking structures, lawyers lubricate the flow of the parties' business. What we see are lawyers and law firms implicated in the creation of structures that minimise risk and uncertainty for investors. While the ability to reduce normative uncertainty is restricted because local rules will not permit their being breached or trumped by others' rules, behavioural uncertainty is substantially reduced by the importation of user-friendly structures via documentation that sidesteps individual peculiarities. Moreover, the complexity of these structures is such that many regulatory authorities within jurisdictions not amenable to their normal usage would be unable to comprehend them. Furthermore, because of that ignorance or lack of comprehension, they are unable to reject them. Thus English law ultimately does 'trump' the other jurisdictions. The real estate finance lawyer therefore demonstrates graphically how lawyers provide solutions and create support structures when cross-border norms do not exist.

REFERENCES

Abel, R and Lewis, P (1989) 'Putting Law Back into the Sociology of Lawyers' in R Abel and P Lewis (eds), *Lawyers in Society: Comparative Theories* (New York, Beard Books) 478.

Davies, P (2006) 'Europe Plunges in at the Deep End' *Financial Times* (19 September 2006) 43.

Dietz, T and Nieswandt, H (2009) 'The Emergence of Transnational Cooperation in the Software-Industry' in V Gessner (ed), *Contractual Certainty in International Trade* (Oxford, Hart).

EBRD (1995) 'Transition Report 1995: Investment and Enterprise Development' (London, European Bank for Reconstruction and Development).

Felstiner, W (2001) 'Synthesising Socio-Legal Research: Lawyer-Client Relations as an Example' 8 *International Journal of the Legal Profession* 191.

Flood, J (1991) 'Doing Business: The Management of Uncertainty in Lawyers' Work' 25 *Law and Society Review* 41.

—— (2005) 'Rating, Dating, and the Informal Regulation and the Formal Ordering of Financial Transactions: Securitizations and Credit Rating Agencies' in M Likosky (ed), *Privatising Development: Transnational Law, Infrastructure and Human Rights* (Leiden/Boston, Martinus Nijhoff).

—— (2007) 'Lawyers as Sanctifiers of Value Creation' 14 *Indiana Journal of Global Legal Studies* 35.

—— and Skordaki, E (1997) 'Normative Bricolage: Informal Rule-Making by Accountants and Lawyers in Mega-Insolvencies' in G Teubner (ed), *Global Law without a State* (Aldershot, Dartmouth).

—— and Sosa, F (2008) 'Lawyers, Law Firms and the Stabilization of Transnational Business' 28 *Northwestern Journal of International Law and Business* 489.

Freund, J (1975) *Anatomy of a Merger: Strategies and Techniques for Negotiation Corporate Acquisitions* (New York, Law Journal Press).

Gessner, V (1996) 'International Cases in German First Instance Courts' in V Gessner (ed), *Foreign Courts: Civil Litigation in Foreign Legal Cultures* (Aldershot, Dartmouth).

—— (2009a) 'Introduction: Toward a Theoretical Framework for Contractual Certainty in Global Trade' in V Gessner (ed), *Contractual Certainty in International Trade* (Oxford, Hart).

—— (2009b) 'Theories of Change—The Governance of Business Transactions in Globalising Economies' in V Gessner (ed), *Contractual Certainty in International Trade* (Oxford, Hart).

Gilson, R (1984) 'Value Creation by Business Lawyers: Legal Skills and Asset Pricing' 94 *Yale Law Journal* 239.

Konradi, W (2009) 'Lex Mercatoria as a Global Law of Transnational Business Exchanges? The Governance of Cross-Border Transactions within the Timber Industry' in V Gessner (ed), *Contractual Certainty in International Trade* (Oxford, Hart).

Luhman, N (1985) A Sociological Theory of Law (London, Routledge).

Neate, F (1987) *The Developing Global Securities Market* (London, Graham & Trotman).

Regan, M (2004) *Eat What You Kill: The Fall of a Wall Street Lawyer* (Ann Arbor, University of Michigan Press).

Smets, M (2006) 'Aligning Local Expertise in Cross-National Legal Work: Translations in Global Law Firm's Banking Group' (unpublished paper).

Sosa, F (2009) 'Cross-Border Dispute Resolution from the Perspective of Midsized Law Firms: The Example of International Commercial Arbitration' in V Gessner (ed), *Contractual Certainty in International Trade* (Oxford, Hart).

Uzzi, B, Lancaster, R and Dunlap, S (2007) 'Weighing the Worth of Social Ties: Embeddedness and the Price of Legal Services in the Large Law Firm Market' in L Empson (ed), *Managing the Modern Law Firm: New Challenges, New Perspectives* (Oxford, Oxford University Press).

Weber, M (1978) *Economy and Society: An Outline of Interpretive Sociology* (Berkeley, University of California Press).

Part III

Debates and New Approaches

7

Theories of Change—the Governance of Business Transactions in Globalising Economies

VOLKMAR GESSNER

INSTITUTIONS AND THE ROLE OF THE STATE

Debates About Market Coordination: Informal versus Formal, Endogenous versus Exogenous Institutions

IN ACCORDANCE WITH the case studies published in this volume (Richman, 2009; Konradi, 2009; Flood and Skordaki, 2009; Dietz and Nieswandt, 2009; Sosa, 2009), most of the literature dealing with market coordination turns on two issues: on the one hand, formal versus informal institutions, and on the other hand, endogenous (rational choice) versus exogenous (embedded) forms of governance. Before discussing contract enforcement and property rights protection (another pair of governance structures), we will briefly summarise the debates about the other two controversial pairs.

i) Max Weber is the most prominent voice in emphasising the regulation of all 'legitimate' coercive power by one universalistic coercive institution (formal rational law) and the disintegration of all particularistic status-determined and other coercive structures. According to him, modern economic life has destroyed those other associations (Weber, 1968: 336–7 and passim).

> The modern capitalist enterprise rests primarily on calculation and presupposes a legal and administrative system, whose functioning can be rationally predicted, at least in principle, by virtue of its fixed general norms, just like the expected performance of a machine (Weber, 1968: 1394).

As is pointed out frequently, this picture of a machine doesn't do justice to Weber's approach as a legal sociologist.[1] Weber's theory of institutional evolution was formed in the earlier periods of his scholarship and was based on Darwinian assumptions of social learning: formal rational institutions are selected by a struggle for survival. He later recognises tensions between formal and substantive rationality and conceives formal structures rather as an iron cage where individual or collective activities are hopelessly imprisoned. In order to act socially responsibly, one cannot only ask what has to be done, but also how it can be done correctly. Despite his own ambivalent attitude, Weber finally seems to make peace with this arrangement since formal rationality mostly leaves some (limited) freedom for pursuing purpose rational goals.

Weber thus clearly recognises informal norms and institutions as equivalent to legal coercion in providing calculability and legal certainty. His belief that those non-legal norms and non-state institutions have ceased to be relevant in a modern economy has been formed before 'legal realism' approaches have started to question legal centralism and begun to empirically evaluate legal institutions (Gessner, 2007)—again arriving at somewhat biased conclusions. There is abundant evidence for private ordering and legal pluralism, but formal law is part of the institutional structure offered for economic coordination. Although New Institutional Economists tend to emphasise informal governance structures (Ellickson, 1991; Dixit, 2004, Williamson, 2005: 3), most of them seem at least to agree with North's statement:

> By 'institutions', I mean three things: (1) the formal rules of the game that are defined in legal terms, (2) the informal norms of behaviour that supplement and compliment and modify institutions, and (3) the effectiveness of enforcement mechanisms. It is the mixture of the three that determines the effectiveness of institutions in influencing transaction costs (North, 1999: 7).

However, North in his historical analyses goes beyond this balanced view, arguing that there is no equivalence between the state's action and

[1] Scheuerman (1999) gives a brilliant interpretation of Weber's legal centralism, but does not mention other more ambivalent passages in Weber's oeuvre which show less 'elective affinity' between capitalism and formal law. Heydebrand (2007: 110) resumes Weber in the following way: 'The upshot of Weber's analysis is that formal legal rationality is "indispensable" when it furthers economic competition and corporate contractual interests in the early market stage of capitalist development. But formal law and justice become obstacles to economic growth and development when economic interests are constrained by, or subordinated to, formal regulations at later stages of corporate and economic concentration. This increasingly contradictory relationship between formal legalism and the political economy was recognised not only by Weber, but by many legal and economic historians on both sides of the Atlantic even when they did not share a Marxian framework.' According to Heydebrand (112), 'Weber despite his admiration for the achievements of formal legal rationality, ... anticipated its decline and commented extensively on the rise of anti-formalism in law'.

spontaneous social norms (and conventions). The role of the state is more significant (Fiani, 2004). A strong argument in favour of formal support structures is delivered by H de Soto (Soto, 1986), who describes and harshly criticises the inefficiencies of informal market mechanisms (in Peru). If textbooks are taken as an indicator for the present state of debates about the relative importance of informal and formal coordination structures, this argument is also the message delivered to the current student generation in economics and business studies (Kasper and Streit, 1998).

ii) Related, but broader and theoretically more ambitious, is the debate about the second pair of forms of government: endogenous versus exogeneous institutions—the former being created by economic actors, the latter imposed or offered by the social environment. Institutional research offers an extremely wide range of approaches from methodological individualism to sociological determinism. Although intermediate positions seem to prevail in recent publications, the scale of opinions remains as wide as ever. If Barzel begins his book by stating, 'In my analysis, institutions emerge as a result of actions of wealth-maximising individuals' (Barzel, 2002: 9), he follows the rational choice methodology of classical economy, the only exception being that actors make choices between institutions rather than between commodities. The other end of the scale is represented by approaches which understand the economy mainly in terms of culture (for example, Hofstede, 1980; 1983; within the same category all 'Asian value' studies and, of course, Weber's classical study on *The Protestant Ethic and the Spirit of Capitalism* (1958)). Intermediate positions are more interesting from our interdisciplinary point of view. Here, the range is from new institutional economists (Williamson, Greif, North) to old institutional economists from the first part of the last century (Veblen, Commons and Mitchell in the United States, as well as Menger, Weber and Hayek in Europe) and to present-day economic sociologists (Granovetter, Nee, Whitley, Hollingsworth, Boyer and Soskice). We will briefly outline their positions.

New institutional economics, in particular Williamson (1985), remain close to classical economics except for the 'boundedness' of maximising rationality (preferences and economic opportunities are shaped by collective political and social processes) and the relevance attributed to institutional trust. Both North (1990) and Greif (2005), the latter using games theoretical models, refer to culture as important for mental models of perception and to social norms as important for uncertainty reduction. This is regarded by critics as a necessary but insufficient recognition of the institutional (exogeneous) environment in transaction-cost economics. Beliefs and norms are relegated to a black box of informal constraints (Nee, 2005: 52). The approach is further problematised for its disregard of power and dependencies in economic transactions (Küpper and Felsch, 2000: 315–32). Old institutional economics offered a complementary knowledge: before Coase (1937), transaction costs as a steering mechanism were unknown and the authors relied on behaviouristic assumptions and demands for state protection. The relationship between the action and system levels—today the core element of institutional research—remains not only unresolved (which is largely true today), but—with the exception for Hayek (1949)—untouched (Rutherford, 1994). Economic sociology claims to address the manner in which informal and formal institutions interrelate in order to shape the performance of economic actors by facilitating, motivating and constraining their behaviour (Nee, 2005: 55–6). This is what new institutional economists also do with superior explanatory power as regards micro-economic decision-making, but economic sociology (already since Weber and Polanyi) better describes the (relational, organisational, communitarian or societal) context in which these institutions operate. Both approaches are clearly compatible and complementary, in particular by using a comparative approach as in the 'varieties of capitalism' (Hollingsworth and Boyer, 1997) and development and transformation studies (Ogus, 2004, with further references).

Contract Enforcement and Property Rights Protection

Contract enforcement[2] in most cases is guaranteed by reciprocity and mutual interest in continuing business relationships. Only beyond these much-debated bilateral aspects of contract emerge institutional approaches to market coordination. Institutions are elements external to the actors and all have in common that they stabilise expectations. This stabilisation is discussed in sociological research as a problem of social order and in economic research as a problem of transaction costs. Both approaches together show a complex picture of how business transactions are coordinated, supported and controlled in a market. Some of the elements of such a market support structure are informal norms and standards, routines, reputation in close-knit communities, informal dispute resolution institutions, legal rules, courts and lawyers. Sociology emphasises how these elements are embedded in the social environment of the business actor; economic research emphasises the rational choice between them and elaborates game theoretical models; legal sociology contributes empirical knowledge of how these institutions (alternative dispute resolution, courts, lawyers) work, what difficulties exist for the individual or business actor to access them and whether the support offered is fairly distributed to

[2] Contract enforcement is in the centre of most other chapters in this volume. In order to avoid repetition, we refer to the literature given and discussed there. Most influential in economic discussions on contract enforcement are Williamson (1985; 2005), Greif (2005) and Dixit (2004). Greif recently goes beyond the narrow contract enforcement perspective (Greif, 2006).

powerful and powerless actors alike. Economic sociology complicates the picture by showing variances between social systems of production and exchange. Institutions, according to these disciplines, 'matter' and are in particular decisive for economic performance. Institutions may or may not create trust and legal certainty, they hinder or facilitate transactions, they may be formal or informal, unstable or path dependent. This kind of knowledge has been recently produced in particular in the context of transformations in Southern and Eastern Europe and Central Asia. Although any assessment is difficult, the research intends to measure the quality of institutions and often prescribes specific institutional reforms. It is not confined to academic discourses, but may also be discovered in publications of international organisations and donor-support institutions. The World Bank (2005) offers a website on 'Legal Institutions of the Market Economy', which not only covers all of these aspects, but also advocates complex approaches to reform and recommends more investigation to address a number of difficult and unanswered questions. It confesses that it is at this stage virtually impossible to sort out the complex and contingent relationship between the different components of real-world institutions. It warns against simply using easily observable characteristics of formal institutions (such as the 'law in the books'). Neglecting informal institutions may, according to the World Bank, not only limit the domain of study, but also seriously skew the findings. Instead of promoting a sort of rule-of-law optimism one might expect from the World Bank, many pages are devoted to reporting experiences with reform strategies: 'What Works, What Hasn't'. Furthermore, if one reads the case studies, it seems that most of them haven't worked.

Contract enforcement studies emphasising the action level select as one (important) aspect the stabilisation of expectations. Actors may or may not sign formal contracts, do business within or beyond social networks, make or buy goods, collect or not all available information before or during the transaction, employ lawyers or avoid legal talk by all means, go to court or withdraw the claim (lump it).

The second element discussed as a prerequisite for a functioning market is the protection of property rights—an aspect largely under-researched and underestimated as a support structure for the stabilisation of expectations.[3] It has to be explained and specified as legal certainty—a term justified later in the chapter.

[3] Much of the property rights discourse is devoted to historical developments in agricultural societies where natural resources were transformed from common ownership to individual property (thus internalising 'externalities' such as predatory activities) (eg the contributions to Anderson and McChesney (2003)). I am not aware of more complex approaches taking account of property rights protection structures in a modern and globalising society. Still unspecific but somewhat close to what I intend to demonstrate in this chapter is the following definition: 'Property rights refer to the sanctioned behavioural

In addition to strategies employed in the business relationship in order to secure specific contractual expectations as far as possible (contract enforcement), the actor relies on complex and often unperceived and hidden structures establishing impersonal trust. Property rights are among the elements protected by such structures of impersonal trust (Shapiro, 1985; 2005). Social control is effective in economic action beyond contract enforcement institutions, hierarchy and social relations. As far as the multiple norms and organisational forms of social control of risk and distrust become relevant, rational choice is pushed to the background. The following is an attempt to review the literature explaining the social control and support of business transactions and the share of the state and its institutions in their control and support.

Shapiro's 'social organisation of distrust' uses agency theory (see also Greif, 2006: 10–11) and focuses on trust. The article is a response to Granovetter (1985) and shows that, in addition to personal trust, economic action relies heavily on impersonal trust. Social differentiation means that all actors ('principals') in society let others ('agents') fulfil most of their tasks on their behalf. Responsibilities are divided between the members of a family, parents entrust their children to professionals such as teachers and housekeepers, employers transfer custody of their property to employees. One's money is deposited in a bank account, assets and properties are turned to experts like stockbrokers, one's health to doctors, future uncertainties to insurance companies and pension funds. Newspapers as well as scientists are agents entrusted with the production of knowledge, the mechanic is an agent who takes care of the security of one's car. This social differentiation requires a complex organisation of risk protection and markets of trust production beyond the stabilisation of expectations created in close social relationships or contractual exchange. Governments are next to private organisations and professions among the guardians of trust substituting for kinship and friendship when dealing with strangers. Contracts are the usual strategy by which principals can assume some control over the behaviour of those who act on their behalf.

relations among economic agents in the use of valuable resources. They range from defining the access and use of natural resources to defining the nature of market exchange and to work relationships within firms. They can assign ownership to private individuals, groups, or the state. Regardless of the nature of the allocation, property rights must be clearly specified and enforced to be effective, and the degree of specificity depends upon the value of the asset covered ... For relatively low-valued assets or in cases where the number of parties is small and where there is a history of interaction, informal norms and local customs are sufficient for defining and enforcing property rights. For high-valued assets where the number of competitors is large and where new entry is common (so that the parties are heterogeneous and have little or no history of interaction), more formal governance structures, such as legally defined private property rights, become necessary. In this latter case, the power of the state usually is necessary to supplement informal constraints on access and use' (Libecap, 2003: 144).

However, they provide only limited control over the agency relationship, future contingencies and non-compliance. Agents rather than principals set the normative agenda: typically the principals are 'one-shotters', whereas agents are 'repeat players' with experience and power. Susan Shapiro and others (eg Zucker, 1986; Luhmann, 1979) conceive trust as social construction. Social control of impersonal trust is neither mainly legal, nor is it only based on rational choices by profit-seeking actors. Still, in explaining in particular economic behaviour, legal as well as economic approaches contribute to the understanding of structures and markets of trust production. In addition, cultural variations of social organisation of distrust have to be taken into account.

Aspects of Shapiro's 'social organisation of distrust' are mentioned in new institutional economics as institutions which reduce transaction costs, in 'old' institutional economics as institutions establishing order and organic solidarity, in systems theory as structures aiming at reduction of market complexities, and in legal sociology as legal guarantee securing market exchange. Recently, political scientists discuss institutional trust as a prerequisite for stable democracies (Hartmann and Offe, 2001). However, looking through this literature it seems that impersonal trust is given far less attention than personal trust. In very general terms, Williamson talks about 'legally sanctioned structures of property rights' (1985: 27), Greif (2006: 6) considers 'tentative results' that 'indicate that more secure property rights, stronger rule of law, and greater trust are correlated with better economic outcomes', and North is equally unspecific wherever he mentions property rights:

> All organized activity by humans entails a structure to define the 'way the game is played', whether it is a sporting activity or the working of an economy. That structure is made up of institutions—formal rules, informal norms, and their enforcement characteristics (North 2005: 48).

Existing theories are surprisingly poor, lacking any reference to the many ways in which a developed economic system is supported by (mostly, but not exclusively, legal) institutions.[4] There are many examples, but no systematic efforts in integrating this concept in sociology or economics. The reasons for this neglect are, as has been frequently observed (Riese, 1996: 422; Stiglitz and Walsh, 2002: 494; Dixit 2004: 2), that economists take the institutional infrastructure underlying a market economy for granted. In all attempts to create market economies in the transformation countries of Eastern Europe and Asia, Western experts[5] had to learn that,

[4] But see Hadfield's discussion of the background legal environment necessary for private ordering (Hadfield, 2009, in this volume).

[5] As Göhler and Kühn (1999: 18) speculate, this seems to be particularly a problem of US-American experts. Europeans have a long tradition of theorising about the state and are more aware of the relevance of state infrastructures.

without support institutions for the establishment and exercise of property rights, market economies simply cannot function.

On the basis of those scattered examples given in the literature,[6] one may list the following elements necessary for the social protection of property rights in any modern business transaction:

a) (constitutional) guarantees against expropriation;
b) protection of intellectual property;
c) reliable monetary systems;
d) banking and credit systems;
e) systems of incorporation;
f) systems of securities;
g) insolvency regimes;
h) tort regimes protecting against damages to property;
i) insurance institutions;
j) criminal protection against fraud, theft, etc;
k) professional services (lawyers, notaries, accountants, etc);

[6] Land registry is mentioned by Barzel (2002: 186) and Ogus (2004: 7), protection and/or registration of intellectual property rights, patents, copyrights, trademarks by Barzel (2002: 186), Riese (1996: 431), Ogus (2004: 2) and Swedberg (2003: 201 and 204), protection of trade secrets by Riese (1996: 431), mortgages, transaction documents and transportation documents by Swedberg (2003: 201), corporations as a legal entity by Swedberg (2003: 201), Ogus (2004: 5) and Dietz (2002: 69), bankruptcy procedures by Carruthers and Halliday (2007), Webb (1999: 167) and Ogus (2004: 5), effective principles of accountability by Ogus (2004: 4), private institutions such as banks, insurance companies by Dietz (2002: 69), credit bureaus and credit card companies by Greif (2006:49), state guarantees of bank deposits by Webb (1999: 167) and regulatory agencies governing securities' exchanges by Whitley (2003b: 20). No doubt, more examples could easily be produced with additional literature research. The point is that not a single author in economic and sociological literature tries to offer a complex picture of the institutional infrastructure needed for a market economy. Relatively comprehensive but on a more abstract level is the following list provided by Ogus (2004: 8):
a) rules published and thus readily accessible;
b) rules which are reasonably certain, clear and stable (thus excluding decisions of unconstrained discretion);
c) mechanisms ensuring the application of rules without discrimination;
d) binding decisions by an independent judiciary;
e) limited delay in judicial proceedings;
f) effective judicial sanctions; and
g) compliance by, and accountability of, the government and its officials in relation to relevant rules.
A World Bank practitioner comes closest to what we mean by institutional infrastructure for the protection of property rights (Webb, 1999: 162–3):
... improving the capacity and quality of law schools; improving lawyer licensing procedures; developing legal information systems; improving the law drafting capacity of governments; improving arbitration and other alternative dispute resolution mechanisms; and improving public understanding of the role of law in a modern economy. We are also placing considerable importance on the development and strengthening of institutions that either provide public registry services, such as corporate registries, land registries, and personal property registries, or that regulate private trading activities, such as securities commissions and competition agencies.

l) transparent substantial and procedural rules (eg contract law, civil procedure);
m) consistency control of rules (legal science);
n) institutions for continuous updating of rules (governments, parliaments, associations); and
o) accessible, competent and reliable intermediary institutions (bureaucracy, commercial and land registers, customs offices).

Hence, business people need stable expectations in regard to their (and their business partners') right of ownership, value of the currency, access to credit, reliability of banking transfers and security of investments, liabilities in corporations, distribution of assets in case of insolvency, insurability of risk, sanctions against criminal behaviour, competent advise by professionals, and adequate, consistent, fair and efficient rules. Business people also depend on trust in licences, professional titles, quality standards and public certificates. All this goes far beyond contractual expectations usually discussed in the contract enforcement literature. Contractual expectations may all be honoured or enforced, but the exchange may break down nevertheless due to lacking or failing property rights protection structures.[7]

Finally, what is the institutional theory of legal science? Lawyers want the law to be reliable, relatively stable, guaranteeing autonomy and securing expectations of how other legal subjects will behave in the future. This is a normative position, which throughout history was based on a wide range of empirical, political or ideological assumptions (Arnauld, 2006) that had their sources in competing social-scientific knowledge. The competition of these sources lies mainly in different explanations for the emergence of property rights protection structures and to a much lesser degree in their assumptions as regards their relevance in a modern economy. The division is again between, on the one hand, new institutional economists who perceive incomplete information and limited mental capacity of human beings as a problem for efficient markets. Since information is costly, institutions are formed to reduce uncertainty and induce the actors to acquire the essential information that will lead them to make rational choices. On the other hand, in old institutional economics and sociology, the emphasis lies on social integration and the establishment of order. A particularly strong representative of this latter aspect was the Freiburg School of *Ordoliberalismus* (Böhm, Eucken) before, during and after the Second World War (Ptak, 2004), and later very influential in the emergent German market economy and economic law discourses. Ptak

[7] See Berman (2005: 519): 'government is always in the background, creating and enforcing the rules of property, contract, tort, employment, and so on. These rules inevitably regulate social life by establishing and maintaining the type of "private" relationships deemed appropriate or desirable. And of course, such regulation is always directed toward the achievement of public goals.'

(99) quotes Franz Böhm with a strong statement in this direction: 'If freedom and order are in conflict it is order which should be given unconditional preference'.[8] Thus, according to German present-day legal dogmatics (Badura, 2005: 1–3), the freedom of the economy is granted only under the conditions imposed or granted by constitutional and legislated provisions. (Private) law is constitutive for the economy, a correspondence is assumed between the market system and the legal constitution of the economy (Mestmäcker, 1978: 10 and 13). This correspondence refers in particular to the freedom in exercising economic activities on the one hand and property rights delimitation and protection on the other.[9]

Whatever the theoretical foundations are, they are not made explicit in legal discourses (eg Badura, 2005). It is generally assumed that law has to offer a complex and coherent institutional structure for a functioning market economy. Enabling law is the core of legal education, disputes based on 'private law' issues form the bulk of the case load in courts and are responsible for the 'litigation explosion' in most Western countries. At least from a legal and socio-legal point of view, the protection of property rights in the range of the above list of elements is best translated as state guarantee of legal certainty. Even those elements which are organised by non-state economic actors (such as banks, insurance companies, legal and other professions, chambers of industry and commerce) produce trust mainly due to state protection and supervision. The coherence of legal institutions is permanently controlled by legal scholars who write commentaries and produce suggestions for law reform. As far as consistency creates legal certainty, it is the result of legal dogmatics and case law—with variations between legal cultures as regards their relative importance. If relevant parts of the institutional structure are 'embedded' in social relations, communities and custom (this is the legal culture element) or are privately created and organised, they remain outside this dogmatic consistency supervision and may jeopardise legal

[8] '*Bei einem Konflikt zwischen Freiheit und Ordnung kommt dem Gesichtspunkt der Ordnung unbedingter Vorrang zu*'. According to Ptak, for Böhm the German National Socialist regime was a welcome guarantee for establishing this *Ordnung*. However, Böhm's political inclinations cannot be generalised. Friedrich Hayek, who was another representative of *Ordo*liberalism, defines order in a way any modern institutionalist could agree with: 'a state of affairs in which a multiplicity of elements of various kinds are so related to each other that we may learn from the acquaintance with some spatial or temporal part of the whole to form correct expectations concerning the rest' (quoted in Fleetwood, 2001: 141). In fact, as Cubeddu (2002: 135) emphasises, Hayek scarcely diverges from Coase and North in theoretical issues about transaction costs and uncertainty. The difference is that Hayek adds ethical goals thought to be superior to the processes of the free market economy.

[9] This idea of a strong constitutive order for the economy is certainly a particular German perspective, but see James M Buchanan for a US-American approach and Adam Smith's classical insights that law and institutions are the basis of society (Buchanan, 1976: 271 and 273).

certainty. This has been frequently observed in regard to the institutional structure of developing countries (Ogus, 2004; North, 2005), but arbitration is also a case in point.

Interim Conclusions

The institutional structure aiming at market coordination consists of informal as well as formal, of endogeneous as well as exogeneous elements. Market coordination may in part be achieved by contract enforcement institutions, but also requires a complex set of property rights protection institutions. They form the infrastructure of a market, a framework which is constitutive for any exchange before, during or after the specific transaction takes place. Unlike contract enforcement, where private institutions prevail, property rights are a collective good (Olson, 1965) and as such protected collectively. In a modern market economy, this protection is predominantly achieved through a *legal* infrastructure, although cultural institutions have an influence and informal (legal cultural) implementation patterns support or hinder the legal institutions to create the required trust in market relations. The importance of law as a constitutive element means that the state is a core player in establishing the institutional framework for markets. This at least was the situation before the markets became increasingly globalised and new actors and global institutions ready to replace or complement the traditional legal infrastructure emerged. We will consider below what is known or speculated about this possible new situation and the role that the state plays in it.

THEORIES OF CHANGE

Defining and Limiting the Scope of the Debate

Law and globalisation has become a popular theme, but the literature mostly refers to regulatory law, which is not the subject of this chapter. Theories of change of (legal or non-legal) market *support structures* emerge slowly and use indicators which are by most authors interpreted in the same way as in the area of regulation, ie towards the 'weak state' paradigm. This debate will first be dealt with, leaving the search for a general theory of enabling law and globalisation for the final section of this chapter.

This section will have to address two problems: what exactly is assumed to change and how the assumed change is measured.

The literature we have reviewed above gives a good idea about the role of the state in market support. This support is modest in contract enforcement (with variations between legal cultures) and high in property rights protection. Taking both elements of institutional infrastructures together, states play an important role in creating legal certainty for national economies. In developed and highly industrialised countries, the state is directly or even 'in the shadow' the core actor in establishing the institutions that help the market to run in an orderly and transaction-costs-saving manner. The scenario might have changed with globalisation. The nation state might offer less support for cross-border transactions due to the limits of legislative power beyond the state's territory. The theory of change then refers to global deals only, to an emerging institutional structure or legal culture of a global market. The state loses power in supporting export business transactions, but remains the key player in the national economy. More ambitious are theories which assume a transformation of the state even within the traditional scenario of national economies. Public or private international organisations or global actors such as multinational corporations may influence or put pressure on domestic institutions so that changes also occur within the nation state's borders. Theories of regulatory law mostly refer to the latter; theories of enabling law to the former scenario. The distinction will be observed in the following discussions. Unless stated otherwise, our theories only try to explain the limits and possible changes of legal support in cross-border deals. Speculations about repercussions to domestic scenarios seem extremely ambitious in the current early phase of research. Heydebrand (2007) and others suggest that once established, transnational rules may influence legal arrangements at the domestic level. Whatever the evidence, the hypotheses seem plausible that the changes observed and discussed in the global context should affect the state in its support for the market. This approach goes beyond studies of isolated phenomena common in the contract enforcement literature.

The measurement of change is quite unproblematic in the regulatory area. Any rule, norm, standard, directive promulgated by globally active organisations or regimes, any decision taken by a global administration or court is weakening the (Westphalian) sovereign power of the nation state. In order to describe changes, it is sufficient to count global rules and keep an eye on their effectiveness. The picture is different in the market support area. A new institution for the global market may or may not affect domestic support structures, may or may not take away legislative power from the nation state, and may substitute for or add something to state support. Many new global support structures are informal, discretionary and autonomously created, but their domestic equivalents might be equally informal, discretionary and autonomously created. Where is the change then? As a consequence, the institutions assumed to build a new global infrastructure will have to be studied one by one and compared to the way in which their support is carried out within the national economies. A related but additional measurement problem which has to be avoided by all means is a comparison of an idealised model of a domestic infrastructure with an empirical model found in the global market. This frequent misunderstanding typically leads to false assumptions about the role of law which, as we learn from legal sociology, is domestically also ambiguous, limited and socially constructed. Where is the change if business people draft a complex contract with a foreign company as they always do within national borders? Is there more autonomous norm creation if an industry branch, with its customs and relational bonds, goes global? Finally, the institutions used as indicators for change will have to survive a property rights protection test. They may look global, but at closer inspection they are in fact as dependent on state support as their domestic predecessors.

Indicators

In an early stage of theory building, single indicators are commonly used for developing hypotheses which may later be falsified or generalised. This is the state of the art in the transformation of the state debate in general and in law and globalisation debates in particular. One debate turns, as shown above, on the transformation of institutional support for the global economy. The indicators most frequently used are contracts, international lawyering, dispute settlement, *lex mercatoria* and arbitration. This list could be easily extended, but will suffice here for demonstrating some of the problems faced by these indicators for making judgements about the role of the state in international business.

Contracts are used as core indicators in the globalisation of law debate, but for opposite purposes. On the one hand, there is the self-enforcing, 'incredibly detailed and completely researched' (Shapiro, 1993: 44) contract, which aims at a maximum of independence from institutional support in general and from state and judicial support in particular. The only support structures are international law firms. Self-enforcement is also—but for different reasons—claimed by those authors who believe in business relationships and networks (Whitley, 2001; Appelbaum, 1998). The relational contract is as self-sufficient as the complex contract. Another version of the 'weak state' paradigm is Scheuerman's 'compression of space and time' hypothesis (Scheuerman, 1999; 2001), which denies the rule of law much significance in economic areas of high capital concentration (multi-national corporations) and rapid communication facilitated by technological innovations.[10] On the other hand, for new institutional

[10] Scheuerman's papers look directly relevant to the 'transformation of the state' theme, eg where he writes that 'economic globalization flourishes precisely where such legal forms (*minimum legal protections*) are lacking' (Scheuerman, 1999: 264). However, his argument

economists the contract supported by formal institutions (in particular law and state courts) is considered to be the most efficient coordination structure (North, 1999) and is therefore also expected to prevail in the global economy. Martin Shapiro (1993) sides this position from a socio-legal perspective. He observes a tendency towards a contractual society (ie a trend 'for reasons I do not profess to understand' (at 40) away from hierarchical forms of coordination) that is dependent on lawyers, judges and litigation. His view of the future is an Americanisation of law, a global economy based on common law and US adversarial civil procedures. Whitley, in a more recent paper (2003a), supports this view from the position of economic sociology by emphasising emergent global institutions for contract enforcement. Finally, global financial institutions put enormous efforts into establishing contractual legal certainty in developing and transformation societies and in global economies (World Bank, 2005). There doesn't seem to exist convincing empirical evidence for any of these controversial positions. All authors argue with examples selected according to their needs. A recent attempt to elaborate a balanced perspective—although on the basis of a small sample of firms—does not clearly support any of these firm positions (Sosa, 2007).

Unlike in the contract controversies, there is almost unanimity and sufficient empirical evidence as regards the role of the international (mega) law firm. This is a relatively new global actor, a core player in international business and finance, in mergers and acquisitions and even in the emergent global law. Governments are advised by those firms and new commercial law is sometimes drafted by a law firm.[11] Bureaucracies are manipulated, legislatures are lobbied and state courts are obliged to decide test cases. In daily legal practice, it is the complex, self-enforcing contract which pushes state law to the background. Other responsibilities are joint ventures, cross-border corporate and tax matters, and licensing and distribution agreements (Silver, 2000; Flood, 2001). Sophisticated international capital market transactions, privatisations and project financing are carried out almost as a matter of routine. An increasing number of mid-sized law firms enter the international market and also show a certain independence from their home countries' law and legal culture (Sosa, 2008). All of this

covers only space and time uncertainties and does not deal with the problems of opportunism, which is the main concern of institutional economists. In addition, he mainly refers to international contracts of selected global players like multi-national corporations, banks and currency traders.

[11] See, eg Cooper (2000: 439): 'the American Bar Association (ABA) has a special Committee on International Legal Technical Assistance Programs. The focus has been on drafting new legislation, model codes for commercial transactions, bankruptcy and insolvency, taxation, and shareholder protection. The ABA has enjoyed some success in the field with its Central and Eastern European Law Initiative, wherein some five thousand judges and lawyers have been involved in pro bono assistance in drafting not just new civil codes, but also criminal codes and constitutions.'

indicates a change, but not necessarily towards the weak-state hypothesis. There is a clear trend towards the Americanisation of international lawyering, law as big business and creative lawyering, the strategic and aggressive use of law in business relations, and highly commercial and pragmatic approaches. The literature, often written by practitioners, emphasises this US style of lawyering all over the world in subsidiaries of US law firms as well as in British and continental firms. All of this seems to affect state prerogatives, but what happens is probably only a transformation of continental, Latin American or Asian state models into the US more-decentralised state model. International law firms don't seem to be a good indicator for a general transformation away from the nation state to global legal pluralism. What they indicate is the power of common law and the hegemony of the United States in the global market.

Dispute settlement has a long tradition as an indicator for the qualities of legal systems. It has helped anthropologists to understand the normative order of tribal communities and was also used by legal sociologists to understand the 'law in action'. Furthermore, it serves economists as a *pars pro toto* for the occurrence of transaction costs and the efficiency of institutions. Recent debates on law and globalisation also follow this tradition by studying, for example, the dispute settlement procedures in the EU, the World Trade Organisation (WTO) or the North American Free Trade Agreement (NAFTA) as regards regulatory disputes and multiple ways of conflict resolution in commercial transactions as regards contract enforcement. Although the evidence provided by this indicator is doubtful (a dispute is a relatively rare and even exceptional occurrence in daily social and legal practice), few efforts seem to exist in current debates to investigate mechanism of order (as opposed to dispute) in daily life and to draw conclusions from a less dramatic picture of social life. Theories of change and state transformation compare developments either in the direction of formal dispute settlement (judicialisation) or in the opposite direction towards informal dispute settlement (alternative forms of conflict resolution, ADR), arriving at sometimes over-simplified conclusions about the rule of law due to the limited value of the indicator. It would not take us very far in challenging these approaches. Instead, two representative approaches are chosen for illustrating the theoretical reach of dispute settlement indicators. Heydebrands's (2003; 2007) complex socio-legal theory on the rise of procedural informalism will be contrasted with theories of emerging economies which claim that the only viable route for successful competition in the global economy is the adoption of (Western) judicial institutions.

Heydebrand represents the affinity of the sociology of law for informal, non-state elements of social order, whereas theories of emerging economies are representative for a strong epistemic and practical movement observing and fostering a change of market support institutions from relational to formal. Both approaches provide impressive empirical evidence in their favour, by showing historical trends in the direction of their hypotheses and by using comparative methods. At the same time, both approaches fail in analysing data which point in the opposite direction. Heydebrand observes a change from the law-based nation state to governance based on negotiated process rationality, informal, privatised, pragmatic and expedient strategies of ad hoc problem-solving, and crisis management. His examples and data are predominantly taken from domestic legal systems, but those developments and changes are presented as a consequence of global trends towards substantive justice, process rationality, logics of negotiation, 'soft law', soft procedure, soft regulation or self-regulation, which have emerged since the 1980s and 1990s. Soft procedures have been emerging in transnational social, political, economic and legal networks. They are regulating global exchanges and the global economy and are specifically linked to the new globality 'where a need for managing global indeterminacy is arising' (Heydebrand, 2003: 329). Heydebrand's vision is a historical transition from the executive-centred state of the twentieth century to the denationalised state and the informal, privatised 'law' of the current round of globalisation (Heydebrand, 2003: 339; but see his discussion on counter-evidence in Heydebrand, 2007: notes 4 and 5). A thoughtful study confirming this trend in the area of cross-border debt collection has been carried out by Budak (1999). Although this development is generally interpreted as a weakening of the state, Heydebrand also refers to Richard Abel's (1982) 'latent functions' of informal justice, which consist of conflict management, the denial of redress, redistribution of state resources, advancement of the interests of professionals and legitimation of state and capital. In contrast to most interpretations, Abel identifies the expansion rather than the reduction of state control through informal dispute procedures. Weak or strong state—Heydebrand's data suggest the rise of alternative dispute processing, but he mainly uses US trial statistics in studying the correspondent development in the judiciary. Recourse to ADR may have increased in some areas and to the courts in others (and recourse to both may have increased in some areas at the same time). Generalisations on the basis of US-American experience seem problematic. Most countries complain about high court case loads and report increasing litigation rates (recently even in East and South-East Asia). Heydebrand's observation that

> ... in the cradle of the civil law (Italy, France, and Germany), informalist trends may be weaker than in Scandinavia, the UK, and the reform societies of Eastern and Southeastern Europe which were influenced by American common law after 1989 (118 and 119)

is interpreted as 'institutional inertia' (111). This view is challenged by the World Bank and Western legal experts who mount policy initiatives that seek to counteract the enduring and putatively corrupting effects of informalisms. Law and economics, institutional economists and to some degree also economic sociologists advocate the economic advantages of rule orientation. 'Institutional inertia' is attributed in those approaches to cultural traditions which resist or undermine the emergence of formal court structures, formal procedures and bureaucracies observing the rule of law.

Nichols (1999) suggests a theory of emerging economies, which he defines as polities in which commercial institutions are changing from a relational to a formal orientation. Notions of contract are used to indicate the orientation of various legal systems between these two variables. This approach is based on North and other new economic institutionalists who strongly believe in formal mechanisms of market support and in particular in state courts as the most reliable and predictable form of dispute resolution and of establishing legal certainty. It legitimises an entire industry of experts who study weak, corrupt and inefficient systems of judicial administration and suggest changes for their improvement (Buscaglia, 1997; Garcia, 1998; Cooper, 2000; Nagle, 2000; for an overview, see Fix Fierro, 2004). The global economy as another emergent economy has also attracted some curiosity. Apart from doctrinal approaches (in the areas of private international law and unified law), there are studies on the use of the UN Convention on the International Sale of Goods (Bonell, 1990; Twibell, 1997; Bailey, 1999; Gordon, 1998) and of domestic courts for the resolution of cross-border disputes (Gessner, 1996; Freyhold, 1996; Stammel, 1998), which describe the relevance of formal (judicial) conflict resolution, but do not explicitly predict a change towards a more active role of courts in cross-border disputes. This latter hypothesis is developed by Slaughter (2000) and Whitley (2003). Slaughter mentions the obvious candidates (the European Court of Justice and the European Court of Human Rights), but also gives examples of cooperation between courts of different jurisdictions in bankruptcy cases, of meetings and international networks between judges, and comes to 'a vision of a global community of law, established not by the World Court in The Hague, but by national courts working together around the world' (1114), a dialogue between the adjudicative bodies of the world community. Still, the empirical evidence is poor despite this vision (shared by generations of jurists) and despite some scattered examples which are available for supporting a theory of change towards the future emergence of more formal dispute resolution structures for business transactions in the global economy.

The *lex mercatoria* as an autonomous (non-state) support structure[12] for the global economy had a glorious past before the advent of the nation

[12] Most authors refer to *lex mercatoria* as a *support* structure for international business. The term 'transnational law' is broader in so far as it refers also to *regulatory* elements of global norms. The debate turns around the autonomy of *lex mercatoria* institutions from the

state (Greif, 2006). It is controversial whether together with and as a consequence of the globalisation of the economy a revival can be observed. Legal scholars, international organisations and lawyers active (although without empirical evaluation efforts) in the unification of law (Wiener, 1999) and elaboration of a global law doctrine are all sceptical. A recent empirical effort shows little to no relevance of *lex mercatoria* norms in international contracts (Drahozal and Naimark, 2005: 249 and 250). Those in favour of this argument (Berman and Kaufman, 1978; Berger, 1996; 2001 with further references) mention formal norms (such as those promulgated by the International Chamber of Commerce or branch organisations) and collections of universal contract principles (such as the Lando Principles), but also contracts (self-enforcing contracts, standard forms, General Conditions), close-knit communities of traders (such as the diamond traders) and even international conventions (such as the UN Convention on Contracts for the International Sale of Goods (CISG) and other UN Commission on International Trade Law (UNCITRAL) conventions). Teubner (1997) refers to an indeterminate normative substance of *lex mercatoria* emerging from 'communicative processes in a given social field that observe social action under the binary code legal/illegal' (at 14). Obviously, the elements mentioned in the discussion as forming an autonomous legal system are strange bed fellows. Some of these elements simply emerge from the state guarantee of freedom of contract, some are relational (and therefore difficult to define as *lex*) and some are of state origin (the international conventions). Trade norms (formal or informal) come closest to an autonomous support structure, but their existence is also nothing new and they are acknowledged as legally relevant in most states' commercial laws.[13] Unlike most other elements[14] of what this

nation state and should not be misunderstood as a debate over the existence of a multitude of global normative orders. It is misleading to call sceptics of the *lex mercatoria* 'traditionalists' adhering to Westphalian-inspired notions of state-centricity. Most of them are aware of the emerging patchwork of global norms and only do not understand why some elements of this patchwork should be given the privileged status of being recognised as 'law' in judicial proceedings.

[13] Article 2 of the Uniform Commercial Code (UCC) provides that usages of trade, courses of dealing, and courses of performance 'give particular meaning to and supplement or qualify terms of an agreement'. Article 9 of the Convention on Contracts for the International Sale of Goods (CISG) similarly provides that the 'parties are bound by any usage to which they have agreed and by any practices which they have established between themselves', including any 'usage of which the parties knew or ought to have known and which in international trade is widely known to, and regularly observed by, parties to contracts of the type involved in the particular trade concerned'. Under such code provisions, judges look directly to what is customary in the trade or between the parties in adjudicating any dispute. For a similar stipulation, see § 356 of the German *Handelsgesetzbuch* (Commercial Code).

[14] Close-knit communities are also well documented (Bernstein, 1992; Richman, 2006; Landa, 1981). Their power as a support structure derives mainly from reputation mechanisms and to a much lesser degree from autonomous norms. The term *lex mercatoria* would be misleading as an analytical tool for the interpretation of these phenomena. In addition, recent

approach calls *lex mercatoria*, these trade norms are well known and documented (in trade publications). Less well known is their relationship to state law—they may complement it, be a substitute for it or may be applied only occasionally (Berger, 1996). Teubner's distinct global communicative processes seem difficult to distinguish from domestic legal/illegal speech acts. All that is new in this area of pluralistic trade support structure is its promotion by a large community of scholars[15] as a kind of legal system 'without a state" (Teubner (ed), 1997). Despite its definitional problems and the almost complete lack of empirical evidence for its autonomy from state law, there is an avalanche of literature 'talking it into existence contrafactually' (Callies, 2002: 207), which by itself might induce a change towards the development and recognition of autonomous global structures.[16]

A broader and more accurate definition of *lex mercatoria* is used by a group of legal scholars within the critical legal studies (CLS) school. It refrains from assuming autonomy and points to the active role of private firms in building institutions or at least in influencing their practice (Santos, 1995; Cutler, 2003; Robé, 1997; Muchlinski, 1997). In addition to private firms, in particular transnational enterprises, private authority over law creation and dispute settlement is exercised by private lawyers and their associations, tax and accounting firms, banks, insurers, representatives of international organisations and government officials, leading to 'different legal spaces superimposed, interpenetrated and mixed in our minds as much as in our actions' (Santos, 1987: 297). If 'interlegality is the key postmodern conception of law' (Santos, 1987: 300), the fiction of an autonomous law merchant is substituted by a neo-Marxist conception of global order created by a transnational managerial class (the CLS school refers to Cox, 1987). States, state bureaucracies and state officials are part of this hegemonic structure, cooperating with private actors in the constitution of a market-friendly environment. The transformation observed by this school is the opposite to the weak state paradigm assumed by the above-mentioned *lex mercatoria* approaches. It is the transformation from the welfare state towards the hyper-liberal state (Cox, 1987). The problem with this approach is that it compares the reality of one society with the

publications (eg Der Spiegel 20, 2006: 136) indicate that their survival is uncertain under pressure of competition and change of market structures.

15 We do not want to speculate about their motivations, but assume a common political (neo-liberal) background. It is significant that economic sociologists do not seem to participate actively in this social construction of the *lex mercatoria*. They know most about the plurality of normative orientations and their variations between cultures. The idea of an *autonomous* set of norms within society is alien to economic sociology and probably also alien to most other sociological disciplines.

16 Religions are similarly socially constructed. Quite accurately therefore, Zumbansen (2004: 198) refers to the debate as a religious war.

ideal type of another. The active role of firms and commercial organisations and the political intervention of the 'mercatocracy' (Cutler) in legislative and norm generation processes on all levels is a common phenomenon in state legal systems and should not come as a surprise in the global economy and international business. There are certainly differences (more and different actors, new forms of state-private cooperation, new forms of law), but Cutler, who describes so well the emerging global inter-legality, uses a surprisingly idealised model for describing law in the nation state (Cutler, 2003: 28; 141–78).[17] 'Law merchant' in the way defined by Cutler is such a ubiquitous phenomenon that it does not seem to be a good indicator for state transformation.[18]

If, for an emergent 'global law without a state', the international arbitration business is used as an example, it is important to note that arbitration agreements of parties with *lex mercatoria* as the chosen law are extremely rare (Drahozal, 2000; Drahozal and Naimark, 2005: 249–50) and that only few cases are known where arbitral awards have applied the *lex mercatoria* as applicable law when parties have not so agreed (these seven cases are listed in Drahozal, 2000: note 229). However, international arbitration is per se used as an indicator for theories on the transformation of the state.

> By and large, parties to international transactions choose to arbitrate eventual disputes not because arbitration is simpler than litigation, not because it is cheaper, not because it is 'final and binding' and therefore substantially unreviewable, and not because arbitrators may have greater relevant expertise than national judges, although any one of those factors may be of interest; they arbitrate simply because neither will suffer its rights and obligations to be determined by the courts of the other party's state of nationality. International arbitration thus is in large measure a substitute for national court litigation (Drahozal, 2000: 95, quoting an international lawyer and arbitrator).

A first qualification of this statement refers to the choices made by the parties. Most international disputes taken to domestic courts are not contractual (Freyhold, 1996: 73–4; Gessner, 1996: 164) and therefore (in practice) not eligible for arbitration.[19] Arbitration is typically chosen by

[17] See Berman (2005) for a socio-legal view on law in the nation-state context. When he talks about the nineteenth-century vision of the sovereign nation state, he adds: 'to the extent it actually existed' (526).

[18] Cutler's critical positions would benefit from observing the crucial differences between regulation and support functions of the law. The regulatory problems in acting against the merchant elite are undeniable. But what is wrong with facilitating economic life and reducing market uncertainties? Support structures are mainly aimed at small and medium-sized businesses. Transnational companies do not need merchant law such as standard contracts, documentary credit or uniform law like the CISG. Their global trade is mostly carried out more or less in-house.

[19] This explains in part the confusion about the frequency of arbitrated cases. The number of arbitration clauses in contracts is not mirrored in the case loads of courts and arbitration

contractual arbitration clauses which seem to be very frequently used in international contracts (Dahozal, 2006: note 1). Since arbitration is confidential and awards are generally not published, there are no reliable numbers. It is assumed that 'general' arbitration offered by arbitral institutions—this institutional arbitration is formal and close to the kind of resolution that would be produced through litigation—is limited to relatively few complex conflicts with high stakes. In addition to formal procedures in arbitral institutions, there exist an unknown number of arbitrations offered by trade organisations with less formal procedures where disputes with lower amounts at stake are also decided. Taken together a considerable increase of arbitration case numbers within the past decades seems to be a fair guess (Drahozal, 2006: 233),[20] although estimates in the literature that international arbitration is now 'the' ordinary and normal method of settling disputes of international trade seem far exaggerated.[21] Whether these arbitrated cases are 'taken away' from domestic jurisdictions or would never have been submitted to a state court is difficult to decide. What is known is that national courts also decide a surprisingly high and presumably also increasing number of international cases (for Germany: Gessner, 1996; for the United States: Freyhold, 1996; for Italy: Olgiati, 1996).[22] The information needed for a transformation hypothesis to be pursued on firm ground is a qualitative and quantitative comparison between international business disputes in arbitral tribunals and domestic courts.[23] Despite in this respect unsatisfactory empirical knowledge,[24]

tribunals. One may speculate that contractual disputes are more frequently taken to arbitration tribunals, whereas all non-contractual disputes are litigated in domestic courts.

[20] However, see Konradi (2009, in this volume), who reports a dramatic decrease of arbitration in the timber industry.

[21] 3,000 arbitration requests filed at the International Chamber of Commerce in a period of 10 years is not a very impressive case load. However, Cutler (2003: 26) refers to 120 other (although less important) private arbitration institutions.

[22] The three countries compared in this project show with 2 to 3% a similar share of international cases in the case load of domestic courts. Although the figures are low compared to the export rates of the three countries, they seem surprisingly high under the impression of estimates in the arbitration promotion literature. The court file studies did differentiate between commercial and non-commercial cases. Within the commercial case load in Germany, 10% of the cases were international. It was estimated in 1996 that, taking all civil courts of first instance of the 15 Member States into account, between 100,000 and 200,000 international disputes are filed every year in the European Union (Freyhold, Gessner and Olgiati, 1996: 269). High estimates for the number of arbitration cases are suspect to be biased in order to promote the lucrative arbitration business.

[23] The arbitration promotion literature avoids any reference to international court cases reported in the legal literature. A recent textbook on *Law of International Trade* shows on 33 pages a list of no less than 1,300 international cases in English jurisdictions only (Chuah, 2005). An empirical comparison of litigated and arbitrated cases in a mid-sized German law firm is currently being carried out by Sosa—the part dealing with arbitration is included in this volume (Sosa, 2009).

[24] The information collected by Dezalay and Garth (1996) has a different focus. The authors are interested in power struggles between arbitrators who, while competing with each other for arbitration business, promote cooperatively the increased use of arbitration and persuade state actors to accept the use of arbitration instead of courts. The survey in Berger *et*

international arbitration has emerged as the standard argument in favour of either paradigm: the weak state (Zürn, 2001; Berger, 2001; Lehmkuhl, 2003) or the strong hyper-liberal state (Cutler, 2003: 225–40).

Limited Scope of the Indicators

All indicators for a transformation of the state discussed above are highly controversial. Sometimes the assumed change is under dispute, most often the empirical evidence is lacking and there is a general tendency of describing global legal phenomena without giving a realistic picture of how the law works domestically. By comparing observable social processes *both* globally and domestically, the 'change' might turn out to be less dramatic or may disappear completely. Hence, there is no general theoretical consent or sufficient empirical evidence that nation-state support for the economy is significantly changing by contractual practices of international business, the activities of international law firms, informal dispute resolution, global legal pluralism or the use of international arbitrators. Speculations in the directions of the weak state or the strong hyper-liberal state paradigms are over-ambitious, come too early and are presently unfounded.

In addition—and this is the main point of this chapter—such speculations under-estimate the complexities of social systems in general and of social systems of production in particular. Single elements such as those discussed above are embedded in a social structural network which is not necessarily changing in the same direction. On the contrary, with its inherent path dependency, the structural environment will either try to slow down the change or create new structures to compensate for the loss of a coordinating factor.

The indicators discussed above are without exception indicators for contract enforcement. This is, as we have shown, an important albeit not the only aspect of institutional support for the economy. The second aspect is those invisible structures mostly taken for granted, but indispensable for a functioning economy: property rights protection structures. However contracts are concluded, honoured or enforced, they rely on stable expectations as to the legal status of the contractual parties, their ownership titles and their legitimation to purchase or sell. In addition, expectations are based on non-legal infrastructures such as banks, the post office, the

al (2001) unfortunately contains no question about the experience with arbitration compared to litigation. A recent report sponsored by PricewaterhouseCoopers based on research by the School of International Arbitration at Queen Mary, University of London, seems to fill the gap by interviewing in-house counsel about their experience with arbitration and litigation. Despite the high costs, they prefer arbitration (Department of ADR News, 2006). Konradi (2009, in this volume) shows that these strong opinions in favour of arbitration are not necessarily supported by the actual choices made in business disputes.

chamber of commerce, the standardisation agencies, etc. These support structures work together with contract enforcement like communicating tubes: if contract enforcement has a low support level, property rights protection may rise in order to reach a sufficient level of certainty and trust—and vice versa. The Italian economy seems to provide a good example: poor contract enforcement, but (since Roman times) strong (more social than legal) protection of property rights. In the transformation states of Eastern Europe and also in Latin America we observe the opposite situation: Western imports have established all kinds of modern contract enforcement institution, but the economies still suffer from uncertainty and lack of trust because little attention was given to modernising institutional elements such as registers, law of incorporations, law of torts, crime control, insurance, securities, etc, which aim to provide the necessary infrastructure. Similar communication effects may be discernible in the globalising economy, but there is no research which examines both types of support institution, contract enforcement and property rights protection (both aspects are at least mentioned in Shihata, 1997; *en passant* Cutler, 2003: 35). Take arbitration: this private form of contract enforcement is not only supported by state law (recognition and enforcement of arbitration awards), in many countries organised as semi-public or public arbitration institutions (Russia, China) or claims tribunals (Iran-US Claims Tribunal), but is also supported by legal dogmatic scholarship trying hard to introduce *ordre public* principles and establish more transparency and consistency in this area of law. Awards use legal arguments developed in domestic legal communication. They also take the entire legal and non-legal infrastructure mentioned above for granted. Where is the transformation of the state if it were true that business people prefer arbitration to litigation?

A transformation of the state due to changes occurring in the global economy is generally assumed and should not be discarded in this chapter. The evidence is strong in the regulation area, but poor in the area of legal certainty. Any hypothesis in the latter field of knowledge needs to cover both contract enforcement and property rights protection institutions. The remaining part of this chapter will deal with theories which seem to be sufficiently complex for rewarding our curiosity.

MERGING ECONOMIC AND LEGAL SOCIOLOGIES

Both economic and legal sociology contribute to current debates on the transformation of the state and aspects of legal and private ordering: the former by observing the context, the latter by adding substance. They stand at the centre between economic approaches (including new institutional economics) with their rationality, market paradigms and legal approaches with their narrow focus on coordination through state law and state bureaucracies. They have both developed a variety of research tools, namely empirical, comparative, cultural, micro-economic and macro-economic as well as historical and political (which refers to power struggles over the constitution and change of institutions). Furthermore, they reach a sufficient level of complexity in regard to our interest when they distinguish between regulation and support, contract enforcement and property rights protection, rational choice and obligation, and market and hierarchies, and when they keep an eye on all relevant actors which may or may not take part in the coordination of the economy. Figure I is based on economic sociological knowledge (Hollingsworth and Boyer, 1997), complemented by what legal sociologists know about the practice of law and private ordering. It illustrates those multiple forms of economic coordination in social systems of production and exchange and locates them within the regulatory field. Each of these coordinating mechanisms has its own logic, norms and ideologies. Hollingsworth's and Boyer's purpose is to demonstrate the interrelatedness of all modes of coordination and to explain variations of those constellations within capitalist societies. They discourage approaches which look for trends towards a universal institutional arrangement or a convergence towards the US model. A classification frequently used for describing the role of the state in business systems is between regulatory states, dominant developmental states, business corporatist states and inclusive corporatist states (Whitley, 2003b; Hall and Soskice, 2001), each developing distinctive ways of organising the institutional environment of the economy. Although from democratic or distributional points of view it is possible to defend preferences between these models, assumptions are not supported according to economic sociology that the models can be ranged on efficiency and rationality scales. There does not seem to exist a single best way to economic growth (Boyer and Hollingsworth, 1997), at least not if the above-mentioned categories are taken as variables. Other studies in economic sociology are more successful in explaining economic growth by using more specific variables like social ties that bind the state to society (Evans, 1995) or the degree of incorporation of Weberian features of bureaucratic structures (meritocratic recruitment and predictable career ladders for civil servants). In a sample of 35 developing countries, there was evidence that growth is fostered by a Weberian state bureaucracy (Evans and Rauch, 1999).

Although the state is represented by only one box in the picture[25] and its relevance for the economy varies like all other elements of the model

[25] This may come as a surprise to approaches which erroneously assume the 'weak state' and private forms of ordering to be a consequence of globalisation. The nation state as the only coordinator of economic (or any other) behaviour has always been a fiction. Also, the legal invention of a new *lex mercatoria* in global trade is losing plausibility if non-state

(Figure I), economic sociology (more so than legal sociology) emphasises not only its current importance in all social systems of production and exchange, but also in the future of an increasingly globalised economy. For Whitely (2003a), the international business environment is just another model of a particularistic business environment with its own peculiar set of institutional frameworks consisting of national, regional or global agencies, cross-border business associations, ad hoc groups of larger firms, financial intermediaries, international business service and law firms, professional and technical societies, and campaigning NGOs.

> If successful, these efforts could generate a common system of rules and procedures governing economic activities throughout the industrial capitalistic world (Whitely, 2003a: 113).

These rules are supposed to govern contracts across national borders and set technical standards and standards governing property rights, corporate control and competitive behaviour. They are administrated by epistemic communities which include government officials in order to develop 'international best practice' (117). Whitley talks about an expansion of international regulatory agencies and a general trend towards more formal rules and procedures, but he is cautious not to take position in the debate about the 'weak state' or 'strong hyper-liberal state' paradigms. What he expects as a future international business environment could be—at least to a large degree—a consequence of nation-state activities.

By contrast, Fligstein (2002) develops a clear position in favour of the continued dominant role of the nation state in a globalising economy. Although one has to keep in mind that Fligstein's state model is the decentralised and relatively weak US governmental structure, this recent publication is by far the most elaborate study on the institutional framework of markets and succeeds in bridging disciplinary barriers with economic, sociological and political-scientific approaches.

Fligstein's position differs from economic approaches in so far as he posits that economic actors are 'totally dependent on social arrangements to make profits' and that 'without laws, states, and the ability to find non-predatory legal methods of competition, firms cannot exist' (23). He differs from most political-scientist approaches in so far as he argues that the conception that globalisation undermines state control of markets is a dramatic hypothesis yet to be tested: 'There is no evidence that state provision of stable and institutional conditions for market actors is diminishing' (192). This position is developed in the tradition of economic sociology on a broad conception of market coordination similar to the one illustrated in Figure I. There are four types of rule relevant to producing

commercial coordination through the establishment of obligations is already common in nation-state systems of production and exchange.

Figure I—Modes of Market Coordination (Adapted from Hollingsworth and Boyer, 1997: 12)

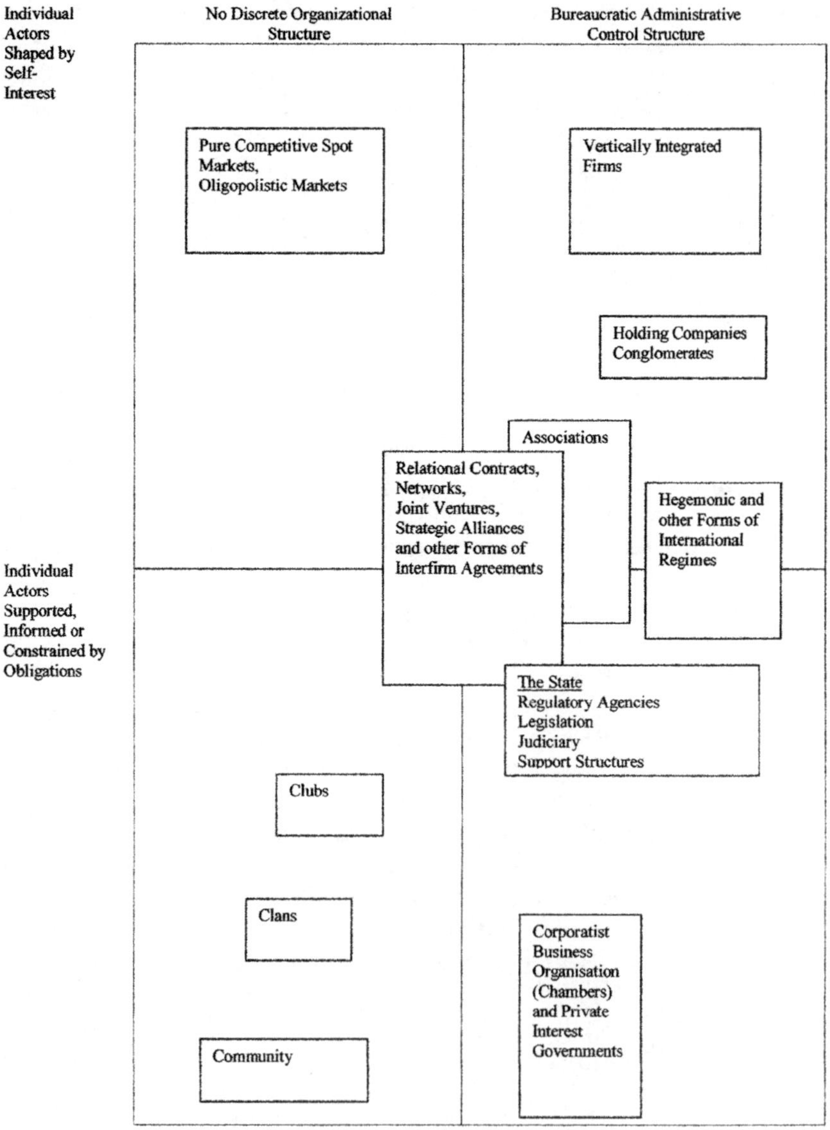

social structures of markets: property rights, governance structures, rules of exchange and conceptions of control. The term 'governance structures' refers to general rules in a society that define competition, cooperation and how firms should be organised. Conceptions of control are cultural patterns—mostly industry specific—about 'how things work in a particular market setting' (35). Fligstein calls his approach 'political-cultural' because the creation of those 'rules of stable interaction' (61) is influenced by culture and the differences at work in different societies mainly reflect the particular power arrangements that exist as societies enter industrialisation (65).

Unlike most other approaches (including globalisation of law debates in the sociology of law), Fligstein is sceptical about globalisation claims and believes that, despite forces of globalisation, economies are mostly organised with firms remaining rooted to a particular system of national property rights and governance (213). This system produces stability and, hence, wealth for the owners and managers of firms—people who still turn to their national authorities for help. Fligstein also presents some statistical evidence against the globalisation hypothesis. In 1996, approximately 83 per cent of the $35 trillion world economy was national, not international. The expansion of global trade is slow: it held a share of 14 per cent of the world economy in 1914 and 16.9 per cent in 1996.

> There are thousands (and maybe hundreds of thousands!) of markets in the world, it is hard to imagine that all of them are suddenly overrun by participants from all capitalist societies (192).

The current instability in global exchanges is a phenomenon of a beginning market.

> The 'networked, learning firm' is a problem to deal with these problems. In essence, it makes a virtue of a vice (225).

Fligstein avoids the fallacies of the above-discussed transformation of the state theories. His approach is complex in so far as he builds his arguments on structural elements of social systems of production which others simply take for granted. He builds on an empirical model of state support for the economy. He also talks about power structures and the interest of political elites in dominating the economy—an aspect desperately missed in most other approaches. One could argue against his way of down-playing globalisation trends and could point to fields of global economic interaction which show a higher globalised share than 16.9 per cent of economic activity. Still, his arguments that current uncertainties are transitory and typical of emergent markets remain thought-provoking. The 'weak state' may be a neo-liberal, ideological, US-American project (220) or an overstatement under the impression of regulatory as opposed to infrastructural problems. In the area of institutional support for the economy, Fligstein's emphasis on state structures as being crucial and without alternatives is striking. Instead of too quickly turning away from nation-state infrastructures for the economy and studying alternative non-state configurations, it seems worth first trying to search for adaptive elements produced by governments in order to cope with global challenges. Alternative forms of coordination may still be relevant—in particular in more globalised areas of economic activity. Fligstein's aggregate data showing a relatively low importance of global exchanges cannot conceal the fact that some branches (for example the internet-based activities) largely lost their domestic roots, that some actors such as international law firms have emerged as key players in international business and that information technology in some globally active branches has radically changed business organisation and the monitoring of ongoing exchange relations. Their dependence on nation-state-provided legal infrastructures and certainty is comparable neither to domestic firms nor to traditional export trade, but Fligstein would probably warn against generalising these observations.

Further discussion and research will have to take into account the 'rootedness' of economic actors in nation-state coordination structures, which Fligstein assumes with no further evidence. His numbers of economic exchanges suggesting that 83 per cent are predominantly domestic are insufficient, since this is certainly not mirrored in every single actor's economic behaviour. Some firms are obviously very global and others are less so or not global at all. The globalisation discourses only focus on the former and these global firms may indeed have largely lost their domestic roots. Fligstein refers to the total of economic exchanges, which then looks much less globalised and more rooted in nation-state structures. Future researchers should (and some of the contributions to this volume do) more explicitly state which type of firm they are talking about and give some evidence for the degree of global (foreign trade) business within the firm's activities. If there is, as the 'globologists' (Fligstein) tacitly assume, a large number of only or predominantly globally active firms, the next research question would be whether they form a global business community (or many of them) with their own structures, communication styles and behavioural patterns. From an empirical point of view, all three aspects have to be operationalised, so that the rootedness and the globalness of a firm and the formation of a global business community become measurable with adequate indicators.

Legal sociology tends to examine more closely than economic sociology how state policies are implemented, how bureaucrats and judges work and how contract law is enforced or negotiated. Fligstein's analysis gives these socio-legal analyses more weight and bridges the gap between economic sociology and theoretical and empirical legal studies. Since the history of law is a history of transformations, the obvious thing to do is to observe more transformations and use for this purpose socio-legal research which has done nothing but that during almost a century. There exists theoretical knowledge which can also be applied to transformations in reaction to the challenges of globalisation and, of course, there is grand theory with ambitious statements. Preferably, the knowledge should be more specific and empirically validated. As regards the transformation of state infrastructures in support for globalised exchange processes, instead of (or in addition to) looking for private ordering, one could trace those slow adaptation processes which happen within the legal infrastructures. Evolutionary economics seems to be a good candidate and research in this direction in cooperation with socio-legal approaches seems to be already under way (Freiling, 2009, in this volume). From legal sociology, two middle-range theories may be used as examples in support of Fligstein's assumption that the nation state, by continuously reacting to new challenges, will remain the core support structure for the global economy. The first example is Kagan's (1984) theory of systemic stabilisation, which refers to the development of large-scale economic and social institutions that ameliorate the conditions that cause individual conflicts or that provide collective, administrative remedies (as contrasted to case-by-case remedies). Empirical evidence is taken from the debt collection area which has been stabilised in the United States in a long historical process by reforms in the banking sector, the offer of insurance for debtors as well as creditors, the diversification of the credit market and the availability of discharge in bankruptcy. As a consequence of law reforms and fundamental changes in the economic and social system (called legal rationalisation), debt collection litigation declined dramatically. It seems possible to observe similar rationalisation processes in the areas of global exchange and dispute resolution. The second example is Edelman's theory of organisational internalisation of law (Edelman 1999), which adds to the current debates on autonomous rule creation of large organisations and transnational corporations— in our context, one not unimportant aspect which fits into Fligstein's state-centred approach. These large firms create their private legal orders by turning to law-like rule-making mimicking the external legal order, by using alternative dispute processing internalising judicial procedures and by employing in-house counsels as quasi-neutral legal experts. By 'legalising' their internal and external relations, they extend the rule of law (by distinguishing between 'legal' and 'illegal') and contribute (in their own interest) to the efficiency of legal systems. Edelman simply adds some more evidence for Fligstein's political-cultural propositions.

CONCLUSIONS

The introductory chapter of the present volume, after resuming the current state of the art in law and economic development studies, compares the global trade miracle with Weber's England problem and the China enigma: some very successful economies operate without formal rational law. England, the birthplace of capitalism, seemed to lack the calculable, logically formal, legal system that Weber identified as necessary for capitalist development. However, according to Francis (1983), the English legal system was predictable for social and economic elites due to strong links between the capitalist class and English lawyers and the lawyers' crucial role in generating precedents. China lacks the rule of law and legal support for contract enforcement, but economic coordination is achieved not through a formal contract law regime, but through government (often bureaucratic) intervention. The state in China and generally in East Asia has, according to Trebilcock and Leng (2006), a critical role in providing predictability in economic transactions. External support for the economy exists in many variations and one should not assume too early that global trade is the exception.

The case studies in this volume offer exciting examples for the private order paradigm and seem to indicate that the crucial role of the state in providing contractual certainty is in many ways disappearing. International mega law firms work together with local lawyers, accountants and credit-rating agencies in structuring real estate investments which under local law would never be created (Flood and Skordaki, 2009, in this volume). Mid-sized international law firms select between different legal solutions on the basis of different legal systems and combine them with different non-legal elements, creating for their mid-sized business clients a level of trust and predictability which for those clients is difficult to achieve in a context of a plurality of competing state legal orders (Sosa, 2009, in this volume). Since state courts are unable to reliably enforce executory contracts for diamond sales, ethnic networks, predominated by Jewish merchants, still—despite current pressures—largely succeed in providing contractual certainty because their community institutions are able to assert extra-legal governance (Bernstein 1982; Richman, 2006; 2009, in this volume). The timber trade relies on relational sanctions, but also on sophisticated standard contracts and arbitration relegating legal advice and litigation to exceptional events (Konradi, 2009, in this volume). International exchanges in the software industry are mainly governed by information and communication technologies. Its capacity and speed of data transfer has increased to such an extent that it has become possible for companies to monitor most actions of their exchange partners in real time. In addition, quality standards provide a normative reference for controversies pushing law and litigation to the background (Dietz and Nieswandt, 2009, in this volume).

These case studies have been chosen on purpose as representing economic activities with a high share in global trade. They cannot and do not claim to represent the average professional or merchant who—as Fligstein emphasises—is predominantly rooted in domestic normative institutions and only occasionally ventures into the global market. As expected, the actors of the case studies form a global business community (in fact, many of them), with their own structures, communication styles and behavioural patterns. However, even apart from their lack of representativeness, these observations can hardly be used as evidence for an emerging global economy without legal institutional support. Contract enforcement remains to a surprisingly high degree structured by state law and to a lesser degree by courts as a somewhat remote sanction in the shadow. Some allegedly autonomous orders are in fact legalising the business branches by mimicking state law. In addition, all observed economic actors depend on state protection of their property rights. Instead of providing evidence of an emergent transnational law or merchant law, the case studies simply offer some more examples of varieties of capitalism and formal/informal patchworks which are or could also be generated in domestic systems of exchange—as has been documented in the law and economic development literature discussed in the introduction to this volume. However, questioning some extreme variants of the private order hypothesis does not necessarily lead us to rejecting the weak state paradigm. The institutional potential of state law observed in our five case studies does not result from state activities like the promulgation of unified law (such as the UN Convention on the International Sale of Goods), reforms of private international law (Wai, 2005) or innovations in judicial systems, but from decisions made by international lawyers, business associations, arbitrators and global firms who make use of state law in an unsystematic way, guided not by superior values, but by economic interests. Law remains important, but states lose control over its application, implementation and its adaptation to new circumstances. As has been discussed previously, this description of a relatively low profile of the state in global legal developments resembles the US-American legal culture. From the point of view of citizens of the common law world, there is nothing fundamentally new in the governance of international trade. Continental Europeans and other civil law cultures are facing developments towards more complex—ie more plural and less hierarchical—institutional structures and less state influence/support in their global exchanges.

REFERENCES

Abel, R (1982) 'The Contradictions of Informal Justice' in R Abel (ed), *The Politics of Informal Justice*, Vol 1, The American Experience (New York, Academic Press).

Anderson, TL and McChesney, FS (eds) (2003) *Property Rights—Cooperation, Conflict, and Law* (Princeton, Princeton University Press).

Appelbaum, RP (1998) 'The Future of Law in a Global Economy' *Social and Legal Studies* 7, 171–92.

Arnauld, A von (2006) *Rechtssicherheit* (Tübingen, Mohr Siebeck).
Badura, P (2005) *Wirtschaftsverfassung und Wirtschaftsverwaltung* (Tübingen, Mohr Siebeck).
Bailey, JE (1999) 'Facing the Truth: Seeing the Convention on Contracts for the International Sale of Goods as an Obstacle to a Uniform Law of International Sales' 32 *Cornell International Law Journal* 273–317.
Barzel, Y (2002) *A Theory of the State—Economic Rights, Legal Rights, and the Scope of the State* (Cambridge, Cambridge University Press).
Berger, KP (1996) *Formalisierte und 'schleichende' Kodifizierung des transnationalen Wirtschaftsrechts* (Berlin and New York, Walter de Gruyter).
—— (2001) 'The New Law Merchant and the Global Market Place' in KP Berger (ed), *The Practice of Transnational Law* (The Hague, Kluwer).
Berger, KP, Dubberstein, H, Lehmann, S and Petzold, V (2001) 'The CENTRAL Enquiry on the Use of Transnational Law in International Contract Law and Arbitration' in KP Berger (ed), *The Practice of Transnational Law* (The Hague, Kluwer).
Berman, H and Kaufman, C (1978) 'The Law of International Commercial Transactions (*lex mercatoria*)' *Harvard International Law Journal* 19, 221–78.
Berman, PS (2005) 'From International Law to Law and Globalization' *Columbia Journal of Transnational Law* 43, 485–555.
Bernstein, L (1992) 'Opting Out of the Legal System: Extralegal Contractual Relations in the Diamond Trade' 21 *Journal of Legal Studies* 115.
Bonell, MJ (1990) 'International Uniform Law in Practice—or Where the Real Trouble Begins' *American Journal of Comparative Law* 38, 865–88.
Boyer, R and Hollingsworth, JR (1997) 'From National Embeddedness to Spatial and Institutional Nestedness' in JR Hollingsworth and R Boyer (eds), *Contemporary Capitalism—The Embeddedness of Institutions* (Cambridge, Cambridge University Press).
Buchanan, JM (1976) 'Public Goods and National Liberty' in T Wilson and A Skinner (eds), *The Market and the State—Essays in Honour of Adam Smith* (Oxford, Oxford University Press).
Budak, AC (1999) *Making Foreign People Pay* (Aldershot, Ashgate).
Buscaglia, E (1997) 'A Quantitative Assessment of the Efficiency of the Judicial Sector in Latin America' 17 *International Review of Law and Economics* 275–91.
Callies, G-P (2002) 'The Privatization of Civil Law and the Civilization of Private Law' *Zeitschrift für Rechtssoziologie* 23, 185–216.
Carruthers, BG and Halliday, TC (2007) 'Law, Economy, and Globalization: Max Weber and how International Financial Institutions Understand Law' in V Nee and R Swedberg (eds), *On Capitalism* (Stanford, Stanford University Press).

Chuah, JCT (2005) *Law of International Trade* (London, Sweet & Maxwell).

Coase, RH (1937) 'The Nature of the Firm' *Economica* 4, 386–405.

—— (1960) 'The Problem of Social Cost' 3(1) *Journal of Law & Economics* 15.

Cooper, JM (2000) 'Latin-America in the Twenty-first Century: Access to Justice' *California Western International Law Journal* 30, 429–39.

Cox, R (1987) *Production, Power, and World Order: Social Forces in the Making of History* (New York, Columbia University Press).

Cubeddu, R (2002) 'Uncertainty, Institutions and Order in Hayek' in J Birner, P Garrouste and T Aimar (eds), *F.A. Hayek as a Political Economist* (London and New York, Routledge).

Cutler, C (2003) *Private Power and Global Authority—Transnational Merchant Law in the Global Political Economy* (Cambridge, Cambridge University Press).

Department ADR News International (2006) 'New Study Reports Multinational Corporations Prefer International Arbitration to Litigation' *Dispute Resolution Journal* 61, 12.

Dezalay, Y and Garth, B (1996) *Dealing in Virtue, International Commercial Arbitration and the Construction of a Transnational Order* (Chicago, University of Chicago Press).

Dietz, M (2002) 'Zur Bedeutung des Rechts für die Ökonomik' in I Pies and M Leschke (eds), *Walter Euckens Ordnungspolitik* (Tübingen, Mohr Siebeck).

Dietz, T and Nieswandt, H (2009) 'The emergence of transnational cooperation in the software-industry' in V Gessner (ed), *Contractual Certainty in International Trade* (Oxford, Hart).

Dixit, AK (2004) *Lawlessness and Economics—Alternative Modes of Governance* (Princeton and Oxford, Princeton University Press).

Drahozal, CR (2000) 'Commercial Norms, Commercial Codes, and International Commercial Arbitration' *Vanderbilt Journal of Transnational* Law 33, 79–146.

—— (2006) 'New Experiences of International Arbitration in the United States' *American Journal of Comparative Law* 56, 233–55.

Drahozal, CR and Naimark, RW (eds) (2005) *Towards a Science of International Arbitration: Collected Empirical Research* (The Hague, Kluwer Law International).

Edelman, LB (1999) 'When the "Haves" Hold Court: Speculations on the Organizational Internalization of Law' *Law & Society Review* 33, 941–84.

Ellickson, RC (1991) *Order without Law—How Neighbors Settle Disputes* (Cambridge, Mass., Harvard University Press).

Estella Nagle, L (2000) 'The Cinderella of Government: Judicial Reform in Latin America' *California Western International Law Journal* 30, 345–79.

Evans, P (1995) *Embedded Autonomy—States and Industrial Transformation* (Princeton, Princeton University Press).

Evans, P and Rauch, JE (1999) 'Bureaucracy and Growth: A Cross-National Analysis of the Effects of "Weberian" State Structures in Economic Growth' *American Sociological Review* 64, 748–65.

Fiani, R (2004) 'An Evaluation of the Role of the State and Property Rights in Douglass North's Analysis' 38 *Journal of Economic Issues* 1003–20.

Fix Fierro, H (2004) *Courts, Justice and Efficiency—A Socio-Legal Study of Economic Rationality in Adjudication* (Oxford, Hart).

Fleetwood, S (2001) *Hayek's Political Economy—The socio-economics of order* (London and New York, Routledge).

Fligstein, N (2002) *The Architecture of Markets—An Economic Sociology of Twenty-First-Century Capitalist Societies* (Princeton and Oxford, Princeton University Press).

Flood, J (2001) 'Capital Markets: Those Who Can and Cannot Do the Purest Global Law Markets' in RP Appelbaum, WLF Felstiner and V Gessner (eds), *Rules and Networks—The Legal Culture of Global Business Transactions* (Oxford, Hart).

Flood, J and Skordaki, E (2009) 'Structuring Transactions: The Case of Real Estate Finance' in V Gessner (ed), *Contractual Certainty in International Trade* (Oxford, Hart).

Francis, CW (1983) 'The Structure of Judicial Administration and the Development of Contract Law in Seventeenth-Century England' 83 *Columbia Law Review* 35.

Freiling, J (2009) 'Institutional Designs in International Transactions—an Evolutionary Economics Perspective' in V Gessner (ed), *Contractual Certainty in International Trade* (Oxford, Hart).

Freyhold, H (1996) 'Cross-Border Legal Interactions in New York Courts' in V Gessner (ed), *Foreign Courts—Civil Litigation in Foreign Legal Cultures* (Aldershot, Dartmouth).

Freyhold, H, Gessner, V and Olgiati, V (1996) 'The Role of Courts in Global Legal Interaction' in V Gessner (ed), *Foreign Courts—Civil Litigation in Foreign Legal Cultures* (Aldershot, Dartmouth).

Gessner, V (1996) 'International Cases in German First Instance Courts' in V Gessner (ed), *Foreign Courts—Civil Litigation in Foreign Legal Cultures* (Aldershot, Dartmouth).

—— (2007) 'Legalisation and the Varieties of Capitalism' in C Antons and V Gessner (eds), *Globalization and Resistance—Law Reform in Asia since the Crisis* (Oxford, Hart).

Göhler, G and Kühn, R (1999) 'Institutionenökonomie, Neo-Institutionalismus und die Theorie politischer Institutionen' in T

Edeling, W Jann and D Wagner (eds), *Institutionenökonomie und Neuer Institutionalismus* (Opladen, Leske & Budrich).

Gordon, MW (1998) 'Some Thoughts on the Receptiveness of Contract Rules in the CISG and UNIDROIT Principles as Reflected in One State's (Florida) Experience of (1) Law School Faculty, (2) Members of the Bar with an International Practice, and (3) Judges' *American Journal of Comparative Law* 46, 361–78.

Granovetter, M (1985) 'Economic Action and Social Structure: The Problem of Embeddedness' 91 *American Journal of Sociology* 481–510.

Greif, A (2005) 'Commitment, Coercion, and Markets: The Nature and Dynamics of Institutions Supporting Exchange' in C Ménard and M Shirley (eds), *Handbook of New Institutional Economics* (The Hague, Springer).

—— (2006) *Institutions and the Path to the Modern Economy—Lessons from Medieval Trade* (Cambridge, Cambridge University Press).

Hadfield, G (2009) 'The Public and the Private in the Provision of Law for Global Transactions' in V Gessner (ed), *Contractual Certainty in International Trade* (Oxford, Hart).

Hall, P and Soskice, D (eds) (2001) *Varieties of Capitalism: The Institutional Foundations of Comparative Advantage* (Oxford, Oxford University Press).

Hartmann, M and Offe, C (eds) (2001) *Vertrauen—Die Grundlage des sozialen Zusammenhalts* (Frankfurt/Main, Campus).

Hayek, F (1949) *Individualism and Economic Order* (London, Routledge & Kegan Paul).

Heydebrand, W (2003) 'Process Rationality as Legal Governance: A Comparative Perspective' *International Sociology* 18, 325–49.

—— (2007) 'Globalization and the Rise of Procedural Informalism in American and European Law' in V Gessner and D Nelken (eds), *European Ways of Law—Towards a European Sociology of Law* (Oxford, Hart).

Hofstede, G (1980) *Culture's Consequences: International Differences in Work-Related Values* (Beverly Hills, Sage).

—— (1983) 'The Cultural Relativity of Organisational Practices and Theories' 14 *Journal of International Business Studies* 1–91.

Hollingsworth, JR and Boyer, R (1997) 'Coordination of Economic Actors and Social Systems of Production' in JR Hollingsworth and R Boyer (eds), *Contemporary Capitalism—The Embeddedness of Institutions* (Cambridge, Cambridge University Press).

Kagan, R (1984) 'The Routinization of Debt Collection: An Essay on Social Change and Conflicts in Court' *Law & Society Review* 18, 323.

Kasper, W and Streit, M (1998) *Institutional Economics—Social Order and Public Policy* (Cheltenham, Edward Elgar).

Konradi, W (2009) 'The role of lex mercatoria in supporting globalised transactions: An empirical insight into the governance structure of the timber industry' in V Gessner (ed), *Contractual Certainty in International Trade* (Oxford, Hart).

Küpper, W and Felsch, A (2000) *Organisation, Macht und Ökonomie—Mikropolitik und die Konstitution organisationaler Handlungssysteme* (Wiesbaden, Westdeutscher Verlag).

Landa, JT (1981) 'A Theory of the Ethnically Homogeneous Middleman Group: An Institutional Alternative to Contract Law' *Journal of Legal Studies* 10, 349–62.

Lehmkuhl, D (2003) 'Structuring Dispute Resolution in Transnational Trade: Competition and Coevolution of Public and Private Institutions' in ML Djelic and S Quack (eds), *Globalization and Institutions. Redefining the Rule of the Economic Game* (Cheltenham, Edward Elgar).

Libecap, GD (2003) 'Contracting for Property Rights' in TL Anderson and FS McChesney (eds), *Property Rights—Cooperation, Conflict, and Law* (Princeton, Princeton University Press).

Luhmann, N (1979) *Trust and Power* (Chichester, Wiley).

Mestmäcker, E-J (1978) *Die sichtbare Hand des Rechts* (Baden-Baden, Nomos).

Muchlinski, PT (1997) 'Global Bukowina' Examined: Viewing the Multinational Enterprise as a Transnational Law-Making Community' in G Teubner (ed), *Global Law without a State* (Aldershot, Dartmouth).

Nee, V (2005) 'The New Institutionalisms in Economics and Sociology' in NJ Smelser and R Swedberg, *The Handbook of Economic Sociology* (Princeton and Oxford, Princeton University Press, New York, Russel Sage Foundation).

Nichols PM (1999) 'A Legal Theory of Emerging Economies' *Virginia Journal of International Law* 39, 229–301.

North, DC (1990) *Institutions, Institutional Change and Economic Performance* (Cambridge, Cambridge University Press).

—— (1999) 'Dealing With a Non-Ergodic World: Institutional Economics, Property Rights, and the Global Environment' 10 *Duke Environmental Law and Policy Forum* 1.

—— (2005) *Understanding the Process of Economic Change* (Princeton and Oxford, Princeton University Press).

Ogus, A (2004) *The Importance of Legal Infrastructure for Regulation (and Deregulation) in Developing Countries*, Working Paper No 65 of the Centre on Regulation and Competition, Institute for Development Policy and Management (Manchester, University of Manchester).

Olgiati, V (1996) 'Cross-Border Litigotiation in Italy' in V Gessner (ed), *Foreign Courts—Civil Litigation in Foreign Legal Cultures* (Aldershot, Dartmouth).

Olson, M (1965) *The Logic of Collective Action* (Cambridge, MA, Harvard University Press).
Ptak, R (2004) *Vom Ordoliberalismus zur sozialen Marktwirtschaft—Stationen des Neoliberalimus in Deutschland* (Opladen, Leske & Budrich).
Richman, BD (2006) 'How Community Institutions Create Economic Advantage: Jewish Diamond Traders in New York' *Law & Social Inquiry* 31, 283–420.
—— (2009) 'Ethnic Networks, Extralegal Certainty, and Globalisation: Peering into the Diamond Industry' in V Gessner (ed), *Contractual Certainty in International Trade* (Oxford, Hart).
Riese, H (1996) 'Institutionenökonomie und Marktökonomie' in R Penz and H Wilkop (eds), *Zeit der Institutionen—Thorstein Veblens evolutorische Ökonomik* (Marburg, Metropolis).
Robé, J-P (1997) 'Multinational Enterprises: The Constitution of a Pluralistic Legal Order' in G Teubner (ed), *Global Law without a State* (Aldershot, Dartmouth).
Rutherford, M (1994) *Institutions in Economics: The Old and the New Institutionalism* (Cambridge, Cambridge University Press).
Saez Garcia, F (1998) 'The Nature of Judicial Reform in Latin America and Some Strategic Considerations' *American University International Law Review* 13, 1267–98.
Santos, B de Sousa (1987) 'Law: A Map of Misreading: Toward a Post-modern Conception of Law' *Journal of Law and Society* 14, 279–302.
—— (1995) *Toward a New Common Sense: Law, Science, and Politics in the Paradigmatic Transition* (London and New York, Routledge).
Scheuerman, WE (1999) 'Globalization and the Fate of Law' in D Dyzenhaus (ed), *Recrafting the Rule of Law: The Limits of Legal Order* (Oxford, Hart).
Shapiro, M (1993) 'The Globalization of Law' *Global Legal Studies Journal* 1, 37–64.
Shapiro, SP (1985) 'The Social Control of Impersonal Trust' 93 *American Journal of Sociology* 623.
—— (2005) 'Agency Theory' 31 *Annual Review of Sociology*, 263–84.
Shihata, IFI (1997) 'The Role of Law in Business Development' 20 *Fordham International Law Journal* 1577–88.
Silver, C (2000) 'Globalization and the US Market in Legal Services—Shifting Identities' 31 *Journal of Law & Policy in International Business* 1093.
Slaughter, A-M (2000) 'Judicial Globalization' *Virginia Journal of International Law* 40, 1103–24.
Sosa, F (2007) *Geschäftsbeziehung und Vertrag im internationalen Rechtsverkehr* (Baden-Baden, Nomos).

—— (2009) 'Cross-Border Dispute Resolution from the Perspective of Midsized Law Firms: The Example of International Commercial Arbitration' in V Gessner (ed), *Contractual Certainty in International Trade* (Oxford, Hart).

Soto, H de (1986) *El otro Sendero—La Revolución Informal* (Bogotá, Oveja Negra).

Stammel, C (1998) *Waving the Gentlemen's Business Goodbye: From Global Deals to Global Disputes in the London Reinsurance Market* (Frankfurt a.M., Peter Lang).

Swedberg, R (2003) *Principles of Economic Sociology* (Princeton and Oxford, Princeton University Press).

Stiglitz, JE and Walsh, CE (2002) *Principles of Macroeconomics* (New York, WW Norton).

Teubner, G (ed) (1997) *Global Law without a State* (Aldershot, Dartmouth).

—— (1997) '"Global Bukowina": Legal Pluralism in the World Society' in G Teubner (ed), *Global Law without a State* (Aldershot, Dartmouth).

Trebilcock, M and Leng, J (2006) 'The Role of Formal Contract Law and Enforcement in Economic Development' 92 *Virginia Law Review* 1517–80.

Twibell, TS (1997) 'Implementation of the United Nations Convention on Contracts for the International Sale of Goods (CISG) under Shari'a (Islamic Law): Will Article 78 of the CISG be Enforced When the Forum is in an Islamic State?' 9 *International Legal Perspectives* 25–92.

Wai, R (2005) 'Comparative Visions of Global Public Order (Part I): Transnational Private Law and Private Ordering in a Contested Global Society' 46 *Harvard International Law Journal* 471–86.

Webb, D (1999) 'Legal and Institutional Reform Strategy and Implementation: A World Bank Perspective' 30 *Law and Policy in International Business* 161–70.

Weber, M (1958) *The Protestant Ethic and the Spirit of Capitalism* (New York, Charles Scribner's Sons).

—— (1968) *Economy and Society: an Outline of Interpretive Sociology* in G Roth and C Wittich (eds), (New York, Bedminster Press, Berkeley, University of California Press).

Whitley, R (2001) 'The Institutional Structuring of Business Transactions' in RP Appelbaum, WLF Felstiner and V Gessner (eds), *Rules and Networks—The Legal Culture of Global Business Transactions* (Oxford, Hart).

—— (2003a) 'Changing Transnational Institutions and the Management of International Business Transactions' in ML Djelic and S Quack (eds), *Globalization and Institutions. Redefining the Rule of the Economic Game* (Cheltenham, Edward Elgar).

—— (2003b) *How National are Business Systems? The Role of Different State Types and Complementary Institutions in Constructing Homogeneous Systems of Economic Coordination and Control*, Proceedings of the workshop on National Business Systems in the New Global Context (Oslo).

Wiener, J (1999) *Globalization and the Harmonization of Law* (London and New York, Pinter).

Williamson, OE (1985) *The Economic Institutions of Capitalism—Firms, Markets, Relational Contracting* (New York and London, The Free Press).

——(2005) 'The Economics of Government' paper downloaded from <http://groups.haas.berkeley.edu/bpp/oew/TheEconomicsOfGovernance. pdf >

The World Bank (2005) http://web.worldbank.org/WBSITE/EXTERNAL/TOPICS/EXTLAWJUSTINST/0,,contentMDK:20934363~menuPK:1989584~pagePK:210058~piPK:210062~theSitePK:1974062,00.html (last accessed on July 28, 2008)

Zucker, LG (1986) 'Production of Trust: Institutional Sources of Economic Structure, 1840–1920' 8 *Research in Organizational Behavior* 53–111.

Zumbansen, P (2004) 'Sustaining Paradox Boundaries: Perspectives on Internal Affairs in Domestic and International Law' *European Journal of International Law* 15, 197–211.

Zürn, M (2001) 'Sovereignty and Law in a Denationalised World' in RP Appelbaum, WLF Felstiner and V Gessner (eds), *Rules and Networks—The Legal Culture of Global Business Transactions* (Oxford, Hart).

8

Transnational Civil Regimes: Economic Globalisation and the Evolution of Commercial Law

GRALF-PETER CALLIESS

PUBLIC LAW AND PRIVATE ORDER IN A GLOBALISED ECONOMY

W*HEREVER WE FIND society, we will find law*. This roman maxim (Sacco, 1995: 456), often ascribed to the Dutch jurist and founder of public international law Hugo Grotius (see Teubner, 2004a),[1] was taken by modern sociology of law as a metaphor for the simple insight, that the globalisation of markets and other social spheres is necessarily accompanied by the emergence of a transnational legal order, although there is no world state as a regulator in sight (Teubner, 1997). In fact, new institutional economics teaches us that economic governance in Organisation for Economic Cooperation and Development (OECD) states, despite an effective legal system, is based on a variety of alternative mechanisms reducing opportunism in contractual exchange (Williamson, 2005: 1; for a comprehensive overview, see Gessner, 2009, in this volume). More radically, the 'New Chicago School' (Lessig, 1998) states that social norms are employed mainly in order to opt out of an inefficient state legal system (Posner, 2000). At least in the absence of an effective state legal system, the normative vacuum left, for example, by low-developed or transformation states, is filled through various phenomena of self-regulation (Dixit, 2004). Occasionally, such phenomena are bundled into private regimes that combine social norms, alternative dispute resolution and non-legal sanctions (Bernstein, 1992: 115; 2001: 1724; Hadfield, 2001: 40). This is well established for the spontaneous evolution of the law merchant, which came about with the commercial expansion in late medieval Europe (Greif, 2006; Benson, 1989). 'Systems Theory of Law' (Luhmann, 1993/2004) claims that the same holds true for modern

[1] However, it is not to be found in Grotius (1625/2001).

times of globalisation, where issue-specific and self-contained non-state legal regimes evolve around functionally differentiated spheres of transnational communication and transaction (Fischer-Lescano and Teubner, 2004). *But do modern private regimes really qualify as law?*

Under the influence of legal positivism (law is the command of a sovereign backed by force: Austin, 1879/2002; identity of state and law: Kelsen, 1945/1961), Western jurisprudence anchored law exclusively in the nation state (see Roberts, 2005), thereby bringing about the domestication of political power under the rule of law. The price for the *internal* formalisation and modernisation of private law produced by the nineteenth century constitutional state was, however, the nationalisation of the once common European law, ie the Roman *ius commune*, as well as the decline of the medieval law merchant (Cutler, 2003: 144; Oldham, 2004: 79). In order to prevent cross-border trade from suffering from the resulting *external* territorial fragmentation of law, soon the idea arose to create a 'world private law' by means of international treaty harmonisation (Zitelmann, 1888; see Berger, 2001). This endeavour, however, turned out to be more difficult than expected. More than 100 years of work within different organisations like the Hague Conference on Private International Law (since 1893), Unidroit (since 1926) and the UN Commission on International Trade Law (UNCITRAL, since 1966) have resulted in little but fragments, for example, the 1980 UN Convention on the International Sale of Goods (CISG) (Ferrari, 2005). The post-Second World War ideological division into the West, the East and the South was, of course, not a particularly fruitful context, but even after the fall of the Iron Curtain, matters did not improve. The negotiations on a Global Judgments Convention, first initiated in the early 1990s in The Hague (Zekoll, 1998; Black, 2000; Traynor, 2000), recently failed for reasons of a purported transatlantic *Justizkonflikt*, a fact proving that even the OECD states are unable and/or unwilling to join for a common constitution of world trade (Baumgartner, 2003; Calliess, 2004). After all, the hopes for a world private law based on multilateral treaties have been deflated (Kronke, 2001, 2003, 2005; Drobnig, 2001).

It was against this background that international law scholars started looking for alternative paths to achieve legal certainty on a global level. As early as in 1956, the Yale law professor and International Court of Justice (ICJ) judge Phillip Jessup presented his functional concept of transnational law, which he defined as 'all law which regulates actions or events that transcend national frontiers' with the aim of founding a branch of jurisprudence more comprehensive than the state-centered law of nations, ie comprising national and international as well as public and private law (Jessup, 1956; Zumbansen, 2006a; Tietje *et al*, 2006). In the same year, French law professor Berthold Goldman, later joined by his British colleague Clive Schmitthoff, promoted a specifically *a*-national understanding of the term transnational law, suggesting that the law merchant might be revived in the context of modern international commercial arbitration (Goldman, 1956; Schmitthoff, 1964; see Berger, 2001).

Today, the literature on transnational law and the new law merchant has become abundant (see, eg Stein, 1995; Berger, 1999; Cutler, 2003). However, there has not yet emerged a theoretical consensus on the concept of transnational law: while many still make use of the expression in functional terms, which remain after all quite vague, others underscore its allegedly 'autonomous' character as a distinct category from national and international law (overview at Zumbansen, 2002). Despite these theoretical divergences, however, in practice scholars of transnational law are united in two aspects of their understanding: they disapprove with the coalition of unwilling nationalists and unable multilateralists, which dominates the international law arena; and, therefore, they engage in alternative modes of constructing a global legal order beyond the nation state. However, this growing school of *transnationalists* is continuously opposed by legal *traditionalists* insisting on the Westphalian paradigm that there is no law except for that produced or at least acknowledged and thus domesticated by the nation state (for a discussion of 'traditionalists' and 'transnationalists', see Berger, 2001).

(Private) Order or (Public) Law? Given the indisputable existence of non-state normative orders in the transnational sphere, the decisive question is how this social reality should be reconstructed from the point of view of legal science (Michaels, 2005). In neglecting the real functional equivalence to state law, which some private regimes accomplish through the bundling of different mechanisms of private governance into an effective private legal system, comprising the jurisdictional functions of legislating, adjudicating and enforcing norms (Bernstein, 2001; Hadfield, 2001; Teubner, 2004b), the traditionalists *on the one hand* take the risk of allowing the law to fall into irrelevance in the face of an accelerating practice of alternative modes of global governance. As a result, these scholars miss the chance of influencing the development of private regimes by constitutionalising them in a comparable way, as the enlightenment's jurists did in subjecting the sovereign nation state to the rule of law (and not of men).

In overemphasising those aspects of private law that help to enable cross-border exchange through the provision of legal certainty, the transnationalists *on the other hand* apply a mere functionalist approach which neglects the cultural and political dimensions of law. As a result, they almost deliberately produce a variety of standard objections regarding the necessary limits to private autonomy with respect to commutative justice (for example, the protection of weaker parties in contract law) as well as public policy (for example, the protection of fundamental common values like competition or human rights) and, thus, the legitimacy of privately created transnational law (Cutler, 2003: 241; see Berger, 1999: 64, 75).

As a reaction to such critique, some scholars propose to limit the extent of the private production of law to issue areas in which the state is disinterested because no public policy is involved. International commerce, where merchants presumably meet on an equal footing, is a prominent example. More generally, Gillian Hadfield draws a line between the *economic* and *justice* functions of a legal system, suggesting that where market efficiency is the sole purpose at stake, the competition of different private legal regimes will lead to a first-best solution. She continues by stating that commercial and corporate law should be privatised, while the justice sphere of the legal system, involving the rights and obligations of citizens, must be delivered by the state for reasons of democratic legitimacy (Hadfield 2001: 44f; Hadfield, 2002: 263; Hadfield and Talley, 2006). This distinction was designed for domestic law-making in the nation state; it is questioned, however, by the current 'postnational constellation' (Habermas, 2001). If Hadfield claims that global political action will have to be taken in transnational settings (Hadfield, 2009, in this volume), this appears to be wishful thinking when the current state of international affairs is taken into account.

For two reasons, I doubt that Hadfield's distinction is useful in the context of transnational (commercial) law. In theory, it seems to be impossible to draw a clear-cut line between the economic and justice functions of a legal system, or—in my preferred terminology—the *coordinative* and the *regulatory* dimensions of law. In practice, transnational governance regimes emerge which actually *do* perform coordinative as well as regulatory functions without being compatible with conventional notions of democratic legitimacy. Transnational Consumer Contract Law (Calliess, 2007) and Transnational Corporate Governance (Zumbansen, 2006b) are prominent examples.

In this chapter, I intend to present an analytical framework, within which an evolutionary theory of transnational commercial law can be developed (see also Freiling, 2009, in this volume). My central thesis is that the debate over transnational law will remain unfruitful as long as it sticks to conceptual distinctions between the private and public which originate in the context of the rising nation state. Once it is acknowledged that the public-private divide cannot prevail when applied to a normative realm that is best described by the term of 'transnational civil regimes' (see 'Transnational Civil Regimes: Overcoming the Public-Private Divide' below), the emergence of transnational law can rightly be perceived as an evolutionary process of legal mutation which is characterised by the innovative recombination of public and private governance mechanisms ('Recombinant Governance: Evolutionary Mutation in Transnational Law' below).

TRANSNATIONAL CIVIL REGIMES: OVERCOMING THE PUBLIC-PRIVATE DIVIDE

In the era of the sovereign nation state, legal theory was based on the paradigm of the public-private divide, which has two dimensions. *Substantively*, the state is ascribed with the task of accomplishing the public good and common welfare (public sphere) in a society composed of self-interested individuals (private sphere). *Procedurally*, the state is constructed as a distinct actor (public sphere), in order to institutionally enable the representation of the whole towards the rest of society (private sphere). A variety of qualifications apply to both dimensions.

On the *substantive plane*, state law is divided into private and public law. The former concerns the relations between individuals; by guaranteeing property rights and enforcing contracts, the state facilitates the cooperation of economic actors on markets, among others; this I call the *coordinative function* of law. The latter regulates the activities of the state in relation to the individual; besides criminal law, mainly tax law and other branches of administrative law are comprised, by which the state interferes with society to steer the behaviour of individuals with respect to public values, for example, free competition, distributive justice or the protection of the environment; this I call the *regulatory function* of law.[2] To be sure, both private and public law are intrinsically related to the fundamental idea of justice; there is no such thing as a purely economic law concerned only with efficiency (but see Hadfield, 2001: 45). For people (including corporations) will not enter a market governed by ever-so efficient rules if the results of such rules with certainty will lead to unjust results. Instead, the coordinative and regulatory functions of law are best reflected in Aristotle's distinction of commutative and distributive justice.[3] For its predominantly coordinative functions, private law is traditionally held to be essentially apolitical in content and, therefore, the making of private law is left mainly to the private parties' autonomy, ie freedom of contract, and, especially in common law, also to judges. The making of public law, in turn, for its regulatory functions, is generally subject to much higher standards of legitimacy; state interference with individual rights is bound to democratic consent expressed in parliamentary legislation. In addition,

[2] For the distinction between *coordinative* and *regulatory* standards, see Lessig, 1999: 759: 'A coordinating standard is a rule that facilitates an activity that otherwise would not exist. A regulating standard restricts behaviour within that activity, according to a policy set by the regulators. A coordinating standard can be imposed from the top down, or emerge from the bottom up; a regulating standard is ordinarily imposed only from the top down. Driving on the right side of the road is a coordinating standard. A speed limit is a regulating standard.' See also Werle and Iversen, 2006: 22; and Schepel, 2005: 2–6.

[3] Aristotle, Nicomachean Ethics, Book V. Another translation for *commutative* justice is *corrective* justice.

any state intervention with the private realm must be based on the rule of law or, in the common law system, is subject to judicial control on due process standards.

On the *procedural plane*, the state is provided with a monopoly in legitimate law-making, adjudication and law enforcement (legal centralism; see for this term Williamson, 1983: 520, 537; Ellickson, 1991: 138 *ff*; Dixit, 2004: 2 *ff*). *Social norms* or *standards* generated by societal self-regulation or private ordering are rejected by the status of law. They may become relevant in the state legal system only indirectly, ie after certain mechanisms of 'degradation' (Michaels, 2005: 1228–37) are applied. While trade usages and the like are turned into facts (deference), other forms of societal self-regulation are domesticated as a subordinate category in order to ensure the supremacy of the state law (delegation or incorporation). However, with regard to *alternative dispute resolution*, the state leaves some space for private judges, recognising and enforcing arbitration agreements, but limits this to the supposedly apolitical issue area of substantive private law (Redfern *et al*, 2004). As a result, arbitration and adjudication do not only coexist, but also complement each other in certain contexts (Sosa, 2009, in this volume). Yet, the *private* threat and execution of *sanctions* is strictly limited by state law, which prohibits not only violence and coercion in the private sphere by means of criminal and tort law, but also limits the exercise of economic power to, for example, legal modes of strike, boycott, discrimination and other forms of social exclusion. A prominent example is state interference with private ordering under anti-trust law.[4]

If both dimensions of the public-private divide are integrated, four categories can be identified, as shown in Table 1 below, where conventional wisdom will have it that regulatory issues have to be treated mainly by the state, whereas coordinative issues are left predominantly to private ordering. In short, under the paradigm of the sovereign nation state, the public-public and private-private categories are dominating (as indicated by dark grey), while the mixed categories of public-private and private-public are of peripheral importance (as indicated by light grey).

[4] See, eg US Supreme Court (1930) *Paramount Famous Lasky Corporation v United States*, 282 US 30 (1930) <http://laws.findlaw.com/us/282/30.html> accessed 19 June 2008.

Table 1—The Public-Private Divide

(Issue Area) Substantive Procedural (Regulator)	Public: Regulation	Private: Coordination
Public: State	Public Law	Private Law
Private: Society	Self-Regulation	Private Ordering

Of course, like any clear-cut distinction, the public-private divide was contested in both dimensions and blurred in manifold ways already under the paradigm of the sovereign nation state. With regard to the substantive dimension, scholars pointed at the fact that the coordinative and regulatory functions of law are deeply intertwined. Especially in the area of 'economic law',[5] public values like free competition or issues of commutative justice, such as the protection of consumers or investors, are often entrenched in norms, which are enforced through private litigation. Prominent examples are punitive damages and class actions in private law.[6] Regarding the procedural dimension, the 'cooperative state' became a popular notion to indicate that the state in modern complex society is no longer able to unilaterally intervene with society, but must be conceived as just one player among others (for example, industry, civil society), moderating and at best catalysing the relevant forces of societal self-regulation by post-interventionist means entrenched in the concept of 'reflexive law' (Teubner, 1993; Calliess, 1999; Zumbansen, 2000). The terms 'new public management', 'public-private-partnerships', 'regulated self-regulation' or 'co-regulation between state, industry and civil society' reflect the modern understanding of the relation between the state and society in governing (Schulz and Held, 2001). A prominent example of the new approach between state and market is the liberalisation of telecommunications and postal services, which came about during the 1980s and 1990s (Schulz, 2001: 101 *ff*; Eifert, 1998).

While this turn in the conception of law and the state was heavily contested in the national realm, the vanishing of the public-private divide—if not its complete absence—cannot be neglected in the context of globalisation (but see Hadfield, 2009, in this volume). The reason for this

[5] Re the German term 'Wirtschaftsrecht', see Wielsch, 2001; and Amstutz, 2002.

[6] See Carrington, 2004, who more generally observes that 'the distinction between public and private law is in America seldom noticed' (1413). For comparable developments in German and European private law, see Wagner, 2006: 352.

is simply that there is no world state at hand which on the global plane could take over the dominating role of the sovereign nation state. If there is no clear-cut actor representing the public, however, it is also impossible to define a restricted area for the private realm. Therefore, the distinction between 'state' and 'society', which is underlying the public-private divide, is about to be replaced by the new and hybrid concepts of 'global governance' and 'global civil society', the former indicating that the activity of governing is no longer reserved for the nation states as the traditional international law actors, the latter proposing that society is no longer identical with the apolitical private realm of self-interested individuals (Czempiel and Rosenau, 1992; Desai and Redfern, 1995).[7]

For the absence of a single player representing the public good, global governance on the *procedural plane* is qualified by a proliferation of actors. This was true already for the traditional sphere of public international law, where many nation states meet on a more or less equal footing, and which, therefore, is based on legal sources quite similar to private law, ie contracts, general principles and custom. The legal centralist's conception of the state as a monopolist in the provision of law is questioned on the global level, where a plurality of states with territorially limited, but partly overlapping, jurisdictions leads to the phenomenon of regulatory competition (Gatsios and Holmes, 1998: 271 *ff*; Kerber, 2005: 296 *ff*, with further references). Moreover, as Slaughter observed, private economic or civil society actors have entered the international law arena recently, engaging in the production of norms and their implementation by alternative modes of governance (Slaughter, 2002: 12 *ff*). For their ambiguous status in terms of traditional international law, such norms are usually referred to as 'soft law', but they may turn into respectable 'hard code' if integrated into transnational legal regimes providing for effective dispute resolution and enforcement mechanisms.

If transnational law comprises private and public law dimensions (Jessup, 1956), the term 'economic law' deserves particular attention in the realm of border-transcending economic relations (Tietje and Nowrot, 2006: 19 *ff*). On the *substantive plane*, transnational private, commercial or business law cannot be purely coordinative in nature. Instead, it has to deal with both the coordinative and regulatory aspects of global economic exchange, since there is no distinct sphere of public economic law available. As a result, transnational civil regimes in praxis deal with both aspects. One example of the intermingling of coordinative and regulative aspects in transnational law is the application of anti-trust provisions by private judges in international commercial arbitration (Mehren, 2003).

[7] A survey of the literature is provided by Mayntz, 2006: 18–25.

If the hybrid dimensions are put together as shown below in Table 2, we get a picture of transnational civil regimes, where in the substantive dimension coordinative (private) and regulatory (public) aspects are merged to what is commonly referred to as economic law, and where in the procedural dimension private (industry), public (states) and civil society actors are involved in co-regulatory efforts of making and implementing transnational private law. I use the term 'civil' for such regimes in order to indicate their hybrid character between or beyond the public-private divide.

Table 2—Transnational Civil Regimes

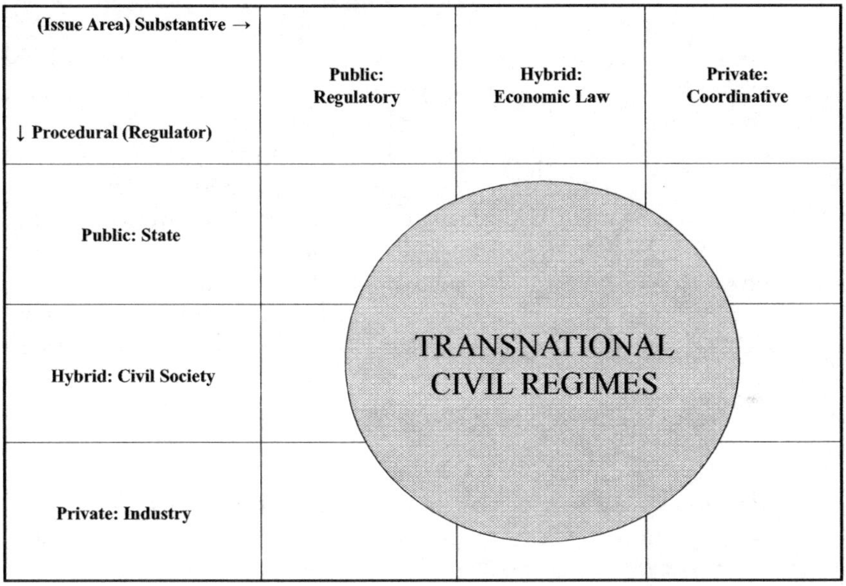

RECOMBINANT GOVERNANCE: EVOLUTIONARY MUTATION IN TRANSNATIONAL LAW

How exactly do transnational civil regimes work? In the literature on 'law and globalisation' as well as on 'law and social norms', we often find the use of the term 'private regime' (Hadfield, 2001: 40, 'private legal regimes'; Teubner, 2004: 'private governance regime'), or even 'private legal system' (Bernstein, 2001: 1725). If the public legal system of a nation state is characterised by the three powers of *legislating*, *adjudicating* and *enforcing norms* in a territorially limited jurisdiction, then a private legal system equally should integrate private governance mechanisms performing these three functions into an effective regime. In identifying such private governance mechanisms, it is useful to build on the theory of private ordering and the economics of governance, which is concerned with the institutional organisation of economic transactions (transaction cost economics: Williamson, 1985: 15 *ff*):

> The economics of governance is an effort to implement the 'study of good order and workable arrangements', where good order includes both spontaneous order in the market ... and intentional order . . . The object is to work out the efficiency logic for managing transactions by alternative modes of governance—principally spot markets, various long term contracts (hybrids), and hierarchies. (Williamson, 2005: 1).

Williamson starts his analysis with the classical distinction between markets and firms. An economic actor in need of a product (good or service) faces the alternatives of 'to make or buy' (Williamson, 2005: 3, 11 *ff*).[8] Economic actors employ governance mechanisms in order to cope with the intrinsic *uncertainty* involved in cooperation, which is founded in *ex ante* bounded rationality, ie the contract parties' inability to draft complete contracts, and ex post opportunism, ie the contract parties' ability to destroy part of the mutual gain from cooperation in order to increase their individual share in it. The relevant criteria for choosing a governance mode for a specific transaction under conditions of such uncertainty are frequency (occasional/recurrent) from the point of view of the buyer and asset specificity with regard to necessary investments made by suppliers (non-specific/mixed/idiosyncratic). Given that the state defines property rights and enforces contracts (lawfulness), *market governance* is the main governance structure for non-specific transactions, for example, the purchase of standard equipment or material. Here, actors mainly rely on market alternatives (prospective exit) and legal rules and litigation (retrospective voice) to protect against opportunism, since the transaction costs of employing additional private governance mechanisms do not pay off. *Unified governance* by means of vertical integration is the most favorable governance mechanism for recurrent transactions with idiosyncratic investment characteristics, for example, the site-specific transfer of an intermediate product across successive stages. Here, access to courts is denied (forbearance) and parties must resolve their disputes internally by means of hierarchy. The firm, therefore, becomes its own court of ultimate appeal (Williamson, 2005: 9).

Private governance comes into focus for transactions with mixed investment characteristics, for example, the purchase of customised equipment or material, as well as for occasional transactions with idiosyncratic investment characteristics, for example, the construction of a plant. Here, specialised investments are exposed by the supplier, a fact which poses

[8] For the following, see also Williamson, 1985: 68 *ff*.

additional contractual hazards, for example, premature contract cancellation. The implied risks will either be priced out by the supplier or the buyer has to offer credible commitments as a relief. Such credible commitments are characteristic for *hybrid governance*, which best fits long-term relational contracts. Since switching costs rise due to relation-specific investments, the exit option characteristic for market governance is of little value. In addition to reliance on the state legal system, parties, therefore, employ mechanisms of private ordering to support the exchange. These may be either bilateral or trilateral.[9] In case of *bilateral governance mechanisms*, the immediate parties to an exchange are actively involved in the provision of order, for example, by posting hostages, engaging in reciprocal trade or otherwise embedding the transaction into a self-enforcing arrangement, where the potential benefits of opportunism with regard to a single transaction have to be offset against the disadvantages of a disruption of the long-term business relationship. The importance of bilateral mechanisms in the governance of cross-border commerce is highlighted by the empirical surveys of the software industry (Dietz and Nieswandt, 2009, in this volume) and the timber trade (Konradi, 2009, in this volume). In case of *trilateral governance mechanisms*, trusted third parties are involved in the provision of private order, for example, arbitration institutions offering alternative dispute resolution services or international law firms specialising in the provision of legal as well as non-legal support structures for global exchange (Sosa, 2009, in this volume).

Because added bureaucratic costs and lower incentive intensity accrue upon taking a transaction out of the market, Williamson concludes that vertical integration is usefully thought of as the governance mode of last resort: 'try markets, try hybrids, and have recourse to the firm only when all else fails' (Williamson, 2005: 12, with an illustrative scheme for contractual governance choice). However, Williamson holds that while the 'main contractual action ... takes places between the parties in the context of private ordering, and court ordering appears late, if at all', 'each generic mode of governance (market, hybrid, hierarchy, etc) is supported by and in significant ways is defined by a distinctive form of contract law' (Williamson, 1985: 10). Thus, the economics of governance is a theory of *private ordering in the shadow of law*, assuming that the state has created and enforces efficacious rules of law, an assumption commonly associated with Western democracies (lawfulness: Williamson, 2005: 1 *ff*; Dixit, 2004: 25 *ff*).

[9] For the distinction of bilateral and trilateral governance, see Williamson, 1985: 74–7. With special attention to bilateral governance mechanisms, cf Williamson, 1983.

Insisting on his premise that even in well-developed countries the state's efforts to protect property rights and enforce contracts are inherently limited, a fact inviting the use of private ordering to infuse order, Williamson, however, acknowledges that circumstances where the state law is 'very costly, slow, unreliable, corrupt, weak, or simply absent' (Dixit, 2004: 3) pose *additional* private ordering challenges (Williamson, 2005: 14). Drawing on a vast array of empirical studies, Avinash Dixit in his book on *Lawlessness and Economics* (2004) recently contributed comprehensive game theoretical analysis to such challenges. Williamson in fact suggests that with regard to his simple scheme of contractual governance choice (try markets, try hybrids and have recourse to the firm only when all else fails) in an institutional environment where the government is unable or unwilling to provide adequate protection of property rights and enforcement of contracts, one could substitute the main explaining variable of asset specificity (ie exposure of specialised supplier investments) by property rights (and one should add contract enforcement) hazards with equivalent results (Williamson, 2005: 15, note 24).

Thus, under conditions of increasing property rights and contract enforcement hazards (lawlessness), there are three options for the organisation of a non-specific transaction (purchase of standard equipment or material), which in an OECD-country would be conducted on the unassisted market: (i) the hazards remain unrelieved and the implied risks will be priced out; (ii) private governance mechanisms are employed in order to add institutional support through credible commitments (hybrids); or (iii) hierarchy is induced by the creation of uniform ownership or other kinds of equity relations (corporate groups, etc).[10]

Taking into account that a situation of *lawlessness* is not only found in low-developed countries and transition economies, but for reasons of a lack of state cooperation through multilateral treaties as well in *global cross-border trade*, where even parties situated in OECD-countries with an internally well-functioning legal system face added institutional uncertainties resulting from the following questions: (i) which court will decide (jurisdiction to adjudicate); (ii) which law applies (jurisdiction to prescribe); and (iii) will a judgment of a court situated in country A be recognised and enforced in country B (see Lowenfeld, 2006; for an economic analysis, Schmidtchen and Schmidt-Trenz, 1990; Streit and

[10] Richman (2004: 2349) rightly observes that it is 'one of the most glaring problems of the legal-centric private ordering literature' to focus on the alternative of public versus private ordering (2338) only, while the alternative of firm versus market (2348) should be included in the analysis in order to get the full picture. For a recent shift from 'private legal system' towards 'hierarchy' in the governance of the global diamond trade, see the contribution of Richman, 2009, in this volume.

Mangels, 1996). The transaction cost economics scheme introduced above, thus, may provide a good explanation for a governance structure of global markets described as follows:

> Recent estimates suggest that there are about 65,000 TNCs (Transnational Corporations) today, with about 850,000 foreign affiliates across the globe ... (which) account for ... one-third of world exports. Finally, if we take into account the value of TNCs' non-equity relationships (eg international subcontracting, licensing, and contract manufacturers) they would account for even larger shares in the global aggregates mentioned above (UNCTAD, 2002: 1).

The increasing importance of intra-firm trade within transnational corporate groups (*unified governance*) and of transnational business networks (*bilateral governance*) is one important institutional facet of economic globalisation. However, these modes of transnational contractual governance work in the spirit of 'think global, act local' in that the employed mechanisms of private ordering are functional only in the shadow of national law. That is to say, transnational corporations (TNCs) work on the assumption of efficacious state enforcement of the underlying equity and non-equity relationships based on local contract and corporate laws enforced by local courts. The same holds true for many *trilateral governance* mechanisms employed by international commerce. One example is international commercial arbitration, the functionality of which depends on the local recognition and enforcement of arbitral awards under the 1958 New York Convention (Lowenfeld, 2006).

Other examples of the involvement of trusted third parties in international commercial transactions (*trilateral governance*) are letters of credit (Levit 2007), escrow services or indirect import and export. Each of these mechanisms work on the basis of nationalising (part of) the contractual relation for the immediate parties to a cross-border transaction by means of involving banks or merchants as intermediaries, which have specialised in international commerce, often on the basis of relational contracting (bilateral governance) with their foreign counterparts. Thus, instead of supplier S contracting directly with buyer B across jurisdictional borders, S sells domestically to exporter E, who has a self-enforcing long-term relationship with importer I, who in turn sells domestically to B. However, note that the intended transfer of the institutional uncertainties implied in cross-border commerce to specialised third parties works on the assumption that the relations S to E and I to B take place under circumstances of lawfulness, ie state enforcement of sales contracts, letters of credit and the like.

However, where transactions become more complex, international networks of law firms are employed in order to tackle the problems arising from multi-jurisdictional transactions. The thus created structures at times reach levels of complexity, which justify a description as private ordering systems of their own (Flood and Skordaki, 2009, in this volume). Where international law firms engage in 'creative lawyering' or 'legal engineering' in order to set up enabling structures for international transactions, lawyers transcend their classical role of simply being organs of a national legal system (Sosa, 2009, in this volume). This kind of 'legal engineering' generates new institutional designs which, in turn, help to overcome institutional gaps in global transactions (Freiling, 2009, in this volume). Thus, lawyers do not only assist their clients in setting up bilateral governance, but law firms also take on an important role in the provision of trilateral governance.

To sum up, the *additional* private ordering challenges resulting from the relative lawlessness implied in international commerce when compared to domestic transactions are tackled by employing bilateral and trilateral governance mechanisms to infuse order (hybrid governance) or by taking such transactions out of the market (unified governance), where all of these mechanisms in one way or the other take place in the shadow of state law. However, one option for transnational contractual governance is left out of the picture so far, and that is *transnational market governance*. The reason for this blank obviously lies in a blind-spot of Williamson's theory, which seems to be a remainder of the legal centralism tradition otherwise criticised by him: that is the underlying assumption that market governance works on the background of contract enforcement by state courts only (see also Gessner, 2009, in this volume). It follows that transnational market governance is not an option unless a world private law is created.

At this point, we finally come back to our initial question which we may now specify as follows: how exactly would *transnational civil regimes* that would enable transnational market governance work? As noted above, a private legal system, which is able to supplant a public legal system in enabling market governance, should bundle private governance mechanisms, which fulfill legislative, adjudicative and enforcement functions, into an effective regime. Thus, for a private legal system being functional autonomously from the state's enforcement mechanisms, it is essential to employ *non-legal sanctions*. The literature basically provides three kinds of example, namely: the reputation mechanism, working best in close-knit groups (informal social control); the exclusion mechanism, working best in organisations (formalised social control); and private force, working best in the mafia (illegal social control) (Charny, 1990; Ellickson, 1991: 126 *ff*; Panther, 2000; Aviram, 2004).[11]

Historical and empirical studies suggest that medieval merchants (Greif, 2006), trade clubs in the cotton industry (Bernstein, 2001) or exchanges in

[11] A slightly different view is taken by Dixit, 2004, focusing on informal, relation-based enforcement (59) or profit-motivated enforcement intermediaries (107).

the diamond trade (Bernstein, 1992) have been successful in implementing effective private regimes. However, how does economic globalisation influence these regimes? The timber industry, where personal business relations, standard contract forms, industry arbitration and network-based sanctioning structures have an important impact, was tentatively able to extend its formerly regional regime to include business partners from other parts of the world (Konradi, 2009, in this volume). Yet globalisation may also have disintegrating effects on traditional forms of industry self-regulation, as seems to be the case with the diamond trade (Richman, 2009, in this volume). This shows that globalisation has multi-level impacts on different modes of governance—private as well as state-based—which are multi-directional. Globalisation may foster private ordering in some cases, but also cause disruption of ancient private ordering systems in others. Such phenomena can be conceived as evolutionary reactions on changing institutional settings in transnational commerce (Freiling, 2009, in this volume).

However, purely private legal systems in praxis are very rare, since any operation of social control which is truly autonomous from the state is delicate. This is obvious for the category of illegal social control conducted by the mafia (Gambetta, 1993), which in OECD countries is more or less effectively tackled as organised crime and, thus, operational only where the state is very weak or even absent. However, it is also true for forms of social control that are in principle legal, since the state heavily regulates non-legal sanctions and, hence, in effect often suppresses any potential concurrence to its traditional plight for being the supreme ruler of society. The operation of any reputation mechanism, for instance, is jeopardised by claims for damages or even prosecution for libel and slander under defamation law. The exclusion mechanism is subject to anti-trust injunctions and remedies, if operated by a market-dominant provider of essential facilities; otherwise it is regulated by anti-discrimination laws or simply by general contract law providing for damages in case of unjustified cancellation of long-term contracts such as memberships.

Where non-legal sanctions are applied in a legal way, however, it often remains unclear whether or not a legal regime, which is driven predominantly by private governance mechanisms, operates autonomously from the state. This ambiguity relates to the fact that legal and non-legal norms and sanctions in these cases do not work in different directions, but mutually support each other in producing order (Panther, 2000). The most prominent example is the 'new law merchant' mentioned above. In light of the three dimensions of legislating, adjudicating and enforcement, only with regard to *adjudication* the exclusive use of a private governance mechanism is indisputable, since the regime evolves from international commercial arbitration offered by private judges. Regarding *enforcement*, however, the states have successfully implemented an international instrument for the global recognition and enforcement of arbitral awards, ie the above-mentioned 1958 New York Convention, which effectively contributes to the attractiveness of arbitration for international commerce since there is no equivalent instrument for international litigation. However, it is often suggested that 99 per cent of arbitral awards are honoured without reliance on state enforcement for reasons of reputation. In fact, there seems to be no positive impact of the New York Convention on international trade between Member States (Leeson, 2005).

Finally, when it comes to *legislating*, reference is made to the fact that the new law merchant is based predominantly on trade usage, which is increasingly codified by private 'norm entrepreneurs' such as the International Chamber of Commerce, by means of model contracts and the like. However, reference to trade usages and model contract forms is also foreseen in national commercial law administered by state courts. In addition, general principles of contract law are often referenced by arbitral tribunals, which recently found their way into so-called 'private codifications' drafted by comparative law experts, such as the UNIDROIT Principles of International Commercial Contracts. The latter, however, are explicitly intended to complement the 1980 UN Convention on the International Sale of Goods. Thus, in practice we find a *mixture* of publicly and privately made norms for international commerce (Sosa, 2009, in this volume). Moreover, the 1985 UN Model Law on International Commercial Arbitration is predominantly interpreted in a way that renders the application of non-state 'rules of law' by arbitrators legal.

To sum up, what we find in the practice of transnational commercial law is a regime based on an innovative *institutional mix of public and private governance mechanisms*. Consequently, Gillian Hadfield refers to a 'privatisation of commercial law' wherever private judges administer private norms, even if the state is present in lending its monopoly on the legitimate use of force to such regimes (Hadfield, 2001: 40, with many examples). Moreover, she suggests extending the model of state-enforced private adjudication to include private legislation in issue areas such as commercial and company law (Hadfield and Talley, 2006). As shown above, however, the institutional mix of public and private governance mechanisms in transnational governance regimes is not limited to the 'black or white' model of private legislation/adjudication and public enforcement. Instead, in each of the three dimensions of legislating, adjudicating and enforcement, public and private elements are often combined in innovative ways to work together in the implementation of effective order, as illustrated in Table 3 below, where the new law merchant is taken as an example. The relative importance of the different governance mechanisms is indicated by white (low), light grey (middle) and dark grey (high).

Table 3—New Law Merchant as a Recombinant Governance Regime

Dimension / Regulator	Legislation	Adjudication	Enforcement
Public	Parliamentary Act	Courts	Legal Sanctions
Private	Social Norms	Arbitration	Social Sanctions

The possible implications of the thus described *recombinant governance mode* are, however, not appropriately described by conventional models of the interrelation of public law and private ordering in the nation state, ie the concepts of incorporation, deference or delegation (Michaels, 2005). Instead, the intermingling of public and private governance mechanisms, which is characteristic to transnational civil regimes, should rightly be perceived as a 'legal mutation' (Amstutz and Karavas, 2006). The processes of institutional evolution in the transnational realm are characterised by regulatory competition and path-dependence (Kerber and Heine, 2003; Freiling, 2009, in this volume). Thus, a transnational civil regime which in practice has successfully established a generally accepted mode of governance in a certain issue area is not susceptible to the traditional forms of degradation that nation states willingly use as a threat in influencing societal self-regulation within their territory. Taking the new law merchant as an example again, it might not suffice for a national legislator who somehow becomes unpleased with international commercial arbitration to simply withdraw from the 1958 New York Convention, because the direct effects of such termination will be limited to a transfer of arbitration business to other jurisdictions, while it may disadvantage resident merchants engaging in international commerce as an unintended side-effect.

CONCLUSION

The theory of transnational civil regimes presented here provides a useful analytical framework to conceptualise the various phenomena of emerging transnational legal orders. It stresses that this process is a deeply political one, which for the involved coordinative and regulatory functions poses questions of due process and legitimacy. In pointing at the dominant praxis of a recombination of private and public trilateral governance mechanisms, at the same time it indicates the crucial mechanisms of cooperation, where the nation states are able to and should influence the evolution of transnational civil regimes in order to safeguard issues of public policy. It remains for further research to show in more detail which selecting factors exactly influence the evolution of the specific forms of the recombination of public and private governance mechanisms in transnational civil regimes and how states may respond to such evolutionary paths.

REFERENCES

Amstutz, M (2002) *Evolutorisches Wirtschaftsrecht* (Baden-Baden, Nomos).

Amstutz, M and Karavas, V (2006) 'Rechtsmutation: Zu Genese und Evolution des Rechts im transnationalen Raum' *Rechtsgeschichte* 14–32

Aristotle (350 BC) *Nichomachean Ethics*, translated by Terence Irwin (Indianapolis, Hackett Publishing Company, 1985).

Austin, J (1879) *Lectures on Jurisprudence, or The Philosophy of Positive Law*, 2 volumes (London, John Murray; Thoemmes Press reprint, 2002).

Aviram, A (2004) 'A Paradox of Spontaneous Formation: The Evolution of Private Legal Systems' 22 *Yale Law and Policy Review* 1–65.

Baumgartner, SP (2003) *The Proposed Hague Convention on Jurisdiction and Foreign Judgements* (Tübingen, Mohr Siebeck).

Benson, B (1989) 'The Spontaneous Evolution of Commercial Law' 55 *Southern Economic Journal* 644–61.

Berger, KP (1999) *The Creeping Codification of the Lex Mercatoria* (The Hague, London, Boston, Kluwer Law International).

—— (2001) 'The New Law Merchant and the Global Market Place. A 21st Century View of Transnational Commercial Law' in KP Berger (ed), *The Practice of Transnational Law* (The Hague, London, Boston, Kluwer Law International).

Bernstein, L (1992) 'Opting out of the Legal System: Extralegal Contractual Relations in the Diamond Industry' 21 *Journal of Legal Studies* 115 –57.

—— (2001) 'Private Commercial Law in the Cotton Industry: Creating Cooperation Through Rules, Norms, and Institutions' 99 *Michigan Law Review* 1724–90.

Black, V (2000) 'Commodifying Justice for Global Free Trade: The Proposed Hague Judgments Convention' 38 *Osgoode Hall Law Journal* 237–66.

Calliess, GP (1999) *Prozedurales Recht* (Baden-Baden, Nomos).

—— (2004) 'Value-added Norms, Local Litigation and Global Enforcement: why the Brussels-Philosophy failed in The Hague' 5 *German Law Journal* 1489–98.

—— (2007) 'Transnational Consumer Law: Co-Regulation of B2C-E-Commerce' in: Olaf Dilling, Martin Herberg & Gerd Winter (eds), *Responsible Business: Self-governance in Transnational Economic Transactions*, Oxford: Hart Publishing 2008, S. 225–258.

Carrington, PD (2004) 'The American Tradition of Private Law Enforcement' 5 *German Law Journal* 1413–29.

Charny, D (1990) 'Non-Legal Sanctions in Commercial Relationships' 104 *Harvard Law Review* 375–467

Cutler, CA (2003) *Private Power and Global Authority: Transnational Merchant Law in the Global Political Economy* (Cambridge, Cambridge University Press).

Czempiel, EO and Rosenau, JN (eds) (1992) *Governance without Government: Order and Change in World Politics* (Cambridge, Cambridge University Press).

Desai, M and Redfern, P (eds) (1995) *Global Governance: Ethics and Economics of the World Order* (London, Pinter).

Dietz, T and Nieswandt, H (2009) 'The emergence of transnational cooperation in the software-industry' in V Gessner (ed), *Contractual Certainty in International Trade* (Oxford, Hart).

Dixit, AK (2004) *Lawlessness and Economics: Alternative Modes of Governance* (Princeton, NJ, Princeton University Press).

Drobnig, U (2001) 'Vereinheitlichung von Zivilrecht durch soft law: neuere Erfahrungen und Einsichten' in J Basedow *et al* (eds), *Aufbruch nach Europa. 75 Jahre MPI Privatrecht* (Tübingen, Mohr Siebeck).

Eifert, M (1998) *Grundversorgung mit Telekommunikationsleistungen im Gewährleistungsstaat* (Baden-Baden, Nomos).

Ellickson, RC (1991) *Order Without Law: How Neighbours Settle Disputes* (Cambridge MA, Harvard University Press).

Ferrari, F (ed) (2005) *Quo vadis CISG? Celebrating the 25th anniversary of the United Nations Convention on Contracts for the International Sale of Goods* (Munich, Sellier European Law Publishers).

Fischer-Lescano, A and Teubner, G (2004) 'Regime-Collisions: The Vain Search for Legal Unity in the Fragmentation of Global Law' 25 *Michigan Journal of International Law* 999–1046.

Flood, J and Skordaki, E (2009) 'Structuring Transactions: The Case of Real Estate Finance' in V Gessner (ed), *Contractual Certainty in International Trade* (Oxford, Hart).

Freiling, J (2009) 'Institutional Designs in International Transactions—an Evolutionary Economics Perspective' in V Gessner (ed), *Contractual Certainty in International Trade* (Oxford, Hart).

Gambetta, D (1993) *The Sicilian Mafia: The Business of Private Protection* (Cambridge, Mass, Harvard University Press).

Gatsios, K and Holmes, P (1998) 'Regulatory Competition' in P Newman (ed), *The New Palgrave Dictionary of Economics and the Law*, Vol 3 (London, Macmillan) 271–5.

Gessner, V (2009) 'The Governance of Business Transactions in Globalising Economies: Theories of Change' in V Gessner (ed), *Contractual Certainty in International Trade* (Oxford, Hart).

Goldman, B (1956) 'Arbitrage International et droit commun des nations' *Revue de l'Arbitrage* 115.

Greif, A (2006) *Institutions and the Path to the Modern Economy: Lessons from Medieval Trade* (Cambridge, Cambridge University Press).

Grotius, H (1625) *De Jure Belli ac Pacis*; AC Campbell (tr), *On the Law of War and Peace* (Kitchener, Ontario, Batoche Books, 2001).

Habermas, J (2001) *The Postnational Constellation* (Cambridge, MA, The MIT Press).

Hadfield, GK (2001) 'Privatizing Commercial Law' 24 *Regulation* 40–45.

—— (2002) 'Privatizing Commercial Law: Lessons from Icann' 6 *Journal of Small and Emerging Business Law* 257–83.

—— (2009) 'The Public and the Private in the Provision of Law for Global Transactions' in V Gessner (ed), *Contractual Certainty in International Trade* (Oxford, Hart).

Hadfield, GK and Talley, E (2006) 'Public Versus Private Provision of Corporate Law' 22 *Journal of Law, Economics, and Organization* 414–41.

Jessup, PC (1956) *Transnational Law* (New Haven, Yale University Press).

Kelsen, H (1945) *General Theory of Law and State* (Wedberg trans.New York, Russell & Russell).

Kerber, W (2005) 'Applying Evolutionary Economics to Economic Policy: The Example of Competitive Federalism' in K Dopfer (ed), *Economics, Evolution and the State: The Governance of Complexity* (Cheltenham, Edward Elgar).

Kerber, W and Heine, K (2003) 'Institutional Evolution, Regulatory Competition and Path Dependence' in P Pelikan and G Wegner (eds), *Evolutionary Analysis of Economic Policy* (Cheltenham, Edward Elgar).

Konradi, W (2009) 'The role of lex mercatoria in supporting globalised transactions: An empirical insight into the governance structure of the timber industry' in V Gessner (ed), *Contractual Certainty in International Trade* (Oxford, Hart).

Kronke, H (2001) 'Ziele—Methoden, Kosten—Nutzen: Perspektiven der Privatrechtsharmonisierung nach 75 Jahren UNIDROIT' *Juristenzeitung* 1149–57.

—— (2003) 'UNIDROIT 75th Anniversary Congress on Worldwide Harmonisation of Private Law and Regional Economic Integration: Hypotheses, Certainties and Open Questions' *Uniform Law Review* 10–30.

—— (2005) 'Methodical Freedom and Organizational Constraints in the Development of Transnational Commercial Law' 51 *Loyola Law Review* 287.

Lessig, L (1998) 'The New Chicago School' 27 *Journal of Legal Studies* 661–91.

—— (1999) 'The Limits in Open Code: Regulatory Standards and the Future of the Net' 14 *Berkeley Technology Law Journal* 759–69.

Leeson, P (2005) 'How Important is State Enforcement for Trade?' Mercatus Center Working Paper 65.

Levit, JK (2007) 'Bottom-Up Lawmaking through a Pluralist Lens: The ICC Banking Commission and the Transnational Regulation of Letters of Credit', University of Tulsa Legal Studies Research Paper No 2007–01 <http://ssrn.com/abstract=1018497> accessed 19 June 2008.

Luhmann, N (1993) *Das Recht der Gesellschaft* (Frankfurt am Main, Suhrkamp); *Law as a Social System* (Oxford, Oxford University Press, 2004).

Lowenfeld, AF (2006) *International Litigation and Arbitration* (3rd edn, St Paul, Minn, Thomson/West).

Mayntz, R (2006) 'From government to governance: Political steering in modern societies' in D Scheer and F Rubik (eds), *Governance of Integrated Product Policy* (Aizlewood Mill, Greenleaf Publishing).

Mehren, RBv (2003) 'The Eco-Swiss Case and International Arbitration' 19 *Arbitration International* 465–9.

Michaels, R (2005) 'The Re-State-Ment of Non-State Law: The State, Choice of Law, and the Challenge from Legal Pluralism' 51 *Wayne Law Review* 1209–59.

Oldham, J (2004) *English Common Law in the Age of Lord Mansfield* (Durham, NC, The University of North Carolina Press).

Panther, S (2000) 'Non-Legal Sanctions' in B Bouckaert and G De Geest (eds), *Encyclopedia of Law and Economics*, Vol I (Cheltenham *et al*, Elgar) <http://encyclo.findlaw.com/0780book.pdf> accessed 19 June 2008.

Posner, EA (2000) *Law and Social Norms* (Cambridge, MA, Harvard University Press).

Redfern, A, Hunter, M, Blackaby, N and Partasides, C (2004) *Law and Practice of International Commercial Arbitration* (4th edn, London, Sweet and Maxwell).

Richman, BD (2004) 'Firms, Courts, and Reputation Mechanisms: Towards a Positive Theory of Private Ordering' 104 *Columbia Law Review* 2328–67.

—— (2009) 'Ethnic Networks, Extralegal Certainty, and Globalisation: Peering into the Diamond Industry' in V Gessner (ed), *Contractual Certainty in International Trade* (Oxford, Hart).

Roberts, SA (2005) 'After Government? On Representing Law Without the State' 68 *Modern Law Review* 1–24.

Sacco, R (1995) 'Mute Law' 43 *American Journal of Comparative Law* 455–67.

Schepel, H (2005) *The Constitution of Private Governance: Product Standards in the Regulation of Integrating Markets* (Oxford, Hart).

Schmidtchen, D and Schmidt-Trenz, HJ (1990) 'The Division of Labour is limited by the extent of the Law' 1 *Constitutional Political Economy* 1–22.

Schmitthoff, C (1964) 'Das neue Recht des Welthandels' 28 *Rabels Zeitschrift für ausländisches und internationales Privatrecht* 47–77.

Schulz, W (2001) 'Regulierte Selbstregulierung im Telekommunikationsrecht. Die informationelle Beteiligung Dritter bei der Regelsetzung des Regulierers in Deutschland und den Vereinigten Staaten' *Die Verwaltung, Beiheft 4 Regulierte Selbstregulierung als Steuerungskonzept des Gewährleistungsstaates*.

Schulz, W and Held, T (2001) 'Regulated Self-Regulation as a Form of Modern Government' Interim Report (October 2001) <http://www.hans-bredow-institut.de/publikationen/apapiere/8selfreg.pdf> accessed 19 June 2008.

Slaughter, AM (2002) 'Breaking Out: The Proliferation of Actors in the International System' in Y Dezalay and BG Garth (eds), *Global Prescriptions, The Production, Exportation, and Importation of a New Legal Orthodoxy* (Ann Arbor, University of Michigan Press).

Sosa, F (2009) 'Cross-Border Dispute Resolution From the Perspective of Midsized Law Firms: The Example of International Commercial Arbitration' in V Gessner (ed), *Contractual Certainty in International Trade* (Oxford, Hart).

Stein, U (1995) *Lex Mercatoria. Realität und Theorie* (Frankfurt a. M., Vittorio Klostermann).

Streit, ME and Mangels, A (1996) 'Privatautonomes Recht und grenzüberschreitende Transaktionen' 47 ORDO 73–100.

Teubner, G (1997) 'Global Bukowina: Legal Pluralism in the World Society' in G Teubner (ed), *Global Law Without a State* (Dartmouth, Aldershot).

—— (1993) *Law as Autopoietic System* (London, Blackwells).

—— (2004a) 'Societal Constitutionalism: Alternatives to State-Centred Constitutional Theory?' in C Joerges, IJ Sand and G Teubner (eds), *Transnational Governance and Constitutionalism* (Oxford, Hart).

—— (2004b) 'Global Private Regimes: Neo-Spontaneous Law and Dual Constitution of Autonomous Sectors?' in KH Ladeur (ed), *Public Governance in the Age of Globalisation* (Ashgate, Aldershot).

Tietje, C and Nowrot, K (2006) 'Laying Conceptual Ghosts of the Past to Rest: The Rise of Philip C Jessup's "Transnational Law" in the Regulatory Governance of the International Economic System' in C Tietje *et al* (eds), *Philip C Jessup's Transnational Law Revisited on the Occasion of the 50th Anniversary of its Publication* (Halle, Institut für Wirtschaftsrecht).

Traynor, M (2000) 'An Introductory Framework for Analyzing the Proposed Hague Convention on Jurisdiction and Foreign Judgments in Civil and Commercial Matters: US and European Perspectives' 6 *Annual Survey of International & Comparative Law* 1–12.

UN Conference on Trade and Development (2002) 'World Investment Report: Transnational Corporations and Export Competitiveness' <http://www.unctad.org/en/docs/wir2002overview_en.pdf> accessed 19 June 2008 overview.

Wagner, G (2006) 'Prävention und Verhaltenssteuerung durch Privatrecht—Anmaßung oder legitime Aufgabe?' 206 *Archiv für die civilistische Praxis* 352–76.

Werle, R and Iversen, EJ (2006) 'Promoting Legitimacy in Technical Standardization' 2 *Science, Technology and Innovation Studies* 19–39.

Wielsch, D (2001) *Freiheit und Funktion. Zur Struktur- und Theoriegeschichte des Rechts der Wirtschaftsgesellschaft* (Baden-Baden, Nomos).

Williamson, OE (1983) 'Credible Commitments: Using Hostages to Support Exchange' 73 *American Economic Review* 519–40.

—— (1985) *The Economic Institutions of Capitalism* (New York, Free Press).

—— (2005) 'The Economics of Governance' 95 *American Economic Review* 1–18.

Zekoll, J (1998) 'Could a Treaty Trump Supreme Court Jurisdictional Doctrine? The Role and Status of American Law. The Hague Judgments Convention Project' 61 *Albany Law Review* 1283.

Zitelmann, E (1888) 'Die Möglichkeiten eines Weltrechts' 39 *Allgemeine Österreichische Gerichts-Zeitung* 193.

Zumbansen, P (2000) *Ordnungsmuster im modernen Wohlfahrtsstaat. Lernerfahrungen zwischen Staat, Gesellschaft und Vertrag* (Baden-Baden, Nomos).

—— (2002) 'Piercing the Legal Veil: Commercial Arbitration and Transnational Law' 8 *European Law Journal* 400–32.

—— (2006a) 'Transnational Law' in J Smits (ed), *Encyclopedia of Comparative Law* 738–54 (Cheltenham, Edward Elgar Publishing).

—— (2006b) 'Spaces and Places: A Systems Theory Approach to Regulatory Competition in European Company Law' 12 *European Law Journal* 534–56.

9

The Public and the Private in the Provision of Law for Global Transactions

GILLIAN K HADFIELD

INTRODUCTION

IN A SERIES of papers, I have discussed the potential and actual role for private profit-making entities to produce commercial law (Hadfield, 2001, 2002, 2004, 2006). Like Bernstein (1992, 2001), I start with the premise that law governing commercial transactions need not be provided by the state—which is to say that the regimes that private parties develop to provide the commitment and coordination necessary to support their transactions are 'law'—a point demonstrated in historical context most forcefully by Greif (1993, 2006). In this volume, two contributions raise interesting questions about the potential for private provision of law in global transactions, a setting beyond the boundaries of the state in which private provision of law takes on particular importance. On the empirical side, Dietz and Nieswandt, based on their study of software contracting between German customers and non-German suppliers, find little if any reliance on private legal regimes. On the theoretical side, Calliess challenges the capacity to distinguish, as a matter of both theory and practice, between a public and private legal regime, or between what I have called the economic and democratic functions of law, particularly in the transborder setting, and urges recognition of the evolutionary process by which mixed public-private governance regimes generate transnational civil order.

In this chapter, I revisit the public/private divide in order to explore more fully the potential for private production of law in global exchange and also to clarify what I think are differences in the way common law and civil legal scholars think about the public and the private in law. These differences stem, I believe, from the centrality of a crisp public/private distinction in traditional civil law theory and the far muddier distinction in common law. As a result, North American scholars such as myself use public and private to refer to a variety of legal dimensions and not only the one I take to be central in civil law. We do have the same starting point: as defined by Calliess (this volume), private law 'concerns the relations between individuals' and 'public law regulates the activities of the state in relation to the individual'. This is also a way in which common law scholars use the terms 'public law' and 'private law', but it is not the only way. In some contexts, 'private law' is defined not by the nature of the relationship (individual to individual or state to individual), but by the private entity status of a producer of legal rules and adjudication and enforcement services. 'Private ordering' is also sometimes called 'private law', but in this context 'private' is defined not by the status of the legal regulator or the nature of the relationship governed, but rather by the source of the content of legal obligations: legal obligations based in private ordering derive exclusively from the intent and consent of the obligated party to be bound. This latter use of the public/private distinction also focuses on the source of legitimacy for the imposition of legal obligation. Finally, 'private' law may be used to refer to the law that parties choose through private ordering to support or coordinate their activities, as distinguished from 'public' law, which is regulatory and imposed on parties' private orderings.

Calliess's analysis suggests that in traditional sovereign nation-state legal theory, all four types of 'private' are lined up: the realm of 'private law' consists of the law governing relationships between individuals, is coordinative, designed by the parties themselves through contract and derives its legitimacy from contractual consent. Public law, on the other hand, governs the state's intervention into private relationships, is regulatory, designed by the state and finds its legitimacy in democratic institutions (parliaments) and procedures (rule of law or due process limits on the state.) As Calliess emphasises, the distinction was challenged 'already under the paradigm of the sovereign nation state' in civil law regimes, largely I believe, as a result of the effort to fit all of the different public/private dimensions into a single category. The law of contracts, for example, has important public dimensions, in that while the content of obligations may be designed by the parties (how many goods to deliver on what date for what price), the rules governing what is a valid contract, a valid excuse, a proper interpretation of written documents, the appropriate remedy for breach and so on are largely developed by the state and adjudicated and enforced by state actors, notably judges. Private relationships between contracting parties are governed not only by obligations of their own design, but also by obligations imposed on them from external sources; obligations of good faith, for example, fit in this category. Indeed, the entire body of tort law, which is quintessentially 'private law' in the sense of governing the relationship between individuals and enforced through private litigation, consists of 'public' obligations that derive their content and legitimacy from outside the parties to the relationship.

As Calliess notes, in common law systems, the public/private distinction is 'seldom noticed'. I think this relative indifference to the distinction arises because in common law regimes, moving from private law (governance of the relationship between individuals) to public law (governance of the relationship between the state and individuals) does not simultaneously bring with it this full set of other transitions from private to public in the nature of law, legal obligation or sources of legitimacy. Furthermore, as Calliess also notes, private law (like public law) in the common law regimes is shot through with legal norms imposed on private individuals which are generated neither by contractual consent nor by 'democratic consent expressed in parliamentary legislation', but rather by judicial authority. Calliess suggests that the law generated by judges in adjudicating private law disputes is apolitical and coordinative, but I do not think that this is how common law scholars would see it. The pressure to see it that way is rooted, I believe, in the traditional effort to keep all of the dimensions of 'private' law lined up, a pressure that common law scholars 'seldom notice'. In a sense, then, Calliess's important effort to disentangle the sharp public/private divide in the transnational context moves us all onto the muddier terrain where there are multiple public/private dimensions which overlap. On this terrain, it is essential to be clear about these different dimensions—to carve some pathways. Some of my disagreements with Calliess's observations about my own effort to draw sharp distinctions between public and private provision of law and the different functions of law stem, I believe, from our failure across the literature to distinguish clearly between the different ways in which scholars in different settings use these terms.

PRIVATE PROVISION OF LAW AND THE DISTINCTION BETWEEN THE ECONOMIC AND DEMOCRATIC FUNCTIONS OF LAW

Let me start, then, by restating the claims I have made about the potential, and motivation, for private production of commercial law. I begin with a distinction, first articulated in Hadfield (2000), between the economic and democratic functions of law, more specifically between the efficiency and non-efficiency goals of a political regime. Calliess suggests that this distinction is the same as his distinction between the coordinative and regulatory functions of law, but for reasons I will explore more fully, I believe these are different.

It is important to emphasise at the outset that efficiency is a normative, value-laden criterion by which we can evaluate relationships and outcomes in a society. It is not a scientific or an apolitical standard. It is a criterion that is adopted only with a view to what a particular society conceives of as the public interest or social welfare. Economic activity is efficient if it is both productively efficient—resources such as labour, time or capital are allocated to their highest valued uses and outputs are produced with the minimum resources possible—and allocatively efficient—final goods and services are allocated to the users that value them the most. Formally, economists speak of Pareto-efficiency to mean an allocation of resources and final goods in which no person can be made better off by a rearrangement of production or allocation without making someone else worse off. Pareto efficiency is grounded in a strict utilitarian calculus in which no interpersonal comparisons are made in deciding who should get what; no external third party can say A should get more at the expense of B because A is more needy or B is less worthy. The only redistributions of goods and services allowed are those to which no individual, based on their private evaluation of utility, will object.

Although the articulation of the Pareto criterion is meant to be non-controversial—presuming that all would agree that productive processes should get the most out of resources possible and there can be no objection, by definition, to the reallocations accomplished in the name of efficiency—it is an overtly normative criterion; it embodies contestable judgments about what is good or bad for society. Economists recognise this: it is a value judgment to say, as the Pareto criterion does, that if B has a lot more than A to begin with, then B should end up with a lot more than A. In many settings we consider it fair, right or just that B, who has much, should give up some so that A, who has little, may be better off. However, to manage this normativity, many economists adopt a separation claim, namely that it is possible to separate concerns about efficiency—making the pie as big as possible—from concerns about equity—how the pie is divided up. So, if B has much and A has little, we can reallocate from B to A, and then apply the Pareto criterion—cannot make anyone better off without making someone worse off—to this redistributed reference point.

Some writers in law and economics, notably Kaplow and Shavell (2001), take this a step further, articulating a strong separation claim: the design of legal rules should be focused, exclusively, on generating efficiency and all other normative concerns, about equity for example, should be handled through redistribution via the tax system. Hadfield (2006) contests this claim, specifically in the context of the potential for a feminist law and economics, arguing that Kaplow's and Shavell's strategy to separate efficiency from other normative goals fails because many 'goods' (particularly rights, such as the right to a harassment-free workplace, and non-market goods, such as own-family care) are not tradeable and thus cannot be purchased with dollars that might be made available through the welfare state. Moreover, building on Sen (1985, 1999), I argue that any coherent use of welfare economics by practitioners of law and economics has to incorporate both the subjective (what we could call 'private' in yet another sense) utility information conventionally used to evaluate efficiency and external (public) judgments about values such as liberty, dignity and fairness. Therefore, I, like Calliess, take it as a given that efficiency concerns and other normative concerns are sometimes not easily, nor at all, separable. However, this does not necessarily obviate all efforts at a public/private distinction: distinguishing the economic and democratic functions of law does not imply that all other public/private dimensions must fall out the same way. Identifying the function of a legal rule as 'efficiency' does not tell us whether the rule governing private relationships must be supplied by private actors and enforced through private litigation, or find its legitimacy only in the consent of private parties.

My claim with respect to the potential for privatising commercial law is not that efficiency is the only criterion of concern or that we can always separate out activities, transactions or organisations in which efficiency is the only concern that we bring to bear in designing a legal regime. Therefore, we are not only interested in efficiency when we think about the organisation of the workplace or the choice of more or less polluting production processes by firms. However, I claim, we can identify legal rules or mechanisms the functions of which are, or can be treated as, exclusively to achieve efficiency: the maximisation of gains from trade and the best use and allocation of resources, increasing the size of the pie.

The rules governing contracts between corporate entities, for example—what causes a contractual obligation to come into existence, how contractual obligations are interpreted, how performance is judged and using what evidence, how breach is remedied—have, I believe, only an efficiency dimension. Corporate entities are not political citizens and do not have moral claims to fair treatment or just distribution. That is not to say that their *shareholders* do not have such claims, but the essence of the corporate entity is that the legal status of the corporation is distinct from the legal status of the shareholders. Similarly, intellectual property ownership rights held by a corporation are economic, not political or moral, instruments; their extent, remedies and use is measured, I argue, exclusively against the efficiency criterion: how does a particular legal rule governing intellectual property (IP) rights affect the efficient production and use of innovative products and processes by corporations? Any moral or political concerns that are rooted in how the state recognises or rewards individual citizens who produce new works and ideas are a separate matter.

When I speak of the potential for privatising commercial law, I am focusing on the production, distribution and pricing of the legal rules that are economic inputs into economic activity. Consider, for example, the transborder software contracts studied by Dietz and Nieswandt. Although they do not present the details of these deals, they presumably include clauses that determine how pricing in the contract will respond to changes in variables, such as the scope of work for the software. These scope-of-work clauses are also likely to be subject to some measure of ambiguity, about what is and is not in the original scope of work and what is and is not the basis for a change in pricing. Widespread principles of contract law see the content of these particular legal obligations—how pricing will relate to scope of work—to be a matter left to the parties, which in my terms is a recognition that efficiency is really the only value at stake. When I speak of the privatisation of commercial contract law, however, I am referring not to the content of the legal obligations per se, but rather to the rules of the regime governing how these obligations will be interpreted and enforced. Therefore, for example, we can imagine that a dispute over the interpretation of an ambiguous scope of work clause will raise issues about what kind of evidence can be introduced to prove the content: can evidence of oral agreements about how the clause would be interpreted be included? What relevance will the ways in which the parties have informally resolved the meaning of the clause in the past have? Will the terms of the clause, in the absence of other evidence, be construed against the drafting party or the more powerful party? Can an expert testify to the ordinary meaning of the clause in the industry? The resolution of these questions makes up a body of contract rules, and it is this body of rules that I claim can be potentially designed and implemented by a private, profit-maximising entity. Parties, such as the German clients and foreign software developers studied by Dietz and Nieswandt, can choose to contract under this body of privately provided rules, much as they now can choose to contract under German law or UN Commission on International Trade Law (UNCITRAL) rules.

If the private law provider operates in a competitive market environment, the set of rules that are likely to emerge through the interplay of demand and supply can be expected to be efficient. The nature of the evidence allowed, interpretive techniques and so on will be offered, which generate marginal benefits (in terms of generating value in the underlying software transaction) that equate with their marginal costs. They will not be designed to satisfy jurisprudential experts about what is fair, just or required by due process in the relationship between software client and software vendor. However, this is not to say, as Calliess suggests, that fairness or due process will never emerge as a component of what the private market produces. If indeed, as he imagines, German firms in need of customised software and foreign providers of that software will not enter a deal governed by rules that fail to assure a fair resolution of a potential dispute about the meaning of a scope of work or pricing term to which they have agreed, then the private market will produce those rules. However, they will not be the rules that necessarily satisfy Aristotelian standards of either corrective or distributive justice; they will just be the rules that satisfy the demand of these corporations for a mechanism that overcomes the obstacles to moving ahead with the deal.

My claim is that, for precisely the same reason that we leave it to a competitive market to determine the particular content of the software development pricing and scope of work provisions, we should also seek to leave it to a competitive market to determine the optimal legal rules governing the interpretation and implementation of those provisions. This is not to say, however, that there is no scope for the state or public law; no role for regulation to accomplish goals other than economic efficiency that may be implicated by the transnational software contract. My proposal that the contract rules governing this private relationship between corporate entities be provided by other private entities does not imply that there are no other relationships affected by the contract (such as the impact the contract might have on German software suppliers, workers in the software industry or consumers of the products produced using the software), relationships that might appropriately be governed by non-efficiency criteria. It does not imply that the contractual relationship might not also be regulated by 'public' entities such as common law judges, state legislatures or transnational political bodies, or that the source of legitimacy for such regulation might not be found in democratic (public) rather than contractual (private) forms of consent. Privatising the *source* of legal rules governing particular dimensions of a relationship does not imply that the entire relationship is allocated to a private legal sphere which, in the traditional sense laid out by Calliess, is strictly coordinative, apolitical and governed exclusively by private entities through private means. I want to discuss three distinct ways in which privatising some aspects of commercial law will inevitably involve, can allow and may require elements of public law.

Combinations of Public and Private Providers of Legal Services

First, as Dietz and Nieswandt set out nicely in their contribution to this volume and Calliess also discusses, the components of any regime which secures legality in structuring a particular transaction—decision-making (adjudication), information processing (legal rules/rule-making) and enforcement—can all be provided by either public or private entities. Enforcement can be provided privately, for example, through the unilateral termination of a valuable contractual relationship by one of the parties in the event of a breach of contract. (This is the self-enforcing contract originally discussed by Telser (1981).) We see widespread use of private decision-makers, applying publicly provided legal rules and drawing on public enforcement of orders, in international arbitration (Dezalay and Garth, 1996). The cotton merchants studied by Bernstein (2001) combine private legal rules with private adjudicators and a mix of public (enforcement of arbitration orders through a court) and private (reputational, collective refusal-to-deal) mechanisms. Any individual legal rule may thus involve both public and private entities as providers of the legal services of rule-making, adjudication and enforcement.

Publicly Provided Infrastructure for Private Provision of Law

Secondly, even if we restrict our attention to legal rules for which all three services of rule-making, adjudication and enforcement are provided by private profit-making entities, like any market, a market for the provision of private law depends on the availability of legal infrastructure. The most obvious sense in which this is true is with respect to contract enforcement: if legal rules or adjudication are privately provided through a market, the transactions (buying and selling legal rules or adjudication services) are likely to require a mechanism for establishing the content of the transactions, judging their performance and remedying their breach. The private provider of legal rules or adjudication makes a commitment, at the time parties choose to draw on the provider's product (such as when they agree to have their substantive transaction—selling cotton, for example—adjudicated under the provider's rules), to provide that service as promised. Often that commitment will be backed by a contract enforceable under publicly provided law.

Even if the legal infrastructure supporting a private legal regime is provided by another private mechanism—such as reputation or private certification by yet another private provider of legality—eventually there is likely to be a point at which publicly provided law plays a role. (Essentially, private displacement of the public legal rules governing an underlying transaction simply moves the locus at which the public law may need to operate, travelling up the commitment chain, as it were.) All of the mechanisms for supporting transactions are embedded in and generally rely on the publicly provided legal environment, in complex and subtle ways. Hadfield (2005) discusses at length the ways in which simple contract law depends on multiple, generally publicly provided, legal institutions such as the organisation of courts and the legal profession, substantive laws of bankruptcy, procedure, corporations, competition, etc, procedural laws related to evidence production and the conduct of hearings or trials, and the enforcement tools (injunction, garnishment orders, identification of assets, bailiff services, etc) necessary to collect on a judgment. Here I want to explore the relationship between publicly provided law and ostensibly non-legal commitment mechanisms, such as self-enforcement, reputation, technological and organisational mechanisms (Hadfield, 2005).

Let us start with the apparently most self-contained commitment devices: self-enforcing mechanisms. The defining feature of these mechanisms, from an economic point of view, is that they can be unilaterally implemented by the party who suffers the default of a transacting partner: a bond or hostage can be retained or a trading relationship suspended. Even these mechanisms, however, depend on the legal environment in which they reside. In particular, they depend on the presence or absence of default or background rules of obligation attached to these unilateral actions. Even a simple suspension of trading is not always and everywhere without legal consequence. The capacity to terminate some relationships is governed by statute. Employment relationships in many countries, for example, cannot be terminated at will; they may require minimal notice or separation payments, or they may prohibit termination without good cause. More generally, any relationship is subject to claims of implicit contractual restrictions on termination, either through the interpretation of explicit terms in the contract or the application of factually or legally implied terms such as the obligation of good faith and fair dealing. Similarly, the capacity to retain a bond or hostage (asset) depends on background laws governing assignment of property rights and potential contract arguments about the nature of the assigned authority over the asset. Moreover, in many settings, a self-enforcing mechanism involving a bond or hostage generates a mirror-image problem, that of the wrongful retention of the bond or hostage by the promisee even after the promise has been performed. Problems such as these are resolved through additional mechanisms such as the use of an escrow agent. The availability of this mechanism, however, depends on the legal environment and specifically the enforceability of claims (common-law or statutory fiduciary duties, for example) on the escrow agent.

Reputational mechanisms, often seen as the epitome of a pure market enforcement mechanism, also depend on the background legal environment. The essence of a reputation mechanism is the communication of information about default to others not involved in the original transaction. The transmission of information is subject to multiple legal rules, including defamation and freedom of expression laws and privacy and confidentiality regulation, whether rooted in statutes or contracts. Laws also affect the extent to which third parties have a right to access information about a potential trading partner, such as credit history, and the extent to which individuals and entities are obliged to disclose information about their past behaviour. The willingness and/or authority of courts to maintain the confidentiality of court settlements that might reveal breach of contract or the obligation to disclose defaults to shareholders, for example, affects reputation. Where reputation is exercised through a community mechanism (Greif, 2006), competition laws may come into effect, controlling boycotts and concerted refusals to deal, for example. Furthermore, where reputation is crystallised into the value of a name or trademark, laws governing the protection of trademarks and the potential to use trademark law to prevent publication of information relating to the trademark can affect the quality and transmission of information.

Organisational commitment mechanisms—which shift decision-making authority to different agents in order to change the nature of the incentives and information that will affect decision-making—depend extensively on the legal environment. The capacity to integrate horizontally or vertically is affected by laws governing corporate form and competition. The availability of other organisational structures that might alter incentives—joint ownership of assets, joint ventures, partnerships—depends on a host of legal rules including those determining the legal capacity of an entity to sue and be sued, the liability of owners and managers for third-party harms and their duties to each other, tax regimes, pension obligations, environmental liability and so on. Other organisational structures to support commitment, such as the delegation of control over information or decisions (such as accounting practices or the handling of confidential data) to a third party, depends on the legal environment in which those third parties operate: their liability for failure to adhere to professional standards, for example, or to comply with the terms of their delegation.

Even a reliance on technology to support commitment—the use of encryption devices, for example, to back up a promise not to distribute confidential data—depends on legal rules: the intellectual property regime, privacy law, the enforceability of agreements established through technological means such as click-ware or shrink-wrap. The use of technology to provide legality on the internet, for example, depends on the enforcement of agreements within certification hierarchies and between service providers and users to permit the technological disabling of access when identification or security requirements are not met, and often the protection of trademarks and symbols intended to signal the use of encryption or other security measures (Hadfield, 2005).

The pervasive role of publicly provided law in structuring even ostensibly extra-legal enforcement mechanisms takes on particular salience in the global context. Although transborder actors may perceive themselves to be operating beyond the bounds of the state, any actions they take under their contracts must of course happen within a particular country. The background legal regime in that country then shapes the legal status of those actions. Parties that perceive themselves to rely heavily on suspension of a trading relationship as an enforcement mechanism may find themselves facing a legal environment in which one of the parties (especially the party that lives in that jurisdiction) is able to raise the cost or lower the effectiveness of this mechanism by taking the matter to a court inclined to find an implied obligation not to suspend. Networks of traders who travel across borders and rely on information exchange within the network to provide enforcement may find that traders in one jurisdiction are able to draw on privacy laws to stymie the exchange of information, or they may find that a weak defamation regime undermines the mechanism by allowing the exchange to become infected with disinformation.

Thus, as a practical matter, the publicly provided law in individual states is inevitably implicated in the development, use and effectiveness of privately provided legal/commitment regimes across borders. Thus, while much of what evolves through private mechanisms to support global exchange may be the product of private actors, there is a continued role for states individually and collectively to design legal regimes that support cross-border transactions.

Public Regulation of Private Legal Regimes

Public and private legal regimes are also intertwined as a normative matter. Private legal regimes, as I have mentioned, will successfully provide the legal inputs demanded by transacting parties only if the market for private law is a competitive one. This is likely to require public regulation to some extent. There is the ordinary need for competition law, as in any market for goods or services, to prevent monopolistic practices and anti-competitive collusion. However, markets for privately provided legal regimes are likely to be especially vulnerable to market imperfections, due primarily to the extent to which information and ideas are a component of legal products. Let me discuss two of these imperfections.

First, because legal rules are essentially ideas, as goods they are subject to appropriation by those who have not paid for them. Non-excludability is the fundamental market problem addressed by intellectual property laws, which prohibit appropriation under certain circumstances by those who have not paid for the use of an idea embodied in a writing, performance, process or good. Effective development of private markets for legal rules, therefore, requires some form of protection for the ideas embodied in legal rules, to the extent that those ideas are the product of investments of time, resources and effort. This need not take the form of patents or even copyright, although it might. Much intellectual property is protected by private arrangements of confidentiality (contracts binding those who have access to the rules not to use them or reveal them without authorisation) and public protection of trade secrets (tort duties of maintaining confidences when information is not publicly shared).

Secondly, again because legal rules are ideas, and often complex ones at that, they are likely to be subject to the phenomenon of network externalities. Network externalities exist when the value of a good to any one consumer of the good is increased when there are larger numbers of others who are also consuming the good. The classic example is a telephone system—the more people who connect onto a particular system, the more people any one subscriber can call. The modern example is the computer operating system: the more people there are who use a particular operating system, the more applications and computers using the system there will be for users to buy, and the more expertise there will be available for help in using or fixing the system. This latter benefit from an increased 'installed base' helps to explain why legal rules can be subject to network externalities. Particularly if they are complex, the larger the group of contracting parties who use the rules, the greater will be the availability of expertise in using the rules: lawyers and legal personnel within corporations will find it worthwhile to invest time and effort in learning how the rules work and how they are implemented by adjudicators. Like the market for computer operating systems, then, a market for legal rules would face a risk of evolving as a monopoly, potentially leading to abuse of monopoly power and the loss of the benefits that arise from private production. Publicly provided competition law would then be necessary to ensure that the private market for legal rules operated competitively.

Both of these forms of public regulation are directed to improving the efficiency of private legal regimes. This is why I do not agree with Calliess that the economic/democratic distinction is the same as his coordinative/regulatory distinction. But what of normative goals other than efficiency that are implicated by the transactions structured using a private legal regime? Calliess raises this as a concern, with examples such as the impact of corporate governance on labour and distributive concerns with respect to consumer contracts. However, the distinction that I aim to draw, and to advocate as an organising principle for thinking about legal design, is not between *transactions or relationships* that are measured exclusively in efficiency terms and those that are not—I think there are some, but this is not important to my point—but rather between *legal rules or mechanisms* that are measured exclusively in efficiency terms and those that are not. From this point of view, I see no difficulty in the observation, with which I agree, that many transactions and relationships implicate both efficiency and democratic or justice-based criteria. The key is to identify the functions of the multiple particular legal rules or legal regimes that regulate a transaction or relationship. A rule of damages for breach of a corporate contract has as its function the achievement of efficiency: giving contracting firms sufficient confidence in the performance of their contracts to encourage them to relinquish alternative deals and invest in a particular one. The content of such a rule is assessed—from a public policy perspective—on the basis of how well it achieves these efficiency objectives. A rule that allows a firm to rescind its contracts without penalty within three days has as its function an external assessment of the need for third-party protection of, for example, smaller or less sophisticated firms.

Such a rule is evaluated in policy terms in light of how well it achieves the fairness goal of protecting weaker firms from unfair bargaining or exploitation of differences in information or sophistication. My claim is that the rule governing damages can be privatised and indeed that the legal rule that emerges will be better if its production is privatised.[1] However, there is no reason to think that private competition between profit-making firms will generate a legal rule governing contract rescission for weaker firms that achieves fairness goals. Fundamentally, fairness is external to the values of the parties, and that is all to which private competition can (if it works) respond.

Moreover, subjecting the transaction to the rescission rule is an action taken by third parties external to the transaction: it imposes on them, and is not, like the rule of damages, chosen by them. This takes us to the question of legitimacy, a topic to which I now turn.

PRIVATE PROVISION OF LAW AND THE PROBLEM OF LEGITIMACY

I suggested in the introduction that it was helpful to distinguish at least four public/private dimensions in legal regimes and not to conflate any of those four with the efficiency/democratic distinction I draw on more generally in thinking about legal design. These four dimensions are: the nature of the *relationship* being governed (individual-individual versus state-individual); the status of the *provider* of legal services (private entities versus state entities); the source of the *content* of legal obligations (the parties themselves or the state); and, relatedly, the source of *legitimacy* (consent or democratic institutions/procedures) for legal obligations. As I discussed in the previous section, legal rules that are directed exclusively to the efficiency function of law can be provided by private or public entities, have their content established by the parties or by the state and their legitimacy rooted in consent or democratic institutions. My distinction between the economic efficiency and democratic functions of law is thus not intended to line up with a distinction between the public and the private on all of these other four dimensions. Indeed, the distinction between the efficiency and democratic functions of law arises from the

[1] Calliess suggests that I claim that the privatised legal rule will be first-best, in economist's terms. This is only true if the market for legal rules is perfectly competitive, which few real markets are and, as I discuss above, the market for intellectual products such as rules is not likely to be. The relevant question is whether private competition between profit-making firms will lead to a better legal rule than public production by the state. I have looked at this question more formally in the context of corporate legal rules in Hadfield and Talley (2006). We develop a model there in which private competition does not lead to the first-best, but private competition between firms does better than regulatory competition between state legislatures.

critical public/private dimension of legitimacy. My claim has been (Hadfield, 2001) that it is for reasons of democratic legitimacy that I have advocated private provision of law only for legal rules which serve, exclusively, efficiency goals. I would like to revisit this question here, particularly in the context of transborder trade and, as Calliess emphasises, the normative challenges of a transnational civil order.

Legal rules serve exclusively efficiency goals when they can be evaluated in policy terms entirely on the basis of the extent to which they promote the allocation of resources to their highest-valued uses and the production of goods and services with minimal expenditure of resources. In competitive markets, this is what private contracting accomplishes and legal inputs (for example, legal rules governing contractual relationships) promote the value of contracting relationships when they help to overcome problems of commitment, private information, costly bargaining, coordination, etc and do so in a way that minimises the expenditure of resources on legal services of a given level of quality. The point is not to spend as little as possible on legal services, but to spend only up to the point at which the marginal value of the legal service is approximately equal to the marginal cost of the legal service.

In market economies, we leave the assessment of costs and values to private actors engaged in private transactions. If consumers express a willingness to pay for higher quality computers, we leave it to the market to allocate more resources to the production of computers. If the cost of some input such as oil goes up, we leave it to the market to reduce the use of oil, innovate substitute inputs and processes, and shift consumption away from oil-consuming products. A key premise for the conclusion that leaving these valuations exclusively to private actors in exchange will lead to efficient resource use and allocation is that in any given transaction there are no externalities that the transacting parties do not take into account: the quality of a shipment of computers and the oil consumed in their production does not impact anyone other than the buyer and seller of this shipment of these computers. Moreover, we assume that the parties to the transaction are the best judge of their own welfare, and so there is no call to substitute external judgments about value for those reached privately by these parties in this exchange.

The legitimacy of a private legal regime, with law produced by private entities, rests in the consent of the parties who choose to subject themselves to the regime. This is always an appropriate regime from a policy perspective when the only public value at stake is the efficiency of private transactions: the parties themselves are the best judge of the value of alternative transactions and the decision to invoke a private legal regime is best left to them. However, as in the underlying transaction, this is only true if there are no externalities and no reason to doubt the capacity of the transacting parties to judge the value of legal rules for themselves.

If these externality criteria are not met, as they are not in some dimension for many transactions—the use of oil does, for example, have an impact on others through phenomena such as pollution and global warming—then there is a basis for imposing legal rules—environmental limits, for example—on the transaction other than the ones the parties will choose themselves. The question is: can *those* legal rules be imposed by private entities? Clearly they can if the parties consent; and clearly parties do sometimes consent to be bound to rules that are put in place for the benefit of others. However, in the absence of consent, the legitimacy of the legal rules must be found elsewhere.

It is this problem of democratic legitimacy that limits my otherwise unreserved proposal for increasing the use of private legal regimes to the commercial setting where efficiency is the only public value at stake. I do not mean to say that private legal regimes, adopted through consent, cannot or will not emerge that will serve other public values such as environmental protection or human rights. There is nothing incompatible with my approach and what Calliess identifies as examples of public/private transnational governance regimes that perform regulatory as well as coordinative functions, imposing limits on corporate governance or consumer contracts. The problem of legitimacy in those cases is resolved through consent.

Furthermore, where the relevant actors are exclusively corporate, and thus the exclusive criterion for evaluating the legal treatment of these entities is efficiency, I see no problem of legitimacy in the imposition of legal rules on these actors without their consent by private legal providers, so long as the private legal providers operate in a competitive market that leads to the production of efficient legal rules. The competitiveness of the market is the protection against outright confiscation of corporate wealth by private legal entities—if the private regulatory rules are efficient, they generate pollution limits, for example, only to the extent that such limits promote efficient use of polluting resources such as oil. There may well be *practical* problems—whether competitive markets for regulation that are not based in the consent of the regulated can exist is a question I have not explored in depth. However, I do not believe that there is a problem of *legitimacy* in this corporate context: as I indicated earlier, I believe corporate entities exist for the purpose of efficient markets and (unlike their shareholders) do not have political or moral claims. The limit on regulatory imposition is determined by what is efficient, not by what is fair or just in the treatment of the corporate entity.

However, where the limits on regulation are rooted in values other than efficiency, where legal rules are imposed without consent on people who do have democratic claims on fair and just treatment, the privatisation of law cannot easily be legitimated. I do not know if it can never be—this is a question I have not explored, although Hadfield (2002) discusses the use of

Internet Corporation for Assigned Names and Numbers (ICANN)—a private non-profit entity—to regulate both corporate and natural persons' access to the domain name registration system on the internet. However, it is clear that there will be many cases in which it cannot be. The democratic nation state draws on a variety of mechanisms to legitimate the imposition of law on individuals without their consent: legislative and administrative bodies subject to the requirements of political accountability to an electorate, constitutionally constrained courts and so on. The challenge is to understand how transnational law-imposing entities can operate democratically in order to legitimate the imposition of legal rules on individuals with democratic claims.

CONCLUSION

Studying the potential for private provision of transnational legal regimes involves several components: empirical/descriptive, theoretical/predictive and normative/ prescriptive work. Empirical work on the kinds of legal regime we see emerging in the transnational setting—such as the work of Dietz and Nieswandt—provides us with important input in understanding what might be theoretically possible for private provision of law as well as what might be normatively desirable. The fact that Dietz and Nieswandt, for example, find little evidence of reliance on private legal regimes in the computer software contracts they studied, for example, indicates that we need to explore whether such regimes have not emerged because they do not meet the needs of the parties or whether they lack the public law infrastructure necessary to come into existence.

Calliess's contribution is not empirical per se, but he does appeal to the patterns of public and private law production in the transnational setting in challenging the value of the efficiency/democratic distinction I advocate, and I think it is important to be clear here about the relationship I see between the empirical evidence and the normative project of evaluating the desirability of privatising law production. I think Calliess is right to point to the emergence of mixed public-private transnational governance regimes which cross over from coordinative to regulatory functions as evidence of the possibility that democratic legitimacy may be rooted in the transnational setting outside of the conventional national legislative setting. Common law scholars are probably less sensitive to this observation than civil law scholars because of the long-standing need to theorise the democratic legitimacy of common law judging within the nation state. However, the fact that mixed public-private transnational governance regimes are, in fact, supplying law that is not only coordinative, but also regulatory in nature, does not, of itself, solve the problem of democratic legitimacy. I suspect that many of the cases Calliess has in mind involve consent to the imposition of the relevant legal rules. However, in any event, it is clearly a project called for in the study of the emergence of transnational civil society. Particularly because, as Calliess notes, so much of what takes place in the transnational setting is driven by commercial corporate actors who can adjust their transactions to shift outside of the reach of national legal regimes, it is important, I believe, to be sharply attuned to the distinction between the economic efficiency and the democratic functions of law. The private market processes that will emerge rapidly in the transnational setting may well serve the efficiency function, but I suspect that achieving the democratic functions will require political, not economic, global action.

REFERENCES

Bernstein, L (1992) 'Opting Out of the Legal System: Extralegal Contractual Relations in the Diamond Industry' 21 *Journal of Legal Studies* 115–57.

—— (2001) 'Private Commercial Law in the Cotton Industry: Creating Cooperation through Rules, Norms and Institutions' 99 *Michigan Law Review* 1724–90.

Calliess, G-P (2009) 'Transnational Civil Regimes: Economic Globalization and the Evolution of Commercial Law' in V Gessner (ed), *Contractual Certainty in International Trade* (Oxford, Hart).

Dezalay, Y and Garth, B (1996) *Dealing in Virtue: International Commercial Arbitration and the Construction of a Transnational Legal Order* (Chicago, University of Chicago Press).

Dietz, T and Nieswandt, H (2009) 'The Emergence of Transnational Cooperation in the Software Industry' in V Gessner (ed), *Contractual Certainty in International Trade* (Oxford, Hart).

Greif, A (1993) 'Contract Enforceability and Economic Institutions in Early Trade: The Maghribi Traders' Coalition' 83 *American Economic Review* 525–48.

—— (2006) *Institutions and the Path to the Modern Economy: Lessons from Medieval Trade* (Cambridge, MA, Cambridge University Press).

Hadfield, GK (2000) 'The Price of Law: How the Market for Lawyers Distorts the Justice System' 98 *Michigan Law Review* 953–1006.

—— (2001) 'Privatizing Commercial Law' 24 *Regulation* 40–45.

—— (2002) 'Privatizing Commercial Law: Lessons from ICANN' 6 *Journal of Small and Emerging Business Law* 257–283.

—— (2004) 'Delivering Legality on the Internet: Developing Principles for the Private Provision of Commercial Law' 6 *American Law and Economics Review* 154–184.

—— (2005) 'The Many Legal Institutions that Support Contractual Commitments' in C. Menard and M. Shirley (eds.) *Handbook of New Institutional Economics* (The Hague, Kluwer).

—— (2006) 'Feminism, Fairness and Welfare: An Invitation to Feminist Law and Economics' 1 *Annual Review of Law and Social Science* 285–306.

Hadfield, GK and Talley, E (2006) 'On Public versus Private Provision of Corporate Law' 22 *Journal of Law, Economics and Organization* 414–41.

Kaplow, L and Shavell, S (2001) *Fairness versus Welfare* (Cambridge, MA, Harvard University Press).

Sen, A (1985) '*Social Choice and Justice*: A Review Article' 23 *Journal of Economic Literature* 1764–76.

—— (1999) 'The Possibility of Social Choice' 89 *American Economic Review* 349–78.

Telser, L (1981) 'A Theory of Self-Enforcing Agreements' 53 *Journal of Business* 27–44.

10

Institutional Designs in International Transactions—an Evolutionary Economics Perspective

JÖRG FREILING

THE RESEARCH PROBLEM

THE GLOBALISATION OF commerce belongs to the group of very few phenomena with an impact on economy and society, not only for recent decades, but for a considerable number of centuries (Kutschker and Schmid, 2005). International trade increased from 7 per cent of the world's gross national product (GNP) in 1950 to (an estimated) 17.2 per cent in 2000 (Schumann, 1999: 126). Pushed by considerable progress in logistics as well as in information and communication technology (ICT), the percentage rate is still on the way up. Despite certain obstacles to trade of different kinds, there is no serious doubt about the future development of increasing globalisation. Reasons can be traced back in particular to: (i) supply factors (eg economies of scale, shorter product lifecycles); (ii) demand factors (eg convergence of the demand, saturation of markets in Western countries, growth of many markets in the Eastern world); (iii) environmental factors (eg deregulation, technological progress); and (iv) competition (eg competitors' moves, chance of first moving for the purpose of attaining competitive advantages).

International business offers many opportunities for economic agents (eg market entry, access to low cost production, international knowledge spill-over effects), but at the same time the respective risks of internationalisation foreclose many transactions (eg monetary investments at stake, threat of reputation losses in case of failure). It is well researched that international business involves numerous risks which are difficult to calculate from the decider's point of view (Groves, 1994; Craig and Douglas, 2000). From new institutional economics we know the differentiation between behavioural and exogenous risks (Williamson, 1985; Anderson and Gatignon, 1986). By taking a look at these two categories of risk, the point is often made that international risks exceed considerably those of national transactions. Due to the high complexity of international business and the usually low level of information from the agent's point of view, the risk of international business might get out of control. In extreme cases, international transactions are inhibited due to uncertainty. Accordingly, economic decision-makers look for mechanisms to reduce the specific risks and to stabilise their expectations (Gessner, 2009, in this volume). In this context, they make use of institutions (Williamson, 1985): 'Institutions are the rules of the game in a society or, more formally, are the humanly devised constraints that shape human interaction' (North, 1990: 3).

To be more precise, we can say that agents typically use not only a single institution, such as a contract or trust, but a mixture of different institutions simultaneously to reduce their problems in connection with uncertainty in decision-making. Thus different institutions will be 'blended' and become 'ingredients' of a particular institutional design in use. An institutional design (synonymous: governance design, transaction design) is therefore the situation-specific mix of institutions to respond to problems of uncertainty from the points of view of the economic agents. How far they are adequate, from an ex post perspective, or even 'efficient' in economic terms is irrelevant to the understanding of institutional designs: the agent's perception to get the transaction managed by the chosen institutional design is decisive – independent of the final result of his or her action.

Obviously, the combination of institutions appears to be a major challenge in case of international transactions. Internationalising actors find themselves in situations with a rather low level of information where—due to the circumstances—they need much information for the purpose of orientation. The question arises of whether and how far adequate institutional designs are at hand. An answer is basic for any further research in this area and the selection of appropriate theories for the sake of understanding the problem. The decision for an adequate design for the specific situation is a matter of selection and specific combination as long as adequate institutions are available and the agents are aware of the potential the institutions offer. According to Williamson (1985), the relevant governance designs undergo an assessment based on criteria that are relevant to transaction cost efficiency. The new institutional economics (NIE) dwell on adapted solutions for transaction-specific situations. How far an 'optimisation' in terms of NIE is possible in the face of incomplete information and the state of uncertainty in decision-making is beyond the discussion of this chapter.

The question arises of whether and how far institutions and institutional designs are available and ready for use in international transactions. What we can observe, first, is that every situation is specific and therefore idiosyncratic. 'Bundling' institutions to find an adequate institutional design is not necessarily an act of innovation. Nevertheless, the situations change due to demand conditions, technological developments, specific risks or even the availability and workability of legal sources, to name a few aspects. This requires at least minor adaptations and modifications regarding the underlying institutional solutions. Secondly, if actors make new steps in the international business, they are not fully aware of how to stabilise their expectations most efficiently. One prominent example among others is the protection of intellectual properties, which is different in almost every country. The case of the PR China shows serious problems of diluting intellectual property rights against the background of product and brand counterfeits. The agents are uncertain due to a lack of knowledge, experience and capabilities in the rather unfamiliar international markets. Building these assets is a time-consuming process, as, for instance, recent contributions in the field of competence-based research suggest (Sanchez *et al*, 1996; Teece *et al*, 1997; Freiling, 2004). Thirdly, international transactions might considerably differ from national transactions. In particular, in cases of inter-cultural transactions, the emotional dimension of the transaction partners is different from that of national transactions. Moreover, the different locations of customer and supplier have an impact on handling the transaction. The significance of electronic coordination is one response in this regard.

Obviously, economic agents need to find ways in which how to cope with the challenges of uncertainty in decision-making. A simple economic consideration would look like this: The given 'supply' of institutional designs does not fit perfectly to the 'demand'. An institutional gap occurs (Dixit, 2004). Therefore, economic actors—be it alone or in cooperation with others—have to develop, modify and test institutional designs by making use of means of public and private ordering (Hadfield, 2009, in this volume; Dorbeck-Jung, 2009, in this volume). Given that this is a real problem in case of international transactions (Streit and Mangels, 1996), and given that the very nature of institutions as mentioned above, we need to analyse how institutional designs evolve and have to be developed. In the context of these development processes, there are some major issues to be considered:

a) How does this kind of institutional change occur?
b) Is the adaptation process straightforward and unidirectional or do several 'trials and errors' of the agents point in different directions?
c) What are the typical rigidities of both actors and institutions?

A research programme like the NIE is—due to its comparative-static nature—not in the position to address these change processes. We need evolutionary theories—be it alone or in connection with other theories (eg Kappelhoff, 2007, who connects evolutionary theory and complexity theory)—to be able to scrutinise and explain the evolution in social systems.

The above-mentioned institutional gap is the research problem of this chapter:

a) In the *descriptive dimension*, it is interesting to know the width of this institutional gap.
b) As to the *analytic dimension*, we ask:
    i) why the institutional gap occurs; and
    ii) what happens in the case of its occurrence.
c) Concerning the *prescriptive dimension*, questions arise as to how to overcome the institutional gap.

It seems hardly possible to develop detailed answers for all of the research problems mentioned above. This chapter will present a general procedure as a basis for further research. It starts with briefly tackling methodological issues of the research endeavour ('Research Methodology' below), followed by scrutinising the 'institutional gap' as it stands ('The Institutional Gap in International Transactions'), the discussion of ways how to overcome it ('Overcoming the Institutional Gap in International Transactions in the Context of Public and Private Ordering'), the application of evolutionary economics as the theoretical reference point of the paper ('Understanding Institutional Evolution—the Contribution of Evolutionary Economics'), the modelling of cause and effect structures by the help of system dynamics ('System Dynamic Modelling'), and a final outlook including open questions ('Outlook and Conclusions').

Although our research problem is an interdisciplinary one, this chapter focuses on a socio-economic perspective.

RESEARCH METHODOLOGY

Research on the topic reveals that the delimitation of the basic research problems is difficult. Important steps are to define the research goals, delimitate the research question adequately and integrate new insights over time. In other words, every single step of generating new findings might go along with changes concerning the basics of the research project in total. In case of such iterative processes, a methodology called 'grounded theory' (Charmaz, 2006) comes into play.[1]

Grounded theory supports and fosters the discovery process of theory from data, systematically obtained and analysed. With the help of this approach, researchers are simultaneously able to describe *and* analyse. This procedure is useful in cases like ours where the subject matter is not well

[1] Grounded theory consists of two different tracks. One is the positivist stream, the other the interpretive kind. See, for more details, Glaser and Strauss (1967); Corbin and Strauss (1990); and Charmaz (2006).

explored. All available knowledge about the subject is used right from the beginning, but in order to avoid making crucial decisions too early, grounded theory proposes an iterative process. Weick (1999) pointed to a typical dilemma of these research constellations by referring to the Kantian adage: 'perception without conception is blind; conception without perception is empty'. The iterative process mentioned above refers to five—closely inter-related—cornerstones of a research project: research question, goals, conceptual framework, methods and validity issues.

a) The basic *goal* is to understand the phenomenon of an institutional gap in international transactions and to develop implications with regard to guaranteeing stable expectations of economic agents.
b) The *research question* is already formulated above and intends to analyse how the gap might be filled.
c) After a longer period of research on the topic and considering the discussion 'The Research Problem' above, it seems that evolutionary approaches could represent a basis for an appropriate *conceptual framework*.
d) From the point of view of *methods*, qualitative research is useful in order to respond adequately to the dynamic nature of the subject matter (see the following discussion).
e) Regarding *validity*, a variety of aspects have to be considered (Miles and Huberman, 1994). How to measure validity is to be discussed in the context of empirical fieldwork.

Burrell and Morgan (1979) remind us that the identification of an adequate theoretical framework for addressing the research problem should not be separated from methodological considerations. In particular, they argue that the relevant theoretical paradigm corresponds to the application of certain methods of empirical research.

Burrell and Morgan (1979) introduce a taxonomy of organisation theories based on two dimensions that help to structure the considerable heterogeneity of approaches. One dimension refers to the debate on subjectivism (individualism) versus objectivism (structuralism) and addresses the very nature of social sciences, whereas the second dimension relates to the assumptions concerning the nature of the society. The latter one addresses the debate between order (regulation) and conflict (radical change). The explanandum of this chapter is the change process in connection with filling the institutional gap in the meaning as outlined above. To put it briefly, if we analyse the ontological and epistemological dimension of the research object of this chapter, the subjective nature turns out:[2] actors as well as situations are

[2] Burrell and Morgan (1979) characterise subjectivism as follows: subjectivists focus on how individuals create, modify and interpret the world, and see things as more relativistic.

unique, developments idiosyncratic, the circumstances complex and dynamic. Moreover, the reality is not to be treated as given. On the contrary and despite their embeddedness in the social context (Granovetter, 1985), economic agents try to find new institutional solutions and the example of law firms as 'legal entrepreneurs' reveals the opportunities to shape external conditions to some extent. 'Moderate voluntarism' seems to be a notion that fits well in the context of the institutional gaps in international transactions. It is important to note that the subjective position goes along with implications regarding the methodology and empirical work. Testing hypotheses in order to generalise findings, valid for a long period of time, is almost impossible. (Longitudinal) observations are required and may lead, at best, to identifying similar patterns in reality (see von Hayek, 1972, as to pattern predictions).

The second dimension of the Burrell and Morgan taxonomy addresses the order-conflict debate within the sociology of regulation on the one hand and the sociology of radical change on the other. In reality, we can observe a complex and non-ergodic interplay of driving and inertial forces. Such an 'in between' position seems to be relevant to most of the phenomena to be analysed in social sciences (Gessner, 2009, in this volume). In particular, we find social and economic actors embedded in institutional contexts which offer, by themselves, a high level of rigidity—as, for instance, fundamental (Dietl, 1993; Picot *et al*, 2005; Schäcke, 2006) and derivative institutions (Hathaway, 2001; Deakin, 2002; Calliess, 2006; 2009, in this volume) reveal. Regulation theories intend to explore the unity of the society and elements of cohesiveness, which is in line with the research objective of this chapter.

Keeping the argument in mind, relevant theories that address the research object belong to the so-called 'interpretive paradigm' in Burrell's and Morgan's (1979) taxonomy. The *evolutionary theories*, as already briefly outlined in 'The Research Problem' above, are part of this paradigm and should be subject to a closer scrutiny. As to the methodological consequences of the argument, longitudinal research—relying for instance on case studies—appears to be useful, as for instance the empirical studies of this volume show (eg Richman, 2009, in this volume; Flood and Skordaki, 2009, in this volume). Although every development might be unique, there could be important similarities regarding how to overcome an institutional gap in international business in general and in international transactions in particular. Identifying general mechanisms, developments and patterns is possible by applying system-dynamic modelling.

THE INSTITUTIONAL GAP IN INTERNATIONAL TRANSACTIONS

What is really different in the case of international business and when do we find ourselves confronted with the institutional gap mentioned above?

A first consideration starts by analysing the typical situation in case of national transactions. Although behavioural as well as exogenous uncertainty will occur, in such situations the economic agents can rely on several established mechanisms that stabilise coordination. These mechanisms rest upon both public and private ordering. The role of public ordering is so far a prominent one, as the national state is in a position to offer an established and acknowledged set of norms, codified in the legal system. In case of conflicts among agents in economic transactions, the national state might represent a 'last resort' (Sosa, 2006a). The economic agents are aware of such a role of the national state and rely upon this, despite the self-defined role of single national states. Due to the history of law and the evolution over time (Calliess, 2005; Heydebrand, 2006), the public/private ordering system is developed and ready for use. Institutional gaps might occur—for instance, in case of innovations. However, this does not disturb coordination too much. In case of international transactions, the situation is different from national transactions because quite frequently it is not clear whether and how far a national state (and its legal system) is responsible for regulation. Accordingly, the actors are uncertain about the applicability and workability of public ordering by a certain national state. This would not be problematic if the gap could be filled immediately by public ordering provided by a supranational organisation. However, as Calliess (2006; 2009, in this volume) points out, such supranational institutions are not existing or unready, unwilling or simply unable to bridge the gap. Supra-nationalisation is, obviously, not the typical response to uncertainty in case of economic globalisation (see also Dorbeck-Jung, 2009, in this volume)—trans-nationalisation, instead, is all the more.

Obviously, institutional gaps might occur. Nevertheless, the question arises of how to specify and substantiate it. The scrutiny, combining findings from international management theory with institutional research, will take place along three discourses: (i) the agent's stage in international business; (ii) the transaction-specific criteria that are relevant to governance problems; and (iii) the type of the transaction in the overall context.

Agent's Stage in International Business

Is it really true that international transactions are completely different when compared with national transactions? We are well advised to formulate our answer precisely and to make use of an important differentiation concerning the internationalisation process of the involved economic agents (Backhaus *et al*, 2003): 'going international' versus 'being international'. The distinction is necessary due to different challenges in coordinating the economic activities in different countries.

a) In case of 'going international', we observe economic agents who find themselves in situations coping with considerable problems of insufficient information. With little experience in international business, they face both exogenous uncertainty and behavioural uncertainty, the latter linking with the threat of opportunism of the transaction partner. In other words, from these agents' points of view, adequate safeguards against the various sources of uncertainty are either not available or simply unknown. Being insufficiently familiar with foreign cultures and the legal system, serious problems in the area of governance might appear. Many small firms miss protection of their sometimes considerable intellectual properties as a basis of their competitive advantage (eg patents, trademarks, brands). An institutional gap is, therefore, one of the most basic barriers when entering the global market.
b) If we regard globalisation, it is useful to understand the word in process terms—as a process of increasing international transactions and connections. Accordingly, globalisation primarily addresses the case of *going international. Being international*, instead, refers to a situation where actors find themselves in international environments that they are more or less familiar with. They are informed about the circumstances in different countries and the institutions of private and public ordering. Most frequently, they have already learned to manage the feedback processes between the countries in which they are doing business. Such a situation is in a certain way nothing more than a new, extended 'domestic business', in particular in case of only small differences as to the culture and the legal systems in the respective countries. Despite these facts, an institutional gap will occur if:
   i) public ordering does not work due to a relative absence of national and supranational authorities; and
   ii) this gap cannot be filled by means of private ordering.

Another differentiation is useful. On the one hand, we find firms acting in new international markets more or less autonomously, while on the other, firms treat the new international base as a hub for intense international activities (new cross-border trade and internal transfers between the subsidiary and the headquarter). Typically, only in the last constellation, delicate governance problems might occur.

Transaction-specific Criteria

Transaction cost theory clearly suggests that the problems of coordination differ significantly depending on criteria describing the transaction. Williamson (1985) pointed out that the specificity, uncertainty and frequency of the underlying transaction are linked to different problems of coordination and governance. In addition to the aspect that coordination is costly and actors are efficiency driven, the institutional design chosen to govern the transaction should take the above-mentioned criteria into account. Empirical research in the first research phase of the Bremen project on 'Transformations of the State' (sponsored by the German Research Foundation) revealed that in case of international transactions, certain transaction-specific criteria apply:

a) Sosa (2006a) confirms in a survey the relevance of *relational contracting* in international transactions and relationships. It turns out that institutional gaps can be filled by relational contracts as a way of private ordering. However, in case of uncertain and highly specific transactions in long-term relationships, the protection offered by this mode of governance is sometimes insufficient. Notably, even in such situations the actors rely on the state as a last resort accompanying the respective instruments of private ordering.
b) Dietz and Nieswandt (2006; 2007; 2009, in this volume) scrutinise the different institutional mechanisms within the scope of *relationship management* in the software industry in their survey. They particularly refer to off-shoring processes and show that *ICT standards* enable a 'real-time monitoring' of the actors' behaviour. Obviously, an institutional gap in international transactions occurs due to the peculiarities of the business relationship. Relational standards, for instance of the technical kind, seem to be useful to fill the gap and provide the relationship with a framework for a number of transactions following up. In the software industry, those technical standards, set up by private actors, reduce the possibilities of opportunistic behaviour.
c) Flood (2005) and Sosa (2006b) observe *mega law firms* participating in international transactions as 'mediators'. They find out that these firms make use of their expertise and network positions to provide economic agents with appropriate governance designs. Moreover, they support the agents in case of claim management and contribute to 'legal certainty beyond the state'.
d) Within the scope of another survey, Sosa and Flood (2006) make similar observations regarding the role of *mid-sized law firms* as *mediators* in the above-mentioned sense (see also Sosa, 2009, in this volume). Those law firms develop innovative governance designs by modifying and combining institutional structures. Hence, uncertainty will be reduced by alert and competent *legal entrepreneurs* who use their skills to find new or modified governance designs instantly. Analysing the role of law firms regarding transaction-specific criteria in general, their legal entrepreneurship seems to go beyond uncertainty issues of transactions. These law firms also support and enable market

processes in case of dynamism and complexity of the transaction-specific situation. The reason for this is their superior competence profile and degree of specialisation.

e) Finally, Konradi (2006; 2009, in this volume) studies the relevance of *merchant law* (*lex mercatoria*) in the international timber trade. In such industries, a (loosely) coupled collective of actors develops *legal standards and norms* for transactions over a long period of time. These standards facilitate or enable economic exchange. *Lex mercatoria* rules work in particular in quite stable settings with a higher level of standardisation as to the product and/or the transaction process.

Empirical evidence suggests that different means of private ordering fill the institutional gap. They respond to different challenges in connection with transaction-specific criteria. Some instruments are applicable more or less instantly (for example, the mechanisms supplied by law firms); others develop over time and are binding for a large group of economic actors. The respective means of private ordering do not stand alone, but are backed up by other institutions. In this respect, the role of the state is not to be underestimated ('last resort'). Nevertheless, trans-nationalisation of commercial law, ie internationalisation in connection with private ordering, seems to play a crucial role.

Business Types

In order to specify the problem of the institutional gap regarding the kinds of business, Backhaus developed an important approach of different business types (Backhaus, 2003; Backhaus *et al*, 2002), which has not yet been transferred to the relevant context of international transactions. The taxonomy, resting on NIE and information economics, helps to identify problems of coordination in transactions and threats of opportunism. Backhaus deals—as transaction cost theory suggests—with investments made by customers and suppliers in business transactions and relationships (so-called 'quasi-rents'[3] which indicate the degree of specific investments and the problems of the other partner's opportunistic behaviour), the

[3] The term 'quasi-rent' was coined by Alfred Marshall (Marshall, 1961: 74). The term indicates specific investments of assets. If, for example, a subcontractor in the automotive industry develops a specialised machine that is dedicated to supplying a particular automotive manufacturer (as the customer), there are most frequently no alternative usages if the automotive manufacturer drops the relationship to the respective part supplier. The quasi-rent represents the value difference between the value of the specialised machine in the relationship with the preferred customer and the value in the next-best relationship with another customer. Such a second-best alternative could be the relationship to another automotive manufacturer with a somewhat different profile of demand. Accordingly, the productivity of the machine decreases in case of a switch due to transaction costs and a loss of effectiveness. A customer, aware of the quasi-rents, could behave opportunistically and try to appropriate the quasi-rent:

uncertainty and the frequency of the transactions. He identifies four different business types (see Figure I).

Figure I—Business Types

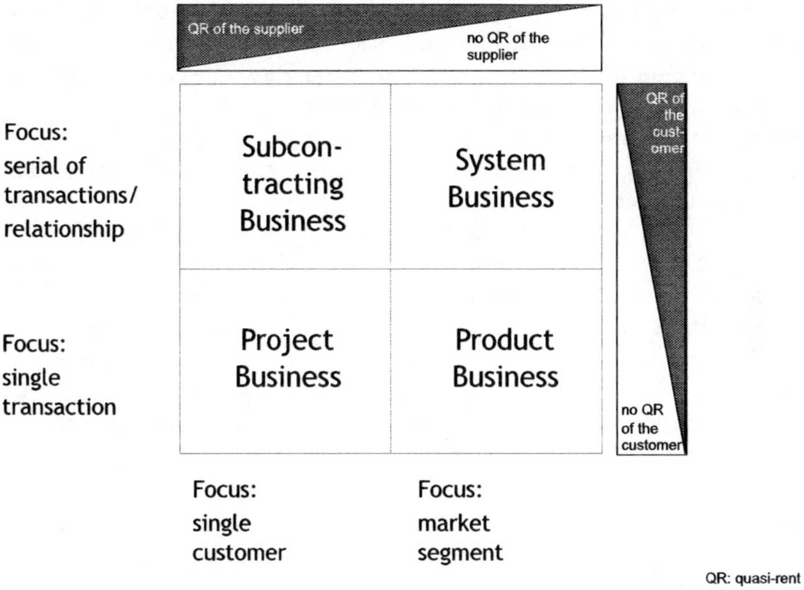

Source: Backhaus, 2003: 324.

Product Business

There are transactions where no specific investments are required because homogenous products are exchanged ('arms-length transactions'). A supplier sells his or her products in a more or less unmodified way to a considerable number of customers with similar needs. In those cases, there is no considerable uncertainty or interdependency between the exchange partners ('hit and run' situation). Quasi-rents do not occur or play an irrelevant role. Due to experience of the handling of transactions, the challenges of opportunism are manageable. Thus problems of governance can be neglected. The *lex mercatoria* can be regarded as one example among many others as an institutional design. Typical market governance

for example, he or she could claim for better prices and simultaneously consider switching to another supplier in case of ignorance. Generally speaking, a quasi-rent refers to the income-related surplus of utilising a specific factor in the first-best application compared to the second-best. In extreme cases, there is no second-best alternative to use a specific asset. In those cases, the quasi-rent equals the specific investment made. In the context of asset specificity in customer/supplier relationships, Klein *et al* (1978) made use of the term 'quasi-rent'.

in terms of 'arms length transactions' is applied in many cases (eg commodity exchanges as an extreme example), as well as forms of trilateral monitoring. Are product business exchanges also problematic in case of international transactions? The answer depends on the considerations mentioned above. As long as agents are familiar with international business, they have most likely established workable transaction designs for governance purposes (in case of 'being international'). However, in case of 'going international', the situation is different.

Although the transactions seem to be uncomplicated, the reliability of typical institutions is not always given due to the international background and the non-applicability of many means of public ordering. Accordingly, typical situations of direct selling will be replaced when it comes to international transactions. Suppliers sell their products to export traders. They cooperate with import traders and replace public ordering by relational modes of private ordering in order to manage the situation. Finally, the import trader cooperates with the customer within the scope of a new national transaction. Since these constellations are the typical case, we can conclude that there must be something about the reliability of public ordering in national transactions.

Project Business

Product business is focused upon a single transaction. The same holds true for project business. In contrast to the product business, however, a rather complex and customised solution is to be negotiated, developed and delivered. Customer and supplier sides need to cooperate intensively in order to cope with the complexity of the project's challenges. This constellation helps to explain why: (i) the supplier has to concentrate the forces on the actual transaction (a second transaction within a relationship is much too far away); and (ii) the supplier has to dedicate assets to the transaction. He or she has to gather information about the customer's problem in order to work out an offer and enter the bidding process. For a longer period of time, the supplier in the project business does not know whether he or she will succeed in winning the order. Specific investments are at stake and the quasi-rent of the supplier might be appropriated by the customer. Moreover, and having won the order, the profitability of the transaction largely depends on the other party's behaviour. Most of the transactions in the area of the project business (eg mechanical engineering, plant engineering) are international. The uncertainty is a major challenge and the way of risk management has a substantial impact on the performance of the project. Accordingly, the problem of an institutional gap becomes a core challenge, in particular in connection with the uniqueness of the performance to be delivered: technical and financial engineering is to be accompanied by 'legal engineering' because a specific solution is to be found so that exogenous and behavioural uncertainty can be controlled by the transaction partners. The expertise of law firms and other specialised players, as well as arbitration courts, is required. Moreover, the 'shadow of the law' is useful in order to monitor the business. Incidentally, it is not unusual that the suppliers of a complex international project found a new company devoted only to the management of the project. This company, often organised as a joint venture, is often created in the country of the customer so that the supplier (as a single firm or a syndicate) can circumvent problems in connection with the institutional gap of international trade.

System Business

Business in the area of computer-integrated manufacturing, software systems or telecommunication services, for example, follows another kind of logic. The supplier offers a prospective solution that he or she is unable to deliver completely at that moment in time. Accordingly, an initial investment of the customer via a buying decision is required, accompanied by the supplier's promise that additional features of the complete solution—the entire system—will follow later on. In other words, the customer is confronted with a lock-in situation when making the first purchase decision because later transactions will follow if the investment he or she made should pay off. Such a system is offered in a similar manner to a group of (often international) customers. In these cases, the situation is quite similar to the project business, with the decisive difference that now the customer makes specific investments causing a quasi-rent. The threat of appropriation by the supplier in connection with exogenous uncertainty (will the solution be feasible thanks to technical progress on time?) indicates the problem of the institutional gap. Trust and stabilised expectations are required and depend on sound institutional mechanisms at hand. To handle the situation requires means of bilateral (eg contingent contracts) or trilateral coordination.

Subcontractor Business

In many industries, we find suppliers and customers working together in long-term relationships. In particular, in case of vertical cooperation there is a long tradition of governance modes that enable and facilitate transactions (Frazier *et al*, 1988; Freiling, 1995). Just-in-time/just-in-sequence delivery is one example among many others; performance contracting is another (Buse *et al*, 2001). In these usually tightly coupled relationships with a high frequency of exchange, specified equipment is required in order to supply the customer adequately. On the other hand, the customer has to make partner-specific investments to ensure the smooth run of processes.

According to that, quasi-rents occur on both sides of the relationship and every partner has certain 'hostages' (Williamson, 1983) in case of the other party's opportunistic behaviour. Despite these interrelations, power asymmetries may play a role so that behavioural uncertainty can also be a latent or manifest problem of relationship management in the subcontractor business. Moreover, the relationships are arranged for a longer period of time and governance modes account for the profitability of the investments. A particular challenge is, therefore, to anticipate potential governance challenges and find corresponding institutional designs. We can conclude that, even in these constellations, institutional gaps are to be filled in order to ensure a workable basis for cooperation. Relational contracting is the typical response of the partners. Accordingly, contractual elements as well as trust and reputation work together in institutional designs (Morgan and Hunt, 1994; Mohr and Spekman, 1994). The 'shadow of the law' is significant in these constellations for enforcement reasons.

The problem of institutional gaps in international transactions and relationships occurs, therefore, predominantly in the project, system and subcontractor businesses. However, we should not underestimate the challenges of product business thanks to the international dimension of business. Compared with domestic transactions and relationships, the problems differ as to intensity and complexity. Moreover, the more organisational networks participate in transactions, the more likely an institutional gap might appear. The reason for this is that every party participating in a transaction is equipped with specific interests and intentions that are often contradictory. In many international transactions, the complexity of the business requires the technological, business, legal, cultural or psychological expertise of different agents so that networking instead of simple dyadic relationships between one customer and one supplier is necessary. However, the governance of a network structure seems to be a much more delicate issue than managing dyads.

OVERCOMING THE INSTITUTIONAL GAP IN INTERNATIONAL TRANSACTIONS IN THE CONTEXT OF PUBLIC AND PRIVATE ORDERING

So far our argument has been that international transactions are accompanied by uncertainty in decision-making. In particular, in case of *going international*, the actors are forced to find new or modified institutional designs for coping with the threatening consequences of uncertainty. What kind of moves will occur in case of an institutional gap? There are public or private potential actors.

Will the state move in case of this problem? A definite answer cannot be given because the state behaves in a different manner all over the world, depending on the nation we scrutinise. Moreover, it is still open why a single state should act in this context. A national state is definitely responsible in case of transactions in its country. In case of international transactions, the situation is different. It depends not only on the nation's and respective state's specific situation, but also on the mission and the self-conception of the state. Whereas, for example, the United States made successful attempts to transfer proven legal structures from national to international settings, similar activities have not yet taken place in Germany. Although it goes beyond the scope of this chapter to scrutinise and assess the respective initiatives of exporting legal structures in detail, it transpires that on an aggregate level the outcome is modest and explains the mentioned institutional gap to some extent.

However, the gap might be filled by international or global law (Calliess, 2006), but there is neither an established global merchant law nor can we find institutions (for example, the UN, OECD or EU) that are powerful enough to drive the supra-nationalisation of law in such a direction (Calliess, 2005; 2006; Calliess *et al*, 2008). The pace of change does not correspond to the development of institutional needs of the economic agents. A crucial reason for inertia is the binding character of legal norms in a supra-national context which meets with strong interest group opposition. Obviously, such complex tasks need time.

The organisational inertia of the national state and international agencies leave opportunities for private actors interested or already involved in the development of new institutional designs for international markets. As the above-mentioned considerations have shown, private actors appear in various functions sometimes autonomously and sometimes in cooperation with others in order to generate new institutional designs:

a) Customers and suppliers involved in international transactions are aware of the possibilities and limitations of the mechanisms of the market. Their alertness and willingness to raise arbitrage profits (Kirzner, 1973) leads to new trials (and errors) to find ways for better coping with uncertainty. The individual customers and suppliers usually act in one-to-one relationships (bilateral coordination), but sometimes also as a part of a loosely coupled network of more or less independent actors (multilateral coordination).
b) The development of institutional designs is the core business of legal entrepreneurs with their specific profile of capabilities. They become mediators (third-party characters) in international transactions and offer an institutional support structure. In many cases, this support structure is subject to a development process which takes place during the transaction. Within this group, we find mega law firms with

considerable expert and resource power as well as small and mid-sized law firms which—due to their structural peculiarities (Freiling, 2008)—rely more on expertise and flexibility to adapt to new situations. The opportunity to shape the business of their clients and raise their profits is their most powerful driving force.

c) Private ordering does not only evolve in case of transactions between single exchange partners. Moreover, strategic and regional networks (Sydow, 1992) develop many institutional solutions on a meta level which are relevant to transactions as a part of the above-mentioned institutional designs. Besides that, in an industry context, such coalitions develop norms and similar autonomous rules.

Some of these numerous initiatives are successful, others fail. The 'trial and error' element in these initiatives helps to explain why the speed of change in case of private ordering is higher compared to the activities of the state. Evolutionary theory could be useful to address these questions in more detail.

UNDERSTANDING INSTITUTIONAL EVOLUTION—THE CONTRIBUTION OF EVOLUTIONARY ECONOMICS

It goes beyond the scope of this chapter to structure the heterogeneity of approaches belonging to the evolutionary theory tradition.[4] In the following parts, emphasis is put on the so-called evolutionary economics which can be regarded as an important part of evolutionary theory. The basic assumptions of evolutionary economics are: (i) incomplete information of (economic) agents in connection with making decisions in situations of uncertainty; (ii) an asymmetrical distribution of knowledge, skills and motivation among the actors; (iii) a permanent change of knowledge and skills available to the agents due to development and erosion; and (iv) actors behaving alertly and permanently trying to shape the conditions creatively and actively in order to improve the situation ('homo agens' according to von Mises, 1949, instead of 'homo oeconomicus'). Innovation, for instance, in such an understanding can be explained endogenously. Moreover, time and history matter due to developments which cannot be reversed. In this context, evolution can be conceptualised as set out below (eg Lehmann-Waffenschmidt and Reichel, 2000).

a) Evolution means a causal determination of the course of actions.
b) In particular, evolution indicates that the course of action depends on

[4] For an overview, see, for instance, Witt (1987; 1992) and, more recently, Kappelhoff (2008), who differentiates between a Darwinian and a Schumpeterian stream of evolutionary approaches.

the chronological order of events. The historical sequence of events determines what can be done in the present and the future. Accordingly, actors can be at least partially 'locked in' by the decisions they—or others—made in the past. These lock-in effects can be so strong that the number of alternatives in later decision-making decreases dramatically: path dependencies of the different kinds might occur which is highly relevant as to the explanation of rigidities and organisational inertia. What we learned from the above-mentioned system business is only one example: customers make buying decisions as to the adoption of a certain system architecture (eg a specific ICT system) that they are bound to for a longer time. Later decisions on revamping and upgrading the system solution depend on the initial decision.

c) Action is determined by available energy and information.
d) Evolution is the process of change of structures over time, characterised by innovation and emergence. The evolution process implies that the former status will be modified—at least gradually.
e) Evolution is driven by a dynamic interplay of variation, selection and retention.

Many scholars in the field of evolutionary economics make use of constructs borrowed from biology or socio-biology (eg Nelson and Winter, 1982). For instance, they deal with genes as analogies. Other scholars regard such a kind of interdisciplinary work as problematic (eg Penrose, 1952).[5] The reason for their scepticism is the problem of making use of these constructs without developing appropriate criteria for a transfer of the findings from one discipline to another (Elschen, 1982). We share this critique and believe that the cause and effect structures in use should be economic or at least belonging to the body of the social sciences in order to avoid incommensurability.

Based on the assumptions and understanding of evolution in terms of this theoretical stream, we can summarise that evolutionary economics contain a certain understanding of change and innovation on the one hand and rigidities on the other. This is useful to scrutinising the notion of an institutional gap. Nevertheless, the question arises as to 'how to bring some flesh to the bones', ie to explain the driving forces and rigidities in this particular context. The following considerations make some first proposals and intend to encourage further work.

[5] In this context, Penrose (1952: 819) states: 'even as a metaphor it [the biological evolution] is badly chosen although in principle metaphorical illustrations are legitimate and useful ... But in seeking fundamental explanations of economic and social phenomena in human affairs the economist, and the social scientist in general, would be well advised to attack his problems directly and in their own terms rather than indirectly by imposing sweeping biological models upon them'.

In the typical situation of agents in international transactions, several institutions and institutional designs are available. As mentioned above, an institutional design governing a transaction and stabilising the agents' expectations depends on the availability of institutions. Institutional designs develop over time and might become a standard in industries or at least in networks of actors. This means that they are acknowledged not only by two transaction partners, but by a number of agents and, moreover, are proven in practice. However, the institutional designs are not to be regarded as static structures. The reason for this is that they are permanently in use and, therefore, adapted to the respective problems which might occur in inter-actor coordination. According to these adaptations, they evolve in the sense of the evolutionary economics which implies that at least minor changes occur. The adaptations in off-shoring agreements in the software industry are only one example of many.

Such changes often remain unperceived by the actors. Nevertheless, they facilitate economic action by private ordering on the micro level and go along with the creation of new knowledge and experience. In contrast to these adaptations, actors might discover new opportunities for governing international transactions. They try out the organisational inventions based on their individual expectations. This is usually a process of 'trial and error' (von Hayek, 1978; Kirzner, 1973), as suggested by scholars belonging to market process theory, an important stream of evolutionary economics. Hume (1779/1980: 131) described the typical procedure of economic actors long ago: 'Much labor lost: Many fruitless trials made.' Inventions will be made continuously, but adapted to the necessities of everyday life. However, every further change is backed up by knowledge (and energy) and leads to new knowledge which is taken into account in future decisions. Evolution takes place, but radical changes of a sustaining kind are not very likely. What we said concerning the behaviour of agents on the micro level can be transferred to the state as an institution and agent as well as to the meta level of groups of actors. As it is considered more important to understand the basics of institutional evolution, these aspects should not be scrutinised here. Instead, the driving and inertial forces should be subject to the following discussion.[6] The process of evolution consists of variation, selection and retention ('VSB') variables, which enable us to shed some additional light on the sequence of events.

[6] At this point, it can be analysed whether and how far the pool of institutions and institutional designs will be changed. This depends on selection and retention. It is discussed in another context in more detail by Rathe and Witt (2000).

Variation

Variation as already mentioned is triggered by making plans or by accident. We need to address these trial-and-error processes of economic agents in order to understand why and how (far) a given status will be changed. Referring once again to the nature of human action, modelled by the 'homo agens' of von Mises (1949), the alertness and the strong drive to improve the actual situation indicate the energy with which actors are equipped. Based on available knowledge and expectations, as well as individual plans, the actors are ready and willing to test new ideas in business life and therefore in transactions with others. Variations take place accordingly. With regard to institutions and institutional designs, a variation could be the design of a new business model of a supplier for marketing his or her goods. The 'hype' phase of e-commerce offers examples about variations of this kind.

Figure II—Variation, Selection, and Retention in Case of Private Ordering

<table>
<tr><th></th><th>Variation</th><th>Selection</th><th>Retention</th></tr>
<tr><td>Customers & suppliers</td><td>Trial & error
• New mixture of available designs
• Design innovations
• New business models</td><td rowspan="2">• Effectiveness of the institutional design
• Justice of the institutional design

in connection with the power and network position of the selecting actors (economic actor, state, society)</td><td rowspan="2">• Commitment
• (Technological, behavioral and governance) Standards
• Routines
• Increasing returns</td></tr>
<tr><td>Legal 'intermediaries' (law firms)</td><td>Legal entrepreneurship
• Design innovations
• Design modifications</td></tr>
</table>

Selection

The 'trial and error' logic implies that not every invention will be accepted in business and social life. Unsuccessful trials cannot be avoided. However, the question remains when and why these variations end up being less effective than alternative institutional designs that are available to the agents. There is obviously a selection process, well known from evolutionary theory in general. A social and economic selection procedure occurs, as indicated by some examples in Figure II. There are at least the following agents relevant to selection:

a) Economic agents select at the basic level of exchange (customers and suppliers). They consider the usefulness of new or modified institutional designs.
b) Economic agents on a meta level (eg law firms) take part in selection as well as in variation procedures. With their assistance, institutional designs can be modified and new institutional proposals questioned.
c) The society on another meta level might react to certain variations. Sanctions of different kinds are possible if new institutional designs are in conflict with basic values.
d) Finally, the state selects because not every variation is desirable from the state's point of view. One crucial issue relates to the selection criteria. Economic agents will primarily employ economic criteria. However, as Figure II indicates, the assumptions of evolutionary economics are to be taken into account. There is no way to optimise when information is incomplete and the decision is to be made in a state of uncertainty. Agents use effectiveness criteria, which are more or less indicators or surrogates, develop trust or mistrust[7] and use similar criteria in order to figure out whether a variation makes sense. Variations with a higher level of perceived effectiveness will be used again. Thus, in terms of evolutionary economics, the reproduction occurs. The other agents will use selection criteria responding to their fundamental goals. The state, for instance, will pay attention to aspects such as justice. The selection takes the relevant environment into account (fit criterion[8]). Notably, not only variation takes place under incomplete information of the actors, but also selection procedures are confronted with the same problem, since not only the best-fitting solutions (here, institutional designs) will be adopted. Inferior designs might be regarded as workable, convenient or simply effective enough—from an angle of incomplete information. Such a position is, indeed, far away from the economic mainstream with its functionalist paradigm.

[7] For a basic understanding of trust, see Zucker (1986); and Morgan/Hunt (1994). Zucker identifies three types of trust which are relevant in this context: characteristic-based, process-based and institutional-based trust.

[8] For a discussion on fit as a construct, see Venkatraman (1989).

Retention

Retention implies that the institutional designs under observation were tested successfully in selection processes. This, however, is not enough for the understanding of retention. Retention includes in our context that successful institutional designs will not only be accepted and internalised by the agents who utilised them at first—for instance by the development of routines.[9] Rather, their acceptance grows by their use in new situations—modified or unmodified. Accordingly, retention goes along with processes of diffusion in the society and, therefore, adoption by other actors. As far as modifications occur, new variations take place. Moreover, new selection procedures are triggered. Retention depends on setting standards in social life. Standards are solutions proven and accepted by a number of actors (Kleinaltenkamp, 1993; Gersch, 1998). If the scope of a standard grows by an increasing adoption, the chances to supersede other standards in use will increase. In the system business, as introduced above, we can find situations where a standard passes the line of the 'critical mass' of users (Backhaus, 2003). Having reached this critical mass, one system wins competition and outpaces other systems more or less definitely ('winner takes all' constellation). These developments are connected with the phenomenon of the so-called 'increasing returns'. Regarding institutional designs, we can at least partly make use of the findings of standardisation theory

Increasing Returns in Case of Institutional Designs

Increasing returns help to explain whether and how far path dependencies occur (North, 1990). Those 'increasing returns' mean positive feedbacks that cause self-reinforcing effects. When, for instance, typewriters were developed, the question arose of what an efficient and ergonomic keyboard could look like. As to mechanical efficiency criteria, the 'QWERTY' keyboard looked promising, although from the user's point of view, 'QWERTY' does not support a fast typing of texts. However, the 'QWERTY' standard succeeded because many firms adopted this standard early and expected the employees to get used to this standard. Thanks to learning and complementarity to other products, this standard produced so many increasing returns that no other standard could compete (David,

[9] Routines can be understood in different ways. See, eg Nelson and Winter (1982). Grant (1991: 121) characterises routines as follows: 'Organizational routines are regular and predictable patterns of activity which are made up of a sequence of coordinated actions by individuals.' Winter (1995: 150) puts it similarly: 'routines connote a menu of previously learned patterns of action'.

1985). In literature, different causes explain this phenomenon of increasing returns (Greif, 1994; Mahoney, 2000; Ackermann, 2001; Lindner, 2003; Schäcke, 2006):

a) *Coordination*: Agents develop benchmarks for coordination of economic or social activities such as technical standards, rules, and routines. These coordination standards are often but not always efficient. However, they are well known and facilitate social life. From the individual agent's point of view, it makes sense to utilise these standards. In case of international transactions, there are certain standards—efficient or not—regarding how to stabilise expectations and proceed by means of private ordering. Once commonly in use and adopted, they force more and more agents to make use of them: They produce increasing returns.
b) *Investments*: Increasing returns will also occur if economic agents make specific investments—be it in technologies or even in governance modes. In those cases, 'sunk costs' will appear if the agent wishes to switch to an alternative. In order to avoid these sunk costs, agents stick to the initial decision they made and quite frequently increase their commitment.
c) *Power*: In case of asymmetric power positions of economic or social agents, the more powerful ones have the opportunity to force others to make certain decisions. In case of institutional designs, agents may favour a certain institutional mix going along with favourable conditions. The institutional designs of many original equipment manufacturers (OEMs) with their subcontractors in the automotive industry are one example of institutional designs which are similarly reproduced due to the power of the automotive manufacturers (Freiling, 1995).
d) *Learning*: The use of institutional designs goes along with the production of knowledge and experience of the agents involved. Once the agents get familiar with the chosen institutional designs, competence develops in handling the problems of coordination. According to the respective conveniences and despite aspects of efficiency, the commitment increases and switches become increasingly unlikely (Arthur, 1989; North, 1990).
e) *Complementarity*: The availability of complementary goods or functional elements of a system can also produce increasing returns. Complementarity goes along with synergies if the respective object is not used in isolation. The more complementarity among objects exists, the more useful it is to adopt a certain object belonging to a system solution. The embeddedness of chosen institutional designs in the context of the hierarchy of fundamental and derived institutions (Dietl, 1993) is one example for complementarity in our context.

The sources of increasing returns show that efficient solutions from an ex post perspective are not necessarily the chosen ones in competition or social life. The evolution helps to explain why certain variations (eg institutional designs) develop faster than others and supersede in the long term—even despite efficiency. This aspect is also relevant to our discussion on the institutional gap in international transactions. The gap will be filled at different levels of action. On the micro level, agents develop individual designs. Once proven (selection), they emerge and have the chance to become a benchmark for other transactions of the same partners or of relationships between other partners. Depending on the adoption, the reproduction might lead to a standardisation (retention) that goes along with self-reinforcing effects as described above in the context of increasing returns. Due to lock-in effects, agents find themselves committed to decisions made in the past. This demonstrates how far history really matters (Teece *et al*, 1994). Private ordering seems to be able to produce variations in a fast manner—faster than the national or transnational state seems to be able to produce binding norms. Accordingly, path dependencies might occur that have a substantial impact on the role of the state as regulator. This consideration shows that we need to take co-evolution of public and private ordering into account. This holds particularly true since regulatory activities of the state are not independent from the evolution of private ordering.

In conclusion, the interdependencies in the emergence of governance modes of public and private ordering are complex. History seems to matter considerably. A major challenge for academic research is to develop hypotheses and model cause-and-effect structures. System dynamics equip researchers with the relevant methodological framework.

SYSTEM DYNAMIC MODELLING

Research based on system dynamics can be traced back to the seminal work of Forrester (1961). In the last 45 years, system dynamics was predominantly applied in the area of innovation and technology management. It turned out that modelling based on system dynamics is able to consider the dynamic interplay of different variables of a system. In particular, recursive effects between key variables can be observed and analysed. This is a key advantage compared to other approaches of modelling, such as modelling based on multi-variate procedures or econometric models: They model relationships between independent, dependent and sometimes also moderating variables. System dynamics, instead, does not necessarily need a dependent variable (Schwarz and Ewaldt, 2005). This is useful in those cases where strong recursive relations among the variables can be observed. Such a situation is possible in the context of developing institutional designs in international transactions.

In connection with Figure II, system dynamic modelling can be characterised as follows (Sterman, 1989; Sterman, 2000; Schwarz and Ewaldt, 2005):

a) It starts with exploring the relevant drivers of developments of a system and takes the agents into account.
b) Then the driving forces are structured by closed and integrated causal loops. Thus, we need to understand cause-and-effect structures thoroughly.
c) Regarding the explanandum, both constructive ('reinforcing loops', 'R loops') and destructive effects ('balancing loops', 'B loops') regarding the run of events are considered and modelled.
d) Time lags between action and result are considered by regarding transmission mechanisms and path dependencies in competition. In Figure III, they are indicated by a grey bar.

To refer to a very simplified reinforcing loop according to Figure III, globalisation of economic activities is the starting point. Following the notion of the institutional gap, the risks of economic agents increase, in particular if they are concerned with a situation of 'going international': globalisation is assumed to be positively related to the actors' risks. This is linked to an additional need for safeguards in the face of exogenous and behavioural uncertainty. Finally, it is assumed that agents of the different kinds will produce matching institutional designs (IDs). At least globalisation and the emergence of institutional designs are linked with lags.

It turns out that things do not run so easily in a unidirectional way. Therefore, it is of interest which factors drive such a development and which factors work in the opposite direction. In system dynamic modelling, we identify and analyse both reinforcing ('R' loops) and balancing loops ('B' loops). Based on these loops, we are in a better position to understand why many trials to establish new institutional designs (part of a reinforcing loop) will fail due to selection in competition (a potential balancing loop) or by intervention of the state (another balancing loop). The respective considerations can be derived in detail from evolutionary economics and tested in reality by making use of the methodological considerations mentioned above (see 'Research Methodology').

System dynamic modelling can be useful in order to model the most important driving and inertial forces and to consider the relevant agents in the area of global business institutions. System dynamics can be useful to facilitate progress in evolutionary institutional research.

Figure III—System Dynamic Modelling in Case of Institutional Designs—a Simplified Example

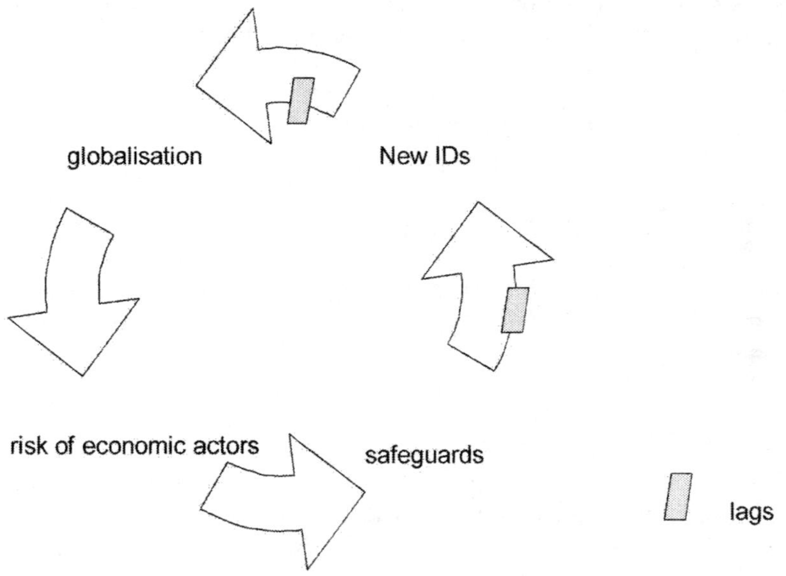

OUTLOOK AND CONCLUSIONS

Trans-nationalisation of governance as an observable phenomenon in reality can be explained by evolutionary economics. However, we are still at the beginning of applying this stream of evolutionary theory to scrutinise phenomena at the interface between jurisprudence, sociology, and business and economics. We need much more exploratory work to better understand the complex causal structures. However, it is obvious that there is a complex dynamic interplay of driving and inertial forces, with results being unpredictable: the principle of non-ergodicity seems to apply. Preliminary empirical evidence suggests that the state will remain an indispensable element in case of governance designs, but with a new role in background and equipped with considerable rigidities.

Further research on this topic is required and should take into account some open questions:

a) How does the development of institutional designs take place? What will be the likely direction and what are decisive criteria of evolution?
b) How does the co-evolution of public and private ordering work? How far and why do rigidities play a role?
c) Are there 'bandwagon effects' in so far as the variations produced by

economic actors will be reproduced in larger groups or in the society in general? If so: how does it proceed?

d) In the face of the rapid evolution of private ordering: is faster really better with regard to criteria going beyond efficiency (such as justice)?
e) What exactly are the mechanisms of variation, selection and retention?

REFERENCES

Ackermann, R (2001) *Pfadabhängigkeit, Institutionen und Regelreformen* (Tübingen, Mohr).

Anderson, E and Gatignon, H (1986) 'Modes of Foreign Entry: A Transaction Cost Analysis and Propositions' 17 *Journal of International Business Studies* 1–26.

Arthur, WB (1989) 'Competing Technologies, Increasing Returns, and Lock-In by Historical Events' 99 *Economic Journal* 116–31.

Backhaus, K (2003) *Industriegütermarketing* (7th edn, Munich, Vahlen).

Backhaus, K, Büschken, J and Voeth, M (2003) *Internationales Marketing* (4th edn, Stuttgart, Schäffer-Poeschel).

Backhaus, K, Mühlfeld, K and Okoye, D (2002) 'Business-to-Business Marketing Textbooks: A Comparative Review' 9 *Journal for Business-to-Business Marketing* 27–64.

Burrell, G and Morgan, G (1979) *Sociological Paradigms and Organisational Analysis. Elements of the Sociology of Corporate Life* (London, Heinemann).

Buse, C, Freiling, J and Weißenfels, S (2001) 'Turning Product Business into Service Business: Performance Contracting as a Challenge of SME Customer/Supplier Networks', Competitive Paper, 17th IMP Conference (Oslo).

Calliess, GP (2005) 'Billigkeit und effektiver Rechtsschutz. Innovation und Evolution des Rechts in der Globalisierung' 26 *Zeitschrift für Rechtssoziologie* 35–55.

—— (2006) *Grenzüberschreitende Verbraucherverträge: Rechtssicherheit und Gerechtigkeit auf dem elektronischen Weltmarktplatz* (Tübingen, Mohr Siebeck).

—— (2009) 'Transnational Civil Regimes: Economic Globalization and the Evolution of Commercial Law' in V Gessner (ed), *Contractual Certainty in International Trade* (Oxford, Hart).

Calliess, GP, Freiling, J and Renner, M (2008) 'Law, the State, and Private Ordering: Evolutionary Explanations of Institutional Change' 9 *German Law Journal* 395–408.

Charmaz, C (2006) *Grounded Theory. A Practical Guide Through Qualitative Analysis* (Thousand Oaks, Sage).

Corbin, J and Strauss, AL (1990) 'Grounded Theory Research: Procedures, Canons, and Evaluative Criteria' 13 *Qualitative Sociology* 3–21.

Craig, CS and Douglas, SP (2000) *International Marketing Research* (2nd edn, Chichester, Wiley).

David, PA (1985) 'Clio and the Economics of QWERTY' 75 *Economic History* 332–7.

Deakin, S (2002) 'Evolution for our Time: A Theory of Legal Memetics' 55 *Current Legal Problems* 1–42.

Dietl, H (1993) *Institutionen und Zeit* (Tübingen, Mohr).

Dietz, T and Nieswandt, H (2006) The Emergence of International Cooperation under Uncertainty', TranState Working Paper, CRC 597 (Bremen).

—— (2007) 'Cross-Border Cooperation. The meaning of Cognitive and Normative Expectations for the Emergence of Global Research and Development Cooperation', TranState Working Paper No 49/2007 (Bremen) <http://www.sfb597.uni-bremen.de/pages/pubApBeschreibung.php?SPRACHE=de&ID=59> accessed 19 June 2008.

—— (2009) 'The Emergence of Transnational Cooperation in the Software Industry' in V Gessner (ed), *Contractual Certainty in International Trade* (Oxford, Hart).

Dixit, AK (2004) *Lawlessness and Economics* (Princeton, Princeton University Press).

Dorbeck-Jung, B (2009) 'Economic Globalization—Changes in the Conceptualization of Legal Certainty?' in V Gessner (ed), *Contractual Certainty in International Trade* (Oxford, Hart).

Elschen, R (1982) *Betriebswirtschaftslehre und Verhaltenswissenschaften. Probleme einer Erkenntnisübernahme am Beispiel des Risikoverhaltens bei Gruppenentscheidungen* (Frankfurt/M., Lang).

Flood, J (2005) 'Large Law Firms: Priests of the New Capitalism', Working Paper, First European Socio-Legal Conference on 'European Ways of Law' (Oñati, Spain).

Flood, J and Skordaki, E (2009) 'Structuring Transactions: The Case of Real Estate Finance' in V Gessner (ed), *Contractual Certainty in International Trade* (Oxford, Hart).

Forrester, JW (1961) *System Dynamics* (Portland, Productivity Press).

Frazier, GL, Spekman, RE and O'Neill, CR (1988) 'Just-in-Time Exchange Relationships in Industrial Markets' 52 *Journal of Marketing* 52–67.

Freiling, J (1995) *Die Abhängigkeit der Zulieferer* (Wiesbaden, DUV).

—— (2004) 'A competence-based theory of the firm' 15 *Management Revue* 1–26.

—— (2008) 'SME Management—What can we Learn from Entrepreneurship Theory?' 6 *International Journal of Entrepreneurship Education* 1–19.

Gersch, M (1998) *Vernetzte Geschäftsbeziehungen* (Wiesbaden, Gabler).

Gessner, V (2009) 'The governance of business transactions in globalising economies: Theories of Change' in V Gessner (ed), *Contractual Certainty in International Trade* (Oxford, Hart).

Glaser, BG and Strauss, AL (1967) *The Discovery of Grounded Theory: Strategies for Qualitative Research* (New York, de Gruyter).

Granovetter, M (1985) 'Economic Action and Social Structure: The Problem of Embeddedness' 91 *American Journal of Sociology* 481–510.

Grant, RM (1991) 'The Resource-Based Theory of Competitive Advantage: Implications for Strategy Formulation' 33 *California Management Review* 114–35.

Greif, A (1994) 'Cultural Beliefs and the Organization of Society' 102 *Journal of Political Economy* 915–50.

Groves, L (1994) *Principles of International Marketing Research* (Oxford, Oxford University Press).

Hadfield, G (2009) 'The Public and the Private on the Provision of Law for Global Transactions' in V Gessner (ed), *Contractual Certainty in International Trade* (Oxford, Hart).

Hathaway, OA (2001) 'Path Dependence in the Law' 86 *Iowa Law Review* 101–65.

Hayek, FA von (1972) *Die Theorie komplexer Phänomene* (Tübingen, Mohr).

—— (1978) 'Competition as a Discovery Problem' in *New Studies in Philosophy, Politics, Economics, and the History of Ideas* (Chicago, Chicago University Press).

Heydebrand, W (2009) 'Contractual Certainty vs Efficiency: The Historical and Institutional Context of Global Trade' in V Gessner (ed), *Contractual Certainty in International Trade* (Oxford, Hart).

Hume, D (1779/1980) *Dialogues Concerning Natural Religion in Focus* (reprint, India-napolis, Hackett).

Kappelhoff, P (2007) 'Die evolutionäre Organisationstheorie im Lichte der Komplexitätstheorie', Working Paper (University of Wuppertal).

—— (2008) 'Kompetenzentwicklung in Netzwerken: Die Sicht der Komplexitäts- und allgemeinen Evolutionstheorie' in A Windeler and J Sydow (eds), *Kompetenz* (Wiesbaden, VS Verlag, forthcoming).

Kirzner, IM (1973) *Competition and Entrepreneurship* (Chicago, Chicago University Press).

Klein, B, Crawford, RG and Alchian, AA (1978) 'Vertical Integration, Appropriable Rents, and the Competitive Contracting Process' 21 *Journal of Law and Economics* 297–326.

Kleinaltenkamp, M (1993) *Standardisierung und Marktprozeß* (Wiesbaden, Gabler).

Konradi, W (2006) 'Lex Mercatoria als globales Recht der Wirtschaft? Die Koordination der grenzüberschreitenden Transaktionen am Beispiel der Holzindustrie', TranState Working Paper, CRC 597 (Bremen).

—— (2009) 'Lex Mercatoria as a Global Law of Transnational Business Exchanges?' in V Gessner (ed), *Contractual Certainty in International Trade* (Oxford, Hart).
Kutschker, M and Schmid, S (2005) *Internationales Management* (4th edn, Munich and Vienna, Oldenbourg).
Lehmann-Waffenschmidt, M and Reichel, M (2002) 'Kontingenz, Pfadabhängigkeit und Lock-In als handlungsbeeinflussende Faktoren der Unternehmenspolitik' in T Beschorner and R Pfriem (eds), *Evolutorische Ökonomik und Theorie der Unternehmung* (Marburg, Metropolis) 337–76.
Lindner, J (2003) 'Institutional Stability and Change: Two Sides of the same Coin' 10 *Journal of European Public Policy* 912–35.
Mahoney, J (2000) 'Path Dependence in Historical Sociology' 29 Theory and Society 507–48.
Marshall, A (1961) *Principles of Economics*, Vol 1 (9th edn, London, Macmillan).
Maxwell, JA (2005) *Qualitative Research Design* (Thousand Oaks, Sage).
Miles, MB and Huberman, M (1994) *Qualitative Data Analysis. An Expanded Sourcebook* (2nd edn, Thousand Oaks, Sage).
Mises, L von (1949) *Human Action: A Treatise on Economics* (Irvington-on-Hudson, Foundation for Economic Education).
Mohr, JJ and Spekman, RE (1994) 'Characteristics of Partnership Success: Partnership Attributes, Communication Behavior, and Conflict Resolution Techniques' 15 *Strategic Management Journal* 135–52.
Morgan, RM and Hunt, SD (1994) 'The Commitment-Trust Theory of Relationship Marketing' 58 *Journal of Marketing* 20–28.
Nelson, RR and Winter, SG (1982) *An Evolutionary Theory of Economic Change* (Cambridge/Mass., Harvard University Press).
North, DC (1990) *Institutions, Institutional Change and Economic Performance* (Cambridge, Cambridge University Press).
Penrose, ET (1952) 'Biological Analogies in the theory of the firm' 42 *American Economic Review* 804–19.
Picot, A, Dietl, H and Franck, E (2005) *Organisation* (4th edn, Stuttgart, Schäffer-Poeschel).
Rathe, K and Witt, U (2000) 'Evolutionäre Ansätze in der Theorie der Unternehmung' in T Beschorner and R Pfriem (eds), *Evolutorische Ökonomik und Theorie der Unternehmung* (Marburg, Metropolis) 153–67.
Richman, B (2009) 'Ethnic Networks, Extralegal Certainty, and Globalisation: Peering into the Diamond Industry' in V Gessner (ed), *Contractual Certainty in International Trade* (Oxford, Hart).

Sanchez, R, Heene, A and Thomas, H (1996) 'Towards the theory and practice of competence based competition' in R Sanchez, A Heene and H Thomas (eds), *Dynamics of Competence-based Competition* (Oxford, Pergamon).

Schäcke, M (2006) *Pfadabhängigkeit in Organisationen* (Berlin, Duncker & Humblot).

Schumann, H (1999) 'Das Jahrhundert des Kapitalismus', *Der Spiegel*, No 25/1999 121–37.

Schwarz, R and Ewaldt, JW (2005) 'Über den Beitrag systemdynamischer Modellierung zur Abschätzung technologischer Evolution' in MG Möhrle and R Isenmann (eds), *Technologie-Roadmapping* (2nd edn, Berlin, Springer) 365–81.

Sosa, FP (2006a) *Geschäftsbeziehung und Vertrag im internationalen Rechtsverkehr* (Baden-Baden, Nomos).

—— (2006b) 'The Role of Midsized Law Firms in Globalized Exchange Processes. The Example of International Commercial Arbitration', TranState Working Paper, CRC 597 (Bremen).

—— (2009) 'Cross-Border Dispute Resolution From the Perspective of Midsized Law Firms: The Example of International Commercial Arbitration' in V Gessner (ed), *Contractual Certainty in International Trade* (Oxford, Hart).

Sosa, FP and Flood, J (2006) 'International Lawyers', TranState Working Paper, CRC 597 (Bremen).

Sterman, JD (1989) 'Misperceptions of Feedback in Dynamic Decision Making' 43 *Organizational Behavior and Human Decision Processes* 301–35.

—— (2000) *Business Dynamics. Systems Thinking and Modeling for a Complex World* (Boston, Irwin/McGraw-Hill).

Streit, ME and Mangels, A (1996) 'Privatautonomes Recht und grenzüberschreitende Transaktionen' 47 ORDO 73–100.

Sydow, J (1992) *Strategische Netzwerke* (Wiesbaden, Gabler).

Teece, DJ, Pisano, G and Shuen, A (1997) 'Dynamic capabilities and strategic management' 18 *Strategic Management Journal* 509–33.

Teece, DJ, Rumelt, RR, Dosi, G and Winter, S (1994) 'Understanding corporate coherence. Theory and evidence' 23 *Journal of Economic Behavior and Organization* 1–30.

Venkatraman, N (1989) 'The Concept of Fit in Strategic Management: Toward Verbal and Statistical Correspondence' 14 *Academy of Management Review* 423–44.

Weick, KE (1999) 'Theory Construction as Disciplined Reflexivity: Tradeoffs in the 90s' 24 *Academy of Management Review* 797–806.

Williamson, OE (1983) 'Credible commitments: using hostage to support exchange' 73 *American Economic Review* 519–40.

—— (1985) *The Economic Institutions of Capitalism—Firms, Markets, Relational Contracting* (New York and London, The Free Press).

Winter, SG (1995) 'Four Rs of Profitability: Rents, Resources, Routines, and Replication' in CA Montgomery (ed), *Resource-Based and Evolutionary Theories of the Firm. Towards a Synthesis* (Dordrecht, Kluwer) 147–78.

Witt, U (1987) *Individualistische Grundlagen der evolutorischen Ökonomik* (Tübingen, Mohr).

—— (1992) 'Evolutionary Concepts in Economics' 18 *Eastern Economic Journal* 405–19.

Zucker, LG (1986) 'Production of Trust: Institutional Sources of Economic Structure, 1840–1920' 8 *Research in Organizational Behaviour* 53–111.

11

Global Trade: Changes in the Conceptualisation of Legal Certainty?

BÄRBEL R DORBECK-JUNG

INTRODUCTION

TRADITIONALLY, THE SUPPORT structures of economic activities are associated with the concept of legal certainty, which here is conceptualised in the Weberian tradition. According to Weber, legal certainty promises calculability of economic activities (Weber, 1980: 487). It creates trust which is indispensable to market capitalism. Calculability of economic activities requires consistent and regular state activity. Stable and predictable legal systems facilitate long-term private planning, where economic expectations have a reasonable chance of gaining satisfaction. Rules which make it possible to foresee with fair certainty how the authority will use its coercive powers in given circumstances enable entrepreneurs to plan their affairs (Hayek, 1944). In the Weberian model, law is regarded as a hierarchical system of rules that is characterised by generality, uniformity, stability, clarity, publicity and predictability. Legal rules are backed by sanctions based on the nation state's monopoly of organised violence. According to this model, capitalism and a legal order based on clear general norms, in conjunction with relatively formalistic modes of legal decision-making, necessarily go hand-in-hand (Scheuerman, 1999; Scheuerman, 2004).

Contemporary globalisation of capitalist economies seems to challenge this view on law and legal certainty. Global trade seems to transform the relationship between capitalism and law. The globalisation-induced 'compression of space and time' occurs systematically to limit the dependence of economic activities on consistent and general forms of legal decision-making that seem to be highly important for relatively small enterprises tied to a specific geographical location. As Scheuerman put it:

> A hitherto unrecognised dialectic has been at work in modern capitalism: by incessantly revolutionising the time and space horizons of economic action, capitalism tends to diminish its reliance on a relatively robust model of the rule of law (1999: 244).

In this chapter, I explore the meaning of Weber's ideas on legal certainty in relation to global trade. My proposition is that Max Weber prepared the ground for a new approach to legal certainty that is indicated by the case studies in this volume. Weber's work is filled with ideas on law and economic action that can be used as departing points for a new approach to legal certainty. To underpin this statement, I first discuss the Weberian model of modern law and legal certainty. I then deal with the implications of global trade on Weber's theoretical frame. Since the institutional structures of economic globalisation are interacting with new public governance structures, attention is also paid to the importance of legal certainty in new public governance approaches. To construct Weber's reply to the challenges of global trade, I build on accounts of Weber's economic theory and dynamic elements in his model of law and legal certainty. Finally, I discuss the need for a revision of Weber's concept of legal certainty which is indicated by the empirical studies included in this volume. How can we update the theory of legal certainty in a society in which global trade seems to prefer non-legal coordination and private regulation?

THE WEBERIAN MODEL OF LEGAL CERTAINTY

Explaining the Quest for Legal Certainty in Modern Rational Capitalism[1]

In his study of the protestant ethic and the spirit of capitalism, Max Weber describes the ethos of the modern 'rational' capitalist enterprise embodying

[1] As Weber focuses on the development and meaning of law and legal certainty in practice, his approach is an empirical one. Regarding law as a phenomenon in the reality of social life, Weber developed a sociological view on law (see Rheinstein, 1967: lv). In his approach to legal certainty, he draws the attention to the *empirical validity* of law. In *normative* approaches to the validity of law, legal certainty is conceived of as one core principle of the rule of law. Other principles are freedom, equality, democracy and effectiveness (see Dorbeck-Jung and De Jong, 2000; Popelier, 1997; Selznick, 1992). In essence, the ideal of the rule of law means the supremacy of law over the state. This ideal refers to a state ruled *by* law. It means also that officials are bound by the law which they themselves have enacted—they must rule *under* law. The rule of law is identified with the separation of the legislative, administrative and judicial powers of the state (Berman, 1983: 294). Law is rooted in human rights, democratic values and other beliefs of Western society (such as legal certainty and, quite recently, efficiency). Accordingly, the substantial basis of the rule of law is broader than the value of legal certainty. In Fuller's approach, legal certainty is related to the internal morality of law (1969).

discipline, systematic action and 'exact' calculation (Weber, 1965). Although he does not define exactly what he means by rational capitalism, his writings indicate that this concept refers to certain type of enterprise that produce for mass markets, use technology and calculate profit using capital accounting (Swedberg, 1998: 20[2]). Rational capitalism presupposes a value system, in which profit-making is the dominant value. It also presupposes a political state where the legal system is predictable and economic activities have their own semi-autonomous space.[3] Discussing the significance of law for economic development, Weber states that the formal rationality of modern law was a necessary precondition of the rise of capitalism. Modern capitalism aspires to achieve maximum predictability in economic affairs. The capitalist preference for 'precise performance' in economic relations leads him to prefer an equally precise and strongly reliable legal institutional frame maximising the chances that his expectations will be satisfied. Furthermore, his desire to 'predict with certainty' makes him an ally of legal forms (for example, clear, calculable and enforceable contracts), tending to reduce economic uncertainty (Scheuerman, 1999: 248). It calls for a rational legality in the sense of general, clear, hierarchic, uniform and stable legal order. Rational legality enhances the economic capacity of the persons affected.[4] As Weber put it:

> To those who had interests in the commodity market, the rationalization and systematization of the law in general and ... the increasing calculability of the functioning of the legal process in particular, constituted one of the most important conditions for the existence ... of capitalistic enterprise, which cannot do without legal certainty (Weber, 1967: 305).

Calculability involves that the state must not make arbitrary interventions in the economy through its legal system, but respect economic autonomy. It covers also a clear, logical, unambiguous legal system that is administered

[2] According to Parsons, the meaning of the term 'rationality' can be derived from Weber's writings as follows: an act is rational in so far as: (i) it is oriented to a clearly formulated unambiguous goal, or to a set of values which are clearly formulated and logically consistent; (ii) the means chosen, are, according to the best available knowledge, adapted to the realisation of the goal (Parsons, 1947: 16). As Parsons pointed out, the question of efficiency, a very important one in defining rationality, is introduced by Weber not earlier than in chapter 11 of *Economy and Society* and then only in a very limited context. In this chapter, Weber maintains that experience tends universally to show that the monocratic type of bureaucratic administration is capable of attaining the highest degree of efficiency (Weber, 1980: 129). Weber thinks this form of administration is superior in intensive efficiency.

[3] In Weber's view, the 'rational' state is characterised by a reliable bureaucracy, an advanced budget system, a systematic economic policy and a special legal system, which provides economic actors with a predictable legal environment (Swedberg, 1998: 19).

[4] Weber assumes that the economic capacity of persons is rather limited (1967: 37). It depends on regularities of conduct, habits and homogeneous norms. In his view, economic conduct can never be adjusted to heterogeneous norms without losses and friction. This friction increases with the increasing interdependence of individual economic units in the market.

in a predictable and professional manner.[5] In this model, legal certainty provides for economic certainty and prosperity.

Weber's explanation of the quest for legal certainty is related to his ideas on the formal characteristics of modern law. According to Weber, legal rules emerge through statutes that are established in a formally correct way. Characteristics of statutes are: compliance with the norms, shared belief in lawfulness and rationality (Weber, 1980: 441). In Weber's view, a legal order exists if coercive means of a physical or psychological kind are available. Comparing law with conventions and customs, the distinguishing characteristic of law is a *staff* of people (including judges, lawyers and prosecutors) who, based on endowed authority, will use physical or psychological coercion in cases of deviance from the prescribed conduct.

According to many socio-legal accounts, Weber's approach to law comes from his theory of politics, and especially his theory that the primary motive force in political life is domination (Berman, 1983: 551; Berman, 1987; Hunt, 1978; Heydebrand, 2009, in this volume[6]). Defining the term 'domination', Weber explains that experience shows that every act of domination will be anxious to raise and cultivate the belief in its *legitimacy*, which supports the probability that certain commands are obeyed (Weber, 1980: 122).[7] In Weber's view, the primary means of domination is coercion. It is the state's monopoly of organised violence ('*politischer Rechtszwang*') that provides for a high degree of certainty regarding the enforceability of objective law.[8] This aspect of legal certainty serves the interests of all stakeholders involved. It motivates entrepreneurs and their legal counsellors ('*Kautelarjuristen*') to explore the opportunities and limits of official law (Weber, 1980: 444). In their search for optimal enforceability, legal counsellors modify existing contracts and 'invent' new ones. In the power relationship between entrepreneurs and states, the first ones exert pressure on the sovereign to provide for legal certainty, while the last ones utilise the quest for legal certainty to the advantage of their own fiscal and political interests (Weber, 1980: 487). Considering the interests of the sovereign and his or her civil servants, Weber stresses that the unity and uniformity of law are essential requirements for effective administration. While civil society calls for certainty relating to the functioning of law, civil

[5] With regard to the calculability of the legal order, Swedberg points out that the concept of calculability covers a host of phenomena (1998: 104).

[6] According to Marcuse, Weber's conception of rationality is closely related to domination inherent in capitalism (Marcuse quoted in Cutler, 2003: 146).

[7] Weber distinguishes three pure types of legitimate domination, ie legal-rational, traditional and charismatic.

[8] Weber admits that the enforceability of legal norms through the state exceptionally may not be essential to particular economic activities. In exceptional cases, pressures of a certain convention, self-interest and loyalty of the other participants provide for enough certainty (Weber, 1980: 443).

servants and sovereign are interested in order and observability of collective action. Dealing with law that emerged after revolutions, Weber discusses a third aspect of legal certainty. This is the quest for legal certainty of those who suffered from the lack of unambiguous, general accessible norms (Weber, 1980: 488). When social conflicts have been pacified, the call for systematic codification of law arises. In summary, the supremacy of formal state law stems from the various benefits that legal certainty provides to the various actors involved.

The Centrality of Law in Modern Capitalism—the Iron Cage of Formal Rational Law

According to Weber, law is central to a capitalist society.[9] It plays a key role in modern economy, owing mainly to the phenomenon of contract.[10] The need for calculability of economic activities is strongly supported by the threat of legal coercion in cases in which contractual agreements are not complied with. In this view, thanks to law, promises will be kept more often and property will be better protected (Swedberg, 1998: 87).[11] In Weber's social theory, formal rationality characterises a certain 'ideal type' of law.[12] With regard to the relation between law and modern capitalism,

[9] Many socio-legal accounts of Weber's sociology of law discuss the centrality-of-law thesis (see, Hunt, 1978). In Weber's ideas, the centrality-of-law thesis is also based on the observation of a strong tendency in Western societies for legal legitimation of public action. Political leaders are obeyed if their actions are based on law. In this case, power is transformed into authority.

[10] Closely connected to the concept of contract is that of the corporation. In Weber's view, the rational corporation is a legal prerequisite for rational capitalism. The modern enterprise can come into being only through permission by the state, but it nonetheless has its own distinct autonomy (Swedberg, 1998: 102).

[11] Interestingly, Weber also recognises the contribution of human rights to the rise of modern capitalism. In the discussion of natural law, he noted that the basic Rights of Man facilitated the expansion of capitalism, because they made it possible to use things and men freely (Weber 1980: 497).

[12] Weber speaks of four ideal types of law: the irrational formal type, the irrational substantive type, the rational substantive type and the rational formal type (1980: 395, 456). In this context, the terminology of rationality refers to a type of law which is guided by general rules. By 'formal rationality', Weber understands independence from external legal forces, as well as a logical interpretation and application of legal rules which is based on abstract concepts created by legal thought itself. Formal rational law is conceived of as constituting a gapless rule system (Rheinstein, 1967: xlii).
Weber repeatedly emphasises that he introduces the ideal types for heuristic and analytical purposes and not to describe concrete historical processes. 'Pure' or 'ideal' types are artificial constructs similar to the pure constructs of geometry (Rheinstein, 1967: xxix). This means that in reality the four types of law do not exist in a 'pure' form. In socio-legal theory, there is much discussion about whether Weber regards ideal types as models for the actualisation of which men ought to strive (see, Berman, 1987; Hunt, 1978; Treiber, 1989; Treiber, 2006). Since Weber idealised formal rationality (eg he speaks of the '*Unentrinnbarkeit*' and '*Überlegenheit*' of bureaucracy, see, Weber 1980: 129), he fell victim, as Treiber pointed out,

Weber seems to suggest that capitalism requires the type of formal rational law. However, Weber's work shows that this connection is not one of absolute correlation.

Weber never postulated simple cause-and-effect relationships.[13] Dealing with anti-formalistic tendencies of modern law, he refers to the 'material' interest of entrepreneurs to evade formal court procedures. According to his analysis, the materialisation of law is also taking place through the introduction of ethical categories into the interpretation of state law. To satisfy the legitimate expectations of private actors, law recognises categories such as 'generally accepted views in trade relations' and 'good faith'. Consequently, the rational qualities of formal law are compromised by material elements which are introduced through a facilitating and protective approach to law.[14]

Discussing the relation between capitalism and the formal quality of law, Weber also admits that the law of England, the leading capitalist country of Europe at his time, was not characterised by formal rationality, but was instead an example partly of the 'traditional' type of law and partly of the 'charismatic' type (Weber, 1980: 511).[15] In Weber's view, capitalist interests were favoured by English judges who were recruited from the capitalists' legal counsellors, as well as by the London location of the English courts, which was inaccessible for ordinary people. Dealing with the Canadian situation of concurring legal systems, Weber concedes that the Anglo-Saxon approach is superior to the continental approach (Weber, 1980: 511). Furthermore, he concludes that capitalism as such does not favour a specific form of rational law. Practical needs for a calculable law may also be gratified, and often better, by a material rational case law.[16]

to the confusion of ideal-typical concept formation and value judgment that he himself so emphatically warns against (Treiber, 2006: 13).

[13] See, Rheinstein (1967: xxvii). In his sophisticated account of the so-called 'England problem', Treiber shows that Weber prefers to view relationships between social phenomena as 'internal correspondent' ('*innere Entsprechung*') or as '*Wahlverwandtschaften*' (Treiber, 1989: 371). See also n 16 below.

[14] In this context, Weber notifies that rational formal law and the particular expectations of entrepreneurs can never match entirely. Law can only guarantee averagely accepted expectations.

[15] Dealing with the Canadian situation of concurring legal systems, he concedes that the Anglo-Saxon approach is dominating the civil law approach (Weber, 1980: 511).

[16] Apparently, this view has not sufficiently been explored by those scholars who discuss Weber's 'England problem' (Swedberg 1998: 105). In summary, the thesis of this discussion is that Weber's identification of calculability with formal legal rationality turns out to be problematic when it comes to England, where the law is characterised by a fairly low degree of formal legal rationality, while capitalism in England had a high degree of rationalism (Trubek, 1972; Kronman, 1983). According to Swedberg, 'the England problem' represents not only a polemical misreading of Weber's argument, but is also based on a simplification of the legal history of England (Swedberg, 1998: 107; see also, Hunt, 1978: 169, fn 131; see also Gessner, 'Introduction', this volume).

Thus it is important to underscore that Weber's conceptual focus of the relationship between modern capitalism and law lies on *calculability* rather than on formal rationality of social structure. One of his basic assumptions is that modern capitalism requires a legal system which guarantees predictability and, in particular, freedom from arbitrary government interference. This guarantee is to a high degree given through the kind of rational formal legality (Rheinstein, 1967: l). As Weber himself put it:

> Conceptually, the 'state' is not indispensable to any economic activity ... It is true (that in the protection of property) individuals are still markedly influenced by convention and usage even today. Yet, the influence of these factors has declined due to the disintegration of tradition, ie, of the tradition-determined relationships as well of the belief in their sacredness . . . The tempo of modern business communication requires a promptly and predictably functioning legal system, ie, one which is guaranteed by the strongest coercive power. Finally, modern economic life by its very nature has destroyed those other associations which used to be the bearers of law and thus legal guaranties (Weber, 1967: 38, 39).

In Weber's view, it is the process of rationalisation of modern life with its increasing 'disenchantment' or 'demagification', and its increasing systematisation of interrelationships of meaning that lead to formally and logically rational law (Treiber, 2006: 2). Modern society seems to be imprisoned in the 'iron cage' of formally rational legal rules.[17] With regard to contemporary economic globalisation, the question arises of whether we can still speak of an iron cage of formal rational law. To answer this question, we will explore the changes of economic globalisation and new public governance with which the Weberian model has to cope. Regarding the focus of this volume, special attention will be paid to the challenges of global trade.

[17] In his historic analysis of the influence of the protestant ethic on the spirit of capitalism, Weber uses the iron cage metaphor to illustrate the irresistible forces of the economic order (Weber, 1965: 181). According to Weber, this order is now bound to the technical and economic conditions of machine production which determine the lives of all the individuals who are born into this mechanism, not only those directly concerned with irresistible force. The iron cage metaphor refers also to formally rational law where individual and collective activities are hopelessly imprisoned (Gessner, 2009b, in this volume; see also, Mitzman, 1970; and Kronman, 1983). Weber himself sketches the picture of legal practice as an advancing machine (1980: 826; see also, Gessner, in this volume).

CHALLENGES TO THE WEBERIAN MODEL OF LEGAL CERTAINTY IN THE AGE OF ECONOMIC GLOBALISATION AND NEW PUBLIC GOVERNANCE

Changes in the Relation between Capitalism and Formally Rational Legal Structures

It is the alliance between capitalism and formally rational legal structures presupposed by Weber that is challenged today by the globalisation of economies. Economic globalisation is characterised by:

a) the growing importance of multinational corporations within the world economy;
b) the transnationalisation of capital and financial markets; and
c) the compression of space and time horizons of action (Hirst and Thompson, 1996; Giddens, 1990; MacGrew, 1998).

Exploring the consequences for legal support structures, we first must look more closely at the implications of economic globalisation. According to most accounts, globalisation is deepening economic concentration in the world economy, in part because of the exorbitant start-up costs entailed by advanced technology. Globalisation appears to be fragmented, rather than uniform. It occurs not exclusively via the internal logics of a capitalist economic sector, but via the internal dynamics of a plurality of social subsystems (Teubner, 1997: 5). Global business interacts efficiently despite the heterogeneity of social, economic and legal cultures (Gessner, 2009a, in this volume). The control of fragmented production processes, spread all over the world, is now exercised by organisations which have themselves spread beyond frontiers. Economic globalisation constantly overcomes geographical barriers and uses technology to speed up production and reduce its costs. Advanced information technologies enable the entrepreneur to perform his or her activities simultaneously and instantaneously. In a globalised economy, enterprises are competing at the world level and are cooperating and competing with states to maximise profits. By making use of the rivalries between countries, large enterprises acquire a strong position. As a consequence of the emergence of multinational corporations and the transnationalisation of financial markets, traditional notions of sovereignty seems to be shaken (Robé, 1997: 46).

> Economic actors of the globalized society themselves decide where to invest and locate their activities, and they do so not as a consequence of allegiance relationships or of sovereignty issues, but after considering the best opportunities offered by a combination of geography, demography, regulations (in particular labour costs and environmental rules), local subsidies, quality of the infrastructure, prospects for political stability and so on (Plantey, 1991: 11).

According to MacGrew, the structural implications of modern globalisation for the modern state are arguably profound (1998: 341). Multinational enterprises succeed in creating a strong internal order that follows it to the territory to which it is moving (Robé, 1997: 53). As Gessner and Budak point out:

> In addition to (or instead of) constitutional lawmaking of global interaction, some local and foreign actors create their own global structures which then may operate entirely autonomously from state law (Gessner and Budak,1998: 6).

As a consequence of factual changes related to new ways of economic production and structural coordination of economic activities, the desire for stable, predictable and coherent state law seems to decrease. According to many accounts, the economic uncertainties on which Weber's model was based have been remarkably reduced by technological and social innovation.[18] The ways in which today's multinational enterprises seek to maximise profits are facilitated by vague, flexible and diverse legal rules rather than by general, clear and uniform ones. Multinational enterprises call for legal institutions providing for flexible modes of conflict resolution (Scheuerman, 1999: 262). They prefer open-ended and flexible guidelines (Atiyah, 1979: 713).[19] They profit from the diversity of national legal systems. Diverse standards of environmental and labour law enable them to play off nation states against each other.

Obviously, the power relationships between states and multinational enterprises have changed remarkably. Economic growth of nation states seems to become more dependent on multinational enterprises. Globalisation has introduced a new element of uncertainty in domestic law-making and implementation which makes it more dependent on domestic and international expertise (Pierre and Peters, 2000: 59). In Scheuerrman's view, this is a weapon to neutralise the regulatory capacities of the nation state (1999: 260). To improve the investment climate, national governments award special rights and privileges to multinational enterprises (for example, special tax cuts for foreign investors). Multinational corporations increasingly seem to possess legally recognised sovereign powers of law-making. We have mentioned above the emergence of strong internal orders

[18] This holds especially in economic sectors in which transactions increasingly rely on high-speed information, communication and transportation technologies. As Scheuerman points out, advanced technology takes care of at least some of the functions performed in an earlier phase in the history of capitalism by a liberal legal code consisting of clear, general and relatively stable norms (Scheuerman, 1999: 255). For example, a present-day currency trader exchanges vast amounts of currency within a few moments merely by pressing a few keys on his or her computer. Certainly, he or she does not experience the same need for a robust rule of law as his or her historical predecessors whose business relied on long and risky voyages. See also Dietz and Nieswandt (2009, in this volume).

[19] One example is the growing recognition of a 'right to change one's mind' in contracts (see Atiyah, 1979: 713).

of multinational enterprises that are competing with state law. Interestingly, the strength of these orders is ascribed to their indeterminate and vague character. Dealing with the legal status of the *lex mercatoria*, Teubner emphasises that the broad principles of which it consists make it relatively resistant to symbolic destruction in the case of deviance (Teubner, 1997: 21). In Teubner's view, stability comes from softness.

The existence and influence exerted by these internal orders on economic regulation question the traditional view of their subordination to state law (Robé, 1997; Teubner, 1997). Given the insight into decreasing efficiency of traditional hierarchic law, governments seek to influence major corporate players through more subtle, cooperative forms of coordination to increase the competitiveness of the domestic industry (Pierre and Peters, 2000: 60). Globalisation breaks the traditional doctrine of legal sources, according to which *lex mercatoria* and other forms of private regulation are regarded as non-law, just facts or delegated law-making that needs recognition by the official legal order (Teubner, 1997).

In this volume, Dietz and Nieswandt, Konradi and Richman point to the significance of non-legal coordination mechanisms (among which are relational contract management, reputation networks, arbitration and *lex mercatoria*). The contributions of Sosa and Flood and Skordaki show how influential law firms and lawyers of real estate finance are with regard to the interpretation and creation of support structures for economic transactions. To these lawyers, the calculability of state law seems to be less important than to Weber's '*Kautelarjuristen*'.

Changes in the Views on Coordination and Steering Capacities of Nation States—from Government to Public Governance[20]

Globalisation has both economic and political dimensions. Above, we saw that the flourishing of transnational activity can depend on state decisions to foster it. Globalisation and public governance are strongly intertwined.[21] The current public governance debate is about shifts in coordination and steering methods, and shifts in approaches and instruments of

[20] According to Benz, the core meaning of governance is 'steering and coordination of interdependent (usually collective) actors based on institutionalised rule systems' (Benz, 2004). For an overview of the discussion of public governance, see Frederiksson and Smith, 2003; Héritier, 2003; Kersbergen and Van Waarden, 2004; Kooiman, 2003; Majone, 1997; Mayntz, 2004; Pierre and Peters, 2000; and Treib, Bähr and Falkner, 2005.

[21] To a certain extent, the economic and political dimensions of globalisation appear to be each other's causes and effects. According to Pierre and Peters, globalisation of political and economic power is accompanied by the 'hollow state' (2000: 58). This means a loss of sovereignty, as well as less power of jurisdictions. Globalisation encouraged the development of transnational institutions, which means also the increasing importance and powers of

collective action. It is a reaction to the critique on the functioning of governments (ie to provide remedies for problems of effectiveness and efficiency of collective action) and an attempt to link the contemporary state to the contemporary society.[22] As law and legislation are crucial instruments of collective action, shifts in the modes of public governance have implications for our model of law and legal certainty. Traditional governance strongly relies on mandatory rules tied to enforcement and sanctions issued by legislatures and courts. New governance draws attention to more non-legal methods of coordination. Its methods establish norms and achieve compliance by encouraging the participation of stakeholders and by requiring transparency and accountability of those participating in decision-making processes. Taking into account the coordination activities of the various public and private actors involved, the new public governance approach is rather heterarchic than hierarchic (Kooiman, 2003; Lagas, 1997). Considering legislation, Teubner concludes:

> When the frame of rule hierarchy with constitutionally legitimated political legislation at its top breaks under the pressures of globalisation, then the new frame which replaces it can only be heterarchical. It decentres political law-making, moves it away from its privileged place at the top of the norm-hierarchy and puts it on an equal footing with other types of social law-making (Teubner, 1997: xiv).

In the methods of new public governance, government still holds a strong position, although a different one (Streeck and Thelen, 2005). According

European and international institutions. To address this development, the terminology of *multi-level governance* is very popular in the contemporary public governance debate.

[22] In *the critique on the functioning of the state*, the most important arguments are: the social welfare state is inhibiting individual freedom, discouraging innovation and entrepreneurship (see Pierre and Peters, 2000: 52). Other critical remarks refer to the bad performance of public organisations. According to critical commentators, the state failed to attain any of its ideological goals such as equality, prosperity, etc. These arguments were related to the financial crisis of the state. This crisis referred to the decline in the financial resources of the states during the 1980s and 1990s. One reason for that related to the increasing public expenditures; another reason was that of the stagnation of economic growth. The financial crisis encouraged the involvement of private actors to deliver public services. As a consequence, the public-private distinction is blurring. This shift from public to mixed delivery was accompanied by an ideological shift towards the market. The introduction of competition in the delivery of public services is regarded as a way to provide more cost-effectiveness. The critical remarks on the performance of public organisation supported the rise of a managerial approach in public service production. *New Public Management* argues that public organisations should be managed in the same way as any private sector organisation. Consequently, elected officials are being assigned a more peripheral role (only goal setting—implementation of public policy is partly delegated to private actors), and input control is partly replaced by performance control and ex post evaluation.

As regards the second point of the public governance discussion, ie to *link the contemporary state to the contemporary society*, this debate seeks responses to the social changes of enhanced participation of civil society (ie deliberate decision-making).

In summary, the contemporary developments in public governance can be regarded as a reaction to ideological shifts and social changes.

to most accounts, governmental intervention is still required, for private actors cannot be relied on to give appropriate weight to public interests over private ones. The government is no longer acting on the basis of command and control, but is taking the role of coordinator and facilitator of social action ('from government to governance'). It focuses on the setting of policy goals ('steering') rather than on the implementation of these goals ('rowing'). Contemporary public governance seeks to find the right mix of traditional regulation and 'soft' coordination (Trubek and Trubek, 2005; Heydebrand, 2009, this volume; Trubek, Cottrell and Nance, 2006). It is closely related to instruments of soft law.[23] Furthermore, it is characterised by a diversification and hybridisation of governance methods, instruments and institutionalisation.[24] As a consequence, the modes used by public actors to support economic transactions are changing.

Implications for Weber's Model of Law and Legal Certainty

Developments of new public governance seem to confirm the picture of a decline for Weber's model of legal certainty I sketched previously with regard to economic globalisation. In the modes of contemporary public governance, the making of rules and legislation is only one way among many to implement public policies. Legal authority is widely delegated. The ideal is to achieve the maximum feasible level of self-regulation. In the debate about new public governance, the assumption is that negotiation, dialogue and compromise can contribute more effectively to problem-solving than hierarchical legislation. The focus of public governance seems to lie on efficiency and effectiveness rather than on legality.

In summary, economic globalisation and new public governance indicate that capitalism and an order of state law based on clear general norms, in conjunction with relatively formalistic modes of legal decision-making, do not necessarily go hand in hand. In contrast, economic globalisation seems to flourish where such legal forms are lacking. According to the empirical

[23] See Senden, 2004: 111–13; 2005: 15, who distinguishes between three categories of soft law. These are: (i) preparatory and informative instruments; (ii) interpretative and decisional instruments; and (iii) steering instruments. However, soft coordination refers also to non-hierarchical instruments like partnership ('co-regulation'), peer pressures, social dialogue and the 'open method of coordination' that are not covered by soft law. It involves a large range of non-hierarchical tools. See also Cutler (2003).

[24] Of course, there is much rhetoric in the 'new' public governance debate. However, according to influential scholars like Frederickson, Pierre and Peters, new public governance must not be regarded as a fashion or hype that will soon disappear. In their view, it implies fundamental changes in collective action. These changes appear to take place evolutionarily rather than revolutionarily, since states are slowly adapting to the changes in their environment and to ideological pressures.

studies included in this volume, global trade is widely supported by non-legal structures. This picture is confirmed by tendencies in contemporary public governance which is intertwined with economic globalisation. There is some evidence that the desire for Weber's model of legal certainty (in the sense of a general, clear, hierarchic, uniform and stable legal order based on the state's monopoly of organised violence) rapidly decreases. Consequently, the ideal type of law that is based on formal rationality may be perceived as an obsolescent form of legal order. Does this mean that we have arrived at an historical turn, where a new model of law and contractual certainty is required? To answer this question, I will first make some critical remarks on the underpinnings of the thesis of a declining need for legal certainty. I will then discuss the 'solutions' provided by Weber's theory to cope with the challenges to his model of law and legal certainty.

REPLIES TO THE CRITIQUE OF WEBER'S MODEL OF LEGAL CERTAINTY

General Remarks

In the critique on Weber's model, the central argument is that the capitalists' need for legal certainty (in the sense of a general, abstract, clear, hierarchic, coherent, uniform, predictable and stable legal order based on the state's monopoly of organised violence) has declined due to:

a) economic uncertainties being remarkably reduced through technological and social innovation;
b) the emergence of strong, autonomous internal legal orders of multinational enterprises;
c) an interest of multinational enterprises in flexible, unstable, open-ended guidelines rather than in stable, predictable state law;
d) an interest of multinational enterprises and their legal counsellors in gaps of legislation rather than in the enforceability of law; and
e) the increasing weakness and dependence of nation states of multinational enterprises.

Considering the influence of technological innovation on the need for legal certainty, Wioletta Konradi's study indicates that the use of modern information and communication technology facilitates the settlement of uncertainties in trans-border timber trade (Konradi, 2009, in this volume). By this, economic uncertainties might be remarkably reduced. According to Dietz and Nieswandt (2009, in this volume), private contract enforcement institutions owe their global functionality to the revolutionary innovation in the field of information technology. Other effects of technological and organisational innovation are pointed out by Barak Richman's study

(Richman, 2009, in this volume). This study indicates that the lawlessness of the diamond industry, which has relied on extra-legal certainty in the sense of a non-state system of contract enforcement that rests on personal exchange and reputation mechanisms, is challenged by the use of new technologies. New coordination strategies based on the internet and other technologies, together with consumer-driven private governance, seem to put an end to lawlessness in the diamond industry. Furthermore, a more general argument is that technological innovation is usually accompanied by risk problems which can lead to economic uncertainties. As the governance of computer crime and software protection shows, economic losses can give rise to a desire for legal structures. In risky global trade, this only seems to be the case when business networks are extended and relation distance increases.

As Konradi and Richman show, trust building in risky cross-border exchanges relies on various interacting forms of private coordination (Konradi, 2009, in this volume; Richman, 2009, in this volume). In their study of transnational cooperation in the software industry, Dietz and Nieswandt conclude that private contract enforcement institutions are the dominant coordination mechanism (Dietz and Nieswandt, 2009, in this volume). According to Sosa, commercial conflicts are usually taken to commercial arbitration and rarely to the courts (Sosa, 2009, in this volume). Even in the current situation where larger and less close-knit networks are emerging, law seems to function only as a *last resort.* However, as Konradi concludes, globalisation seems to increase the interactions between public regulation and *lex mercatoria.* This is why she considers the *lex mercatoria* only as a partly autonomous order. Regarding the emergence of autonomous strong internal orders of multinationals, I mentioned above other examples of 'law-like' generally accepted commercial customs (Gessner and Budak, 1998; Robé, 1997). It occurs to me, however, that there is no evidence that these internal orders are entirely autonomous. As Muchlinski concludes in his investigation of 'law-making' activities of multinational enterprises:

> The history of commercial law and regulations rests on the response of the 'official' order to discrete business practices. It is through the absorption of such practices into the 'official' legal order that their interpretation in accordance with the binary code legal/illegal most vividly emerges (1997: 101[25]).

[25] According to Muchlinski, another argument against the strength of these orders is that it depends on the capacity of local communities to destabilise such emerging 'law' (1997: 102).

Apparently, these internal orders are partly autonomous and co-evolving in interaction with state law (Gessner, 1998; Gessner, 2009b, in this volume[26]). Hence, the picture is much more complex than the one drawn by the critique on Weber's model.

With regard to the need for stable, predictable state law, the empirical studies included in this volume point out that global trade primarily relies on private coordination mechanisms which are tailored to the specific needs and contextual circumstances of the industry (Konradi, 2009; Richman, 2009; Sosa, 2009, all in this volume). Obviously, the business community is interested in specific norms and particularistic solutions rather than in open-ended guidelines. There seems to be a strong interest in the flexibility, but also in the stability of private governance.

Considering the activities of the legal counselors, the case studies of Flood and Skordaki and Sosa point out that the functions of Weber's '*Kautelarjuristen*' have remarkably changed (Flood and Skordaki, 2009; Sosa, 2009, both in this volume). Due to the weakness and fragmentation of international legal structures, certain law firms and highly qualified lawyers have attained a crucial influence on the support structures of global economic transactions. Working within the confines of law, these experts are shaping the support structures rather than interpreting state regulation. It is up to the expert, as Flood and Skordaki show, to create a structure that will satisfy not merely the immediate needs of investors and funders, but accommodate local jurisdictional needs without compromising the essential aspects of the transaction. At present, legal counsellors seem to *fill* the regulatory gaps rather than *find* the regulatory gaps of legal regulation. It is striking that the properties of English common law facilitate this new key function of legal counsellors, which, according to Flood and Skordaki, would be difficult, if not at times impossible, for civil law. Obviously, various forms of capitalism seem to flourish with the Anglo-Saxon legal system.

With regard to the argument of the increasing weakness and dependence of the nation state, empirical studies show contradictory findings (Heydebrand, 2009, in this volume). It is not yet clear whether states are weakened in situations of shared legal sovereignty. Furthermore, there are other influential developments that call for state law and legal certainty. For example, the World Bank asserts in its 2001 centrepiece document on insolvency law that:

[26] See also Streeck and Thelen, 2005. In the papers on Better Regulation, the EU focuses on an incremental co-evolutionary approach (Task Force Group Better Regulation <http://archive.cabinetoffice.gov.uk/brc/upload/assets/www.brc.gov.uk/betterroutes.pdf> accessed 28 July 2008.

> Effective insolvency systems include rules that are reasonably predictable, transparent and hold all parties duly accountable throughout the process. There is no substitute for a clear law (quoted in Carruthers and Halliday (2007: 9)).

In summary, there is some evidence that the importance of various aspects of Weber's model have changed. Due to the global trade's interest in specific and tailored norms, the capitalists' requirement for general, abstract, uniform and coherent law seems to decrease. Global trade business seems to be more interested in the calculability of private norms than in the predictability of law. Regarding the modes of new public governance, a heterarchic approach to law appears to be more appropriate for legal theory rather than Weber's hierarchic view. Presently, the focus of multinationals' interest in legal certainty seems to lie in the functioning of law as a last resort. For the revision of the concept of legal certainty, however, the multinationals interest must be put in perspective. It must be related to other interests in legal certainty, such as the call of citizens and small enterprises for general and uniform law. It is obvious that Weber's model of legal certainty must be revised to cope with the focus on private support structures and the fragmentation, diversification and hybridisation of governance. It seems to me, however, that we have not arrived at a historical turn where a new model of legal certainty is required, but instead at a period of transition in which new conceptual ideas around legal certainty must be worked out. In the introduction to this chapter, I claimed that Max Weber prepared the ground for the revision of his model of law and legal certainty. In the next section, I will underpin this proposition.

The Open Doors of the Iron Cage of Formal Rational Law

In our search for an approach to legal certainty that can cope with the implications of economic globalisation and new public governance, Weber's work provides us with some basic ideas regarding the dynamics, diversity and pluralism of law. Before discussing these ideas in more detail, attention must be paid to Weber's conceptualisation of the relation between economic action and law.

Weber's writings on 'economic sociology' provide interesting ideas on the interaction between law and economic activities.[27] In *Economy and Society*, he sketches what he calls the most general relationships between

[27] In his illuminating exploration of Weber's ideas of economic sociology (in Weber's terminology '*Sozialökonomik*'), Swedberg shows that Weber's (late) work is filled with ideas on economic action, many of which have never been explored (Swedberg, 1998). Swedberg's study puts the socio-legal focus on Weber's political theory in perspective. Earlier, Talcott Parsons pointed out that in Weber's earlier development the emphasis laid on economic rather than formal legal factors (Parsons, 1947: 6). According to Rheinstein, the main problem on which Weber focuses in his sociology of law is whether the rise of formal rationality in legal

law and economy (Weber, 1980: 181). He concludes that the influences between law and economy are very complicated.[28] Economic conditions have played an important role in the evolution of law, but they have not been decisive alone and by themselves. Weber developed a flexible and social version of an interest theory, in which interest-driven behaviour and social behaviour are united in the conception of economic social action (Swedberg, 1998: 5).[29] Interestingly, this notion implies a strong connection between law and economy. Embarking on his concept of social behaviour, which is constituted by social interaction[30] and social structures, Weber presupposes that an economic actor naturally orients him- or herself to the behaviour of other economic actors and to the conventional and legal rules which he or she recognises as valid.[31] Hence, legal structures are incorporated in a rather dynamic way in economic action. Furthermore, with regard to the interaction between law and economy, Weber suggests in his discussion of law's centrality that the constant expansion of the market has favoured the monopolisation of all 'legitimate' coercive power by *one* universalist coercive institution (Weber, 1980: 518). Furthermore, he states that economic interests are among the strongest factors influencing the creation of law. Because any authority guaranteeing a legal order depends, in some way, upon consensual action of the constitutive social groups, and the formation of social groups depends, to a large extent, upon constellations of material interests (1967: 37).

As shown above, Weber was aware of contradictory tendencies ('materialisation') in the development of the formal qualities of law (1980: 512).

thought contributed to the rise of capitalism; and whether capitalism has contributed to the rise of logical rationality in legal thought (Rheinstein, 1967: xlii).

[28] In this chapter, Weber partly discusses the relation between law and economy, criticising Stammler's approach (Weber, 1980: 191).

[29] First, Weber distinguishes between material and ideal interests. Both can motivate social action. In economic behaviour, material interests count most. Interestingly, Weber also argued that not only interests, but also emotions and tradition play a part in the behaviour of the individual. Secondly, in his definition of economic social action, Weber distinguishes between economic and economically oriented action (1980: 31). According to this distinction, multinational enterprises conduct economic action when their action is primarily oriented to the goal of profit-making. Actions of public governance which are not primarily oriented to economic ends, but in their orientation to public goals take economic considerations into account (such as to give tax advantages to multinationals in order to safeguard the nation's welfare), fall under the category of economically oriented action.

[30] In Weber's theory, social interaction means taking into account the behaviour of others.

[31] By validity, Weber refers to the knowledge of the economic actor related to the fact that a violation of the rules would call forth a given reaction of other persons (Weber, 1980: 181; see also, n 1; and Swedberg, 1998: 87). It has to be mentioned that Weber explains compliance with the law by self-interest rather than obedience to authority. However, Weber emphasises that the various reasons why some behaviour takes place are not relevant, since economic theory does not rest on psychological foundations. What counts is that some behaviour indeed takes place and whether it complies with the established social structure.

He also concedes that the calculability of economic activities can be provided by material rational law (like the English case law), which is more adaptive to existing demands and needs because of particular structures based on tradition (Treiber, 1989: 364). Additionally, Weber acknowledges that in the modern occidental society the power of law over economic conduct has in many respects grown weaker rather than stronger. He admits the strong influence of economic forces on state sovereignty and law, as well as the interdependence between public and private institutional structures. He concedes that the power of law is weakening in increasingly complex economies. Discussing the relation between law and economic activity, he acknowledges the dependence of legal authority on consensual action of social groups. This applies particularly to those situations where the determinants in production and consumption do not lie within a completely perspicuous and directly manageable complex of consensual contract. In an economy based on all-embracing interdependence on the market, the possible and unintended effects of a legal measure must to a large extent escape the foresight of the legislator and enforcement officers, simply because they do not have the rational knowledge of the market and the interest situation.[32] Regarding these difficulties, the factual impact of the law on economic conduct cannot be determined generally, but must be calculated for each particular case (Weber, 1967: 38). Hence, in market societies, certainty cannot be exclusively provided by general and abstract legal norms. With regard to the diversity of law, Weber mentions legal particularism arising in monopolised markets from competing political associations (Weber, 1967: 40). Obviously, Weber was aware of the limits of a static model of formal rational law.

This conclusion is also confirmed by his general ideas about the four stages of legal development (Weber, 1980: 504).[33] Weber developed an evolutionary approach to law which implies a dialectic interaction between revolution and evolution.[34] In this view, legal innovation is caused by a new line of conduct, which is spread by imitation and selection of the

[32] In this context, it is important to note that Weber maintains that bureaucracy is superior in knowledge, including both technical knowledge and knowledge of the concrete fact (see Parsons, 1947: 339). In Weber's view, bureaucracy refers to state administration, as well as to the administration of large-scale corporate groups.

[33] See n 12.

[34] As Gessner points out, Weber's theory of institutional evolution was formed in the earlier periods of his scholarship and was based on Darwinian assumptions of social learning: formal rational institutions are selected by a struggle for survival (Gessner, 2009b, in this volume). In the socio-legal literature there is some debate about the question of whether Weber's approach to law was an evolutionary one (Berman, 1983: 504; Habermas, 1981; Rottleuthner, 1986; Seyfarth, 1981; Teubner, 1982; Treiber, 1989). In this debate, the main question is whether Weber's four types of law must be regarded purely as a classification or whether they can be viewed as stages of legal development. According to most accounts, Weber's focus is the evolution of law. Even those scholars who contest this conclusion (eg

persons involved. In the selection process, economic forces, as well as the interdependence of institutions, play an important role. On the basis of these ideas, the image of dynamic co-evolving social structures arises. As such, Weber's iron cage provides a 'window' to a co-evolutionary approach to law.

With regard to legal pluralism, interesting ideas can be derived from Weber's broad definition of a law and legal order. As we mentioned above, a Weberian legal order is said to exist wherever statutes are established in a formally correct way, when they are complied with, where there is shared belief in the lawfulness and rationality of the rules emerging from these statutes, and where there is a *staff* of people whose members are endowed with a specific authority and use the available means of a physical or psychological kind.[35] This staff must not necessarily be, as Rheinstein convincingly pointed out, an agency of the sovereign (Rheinstein, 1967: lix). In cases where the internal order of multinational enterprises has been established according to the authority and procedural rules of the organisation, and if it is likely that it will be enforced by its enforcement staff, we could speak of a legal order, as proponents of legal pluralism claim.[36] In sum, Weber's 'iron cage' is much more permeable than many commentators suggest.

CONCLUSION

My conclusion is that Weber's concept of legal order and some of his ideas related to the interaction between law and economic activity provide inspiration for the revision of the concept of legal certainty. 90 years ago, Weber already identified important theoretical topics with which contemporary socio-legal theory has to cope. Considering the challenges of

Treiber and Seyfarth) speak of a minimal programme of evolutionary theory (see Treiber, 1989: 386). Weber himself refers to the dialectic of legal evolution and revolution in his debate of natural law (1980: 496).

[35] Weber admits that the existence of an 'enforcement agency' does not require any specifically 'judicial' authority (1947: 128). The clan, as an agency of blood revenge and of the prosecution of feuds, is such an enforcing agency, if there exists any sort of rules which govern its behaviour in such situations. In any case, the means of coercion are irrelevant.

[36] See Gottlieb, 1983: 570; and Robbé, 1997: 52. Whether internal statutes of enterprises can be interpreted as law in the Weberian terminology does not only depend on the formal correct way of rule establishment, the available coercive means, the perception of the members of these enterprises of the statutes as being legitimate and mandatory, but also on the existence of a *staff*. In Weber's view, the *staff* includes officials (ie lawyers, judges, police officers and prosecutors), 'the people with the spiked helmets', as he put it more colloquially (see Swedberg, 1998: 85, with references to Weber's writings). In cases where internal statutes meet the first three requirements of Weber's definition, it has to be explored whether the people in charge of enforcement can be regarded as a 'staff'. With regard to legal pluralism, we must bear in mind that Weber's concept of law is that of a sociologist (see Rheinstein, 1967: lxiii).

economic globalisation to the Weberian model, it occurs to me that the first step of the revision of legal certainty must be to re-conceptualise the basic needs of calculability of social economic action. Which are the factual and which are the legitimate interests in calculable support structures? In doing this, the various interests of multinationals in calculable structures, but also the concerns of small enterprises, citizens, the EU, NGOs, the World Bank and nation states must be explored. As the case studies of this volume indicate, special attention should be paid to the gaps in transnational support structures, as well as to the multinationals' interest in tailored solutions.

Regarding the discussion about the recognition of internal orders of economic enterprises and co-regulation of private and public actors, Weber's concept of law provides a pluralistic approach. Hence, on our way to revising legal certainty, a second step is to explore the persuasiveness of a polycentric approach.[37] This raises the question of whether legal thought can cope with law and legal certainty being engendered in many centres. How can arbitrary decision-making be reduced in cases of competing and conflicting 'legal' orders? What are the implications of heterarchy and diversity on the effectiveness of law? How can legal thought cope with the hybridisation of legal governance? In this regard, we should keep Weber's warning in mind that economic conduct cannot be adjusted to heterogeneous norms without losses and friction.[38] Furthermore, we can refer to his study of English law, which indicates that material rational case law can respond more effectively to a dynamic environment than formal rational law.

In another approach to legal certainty, we can learn from the insights of the empirical studies included in this volume, as well as from evaluations of hybrid approaches to law and regulation (amongst which is the notion of legally structured and conditioned self-regulation[39]). There are many uncertainties and risks lying on our road to a new approach to legal certainty. One thing is for sure: we have left the iron cage of formal rational law behind us. And this is partly the case because Weber himself opened many doors.

REFERENCES

Atiyah, PS (1979) *The Rise and Fall of Freedom of Contract* (Oxford, Clarendon Press).

[37] See also Petersen and Zahle, 1995.
[38] See n 4.
[39] See, eg Dorbeck-Jung, Oude Vrielink and Reussing, 2006.

Benz, A (2004) 'Einleitung: Governance—Modebegriff oder nützliches sozialwissenschaftliches Konzept?' in A Benz (ed), *Governance—Regieren in komplexen Regelsystemen: eine Einführung* (Wiesbaden, VS Verlag für Sozialwissenschaften).

Berman, H (1983) *Law and Revolution* (Cambridge, Harvard University Press).

—— (1987) 'Some False Premises of Max Weber's Sociology of Law' 65 *Washington University law Quarterly* 758–70.

Carruthers, BG and Halliday, TC (2007) 'Law, Economy and Globalisation: How Modern International Financial Institutions Embraced Adam Smith and accidentally discovered Max Weber' in V Nee and R Swedberg (eds), *On Capitalism* (Stanford, Stanford University Press).

Cutler, C (2003) *Private Power and Global Authority. Transnational Merchant Law in the Global Political Economy* (Cambridge, Cambridge University Press).

Dietz, T and Nieswandt, H (2009) 'The emergence of transnational cooperation in the software-industry' in V Gessner (ed), *Contractual Certainty in International Trade* (Oxford, Hart).

Djelic, ML and Quack, S (eds) (2003) *Globalisation and Institutions. Redefining the Rules of the Economic Game* (Cheltenham, Edward Elgar).

Dorbeck-Jung, BR and Jong, HM de (2000) 'Legitimate Governance within the State' in H Wagenaar (ed), *Government Institutions: Effects, Changes and Normative Foundations* (Dordrecht/London, Kluwer).

Dorbeck-Jung, BR, Oude Vrielink-van Heffen, MJ and Reussing, GH (2006) *Open normen en regeldruk—een onderzoek naar de kosten en oorzaken van irritaties bij open normen in de kwaliteitszorg* (Enschede, IGS).

Flood, J and Skordaki, E (2009) 'Structuring transactions: The case of real estate finance' in V Gessner (ed), *Contractual Certainty in International Trade* (Oxford, Hart).

Frederickson, HG and Smit, KB (2003) *The Public Administration Theory Primer* (Boulder, CO, Westview Press) chapter 9.

Fuller, L (1969) *The Internal Morality of Law* (2nd edn, New Haven, Yale University Press).

Gessner, V (1998) 'Globalisation and Legal Certainty' in V Gessner and AC Budak (eds), *Emerging Legal Certainty. Empirical Studies on the Globalisation of Law*, ISSJ Series (Ashgate, Dartmouth).

—— (2007) 'Legislation and the Varieties of Capitalism' in C Antons and V Gessner (eds), *Globalisation and Resistance* (Oxford, Hart).

—— (2009a) 'Introduction: Toward a theoretical framework for contractual certainty in global trade' in V Gessner (ed), *Contractual Certainty in International Trade* (Oxford, Hart).

—— (2009b) 'The Governance of Business Transactions in Globalising Economies: Theories of Change' in V Gessner (ed), *Contractual Certainty in International Trade* (Oxford, Hart).

Gessner, V and Budak, AC (1998a) 'Introduction' in V Gessner and AC Budak (eds), *Emerging Legal Certainty. Empirical Studies on the Globalisation of Law*, ISSJ Series (Ashgate, Dartmouth).

Giddens, A (1990) *The Consequences of Modernity* (Cambridge, Polity Press).

Gottlieb, G (1983) 'Relationism: Legal Theory for a Relational Society' 50 *University of Chicago La Review* 567.

Habermas, J (1981) *Theorie des Kommunikatieven Handelns* (Frankfurt, Rowolt).

Hayek, FA (1944) *The Road to Serfdom* (Chicago, University of Chicago Press).

Héritier, A (2003) 'New Modes of Governance in Europe. Increasing Political Capacity and Policy Effectiveness' in TA Borzel and RA Cichowski (eds), *The State of the European Union* (Oxford, Oxford University Press).

Heydebrand, W (2009) 'Contractual certainty vs efficiency: The historical and institutional context of global trade' in V Gessner (ed), *Contractual Certainty in International Trade* (Oxford, Hart).

Hirst, P and Thompson, G (1996) *Globalisation in Question* (Cambridge, Polity Press).

Hunt, A (1978) *The Sociological Movement in Law* (London, Macmillan Press).

Kersbergen, K van and Waarden, F van (2004) 'Governance as a bridge between disciplines, cross-disciplinary inspiration regarding shifts in governance and problems of governability, accountability and legitimacy' 43 *European Journal of Political Research* 143–71.

Konradi, W (2009) 'The role of *lex mercatoria* in supporting globalised transactions: An empirical insight into the governance structure of the timber industry' in V Gessner (ed), *Contractual Certainty in International Trade* (Oxford, Hart).

Kooiman, J (2003) 'Societal Governance: Levels, Models and orders of Social-Political Interaction' in J Pierre (ed), *Debating Governance: Authority, Steering and Democracy* (Oxford, Oxford University Press).

Knill, Ch and Lenschow, A (2003) 'Modes of regulation in the Governance of the European Union: Towards a Comprehensive Evaluation' 7 European Integration Online Papers <http://papers.ssrn.com/sol3/papers.cfm?abstract_id=380680> accessed 28 July 2008.

Kronman, AT (1983) *Max Weber* (Stanford, Stanford University Press).

Lagas, P (1997) 'Heterarchy as trigger for Public Governing and Governance' in J Kooiman *et al* (eds), *Social-political Governance and Management* (Rotterdam, Rotterdam University Press).

MacGrew, A (1998) 'Global Legal Interaction and present-day Patterns of Globalisation' in V Gessner and AC Budak (eds), *Emerging Legal Certainty: Empirical Studies on the Globalisation of Law*, ISSJ Series (Ashgate, Dartmouth).

Majone, G (1997) 'From the Positive to the Regulatory State: Causes and Consequences of Changes in the Mode of Governance' 17(2) *Journal of Public Policy* 139–67.

Mayntz, R (2004) 'Governance Theory als fortentwickelte Steuerungstheorie?' 04/1 MPIfG Working Paper (Cologne, Max-Planck-Institute for the Study of Societies).

Mitzman, A (1979) *The Iron Cage* (New York).

Muchlinski, P (1997) '"Global Bukowina" Examined: Viewing the Multinational Enterprise as a Transnational Law-Making Community' in G Teubner (ed), *Global Law without a State* (Aldershot, Dartmouth).

Parsons, T (1947) *Max Weber: The Theory of Social and Economic Organization* (New York, Oxford University Press).

Petersen, H and Zahle, H (eds) (1995) *Legal Policentricity: Consequences of Pluralism in Law* (Aldershot, Dartmouth).

Peterson, MJ (1992) 'Transnational Activity, international Society and World Politics' 21 *Millennium*.

Pierre, J and Peters, BG (2000) *Governance, Politics and the State* (Houndsmills, Macmillan Press).

Plantey, A (1991) *De la politique entre les Etats—principes de diplomatique* (Paris, Pédone).

Popelier, P (1997) *Rechtszekerheid als beginsel voor behoorlijke regelgeving* (Antwerpen/Groningen, Intersentia Rechtswetenschappen).

Richman, BD (2009) 'Ethnic Networks, Extralegal Certainty, and Globalisation: Peering into the Diamond Industry' in V Gessner (ed), *Contractual Certainty in International Trade* (Oxford, Hart).

Rheinstein, M (1967) 'Introduction' in E Shils and M Rheinstein (tr), *Max Weber on Law in Economy and Society* (New York, Clarion).

Robé, JP (1997) 'Multinational Enterprises: The Constitution of a Pluralistic Legal Order' in G Teubner (ed), *Global Law without a State* (Aldershot, Dartmouth).

Rottleuthner, H (1986) 'Theories of Legal Evolution: Between Empiricism and Philosophy of History' *Rechtstheorie* (Beiheft 9) 217–30.

Scheuerman, WE (1999) 'Globalisation and the Fate of Law' in D Dyzenhaus (ed), *Recrafting the Rule of Law* (Oxford, Hart Publishing).

—— (2004) *Liberal Democracy and the Acceleration of Time* (Baltimore and London, Hopkins University Press).

Selznick, Ph (1992) *The Moral Commonwealth. Social Theory and the Promise of Community* (Berkeley, University of California Press).

Senden, L (2004) *Soft law in European Community Law* (Oxford, Hart Publishing).

—— (2005) 'Soft law, Self-regulation and Co-regulation in European Law' 9 *Electronic Journal of Comparative Law*.

Seyfarth, Ch (1981) 'Gesellschaftliche Rationalisierung und die Entwicklung der Intellektuellenschichten. Zur Weiterfuehrung eines zentralen Themas Max Webers' in WM Sprondel and C Seyfarth (eds), *Max Weber und die Rationalisierung sozialen Handelns* (Stuttgart, Enke).

Sosa, F (2009) 'Cross-Border Dispute Resolution from the Perspective of Midsized Law Firms: The Example of International Commercial Arbitration' in V Gessner (ed), *Contractual Certainty in International Trade* (Oxford, Hart).

Streeck, W and Thelen, K (2005) *Beyond Continuity. Institutional Change in Advanced Political Economies* (Oxford, Oxford University Press).

Swedberg, R (1998) *Max Weber and the Idea of Economic Sociology* (Princeton, Princeton University Press).

Teubner, G (1982) 'Reflexives Recht' 68 *Archiv für Rechts- und Sozialphilosophie* 13–59.

—— (ed) (1997) *Global Law without a State* (Aldershot, Dartmouth).

Treib, O, Bähr, M and Falkner, G (2005) 'Modes of Governance: a note towards Conceptual Clarification' *European Governance Papers (EUROGOV)* No N-05–02.

Treiber, H (1989) *Vollzugskosten des Rechtsstaates und andere Studien zum Recht* (Baden-Baden, Nomos).

—— (2006) *Max Weber and Eugen Ehrlich: on the Janus-headed construction of Weber's ideal type in the Sociology of Law*, Oñati Workshop.

Trubek, DM (1972) 'Max Weber on Law and the Rise of Capitalism' 3 *Wisconsin Law Review* 720–53.

Trubek, DM and Trubek, LG (2005) 'Hard and Soft Law in the Construction of Social Europe: the Role of the Open Method of Coordination' 11(3) *European Law Journal* 343–64.

Trubek, DM, Cottrell, P and Nance, M (2006) 'Soft law, hard law and EU integration' in G de Burca and J Scott (eds), *Law and new governance in the EU and the US* (Oxford, Hart Publishing).

Weber, M (1965) *The Protestant Ethic and the Spirit of Capitalism* (T Parsons (tr)) (London, Unwin).

—— (1967) *Max Weber on Law in Economy and Society* (E Shils and M Rheinstein (eds)) (New York, Clarion).

—— (1980) *Wirtschaft und Gesellschaft* (J Winkelmann (ed)) (5th edn, Tübingen, Mohr).

12

Contractual Certainty versus Efficiency: The Historical and Institutional Context of Global Trade

WOLF HEYDEBRAND

INTRODUCTION

IN THIS CHAPTER, I examine the concepts of contractual certainty and efficiency from a critical and historical perspective. This analysis suggests that the contemporary processes of economic globalisation not only entail the institutional transformation of contract law and the rise of new mechanisms of governance and regulation, but that the legal and economic categories embodied in these institutions and mechanisms are themselves changing in terms of their meaning and relevance. I begin with Weber's notion that contractual certainty is intimately linked to contractual formalism and the belief in the capacity of the nineteenth century liberal nation state to guarantee adequate contract performance and norm enforcement. A subsequent section of the chapter briefly refers to the largely relational or informal alternatives to Weber's classical notion of contractual certainty (for a systematic overview of the empirical studies involved, see Gessner, 2009a, in this volume). I then turn to the issue of contractual efficiency as framed by the economic analysis of law and the evolving historical context of the debate on certainty versus efficiency.

In focusing on the continuities and discontinuities of the historical context which partially overlaps with the early phases of economic globalisation, I distinguish four periods of political and legal development: a pre-national period of customary pre-formal law and equity; a nation-state-based period of formal law, a supra-national period with anti-formalistic tendencies, and a post-national period which coincides with the contemporary round of globalisation since 1989 to 1991. These four periods can also be identified in terms of progressive phases of commercial, industrial and financial globalisation and the transitions among them. Finally, I examine the theoretical tensions surrounding the concepts of legal autonomy and economic embeddedness. This analysis is prompted by the mutually contradictory assumptions that formal contract law is autonomous with respect to substantive institutional spheres like state, economy and society (from Weber to Luhman and Teubner), while economic sociology views contractual practices in law and economy as institutionally embedded in society (for example, Macaulay, Macneil), hence as non-autonomous. The state-based periodisation of legal development relative to globalisation used in this chapter overlaps partially with Weber's (1966) implicit periodisation of legal development, as well as with Cutler's (2003) explicit periodisation of merchant law. My own periodisation of economic globalisation has a different purpose, namely, to emphasise the importance of finance capital in the form of foreign direct investment (FDI) for the nexus between economic globalisation and legal development (Heydebrand, 2003: 162–73; 2007). As will become apparent, there is a sufficient degree of overlap among these slightly different approaches to justify a combined perspective for present purposes.

THE CONTRACTUAL CERTAINTY OF LAW

Max Weber's thesis on the role of formal law and the nation state in providing contractual certainty is still widely believed to be a general theoretical proposition in the sociology of law rather than a descriptive statement applicable mainly to continental European states in a specific historical period (see Weber, 1966: 11–20) and the 'significance and limits of legal coercion in economic life' (33–40; see also Gessner, 2000; and Dorbeck-Jung, 2009, in this volume). The thesis asserts not only the efficacy of interactive links and mutual causation between law and economics, such that nineteenth century capitalism might not have flourished without the legal foundations and guarantees provided by the state, but also that the capitalist economy gave rise to property, contract and tort law because entrepreneurs 'required' those kinds of rules and guarantees. Weber's concept of sociological 'causality' was expansive and included the notion of 'elective affinity' among historical actors and ideologies, a notion which mixes strategic rationality with a touch of manifest functionalism (Heydebrand, 2006).

Weber's sociology of law implicitly refers to three historical periods and two major transitions: (i) a long period of customary law and contract relations in ancient and medieval history before the arrival, or outside of, the nation state; (ii) a period of formal legal rationality linked jointly to the 'modern' capitalist economy and 'modern' nation state and gradually tending toward economic concentration and monopolisation; and (iii) the rise of the 'anti-formalistic tendencies of modern legal development', the decline and transformation of formally rational law, and the emergence of various types of substantively rational, non-rational or mixed formal-informal, proceduralist legal regimes (Weber, 1966: 303–21; Neumann, 1957; see also Kennedy, 2003, on the 'two globalizations of law'). It is important here to remember that Weber's usage of the term 'modern' and 'present-day' refers largely to the late nineteenth and early twentieth century, whereas Neumann's frame of reference is the growing impact of economic concentration on law and 'modern society' during and after the Second World War. Moreover, Weber's viewpoint is largely 'Eurocentric' and does not yet reflect the second and third round of economic globalisation and the rise of transnational legal governance under US auspices (but see Dorbeck-Jung, 2009, in this volume, on Weber's intuitions about future developments).

There is a curiously 'contemporary', post-modern, pessimistic (and almost Foucaultean) vision that dominates Weber's work from the Protestant ethic to the sociology of law (see also Kennedy, 2004). This is striking, especially if one looks at the last two paragraphs of Weber's chapter on the eclipse of the 'formal qualities of modern law' where he uses the term 'inevitable' twice. Let me quote the key sentence.

> Inevitably the notion must expand that the law is a *rational technical apparatus*, which is *continually transformable in the light of expediential considerations* and devoid of all sacredness of content (Weber, 1966: 321, emphasis added).

This continuous transformability of legal and contractual procedures under the impact of both internal and external challenges has become visible especially in the last two decades of the political economy of globalisation.

Given the centrality of the idea of 'formal-legal rationality' in Weber's sociology of law, let me briefly examine the first period identified above as the pre-history of legal formalism (although I do not share the implicit teleological assumption of formalism being the ultimate vanishing point of this historical portrait). In historical periods and social formations *preceding the formal rationality of law*, local customary law and 'traditional authority' (for example, patriarchal, patrimonial and feudal social arrangements or relatively 'autonomous' merchant law) provided private legal regimes based on traditional, communal, occupational, pre-national or sub-national institutions (see also Greif, 2006). Medieval merchant law is an important example of this pre-history (Berman and Kaufman, 1978; Cutler, 2003: 108–40). It can be described as a medieval, trade-based internationalism exhibiting a certain universality of mercantile customs and rules. It is a type of customary common law based on principles of equity and fairness. It is marked by informal, participatory and speedy procedures of dispute resolution. It operated outside and independent of local feudal legal orders and was administered not by public courts or professional judges, but by the merchants and their peers themselves. Thus, the *lex mercatoria* was an autonomous, informal and private regulatory system that developed its own procedures of law creation and dispute resolution. In this respect, it shares certain characteristics with the traditional, autonomous regulatory practices of the international diamond trade (which offered the additional advantage of ethnically relatively homogeneous Jewish in-group solidarity, for which international borders did not present a special obstacle (Bernstein, 1992; Richman, 2009, in this volume)).

In general, we may conclude that the extra-legal social support structures for traditional transactions typically do not rely either on considerations of contractual certainty or economic efficiency, although they are apparently very fast, accurate and 'efficient' in a colloquial sense, as Barak Richman (2009, in this volume) points out. Instead, they depend on traditional notions of reciprocity and a 'mutual interest in continuing business relationships' (Gessner, 2009b, in this volume). In other words, they rely on a combination of close-knit, long-term, traditional, communal, family and network ties, on the one hand, and relational contracting, inter-industry arbitration, as well as reputation, blacklisting and exclusion, on the other. Both traditional 'trust' (Gambetta, 1990; Sabel, 1993) and 'rational expectations' (Sheffrin, 1996) come into play (see also Weber's distinction between 'external' (law enforcement) and 'internal' (ethical or religious) guarantees of a social order (1966: 7)). As Wioletta Konradi points out for the German timber industry:

> ... the businessmen who conceive their business relation as a friendship do not care much about detailed contracts or legal methods to enforce their rights . . . they favor simple solutions. In their eyes, the bureaucracy connected with drafting detailed contracts is not worth the time and energy and is viewed as rather damaging. However, whereas contracts by handshake are common in the *domestic* timber trade where the same people meet like a club, written contracts are drafted for *cross-border transactions* characterized by a diversity of suppliers and clients (Konradi, 2009, in this volume, emphasis added).

Konradi's observations are supported by empirical studies of very similar sets of informal norms and attitudes governing the local network relations within and among contemporary new media start-ups in Silicon Valley and Silicon Alley at the turn of the last millennium (Suchman and Cahill, 1996; Heydebrand and Miron, 2002). While the new media start-ups largely 'opted out of the legal system', this was true mainly for domestic and local business relations, not so for cross-border (for example, US-Sri Lanka) relations. This suggests that 'structural' factors (for example, national borders and institutions) may be as important as 'historical' ones (time period) in determining the nature of the formal/informal divide.

Much of Weber's treatment of the pre-history of 'modern' formal law deals with selected issues of legal history such as the emergence and creation of legal norms and rights, the development and limits of freedom of contract (Weber, 1966: 98–140), types of substantive law, and the formal qualities of revolutionary law as a transition to modern law. When Weber reaches the 'formal qualities of modern law', however, only three pages of his 20-page chapter are devoted to formal law; the rest of the chapter focuses on the next transition, namely the 'anti-formalistic tendencies of modern legal development' (Weber, 1966: 303–21). I take this to mean that Weber was aware that his most famous ideal-type, formal legal rationality, was itself a transitional phenomenon that pointed toward an uncertain and potentially chaotic future.

For the purposes of this chapter, it is sufficient to recall Weber's profound ambivalence about the role of the state in the relation between law and economy. 'From the purely theoretical point of view', Weber argues:

> ... legal guaranty *by the state* is not indispensable to any basic economic phenomenon. The protection of property, for example can be provided by the mutual aid system of kinship groups . . . but contracts [among the ancient Babylonians] were apparently in use under which payment was to be made in pieces of a fifth of a shekel designated as such by the stamp of a certain 'firm' (as we would say). There was thus lacking any guaranty 'proclaimed' by the state; the chosen unit of value was derived, not from the state, but from private contract. Yet the means of payment was 'chartal' in character, and the state guaranteed coercively the concrete deal (1968: 39).

Weber insists that, 'conceptually', 'the "state" is not indispensable to any economic activity' (39), presumably even under conditions of formalism and modernism. However, he then goes on to argue that a 'modern' economic system could not

> ... exist without a legal order with very special features which could not develop except in the frame of a 'statal' legal order. Present-day economic life rests on opportunities acquired through contracts. It is true, the private interests in the obligation of contract are . . . still considerable, and individuals are still markedly influenced by convention and usage even today. Yet the influence of these factors has declined due to the disintegration of tradition, ie, of the tradition-determined relationships as well as of the belief in their sacredness. Furthermore, class interests have come to diverge more sharply from one another than ever before. The tempo of modern business communication requires a promptly and predictably functioning legal system, ie, one which is guaranteed by the strongest coercive power. Finally, modern economic life by its very nature has destroyed those other associations which used to be he bearers of law and thus of legal guarantees. This has been the result of the development of the market. The universal predominance of the market . . . requires on the one hand a legal system [whose] functioning is *calculable* in accordance with rational rules. On

> the other hand, the constant expansion of the market . . . has favored the monopolization and regulation of all 'legitimate' coercive power by *one* universal coercive institution through the disintegration of all particular status-determined and other coercive structures, which have been resting mainly on economic monopolies (Weber, 1966: 39–40).

Thus, state-centrism, contractual formalism and economic concentration are seen as characterising the second, modernist period of legal development and as increasingly unstable institutional structures. For Weber, then, the modernist period of formal, contractual certainty is both the high point of Western legal development and the beginning of an unstable transition toward new constellations of political and economic dominance. This is so because, in contrast to pre-national and national legal systems, the emerging supra-national and post-national legal systems are either 'integrated' with state and economy (as for instance, in the case of the substantive legal rationality of state-socialist economies), or they are more or less 'dominated' by capitalist or neo-imperialist political economies.

The process of economic globalisation exhibits a dynamic that passes like a *tsunami* through Weber's national constellations from the middle of the nineteenth century to the end of Polanyi's '100-year peace' in 1913. Two rounds of globalisation were to follow. Between 1914 and 1989, a second, politically highly fractious and economically stagnant period of 'negative globalisation' is dominated by the long 'cold war' between two supra-national powers representing capitalism and socialism, respectively. After the collapse of the Soviet Union in 1989 to 1991, this period is followed by a third round of globalisation and the emergence of 'post-national constellations' such as the European Union and the de-nationalised 'new world order' under US auspices (see also Habermas, 2000; Zuern, 2001: 39–71).

The historical periodisation of this process is controversial and depends in part on whether one uses global trade and commercial capital as the main indicator (for example, Wallerstein and Hopkins, 2000), or the movement and expansion of finance capital (for example, Bairoch, 2000; Eichengreen, 2003; Heydebrand, 2003; see also Flood and Skordaki, 1997; Flood and Skordaki, 2009, in this volume), or a combination of political and economic indicators which also include the expansion of multinational and transnational corporations and other forms of 'industrial capital' (Held and McGrew, 1999; 2003; Sklair, 2000; Cutler, 2003). For example, if one uses the globalisation of trade ('markets') as the main indicator, the 1989 to 1991 transition may appear to be negligible (see, for example, Fligstein, 2002: 192, on comparing global trade as a share of the world economy in 1914 (14 per cent) and 1996 (less than 17 per cent), as quoted by Gessner, 2009b, in this volume). This comparison suggests a 'slow' rate of growth, but neglects the 75-year period of what one could call no-growth or 'negative' globalisation between 1914 and 1989 to 1991.

By contrast, the growth of FDI, also slow or absent after 1913, increased in the late 1960s, but then jumped significantly after 1991, thereby surpassing the 1913 threshold for the first time in history (see Bairoch, 2000).

Alternatives to Contractual Certainty in Global Trade

The continuing debate on the theoretical and empirical alternatives to 'contractual certainty in global trade' documented in the present volume suggests the likelihood that the category of contractual certainty has itself begun to lose its legal and empirical relevance. This possibility is already apparent in earlier publications, for example, in an introductory essay on the 'Legal Culture of Global Business Transactions' (Gessner, Appelbaum and Felstiner, 2001). In their introduction, the authors reflect inter alia on:

> Ian Macneil's critique of 'classical' notions in contract law . . . a critique which runs parallel to the critique that transaction cost economists and sociologists raise against the faceless buyer and seller myth of classical economics (Gessner, Appelbaum and Felstiner, 24; Macneil, 1985).

For example, following Joerges (1985), the authors show how relational transactions can be characterised in terms of seven elements:

a) the relational exchange does not begin at a precise point in time and has no definite end;
b) the commencement is characterised by ongoing negotiations and the duration of the contract may remain indefinite;
c) the performance can and must often be measured and specified not at the commencement of the agreement, but during the course of the contract;
d) the parties' planning refers not only to the exchange conditions, but also to future interaction and performance;
e) the planning may be cooperative or unilateral;
f) unlike discrete transactions, the contractual relations cannot afford to neglect expectations resulting from ongoing interactions; and
g) in contrast to discrete transactions, with relational contracts there is no set, long-term power structure.

As Gessner, Appelbaum and Felstiner (2001: 24) note, Campbell (1990) points to the consequences of relational contract theory for 'classical contract law in areas like contract formation, performance, variation, termination and application of remedies', although its applicability to 'international business exchanges still needs to be established' (*ibid*). These and other variables that may intervene in the life course of a relational contract suggest a shift from determinacy to probability, in line with Frank

Knight's fruitful distinction between the binary opposition of certainty/uncertainty, on the one hand, and the statistically estimated probability of risk, on the other. Thus, many of the contributions to the present volume deal either with contractual *un*certainty and degrees of uncertainty or, in the language of the globalising 'risk society', the relative probability of risk (see Beck, 1998; 2000: 99; Gessner, 2000: 172, both in Held and McGrew, 1999).

The identification and measurement (or informed estimate) of the risks in transnational contracting, in turn, improves the chances of facing the challenges of risk management through, inter alia, 'reputational networks' and 'bi-lateral contract management' based on the 'revolutionary innovations in the field of ICT [information and communication technology]'(see also the suggestive typology of 'contract enforcement institutions', Dietz and Nieswandt, 2008). In 'fast developing market economies' and in the absence of 'trust and relational norms . . . the exchange partners feel the risks of being vulnerable to the action of the other' (Dietz and Nieswandt (2006: 1). As the authors point out, the classical 'contractual certainty' response to risk is to 'draft detailed contracts and plan for enforcement institutions to safeguard the transaction', as noted by Hadfield (2005: 178). However, as the contributions to this volume show, alternative approaches are emerging. They range from the efficiency goals of economic regimes and the non-efficiency (democratic) goals of political regimes (Hadfield 2000; 2005; 2009, in this volume), to Calliess's (2009, in this volume) public-private governance regimes that produce, or evolve into, transnational civil order, to 'relational contracting in the context of long-term business relations' in the international timber industry (Konradi, 2009, in this volume), although 'self-created rules and intra-industry arbitration' also play a role (*ibid*, 24; on other governance mechanisms and institutional designs, see Freiling, 2009, in this volume; Gessner, 2009b, in this volume; Trubek and Trubek, 2005; Williamson, 1996; Heydebrand, 2003a; and Sosa, 2009, in this volume).

THE ECONOMIC EFFICIENCY OF CONTRACT LAW

In view of advancing economic globalisation, the decline or 'limits' of traditional 'international law' have become more and more apparent (for example, Koskenniemi, 2001; Kingsbury, 2003; Scheuerman, 2004b; and Goldsmith and Posner, 2005). As a result, the category of contractual certainty is being superseded by the concept of the economic efficiency of private international legal rules. In line with the rising influence of the economic analysis of law in the United States, then, legal efficiency tends to become a central normative criterion for evaluating the viability and performance of international contract and trade relations.

Gillian Hadfield provides one of the clearest statements of the definitional issues surrounding the idea of the economic efficiency of legal rules. Granting from the outset that 'efficiency is a normative, value-laden' concept, Hadfield (2009, in this volume) points out that it 'is adopted only with a view to what a particular society conceives of as the public interest or social welfare'. This formulation implies that the efficiency of processes of production and reproduction can have both quantitative and qualitative aspects, and that it is theoretically possible to distinguish, for example, capitalist efficiency from socialist efficiency (Gordon, 1976). Thus, Hadfield (2009, in this volume) states that:

> ... although the articulation of the Pareto criterion is meant to be non-controversial—presuming that all would agree that productive processes should get the most out of resources . . . and that there can be no objection, by definition, to the re-allocations accomplished in the name of efficiency—it is an overtly normative criterion; it embodies contestable judgments about what is good or bad for society.

In discussing the potential for privatising commercial law, Hadfield (2009, in this volume) is 'focusing on the production, distribution, and pricing of the legal rules that are economic inputs into economic activity'. In short:

> ... we can identify legal rules or mechanisms the functions of which are, or can be treated as, *exclusively to achieve efficiency* : the maximization of gains from trade and the best use and allocation of resources, increasing the size of the pie (*ibid*, emphasis added).

Historically speaking, the concept of the efficiency of contractual rules is a product of the second phase of globalisation and can be linked to the emergence of the law and economics movement at the University of Chicago in the late 1930s (Medema, 2007: 167–70). The movement included the work of Ronald Coase and Guido Calabresi and culminated in Richard Posner's *Economic Analysis of Law* (1973), a text that is now in its sixth edition (2003). In recent years, and not coincidentally related to the exigencies of economic globalisation, Posner's position has moved toward the pragmatic, neo-liberal 'overcoming' of formalist law by means of the positive economic analysis of law (Posner, 1995, 1–25; Kornhauser, 1989; and Cooter, 1996). The new approach to law values efficiency over certainty, or more accurately, certainty and other values only in so far as they can serve as 'efficiency justifications for legal doctrines' (Posner, 1995: 272). Thus, contractual certainty *per se* is no longer of any concern in this analysis. Instead, it is argued that 'efficiency provides the most appropriate criterion for allocating limited resources among competing claims' (Parisi, 2007: 457). Recent descriptions of the law and economics movement extend the economic analysis of law to positive, functional and other social science approaches to law, an exercise that requires a critical response, but transcends the scope of the present chapter (see Parisi, 2007: 451–8; and Posner and Parisi, 2002, a justification of efficiency applicable to private international contract law).

HISTORICAL CONTINUITIES AND DISCONTINUITIES IN CONTRACTUAL CERTAINTY

A historical perspective on the notion of contractual certainty suggests that the autonomy of social institutions and legal structures is not only relative, but a relatively rare phenomenon. Indeed, under conditions of the increasing frequency, scale and scope of transnational exchange and its growing complexity, the degree of interdependence among transnational exchange partners tends to rise, thus restricting their relative autonomy and sovereignty (Held, 2003b). Moreover, just as relative state autonomy and sovereignty are declining under the progressive competition and denationalisation of economic transactions, the de jure legal autonomy of national and international law becomes increasingly circumscribed and limited by the de facto power of corporations, finance capital and the exigencies of transnational governance (Strange, 1998). Nevertheless, certain historical pathways of international legal development are instructive. Claire Cutler's (2003) work is useful in this respect (see also Heydebrand, 2004).

Cutler's tripartite periodisation (which is based in part on Berman and Kaufman, 1978) seeks to capture the significant developmental phases of the law merchant which stands as one model of relative autonomy, although not the only one. The often-cited diamond trade, the Mafia, the use of ethnic iron workers in the high-rise construction industry, and other ethnic and immigrant minorities are examples (Portes and Sensenbrenner, 2001). Modern inter-firm networks and transnational economic, political and criminal networks, especially if they remain small, informal and clandestine, have the organisational capacity to act as relatively autonomous structures of global exchange and interaction. At the top, a unified, integrated and relatively autonomous meritocracy would, of course, seek to insinuate itself into, and form alliances with, institutionalised organisations in the domestic and transnational private and public sectors, if only to raise its efficacy and legitimacy.

After the early pre-capitalist and pre-national period which had broadly feudal characteristics (also Cutler's first phase), I distinguish three additional phases of legal development: national (1848–1913), supranational (1914–89) and post-national or global (1990 to the present). They are closely related to the main phases of financial globalisation from 1848 onward (for details, see Heydebrand, 2003: 165–80). Cutler's third phase collapses the supranational and transnational phases into one: from 1900 to the present. I believe that this obscures the acceleration of the global time/space compression in the twentieth century. It relegates the legal consequences of the Cold War to a minor role and underestimates the historic significance of the end of the Cold War for the onset of the contemporary round of globalisation betweem 1989 and 1991.

The Pre-national Phase (Before the Seventeenth Century)

In early modern forms of law before the seventeenth century, legal norms are established and enforced by pre-national and sub-national polities based on traditional forms of authority, ie on forms of social and political power justified and legitimated by patriarchal, patrimonial and feudal rules and enforced by the corresponding political structures. As mentioned above, in this period, we find types of customary law and legal pluralism that are based on the whole range of territorial (local, regional), ideological, hierarchical, and especially occupational authority structures of which the '*lex mercatoria*' or merchant law is one suggestive proto-type. Since I have already discussed this period, I will not go into further details here.

The Nation-state Phase (Seventeenth to Nineteenth Centuries)

If the first phase represents a kind of traditional or customary legal certainty before the state, the second phase is associated with the relative rationality of national, state-based legal systems in the modern period. The 1648 Westphalian peace accord among 'states' is a convenient marker. To be sure, these states were not democratic. Moreover, as part of the 'lineage of the absolutist state' (Anderson, 1974), authoritarian and totalitarian regimes have tended to rely on varying degrees of coercion and antagonistic cooperation by referring to the 'need' for discipline as a basic method of maintaining social order and legal compliance (Gorski, 2003; O'Neill, 1986; Treiber and Steinert, 2005: 105–18; Foucault, 1995; and Tilly, 1992). However, because of its arbitrary nature and potential for generating protest and revolutionary movements, absolutist power cannot be said to have produced absolute legal certainty, except by way of its dialectical transmutation into formal revolutionary law (Weber, 1966: 224–55; and Berman, 1983).

State-guaranteed legal certainty is the general prototype for both the legal ideal and the real-political enforcement under-girding expectations of the stability of property, contract, trade, as well as civil procedure and criminal sanctions (Hazard, 2003; 2004; and Hazard, Taruffo, Stuerner and Gidi, 2001). Especially from about 1850 onwards, the problem of 'legal formalism' emerges as one of the central issues. As is well known, Weber's definition relies on two variables: a legal system is 'formally rational' to the extent that it is autonomous (independent of politics and religion, but not of 'quasi-scientific' economics, according to Friedman, 1994: 647 and Posner, 1995: 1–29), and that its norms are general, rather than specific, particularistic and case-based (Weber, 1966). Crucially, it was the national state that was expected to 'guarantee' the legal system and to carry out the enforcement of legal norms, an expectation that taxed legal positivism to the breaking point (see, for example, Rosenbaum's insight that 'under legal positivism, the problem of law is reduced to its application' (1972: 60)). Different versions of such legal regimes, for example, the modern capitalist developmental state, the bureaucratic state and the liberal-democratic state permitted different degrees of autonomy of the state from economy and society (Evans, 1995; and Held, 2003a). As territorial states assumed greater control over international commerce, the localisation and nationalisation of merchant law began to expand and cement the mutual ties between law and state. The merchant class and its 'courts' (juries of peers) were incorporated into national legal systems and became part of the formal juridification and commercial relations among states.

The Supra-national Phase (1919–89)

The historic confrontation between the United States in alliance with Western Europe (the first or 'free' world), on the one hand, and the Soviet Union (second world or 'communism') on the other, between 1919 and 1989, did not only frame the specific conflict between state socialism and national socialism, but between socialism and capitalism. It also created the political construct of the 'third world', consisting of the less-developed countries of the world and various 'modernising' developmental states, most of them remnants of the colonialism and imperialism of the nineteenth-century European powers.

Thus, in certain respects, supra-nationalism was a continuation of the system of national states created in the previous phase, but now under the auspices of a substantive legal rationality that Weber had anticipated as part of the 'anti-formalist' turn. Much of the first half of the twentieth century featured state-sponsored, substantive 'hard law' and regulation, even though it was politicised as well as de-formalised under European national and state socialism and turning toward 'legal realism' and 'procedural informalism' in the United States (Heydebrand, 2007). The policies and actions of the Soviet Empire in that period, as well as the rise of fascism, on the one hand, and the eventual consolidation of the US 'administrative state' during the New Deal and the Bretton Woods periods (1944–71) showed signs of super-power confrontation. All were major factors in the 'long' Cold War and the temporary stagnation of transnational capital flows and trade. None seemed designed to generate much contractual certainty.

Moreover, two supra-national legal systems faced each other competitively. 'Socialist legality', which had been adopted by most of the client states of the Soviet Union and China began to confront, and interact with, US liberal capitalist democracy, which, in turn, began to change in an illiberal direction under the impact of this confrontation (for example, the national security state, the McCarthy period, the arms race, two bloody and costly wars in Korea and Vietnam, continuous mutual surveillance and covert intelligence activities, and competition for the allegiance of the third-world countries in the United Nations).

In the Soviet Union after 1919, Western-style private property and contract law were abolished and replaced by an elaborate system of public law and a state-based system of contract law. After 1949, the East German version of this 'contract system' (*Vertragssystem*) became an officially sanctioned, dominant model in Eastern Europe, although countries such as Poland and Hungary dissented and deviated more or less successfully (for details and further references, see Heydebrand, 1996). Local dispute settlement in this 'public' contract system was based on 'factory councils' or 'works councils' which resembled in many ways the US approaches to 'informal' justice and alternative dispute resolution in 'neighbourhood' and 'community' mediation emerging in the 1960s and 1970s (Harrington, 1985; see also the later concepts of 'procedural justice' (Tyler and Huo, 2002) and 'restorative justice' (Braithwaite, 2001). The question of to what extent the 'politics of informal justice' (Abel, 1982) is truly 'private' or an extension of the 'public' arm of the state remains controversial (see, for example, Spitzer, 1982). It is true that state functions were increasingly 'outsourced' to the private sector, that industry-government cooperation in cities and selective industries were promoted under the slogan of 'public-private partnerships', and that government institutions were criticised as inherently inefficient. Thus, the financial shift involving the ascendancy of neo-liberal monetarism over neo-Keyneseanism is often seen as the beginning of the contemporary round of globalisation. However, I believe that this shift, together with the widely cited emergence of 'post-Fordism' and 'flexible specialisation' as a watershed in 1973, while important and valid, tends to exaggerate the internal economic dynamics of Western capitalism as a certain kind of technological determinism. Most importantly, it neglects the external political dynamics of the post-1949 phases of the Cold War, the emergence of the European Union as a competitor and/or mediating partner, and the 'second cold war' ('Star wars') initiated by the Reagan administration in the early 1980s (see also Helleiner, 1994; and Scherrer, 1999).

Speaking of the rise of the consolidation of a 'mercatocracy' as part of the 'modern internationalism and trans-nationalism' of the unification movement of the law merchant 'from the nineteenth century to the present', Cutler (2003: 105) mentions the 'shift to highly privatised and discretionary dispute resolution' and other privatising tendencies. However, while these tendencies were becoming more visible in Europe and the United States from the 1970s onward, they no longer reflected the 'intensifying legal regulation and the juridification of commerce' (*ibid*) that had occurred at the beginning of that period in the nineteenth and early twentieth centuries. The global divide due to the Cold War persisted and helped to retard wholesale privatisation and de-regulation.

In summary, the weaknesses of the respective supra-national legal systems seem to have been over-determined by the exigencies of the political and economic confrontation between the two super-powers during much of the twentieth century. Contrary to Cutler, then, the 'mercatocracy' could not and did not emerge fully 'as a cooperative strategy for managing conflicting nationally-based commercial laws' until the end of the Cold War between 1989 and 1991, 'thereby facilitating the mobility of capital and the expansion of capitalism' (Cutler, 2003: 182). It is largely after this transition, then, that the economic policies of Maastricht and the European Union, the economic summits by the G8, and ministerial meetings by the WTO and other agencies of transnational governance began to merge with the policies and decisions of the 'mercatocracy'.

The Post-national or Denationalised phase (1989 to Present)

The fourth phase is characterised by the 'new world order' and the emergence of what has been called the 'new informal imperialism' or the 'Washington Consensus' (Held and Koenig-Archibugi, 2004). The network of current international agreements is an outgrowth of the formation of the European Union and the contemporary process of globalisation since the collapse of the Soviet Union (1989 to 1991). In contrast to the medieval trans-nationalism of the first phase, modern internationalism and contemporary trans-nationalism are 'distinctive and particular to conditions of post-modernity and late capitalism' (Cutler, 2003: 31). Twentieth-century nation states had begun to adopt procedures for integrating and regulating international commerce (for example, the US Uniform Commercial Code) and establishing uniform policies and rules for commercial dispute processing. Other examples include the International Council for Commercial Arbitration, the International Center for Settlement and Investment Disputes and the International Chamber of Commerce in Paris and other regional venues for transnational dispute processing. According to Dezalay and Garth (1995), these are all extra-legal, non-state, semi-private and private arrangements. Arbitration-based mechanisms of dispute resolution have also been established within many other agencies of transnational governance. There is little formal accountability, oversight and regulation, only internal regulation or so-called self-regulation and 'soft law' (see also Cutler, 2003: 225–36; Trubek and Trubek, 2005; and Heydebrand, 2007). The shift from super-power competition to neo-liberal globalisation seems to have begun to reduce the relative autonomy and sovereignty of the 'average nation state' (except, of course, the United States as the central power of the new informal world order). It also seems to have transformed the remnants of international law into new modalities of transnational governance (Held and Koenig-Archibugi, 2005).

Given the potential diversity, complexity, interdependence and variability of transaction channels, it seems obvious that there might be a strong interest, among neo-liberal economic policy makers, in a movement towards unification, harmonisation and integration under a global system or 'mercatocracy' (Cutler, 2003: 180, 207 and 236).

Cutler (at 181) quotes Leslie Sklair (2001) to the effect that:

> ... the transnational capitalist class is the main driver of a series of globalising practices in the global economy. It is, therefore, the leading force in the creation of a global capitalist system. The global is the goal, while the transnational, transcending nation-states in an international system . . . is the reality. The global capitalist system and the global economy exist to the extent that private rather than national interests prevail across borders.

The 'mercatocracy', argues Cutler (181–2):

> ... plays a very significant role in the furtherance of these goals. Its contemporary focal point is the unification movement: a movement engaged in harmonising, unifying, and globalising merchant law.

This transnational movement seeks to develop a new, *efficiency-oriented legal-economic framework*. As Cooter (1996: 1647) puts it, 'following private international law, I refer to all [emerging] norms of business communities as the "new law merchant"' which 'arises outside of the state's apparatus for making law'. The unification of commercial law under transnational auspices 'facilitates exchange through delocalised laws, procedures, and dispute settlement mechanisms' (Cutler, 2003: 182). The rise of the 'primacy of the private' is related to 'the advent of the competition state and a shift in structural power from nationally to transnationally based interests' (183). The structural shift is evident, among other things, 'in the corporate legal preference for non-binding "soft law" over binding "hard law"' (*ibid*). The goal of corporate strategies is to:

> ... disembed commercial law and practice from the 'public' sphere and to reembed them in the 'private' sphere, free from democratic and social control.

This, Cutler argues, is 'reordering state-society relations both locally and globally' (183). Cutler concludes, however, that 'the influence of the mercatocracy is neither complete nor hegemonic . . . for the crisis also involves a crisis of representation and legitimacy' (183). This counter-hegemonic perspective is well represented by those who see a rising tide of emancipatory globalisation from below, for example, Smith, 1998; Barlow and Clarke, 2002; Broad, 2002; Santos and Rodriguez-Garavito, 2005; and Tabb, 2002.

CONTRACTUAL AUTONOMY VERSUS ECONOMIC EMBEDDEDNESS

In this final section of the chapter, I want to return to a point made at the beginning, namely that globalisation is transforming not only the nature and interrelation of socio-legal institutions, but also the categories and theories in terms of which we comprehend the trajectories of *law, economy and the state* in relation to each other and to society as a whole (see also Gessner, 2009b, in this volume). Thus, we are dealing with a theoretical triangle whose structure and boundaries are in motion, a constellation not of fixed stars, but of historically changing key institutions. However, at the same time, the causal interrelations of the elements do not all point in the same direction. Their relative autonomy is contested as much as is their relative embeddedness in each other and in society. Their postulated structural-functional differentiation from each other, once the centerpiece of systems theory from Parsons to Luhman, has given way to their growing interdependence and interpenetration (de-differentiation) in the wake of globalisation. For example, the normative autonomy of positive law from politics, religion, morality and the economy, once seen by Weber and others as the signal achievement of Western formal-legal rationality, is now a contested, if not forgotten, ideal. The idea of legal autonomy certainly lives on in Luhmann's and Teubner's theory of the auto-poietic, self-observing and self-regulating legal system that operates at the global level beyond the state. However, its meaning has changed, and its conceptual framework of 'normative closure' and 'cognitive openness' may not be sufficiently flexible to symbolically incorporate law's globalising environment and withstand the assault of neo-liberal economic policies on constitutional protections and the legal regulation of the economy. The economic analysis of law moves closer to a vision of law being embedded in economics and evaluated by the criterion of efficiency, as we have just seen. At the same time, the new institutionalism in economics looks at this process from the other side, as it were, emphasising new mechanisms of economic governance such as social networks that mediate between markets and hierarchies. However, the contradictory forces of economic concentration and wealth maximisation have begun to limit freedom of contract and curtail the institutional autonomy of law for some time (Atiyah, 1979; Gilmore, 1997; and Feinman, 2004).

Moreover, economic sociology speaks of the embeddedness of economic rationality and action in the social and cultural infrastructure of the institutional environment (Smelser and Swedberg, 2005). However, transnational opportunism, deviance, corruption and crime, mediated as they are themselves by unaccountable social and relational networks, impinge on the efficacy of law and the institutional structure of corporations and states (Nelken, 1997). Each of the theoretical positions mentioned above offers its own answers and solutions, yet each is typically silent about the queries raised by the other perspectives or by critical analysis.

Under the impact of these contradictory tendencies, each of which validly represents different and separate aspects of globalisation, contemporary societies can no longer be said to experience the orderly processes of 'integration' and 'differentiation' as if they were a part of a socio-legal or contractual calculus. On the contrary, they are confronted by fragmentation and the challenges of de-formalisation, de-differentiation, and de-institutionalisation. For example, trial rates in the category of US federal contracts have been declining in the last half century, and probably longer—not that high levels of litigation are a sign of social health. However, the underlying institutional trends are indicators of the transformation of contract law and civil procedure. The number of jury and bench trials involving diversity (inter-state) contract cases as a percentage of total dispositions declined from 16.6 per cent in 1962 to 2.7 per cent in 2002. During the same period, regular contract disputes declined from 7.5 to 1.9 per cent (Galanter, 2004: 462–3). Next to reasons due to declining filings, high rates of settlements and diversion to alternative dispute resolution (ADR), Galanter (2004: 517) ascribes the decline in percentages and absolute numbers to 'economic' causes, ie 'going to trial has become more costly as litigation has become more technical, complex, and expensive' (Galanter here refers to Gillian Hadfield, 2000; see also Heydebrand, 2007: 119–20).

It is true, as Gessner argues, that these figures do not show the trends in transnational contract litigation, arbitration, mediation and settlements (but see, for example, Dezalay and Garth, 1996; Sosa, 2009, in this volume; and the extensive literature on international arbitration and mediation, as well as 'administrative adjudication' by US national regulatory commissions and 'dispute settlement' by international agencies like the World Trade Organisation (WTO) or North American Free Trade Agreement (NAFTA)). However, there is no reason to assume that Galanter's 'economic argument' (the high transaction cost of formal trials) does not apply equally, if not more so, to international contract litigation. If one looks at the rising use of ADR, the decline of trials and the restructuring and/or marginalisation of formal judicial functions and legal institutions, the claim of de-formalisation and de-institutionalisation as well as de-differentiation via informal bargaining and network-based transactions does not seem to be exaggerated. Indeed, the autonomous legal and judicial practices of nation states can have transnational and global effects without necessarily encroaching on the autonomy of other nation states (Stewart, 2005; Kingsbury, Krisch and Stewart, 2005; and Wiegand, 1991).

Technically, the opposite of legal autonomy is heteronomy. Heteronomous structures are subject to the sovereignty and laws of another state, an association or federation of states, or some other social, economic or political structure of power. However, a movement that is underway in the social sciences uses the term 'embeddedness' to signal the presumed dependence of one institutional sphere or set of actors on another. The preferred opposite of institutional embeddedness is not autonomy, but 'atomisation' or 'atomised actors' (Granovetter and Swedberg, 2001: 507–8 and 516). Thus, Granovetter (2001) talks about the social embeddedness of economic action, ie the assumption that economic transactions tend to be embedded in social relations (see also Hollingsworth and Boyer, 1997, on capitalism as an embedded institution; and Ruggie, 1982). However, while the conceptual embedding of exchange in interpersonal relations avoids the construct of 'atomised individual action' and pure 'rational choice' as used in neo-classical economics, it excludes from consideration the opposite possibility: that in a highly developed capitalist society, *social relations* may be permeated by, or embedded in, *economic relations* such as the profit motive, opportunism, competitive advantage, the 'cash nexus', the 'market', commodification and alienation. Similarly, Evans (1995) refers to the 'embedded autonomy of the state' to stress the desirability of the state being anchored in, and responsive to, social relations, status groups and even social movements (but see Mann, 1984, on the autonomous power of the state versus Domhoff, 1996 and Sklair, 2001, who emphasise the class basis of states and transnational governance). Yet, even though the twentieth century state-socialist or national-socialist states were socially embedded, they abused their 'absolutist' autonomy by assuming more or less total control over their social base.

The contemporary literature on 'embeddedness' uses the term to claim a determinate relationship between economic, political and social phenomena and their institutional environment, context or infrastructure. For example, Brian Uzzi's (2001: 207–38) distinction between personally embedded network ties and instrumental, arm's-length ties is extended to an imaginary scale stretching between over-embedded social ties (personally too involved; dysfunctional for relations with actors in other networks) and under-embedded ones (too impersonal and atomistic; dysfunctional for internal network cohesion). The paradox of embeddedness, then, is that:

> ... the same processes by which embeddedness creates a requisite fit with the current environment can paradoxically reduce an organisation's ability to adapt (Uzzi, 2001: 227).

While these distinctions are useful in countering the implicit value judgments embedded in the literature on embeddedness, their functionalist undertone is unmistakeable. The argument abounds with references to the positive functions of ties and exchange relations for the fit, adaptive capacity and viability of organisations relative to their environments. To his credit, Uzzi offers a series of empirically testable propositions, even though functionalist theory is notoriously difficult to falsify.

Disembedding Global Contractual Relations (Dialectical and Historical Reversals)

It is not my intention here to criticise the concept of social embeddedness as such, but to raise the question of to what extent it implies (or obscures) reductionist explanations of contractual certainty and similar constructs. The concept of embeddedness, as used in economic sociology, refers to a variety of causal mechanisms or determinative schemata, for example, the relative ontological priority of 'culture' and 'society' over law, politics or economy. Thus, law or the economy may be seen as embedded in the autonomy of social and cultural institutions; autonomous law as embedded in the economy; law as embedded in politics or political culture; the state as embedded in class society or, conversely, as dominating society.

In each case, there is an explanatory strategy at stake. Typically, there is the imagery of a level (A) which is claimed to be more autonomous relative to another level (B) and in which B is less autonomous or embedded. Since it is difficult to prove or disprove the operation of a single, one-way causality in the social sciences, the preferred method is to give narrative reasons that have a degree of common sense and empirical plausibility (see Tilly, 2006).

The point is that the imagery of 'embeddeness' has a static, trans-historical, ontological quality. It is intrinsically reductionist (ie non-autonomous) and seems to preclude the possibility of an empirical reversal of the implicit causal relationship, forcing us to speak of the two contenders in either-or (dualistic) terms. This suggests that the concept of embeddedness may have an ideological purpose: to guard against determinism, especially economic or materialist determinism. At the same time, this strategy may create counter-determinisms such as social, institutional, cognitive or cultural determinisms that seem broad and abstract enough to accommodate the other social sciences and to avoid provoking the wrath of the idealist determinist camp.

However, it stands to reason, and could be empirically demonstrated, that if an economy is embedded in a society at time 1, it is possible that, as both develop over time, society becomes embedded in the economy at time 2, especially when we are dealing with a dynamic, self-revolutionising 'productive force' like industrial and financial capitalism. A dialectical and historical reversal of the relationship between economy and society suggests that in the early stages of social development, say in early seventeenth-century England, capitalist economic practices might develop within the womb of that particular historical society. However, this stage of embeddeness might be temporary and limited like a pregnancy that is followed by birth and the development of the newborn child into an adult. The erstwhile primacy of the nurturing society over the fledgling economy may end up as the encompassing dominance of a globalising capitalist economy over the society which gave birth to it. In other words, the *determination* of B (the economy) by A (the society) may eventually lead to the *domination* of B over A. Colloquially speaking, one might 'see the tail of the military-industrial complex wagging the dog of American life', as Eisenhower put it in his farewell speech in January 1961 (Bob Herbert, 2006; see also Susan Strange's image of 'markets outgrowing governments' (1998)). Ordinary language abounds with everyday examples such as the sorcerer's lesson for his wayward apprentice: 'once you exorcise evil spirits to help you, you can't get rid of them (unless you know the secret word)', or sardonic sayings like 'the chickens are coming home to roost', or 'you reap what you sow'). A related 'historical reversal' is described by Scheuerman (1999b: 261) as one of the negative side-effects of globalisation: 'discretionary authority for the sake of international business now threatens the democratic nation-state'. One could conduct similar thought experiments with the development of the state as a product of society and its subsequent dominance over that society in the form of the bureaucratic, authoritarian or totalitarian state under nationalist socialism or state socialism (see also Evans, 1995, whose framework is flexible enough to accommodate various state forms in relation to society). The idea of a historical, dialectical reversal, of course, dates back to Marx who, unlike Hegel, saw the state not as the perfection of society, but in its 'alienated form'. He also anticipated capital's inherent tendency to create the world market which might end up controlling local markets.

Thus, the concept of *embeddedness* may be descriptively useful, even enticing up to a point, but it should perhaps not be turned into a structural 'explanation' of the trans-historical stability and continuity of an institution. On the contrary, the dynamic relationships among analytically differentiated spheres such as law, economy and state might be more fruitfully seen as *interactions* in a force field (a la Bourdieu), even though the outcomes of social interaction are less predictable than those of permanently embedded social arrangements. Unfortunately, like all social theory, positivism, functionalism and institutionalism can easily turn into an ideology that mystifies, but does not explain. For example, to deal with the problem of control of uncertainty or risk management and to make contractual outcomes predictable, social 'interactions' are often theoretically reified as social 'relations' and social roles that can then be treated as 'embedded' enactments of institutional norms and rules (as, for example, in legal formalism and codification).

DISCUSSION AND CONCLUSION

I conclude that the criterion of 'contractual certainty' is no longer deemed central under conditions of economic globalisation; rather, the new neo-liberal governing norms are 'efficiency' and pragmatism (Cooter, 1996; and Posner, 1980; 1995: ch 3). Whatever *economic-legal* efficiency is generated by progressive global integration appears, therefore, to be the result of the neo-liberal policies and decisions of the mercatocratic unification movement. Thus, whatever level of efficiency is considered socially desirable or practically attainable by the relevant policy-makers should not be so much determined by already existing, path-dependent mechanisms of economic governance and political control, but rather by democratic and social processes of interaction, bargaining, negotiation and cooperation (Okun, 1975). Most importantly, the top-down policies of globalisation need to be tempered and tamed by 'globalisation from below'.

Current thinking about procedural informalism (arbitration, mediation, negotiation, soft law), and network-based transnational governance (without government) suggests that neither of them is autonomous, authoritative or democratic (Cotterrell, 1983; and Roberts, 2005). The problems of 'informalism' include the uncertainty, ambiguity and problematic validity of international legal norms, risky outcomes under conditions of bargaining and negotiation, and the almost unlimited conditionality and flexibility of norm enforcement (see also Macaulay, 1963; 1986; Aman, 2004; and Held, 2004). The problems of quasi-legal governance include the pervasive structural inequality among both state and non-state actors and, hence, the continuing possibility of unilateral action by a sovereign super power and its informal coalition partners.

Therefore, the concepts of sovereignty and contractual certainty have become highly problematic and require redefinition and rethinking (Giddens, 1985; Kingsbury, 1999; Zuern, 2001; and Held, 2003b). In addition, transnational governance has technocratic and corporatist (hence potentially non-democratic and non-legal) implications (Aman, 2001; Heydebrand, 1983; 2003a; and Joerges and Everson, 2004: 174–5). Moreover, due to the informal, soft and usually non-contractual and non-binding character of social relations supporting quasi-legal, quasi-voluntary arrangements, there are generic problems of 'getting action' and 'blocking action' (White, 1992), sometimes also referred to as problems of 'collective action', opportunism, free riders or shirking.

Strategic networks and procedural informalism serve to deconstruct contractual certainty in favour of contractual efficiency. They legitimise the one-sided support of privatised, governance-oriented or unregulated neo-liberal globalisation. By the same token, they weaken normative and broadly democratic efforts (ie not just formal and political, but social and economic) to regulate rampant expansion. A related but separate analysis would also need to examine the widely discussed shift to privatised and discretionary processes of dispute resolution and business mediation and their easy relationship to legal and process pluralism as well as 'inter-legality'.

Finally, there is the question of under what conditions the tension between privatising and rationalising initiatives, on the one hand, and public, regulatory policies of transnational agencies or bodies like the UN or EU, on the other, can be transcended and integrated by the relative certainty of a (supra-positive) democratic social contract, if not a constitution. As a minimum, such a civil contract would have to be justified and guaranteed by a transnational public charter, capable of effective enforcement, and supervised by transnational agencies of financial and political governance like the United Nations, the European Union, as well as African, Asian and South American organised constituencies. Moreover, global trade relations and their embedded 'institutionalisation' would have to be regulated by regional international courts of social, economic and human rights. All of these questions are, of course, issues for another project.

REFERENCES

Abel, R (1982) 'The Conradictions of Informal Justice', in R Abel (ed), *The Politics of Informal Justice*, Vol 1 (New York, Academic Press).

Aman, AC (2001) 'The Limits of Globalization and the Future of Administrative Law: From Government to Governance' 8 *Indiana Journal of Global Legal Studies* 2 379–400.

—— (2004) *The Democracy Deficit: Taming Globalization through Law Reform* (New York, New York University Press).

Anderson, P (1974) *Lineages of the Absolutist State* (London, Verso).

Atiyah, PS (1979) *The Rise and Fall of Freedom of Contract* (Oxford, Clarendon Press).

Bairoch, P (2000) 'The Constituent Economic Principles of Globalization in Historical Perspective: Myths and Realities' 15 *International Sociology* 2 197–214.

Barlow, M and Clarke, T (2002) Global Showdown: How the New Activists are Fighting Global Corporate Rule (Toronto, Stoddart).
Beck, U (1998) *World Risk Society* (Cambridge, Polity Press).
—— (2000) 'What is Globalization?' in D Held and A McGrew (eds), *The Global Transformations Reader* (Cambridge, Polity Press).
Berman, H (1983) *Law and Revolution: The Formation of the Western Legal Tradition* (Cambridge, MA, Harvard University Press).
Berman, H and Kaufman, C (1978) 'The Law of International Commercial Transactions (Lex Mercatoria)' *Harvard International Law Journal* 19(1) 221–78.
Braithwaite, J (2001) *Restorative Justice and Civil Society* (Cambridge, Cambridge University Press).
Broad, R (2002) *Global Backlash: Citizen Initiatives for a Just World Economy* (Lanham, MD, Rowmanand Littlefield).
Calliess, GP (2009) 'Transnational Civil Regimes: Economic Globalization and the Evolution of Commercial Law' in V Gessner (ed), *Contractual Certainty in International Trade* (Oxford, Hart).
Campbell, D (1990) 'The Social Theory of Relational Contract: Macneil as the Modern Proudhon' *International Journal of the Sociology of Law* 18 75–95.
Cooter, RD (1996) 'Decentralized Law for a Complex Economy: The structural approach to adjudicating the New Law Merchant' 144 *University of Pennsylvania Law Review* 5 1643.
Cotterrell, RMB (1983) 'The Sociological Concept of Law' 10 *Journal of Law and Society* 241.
Cutler, AC (1995) 'Global Capitalism and Liberal Myths: Dispute Settlement in Private International Trade Relations' 3 *Millennium Journal of International Studies* 24 377–97.
—— (2003) *Private Power and Global Authority: Transnational Merchant Law in the Global Political Economy* (Cambridge, Cambridge University Press).
Dezalay, Y and Garth, B (1995) 'Merchants of Law as Moral Entrepreneurs: Constructing International Justice from the Competition for Transnational Business Disputes' 29 *Law & Society Review* 27.
—— (1996) *Dealing in Virtue: International Commercial Arbitration and the Constitution of a Transnational Legal Order* (Chicago, University of Chicago Press).
Dietz, T and Nieswandt, H (2009) 'The emergence of transnational cooperation in the software industry' in V Gessner (ed), *Contractual Certainty in International Trade* (Oxford, Hart).
Domhoff, GW (1996) *State Autonomy or Class Dominance? Case Studies on Policy Making in America* (New York, Aldine de Gruyter).

Dorbeck-Jung, B (2009) 'Economic Globalization—Changes in the Conceptualization of Legal Certainty?' in V Gessner (ed), *Contractual Certainty in International Trade* (Oxford, Hart).
Eichengreen, BJ (2003) *Capital Flows and Crises* (Cambridge, MA, MIT Press).
Evans, P (1995) *Embedded Autonomy: States and Industrial Transformation* (Princeton, Princeton University Press).
Feinman, J (2004) 'Un-making Law: the Classical Revival in the Common Law' 28 *Seattle University Law Review* 1–59.
Fligstein, N (2002) *The Architecture of Markets: An Economic Sociology of 21st Century Capitalist Societies* (Princeton, Princeton University Press).
Flood, J, and Skordaki, E (1997) 'Normative Bricolage: Informal Rule-Making by Accountants and Lawyers in Mega-Insolvencies' in G Teubner (ed), *Global Law without a State* (Aldershot, Dartmouth).
Flood, J and Skordaki, E (2009) 'Structuring Transactions: The Case of Real Estate Finance' in V Gessner (ed), *Contractual Certainty in International Trade* (Oxford, Hart).
Foucault, M (1995) *Discipline and Punish* (New York, Vintage Books).
Freiling, J (2009) 'Institutional Designs in International Transactions—an Evolutionary Economics Perspective' in V Gessner (ed), *Contractual Certainty in International Trade* (Oxford, Hart).
Friedman, M (1994) 'The Methodology of Positive Economics' in M Martin and LC McIntyre (eds), *Readings in the Philosophy of Social Science* (Cambridge, MIT Press) 647–60.
Galanter, M (2004) 'The Vanishing Trial: An Examination of Trials and Related Matters in Federal and State Courts' 1 *Journal of Empirical Legal Studies* 3 459–570.
Gambetta, D (ed) (1990) *Trust: Making and Breaking Cooperative Relations* (Oxford, Blackwell).
Gessner, V (2000) 'Globalization and Legal Certainty' in D Held and A McGrew (eds), *The Global Transformation Reader* (Cambridge, Polity Press).
—— (2009a) 'Introduction: Toward a theoretical framework for contractual certainty in global trade' in V Gessner (ed), *Contractual Certainty in International Trade* (Oxford, Hart).
—— (2009b) 'The governance of business transactions in globalising economies: Theories of Change' in V Gessner (ed), *Contractual Certainty in International Trade* (Oxford, Hart).
Gessner, V, Appelbaum, R and Felstiner, W (2001) 'The Legal Culture of Global Business Transactions' in R Appelbaum, W Felstiner and V Gessner (eds), *Rules and Networks: The Legal Culture of Global Business Transactions* (Oxford, Hart).
Gilmore, G (1997) *The Death of Contract* (New York, Gryphon Editions).

Goldsmith, JL and Posner, EA (2005) *The Limits of International Law* (New York, Oxford University Press).

Gordon, D (1976) 'Capitalist Efficiency and Socialist Efficiency' 28 *Monthly Review* 3 19–39.

Gorski, PS (2003) *The Disciplinary Revolution: Calvinism and the Rise of the Early Modern State* (Chicago, University of Chicago Press).

Granovetter, M (2001) [1985] 'Economic Action, Social Structure, and Embeddedness' in M Granovetter and R Swedberg (eds), *The Sociology of Economic Life* (Cambridge, MA, Westview-Perseus).

Granovetter, M and Swedberg, R (eds) (2001) *The Sociology of Economic Life* (2nd edn, Cambridge, MA, Westview-Perseus).

Grant, RW and Keohane, RO (2005) 'Accountability and Abuses of Power in World Politics' 99 *American Political Science Review* 1 1–15.

Greif, A (2006) *Institutions and the Path to the Modern Economy: Lessons from Medieval Trade* (Cambridge, Cambridge University Press).

Habermas, J (2000) *The Post-national Constellation* (Cambridge, MA, MIT Press).

Hadfield, GK (2000) 'The Price of Law: How the Market for Lawyers Distorts the Justice System' 98 *Michigan Law Review* 953–1006.

—— (2005) 'The Many Legal Institutions that support Contractual Commitments' in C Menard and M Shirley (eds), *Handbook of New Institutional Economics* (Dordrecht, Springer).

—— (2009) 'The Public and the Private in the Provision of Law for Global Transactions' in V Gessner (ed), *Contractual Certainty in International Trade* (Oxford, Hart).

Harvey, D (1989) *The Condition of Postmodernity* (Oxford, Blackwell).

Hazard, GC (2003) 'International Civil Procedure and Transnational Civil Procedure: The Impact of Regional Economic Integration—An Overview' 8 *Uniform Law Review* (1, 2) 437.

—— (2004) 'ALI/Unidroit Project' in M Adenas, N Andrews and R Nazzini (eds), *The Future of Transnational Civil Litigation* (London, British Institute of International and Comparative Law).

Hazard, GC, Taruffo, M, Stuerner, R and Gidi, A (2001) 'Principles and Rules of Transnational Civil Procedure' 33 *Journal of International Law and Politics* 3 769–859.

Held, D (2003a) 'From Executive to Cosmopolitan Multilateralism' in D Held and M Koenig-Archibugi (eds), *Taming Globalization: Frontiers of Governance* (Cambridge, Polity Press).

—— (2003b) 'The Changing Structure of International Law: Sovereignty Transformed?' in D Held and A McGrew (eds), *The Global Transformations Reader* (2nd edn, Cambridge, Polity Press).

—— (2004) *Global Covenant: The Social Democratic Alternative to the Washington Consensus* (Cambridge, Polity Press).

Held, D and Koenig-Archibugi, M (eds) (2004) *American Power in the 21st Century* (Cambridge, Malden, Polity Press).

—— (2005) *Global Governance and Public Accountability* (Oxford, Malden).

Helleiner, E (1994) *States and the Reemergence of Global Finance: From Bretton Woods to the 1990s* (Ithaca, New York, Cornell University Press).

Herbert, B (2006) 'Ike saw it coming' OP-ED article, *New York Times* (27 February 2006) A19.

Heydebrand, W (1996) 'The Dynamics of Legal Change in Eastern Europe' 15 *Studies in Law, Politics, and Society* 263–313.

—— (2003a) 'Process Rationality as Legal Governance' 18 *International Sociology* 2 325–49. Reprinted in R Cotterrell (ed) (2006) *Law in Social Theory* (Aldershot, Ashgate).

—— (2003b) 'The Time Dimension in Marxian Social Theory' 12 *Time & Society* 2/3 147–88.

—— (2004) 'Review of A. Claire Cutler, 2003. Private Power and Global Authority' 11 *Constellations* 4 591–4.

—— (2006) 'Structural Functionalism' in D Clark (ed), *Encyclopedia of Law and Society: American and Global Perspectives* (Thousand Oaks, Sage).

—— (2007) 'Globalization and the Rise of Procedural Informalism in American and European Law' in V Gessner and D Nelken (eds), *European Ways of Law* (Oxford, Hart).

Heydebrand, W and Miron, A (2002) 'Constructing innovativeness in new-media start-up firms' 34 *Environment and Planning* 1951–84.

Hollingsworth, JR and Boyer, R (1997) *Contemporary Capitalism: The Embeddedness of Institutions* (Cambridge, Cambridge University Press).

Joerges, C (1985) 'Relational Contract Theory in a Comparative Perspective' *Wisconsin Law Review* 37 581–631.

Kennedy, D (2003) 'Two Globalizations of Law and Legal Thought: 1850–1968' 36 *Suffolk University Law Review* 631–79.

—— (2004) 'The Disenchantment of Logically Formal Legal Rationality, or Max Weber's Sociology in the Genealogy of the Contemporary Mode of Western Legal Thought' 55 *Hastings Law Jounral* 1031.

Kingsbury, B (1999) 'Sovereignty and Inequality' in A Hurrel and N Woods (eds), *Inequality, Globalization, and World Politics* (Oxford, Oxford University Press).

—— (2003) 'The International Legal Order' in P Cane and M Tushnet (eds), *Oxford Handbook of Legal Studies* (Oxford, Oxford University Press).

Kingsbury, B, Krisch, N and Stewart, R (2005) 'The Emergence of Global Administrative Law' 68 *Law and Contemporary Problems* 3 7–54.

Konradi, W (2009) 'Lex mercatoria as a global law of transnational business exchanges? The governance of cross-border transactions within the timber industry' in V Gessner (ed), *Contractual Certainty in International Trade* (Oxford, Hart).

Kornhauser, L (1989) 'The New Economic Analysis of Law: Legal Rules as Incentives' in N Mercuro (ed), *Law and Economics* (Boston, Kluwer Academic).

Koskenniemi, M (2002) *The Gentle Civilizer of Nations: The Rise and Fall of International Law, 1870–1960* (Cambridge, Cambridge University Press).

Luhmann, N (1969) *Legitimation durch Verfahren (Legitimation by Procedure)* (Neuwied, Luchterhand).

Macaulay, S (1963) 'Non-contractual relations in business: A preliminary study' 28 *American Sociological Review* 55–69.

—— (1986) 'Private Government' in L Lipson and S Wheeler (eds), *Law and the Social Sciences* (New York, Russell Sage).

Macneil, I (1985) 'Reflections on Relational Contract' *Journal of Institutional and Theoretical Economics* 141 541–6.

Mann, M (1984) 'The Autonomous Power of the State: its origins, mechanisms, and results' 25 *Archives Europeennes de Sociologie* 185–213.

Mensch, E (1998) "The History of Mainstream Legal Thought" in D Kairys (ed), *The Politics of Law*, 3rd.ed. (New York, Basic Books).

Merton, R K (1968) 'Manifest and Latent Functions' in *Social Theory and Social Structure* (enlarged edn, New York, Free Press).

Meyer, J and Rowan, B (1991) [1977] 'Institutionalized Organizations: Formal Structure as Myth and Ceremony' in W Powell and P DiMaggio (eds), *The New Institutionalism in Organizational Analysis* (Chicago, University of Chicago Press).

Nelken, D (1984) 'Law in action or living law? Back to the Beginning in Sociology of Law' 4 *Legal Studies* 2 157–74.

—— (1997) 'The Globalization of Crime and Criminal Justice' in M Freeman and A Lewis (eds), *Current Legal Problems* (Oxford, Oxford University Press) 50.

Okun, AM (1975) *Equality and Efficiency, the big tradeoff* (Washington DC, Brookings).

O'Neill, J (1986) 'The Disciplinary Society: From Weber to Foucault' 37 *British Journal of Sociology* 1 42–60.

Parisi, F (2007) 'Law and Economics' in D Clark (ed), *Encyclopedia of Law & Society* (Thousand Oaks, Sage).

Portes, A and Sensenbrenner, J (2001) 'Embeddedness and Immigration: Notes on the Social Determinants of Economic Action' in Granovetter and Swedberg (eds), *The Sociology of Economic Life* (2nd edn, Cambridge, Westview).

Posner, RA (1980) 'The Ethical and Political Basis of the Efficiency Norm' 8 *Hofstra Law Review* 489.

—— (1995) *Overcoming Law* (Cambridge, MA, Harvard University Press).

—— (1998) *Economic Analysis of Law* (5th edn, New York, Aspen Law and Business).

Posner, R and Parisi, F (2002) *Economic Foundations of Private Law* (Cheltenham Edward Elgar).

Richman, BD (2009) 'Ethnic Networks, Extralegal Certainty, and Globalization: Peering into the Diamond Industry' in V Gessner (ed), *Contractual Certainty in International Trade* (Oxford, Hart).

Roberts, S (2005) 'After Government? On Representing Law without the State' 68 *Modern Law Review*1 1.

Rogowski, R (2006) *Reflexive Coordination: Thoughts on the Social Model of the European Union* (New York, New York University School of Law, Jean Monnet Center for International and Regional Economic Law and Justice).

Rosenbaum, W (1972) *Naturrecht und positives Recht (Natural Law and Positive Law)* (Neuwied, Luchterhand).

Ruggie, JG (1982) 'International Regimes, Transactions, and Change: Embedded Liberalism in the Postwar Economic Order' 36 *International Organization* 379–415.

Sabel, C (1993) 'Studied Trust: Building New Forms of Cooperation in a Volatile Economy' in R Swedberg (ed), *Explorations in Economic Sociology* (New York, Russell Sage).

Santos, B de Sousa (2003) *Toward a New Legal Common Sense: Law, Globalization, and Emancipation* (2nd edn, Evanston, Northwestern University Press).

Santos, B de Sousa and Rodriguez-Garavito, CA (eds) (2005) *Law and Counter-Hegemonic Globalization: Toward a Cosmopolitan Legality* (Cambridge, Cambridge University Press).

Scherrer, C (1999) *Globalisierung wider Willen? (Involuntary Globalization? The implementation of liberal economic foreign policy in the US)* (Berlin, Edition Sigma).

Scheuerman, W (1999a) 'Economic Globalization and the Rule of Law' 6 *Constellations* 1 3–25.

—— (1999b) 'Globalization and the Fate of Law' in D Dyzenhaus (ed), *Recrafting the Rule of Law: The Limits of Legal Order* (Oxford, Hart).

—— (2001a) '"False Humanitarianism"?: US advocacy of transnational labour protections' 8 *Review of International Political Economy* 3 359–8.

—— (2001b) 'Global Law in our High-Speed Economy' in R Appelbaum, W Felstiner and V Gessner (eds), *Rules and Networks: The Legal Culture of Global Business Transactions* (Oxford, Hart).
—— (2004a) *Liberal Democracy and the Social Acceleration of Time* (Baltimore, Johns Hopkins).
—— (2004b) 'International Law as Historical Myth' 11 *Constellations* 4 537–50.
Sheffrin, SM (1996) *Rational Expectations* (2nd edn, Cambridge, Cambridge University Press).
Sklair, L (2001) *The Transnational Capitalist Class* (Oxford, Blackwell).
—— (2002) *Globalization: Capitalism and its Alternatives* (3rd edn, Oxford, Oxford University Press).
Smelser, N and Swedberg, R (2005) *Handbook of Economic Sociology* (2nd edn, Princeton, Princeton University Press).
Smith, MP (ed) (1998) *Transnationalism from Below* (New Brunswick, New Jersey, Transaction Publications).
Sosa, F (2009) 'Cross-Border Dispute Resolution from the Perspective of Midsized Law Firms: The Example of International Commercial Arbitration' in V Gessner (ed), *Contractual Certainty in International Trade* (Oxford, Hart).
Spitzer, S (1982) 'The Dialectics of Formal and Informal Control' in R Abel (ed), *The Politics of Informal Justice*, Vol1 (New York, Academic Press).
Stewart, RB (2005) 'US Administrative Law: A Model for Global Administrative Law?' 68 *Law and Contemporary Problems* 3 55–89.
Stiglitz, JE (2002) *Globalization and its Discontents* (New York, Norton).
Strange, S (1998) *Mad Money: When Markets Outgrow Governments* (Ann Arbor, University of Michigan Press).
Suchman, M and Cahill, M (1996) 'The hired-gun as a facilitator: lawyers and the suppression of business disputes in Silicon Valley' 21 *Law and Social Inquiry* 619–712.
Tabb, WK (2002) *Unequal Partners: A Primer on Globalization* (New York, New Press).
Teubner, G (1992) *Law as an Autopoietic System* (Oxford, Blackwell).
—— (ed) (1997) *Global Law without a State* (Aldershot, Dartmouth).
Tilly, C (1992) *Coercion, Capital, and European States, 1990–1992* (Cambridge, Blackwell).
—— (2006) *Why?* (Princeton, Princeton University Press).
Treiber, H and Steinert, H (2005) *Die Fabrikation des zuverlässigen Menschen (The fabrication of reliable man)* (Münster, Westfälisches Dampfboot).
Trubek, D and Trubek, L (2005) 'Hard and Soft Law in the Construction of Social Europe: the Role of the Open Method of Coordination' 11 *European Law Journal* 3 343–64.

Tyler, TR and Huo, YJ (2002) *Trust in the Law* (New York, Russell Sage).
Uzzi, B (2001) 'Social Structure and Competition in Interfirm Networks: The Paradox of Embeddedness' in Granovetter and Swedberg (eds), *The Sociology of Economic Life* (Boulder, Westview Press).
Weber, M (1966) *Law in Economy and Society* (Cambridge, Harvard University Press).
—— (1978) *Economy and Society*, 2 volumes (G Roth (ed)) (Berkeley, University of California Press).
Wiegand, W (1991) 'The Reception of American Law in Europe' 39 *American Journal of Comparative Law* 229.
White, H (1992) *Identity and Control* (Princeton, Princeton University Press).
Williamson, O (1996) *The Mechanisms of Governance* (New York, Oxford University Press).
Zuern, M (2001) 'Sovereignty and Law in a Denationalized World' in R Appelbaum, W Felstiner and V Gessner (eds), *Rules and Networks—The Legal Culture of Global Business Transactions* (Oxford, Hart).

Index

Introductory Note

References such as '178–9' indicate (not necessarily continuous) discussion of a topic across a range of pages. Wherever possible in the case of topics with many references, these have been divided into sub-topics and/or only the most significant discussions of the topic are listed. Because the entire volume is about 'contractual certainty' and 'international trade', the use of these terms (and certain others which appear throughout the work) as an entry point has been minimised. Information will be found under the corresponding detailed topics.